The Great Radio
Audience Participation Shows

For Jordan Elizabeth and Hannah Lynn,
who bring smiles to rainy days,
and joy to their Pawpaw's heart

The Great Radio Audience Participation Shows

Seventeen Programs from the 1940s and 1950s

by Jim Cox

McFarland & Company, Inc., Publishers
Jefferson, North Carolina, and London

ALSO BY JIM COX

The Great Radio Soap Operas
(McFarland, 1999)

Library of Congress Cataloguing-in-Publication Data

Cox, Jim, 1939–
The great radio audience participation shows : seventeen
programs from the 1940s and 1950s/ by Jim Cox.
p.   cm.
Includes bibliographical references and index.
ISBN 0-7864-1071-X (illustrated case binding : 50# alkaline paper) ∞
1. Quiz shows— United States.
2. Game shows— United States.
I. Title.
PN1991.8.Q58C69   2001   791.44'6 — dc21   2001044063

British Library cataloguing data are available

Manufactured in the United States of America

On the cover: Bert Parks on the air and on the phone as vocalists Kay Armen and
Dick Brown back him up on the ABC radio program *Stop the Music!*

*McFarland & Company, Inc., Publishers
Box 611, Jefferson, North Carolina 28640
www.mcfarlandpub.com*

Acknowledgments

This is my sixth book. I never complete a project like this without reaffirming my inescapable dependency on so many individuals and sources. No author works by himself, and the more I write, the more palpable that fact becomes.

In contemporary times I have connected with what some would call a rather clandestine subculture that proudly recalls radio as our principal means of news, information and entertainment. Those halcyon days of the first half of the twentieth century are often referred to as radio's Golden Age. Numbering into the thousands, my cohorts join vintage radio clubs, subscribe to pastime newsletters, buy and trade premiums and memorabilia and books and tapes and CDs, attend annual conventions that draw some of the last vestiges of living network radio performers, and speak passionately of their hobby in near–reverent tones to anyone who expresses even passing interest. Gerald Nachman tagged us as "radiophiles," likening our wait for the return of a bygone era to "members of some cult huddled in remote mountain outposts watching for signs of the true messiah."

I am constantly gaining useful information from such companions as we exchange data and reminisce electronically and in hallway conversations at club and convention events. Many of these are not only knowledgeable but pervasively generous, bestowing tapes, books, photos and the like while pointing to obscure databases—asking for little or nothing in return, justifying their actions with statements like, "It's just my little contribution to research." In their own way, they are helping those of us who write to preserve something for future generations.

Among those making substantive additions to my research (several of whom share a love for radio in various fraternal clusters) are Sue Chadwick, Larry Gassman, Ted Kneebone, Howard Mandelbaum, Tom McConnell, Tom McNeill, Gary Mercer, Charles Niren, James Snyder and Eric Spilker. Several more—most of them "radiophiles"—have been in the wings, offering moral support while prodding me along: George Ansbro, Dennis Crow, Ted Davenport, Doug Douglass, Jack French, Lou Genco, Denise George, Eddie Ginsburg, Jay Hickerson, Oscar Hoffmeyer, Al Hubin, John Leasure, Ken Krug, Patrick Luciano, Jack Rothwell, Hal

Sampson, Jerry Siebel, Paul Urbahns, Stewart Wright and Harlan Zinck. I'm especially grateful to the members of the Kentuckiana Radio Addicts alliance, whose upbeat patronage has helped me realize completion of this quest.

The competent and tireless staff of the Louisville (Kentucky) Free Public Library never failed me, willingly researching every request I made.

A list of secondary sources appears in the Bibliography section. Special thanks go to three authors for not only providing vital data and colorful descriptions of shows and personalities, but particularly for their interviews: Tom DeLong's *Quiz Craze*, John Dunning's *On the Air* and Gerald Nachman's *Raised on Radio*. Some of their subjects have since passed away. Were it not for these scribes, we wouldn't have some of the priceless insights that have been recorded and preserved. I'm grateful for their efforts.

I'm also indebted to the men and women who created, aired and performed in the audience participation shows. Without renaming them individually, they brought us hundreds of thousands of hours of listening pleasure at the flick of a dial. They are the reason why such a volume is worthy.

I'm also deeply appreciative to my helpmate, Sharon Cox, for her willingness to share me with an ongoing airwaves pursuit. In understanding my preoccupation, she gives me the latitude I need to complete such tasks.

Actress Virginia Payne summarized it for me on her final broadcast, after playing *Ma Perkins* for 27 years: "I give thanks that I've been given this gift of life, this gift of time to play my little part."

Contents

Preface

One of the games people played in the 1940s in the era of the audience participation shows was a carryover from some commercials whose origins could be found in 1930s soap operas. Procter & Gamble, for instance, sponsored a giveaway on *The Guiding Light* in the spring of 1938 that was typical of a myriad of radio contests of that day. Listeners were asked to complete the following statement in 25 words or less: "I like P&G White Naptha soap because…." By attaching the panels from five packages of White Naptha soap (a popular brand then) to their submissions, they were automatically entered into competitive drawings for refrigerators, gas ranges, radios and various other home appliances.

So accepted was the phrase "in 25 words or less" that it became a fixture in the national vernacular of the epoch, frequently falling from the lips of the commoners who used it either emphatically or humorously. It's easy to see then why such shows as *Truth or Consequences* encouraged fans at home to enter a multiplicity of contests, like those seeking to reveal the hidden identities of "Mrs. Hush" and "The Walking Man" by requiring entry submissions in 25 words or less with charitable preambles such as, "We should all support the March of Dimes because…."

Thinking back over the legions of individuals who were engaged in entertaining Americans in audience participation series during radio's Golden Age, I selected a handful who—if I had my life to live over—I really wouldn't mind being. Borrowing from the timeworn expression of long ago, I'll share a few of them here, without regard to any order.

• I would like to have been John Kieran because … while adept at so much and dubbed "the man who knows everything," a colleague also labeled him "the sweetest, most gentle man I've encountered." (Wow! Smart *and* tender!)

• I would like to have been Warren Hull because … his heart was genuinely touched by the less fortunate; he was willing to work for scale; and—an associate allowed—he had those "bedroom eyes"! (Compassionate, humble, exciting!)

• I would like to have been Ralph Edwards because … he loved to make people laugh, but got serious in support of great causes. (Playful yet beneficent to a fault.)

• I would like to have been Bert Parks

1

because ... he was "the most excitable man in radio," possessed a contagious smile and was typified as "handsome, virile, supercharged." And could he carry a tune! (Energetic, masculine, charming, while talented, too!)

• I would like to have been Art Linkletter because ... he overcame adversity in early life, maintained a toothy grin, developed an extroverted personality and winsomeness that tagged him as "the smoothest man in radio." (Confident, gregarious, suave.)

• I would like to have been Don McNeill because ... he was simple, genial, witty, devout, rose above rancor and encouraged everybody to "be good to yourselves!" (Down-to-earth, reverent, unflappable and forever a cheerleader!)

• I would like to have been Walt Framer because ... imbued with a strong work ethic from his immigrant father and a love for humanity, he practiced those precepts throughout his life. (Committed, compassionate, consistent.)

• I would like to have been Edwin Wolfe because ... he was widely respected by his peers and subordinates for maintaining high standards, firmness and fairness, a man of personal integrity in business practices. (Accepted, idealistic, evenhanded, ethical.)

• I would like to have been Garry Moore because ... he was refreshingly entertaining, simply delightfully so. (Appealing, satisfying and, at times, exceptional.)

• I would like to have been Bill Cullen because ... he overcame physical malady, mastered the one-liners and made his job appear absolutely effortless— while having such obvious fun emceeing so many shows! (Invincible, hilarious, natural, gratified.)

There were others, of course, who embodied admirable traits.

Walter O'Keefe said that his life's greatest achievement was in conquering an addiction, definitely a laudable triumph.

A biographer characterized Tommy Bartlett's laid-back style as unique among the "most able and least offensive" human-interest emcees.

When Clayton "Bud" Collyer bade farewell to parting guests with a cheery "God bless you!" his deep personal faith visibly supported it.

Jean Hersholt refused to accept any acting jobs that conflicted with the helping-hand character that he was typecast as both on and off the stage.

Peter Donald possessed an uncanny yet brilliant ability to dissolve into character dialects, no matter what a culture required, for his joke-telling sprees. Few could have done it as well.

And on and on they went.

And what of the women? Audience participation shows were hardly their domain — seldom as hostesses, for sure. Few besides Arlene Francis, Irene Beasley and a handful of others made it as quizmasters. More often the distaff side was to be found on such programs as assistants, vocalists, instrumentalists, actresses, comediennes, advice-givers, panelists, writers and occasionally co-hosts who, like Johnny and Penny Olsen, and Ed and Polly East, often shared the spotlight with a spouse. The audience participation shows may have been one of the true bastions of near-male supremacy in vintage radio. Nevertheless, it apparently didn't faze the feminine gender, who flocked to those shows and for whom many of them were singularly created.

The reader will encounter biographical vignettes of 177 figures who were connected with the genre, woven into the body of the text. Nearly all of those individuals were aligned with more than one show. In most cases a biography appears in the chapter in which a personality's most prominent role is introduced. (Those who appeared on several series sometimes made this difficult!) Refer to the Index at the back of the book if you need help in locating an individual's summary.

If some of your favorite performers and their shows are not highlighted as separate chapters in this text, let me assure you that some of mine are missing, too. There was no way to do justice to all those who merited recognition. In determining the series and celebrities who are included, I attempted to select one or more features from each of the representative types of audience participation shows (which will be examined presently). If there was an unmistakable leader or otherwise a unique contender among the varied areas, such programs were included.

One of the more interesting departures (yet not a digression) is the opportunity to examine the familial lineage of some of the field's principal subjects. For instance, the reader will observe that there were some distinct similarities in the backgrounds of Arthur Godfrey and Groucho Marx.

Both had at least one first generation immigrant parent (Marx had two) who settled in the environs of greater New York City. The mother of each was stage-struck, dreaming of notoriety as a performer. As it turned out, those dreams were delayed, realized in the famous son (or sons) they bore. Both households fell on lean times, and the kids were forced to support the clan. Marx had the encouragement of his siblings early in life, whom his mother guided onto the stage. Godfrey, on the other hand, left his home environment to go out on his own — and became renowned as a solo act.

The glimpses, though brief, into the domiciles of Ralph Edwards, Art Linkletter, Don McNeill and others presented here may be a treasure-trove for any who love old time radio and the personalities who comprised it. This data may also be helpful to those doing serious research in the field.

Quizmaster Bob Hawk, one of the more intrepid masters of ceremonies of some of the audience participation shows, expressed some thoughts about the quiz-show sphere of the genre — easily its largest specialty, incidentally — that seem worthy of note:

There's nothing on the air that can top a good quiz. What other type of show can compare to it in mass appeal, in audience participation, in spontaneity, in unrehearsed humor and in, above all, just plain, downright folksiness?

Let me prove my point.

Let's watch an audience listening in to a comedy show, for instance (and you can name your own comedian, too), and then let's compare it to an audience listening in to a quiz program.

The comedy show audience is thoroughly relaxed; they lean back in their chairs, puffing away on their cigarettes and, in general, taking things very, very easy. No matter how funny the act, how loud the laughter, their reaction is, nevertheless, purely passive. Their participation in the show is nil. At the most, the audience plays the role of amused observers.

Now let's take an audience listening to a good quiz program.

Watch the way they lean forward in their chairs, the intent expressions on their faces, the breathless hush when the quiz master fires his question. Hear their exclamations of pleasure when the contestant answers the question correctly; hear their groans of dismay if he fumbles with the question or can't answer it. Observe how they then urge on the contestant, encourage him, pray for him and, in the end, call out the correct answer in the vain hope that he'll hear it.

Nothing passive about this audience![1]

Hawk appears to be on target in his assessment of quiz shows. Author Tom DeLong adds: "Never has there been a bigger crowd-pleasing spectator sport in any American arena — a field where the voice of the people can be heard and common people have a chance to 'come on down' and play."[2]

Since the quiz derivative of the audience participation breed produced the largest number of shows, could you identify the very first true radio quiz? John Dunning, one of the more creditable researchers among us, submits that *Professor Quiz*— a CBS entry in the spring of 1936 — lays claim to the honor. If that is true, what a door-opener the series was! And who hosted it in its early days? A man most people would probably never associate with quiz shows in their purest sense: Arthur Godfrey, a foremost contributor to the genre of audience participation shows and to radio itself.

In the late 1940s, at the apex of such programming, advertising agency executive Charles Hull Wolfe, of Batten, Barton, Durstine & Osborn, limited this field to four types of programming, all linked to a quiz (or, in modern parlance, game show) construction:

1. Those that highlighted information (e.g., *Information Please*).
2. Those that highlighted money giveaways, in two sub-categories: the ones that called listeners at home (e.g., *Pot o' Gold*) and the ones that drew participants from the studio audience (e.g., *Take It or Leave It*).
3. Those that highlighted stunts (e.g., *Truth or Consequences*).
4. Those that highlighted prearranged comedy (e.g., *It Pays to Be Ignorant*).[3]

While the game show easily predominated the form — and as inclusive as Wolfe's list is— by no means does this cover the waterfront. There is considerably more to the category than mere question-and-answer brainteasers. Before we proceed, to be certain that both the reader and author are working on the same page in a comprehensive view of audience participation

shows, it's reasonable to suggest some specific parameters of the breed.

Into which category, for instance, should the auditions of amateur and semi-professional aspirants be placed? There is no spot on Wolfe's list for *Arthur Godfrey's Talent Scouts* and shows of its ilk. Nor is there room for interview series like *Vox Pop*, or for advice columns like *The Goodwill Hour*, or group harmony fests like *Community Sing*. And while gifts galore were dispersed on *Welcome Travelers* and *Bride and Groom*, wasn't the overriding outlook in both features one of human interest? Certainly the stashes their guests carried away were simply incidental to the shows' programming themes.

The audience participation category must be opened further to embrace all those programs on which there were frequent exchanges between a host (or other figures) and a live, on-premises audience. This happened daily on shows like *The Breakfast Club* and various Garry Moore outings, plus others.

The participatory concept can sensibly be broadened to include "the only show in radio where the audience writes the script"— the dramatic *Dr. Christian* half-hour, and expanded to encompass at least three series on which a live studio audience contributed audibly to the commercials and program content: *The Adventures of Archie Andrews*, *Let's Pretend* and *Smilin' Ed's Buster Brown Gang*.

The author's definition of what constitutes an audience participation show, then, incorporates giveaways of several persuasions while adding those series in which a host bantered back and forth with spectators, along with a myriad of deviant branches. In short: *all of the programming for which any observers shared in an active way in the content.*

George Ansboro, an astonishingly long-winded broadcaster who still maintains the durability record (60 years) with a network, recalls what he believes to have been the very first audience participation show. Following the death of theatrical producer Florenz Ziegfeld in 1932, NBC rented a small venue that Ziegfeld had provided above the New Amsterdam Theater on New York's West 42nd Street, site of the world-famous *Ziegfeld Follies*. Transposing that facility into a broadcast studio, NBC left the audience-seating layout as it was. But it installed an all-glass curtain on the stage to protect the listening fans' ears from any sounds that might diminish a show in progress. "The thinking then was to accommodate an audience's curiosity in wanting to view a program but not allow that audience to be heard on the air as part of the action," Ansboro explained.[4]

All went well until the day the curtain was stuck in the "up" position. The scheduled program proceeded as usual, but along with it the folks at home heard gales of laughter and thunderous applause—something their radios had never brought them before. While it was totally unintentional, the experience confirmed the inevitability of audience participation shows, surmised Ansboro.

I must call your attention to the Appendix near the back of this book, "An Annotated Guide to Network Radio Audience Participation Shows." At the outset I make no claim that this is the ultimate list of such programming—the most complete, exhaustive and unabridged inventory available. If I did, some jokester would soon be contacting me with a dozen more shows that I had inadvertently overlooked. (I couldn't help but be amused by the Appendix in another scribe's discourse, which appeared under the heading "Every Game Show Ever." To this, at the bottom of the first page of the Appendix, the author had provided the disclaimer: "Any additions submitted by readers will be excitedly received." *Every* show *ever*?) All I can argue about my list of 400+ series is that I believe it to be the most comprehensive record of audience participation programs to date, and just possibly the first ever published. Nothing more.

Allow me to also reiterate what I pointed out in an earlier tome: "I make no claim of infallibility. Every human effort has been made to produce correct data and avoid perpetuating falsehoods that sometimes creep into print to be repeated by others. Still, the discerning reader may discover an inconsistency here and there. I have relied on some sources that occasionally conflicted with others. If I found obvious errors or questionable statements, I examined multiple sources. Accounts proving to be unreliable were simply discarded."[5] The same holds true in this volume.

Most of the people who were directly associated with these programs are no longer with us. The passing of time has left others with fuzzy memories. Be assured that any mistakes you find are mine alone and are of the head and not the heart. The possibility of error weighs on me heavily, and I beg your indulgence.

It is also helpful to guide the reader in separating the networks that are designated in the text. This will eliminate some of the confusion that a neophyte in old time radio might encounter through a casual reading. From its earliest days, the National Broadcasting Company (NBC) owned two radio chains. They were easily illustrated on a United States map by red or blue lines that connected their affiliates. The dual systems thus became commonly known as the Red and Blue networks. In the early 1940s the Federal Communications Commission ruled—primarily for competitive reasons—that the networks could not be jointly owned. The requirement forced NBC to sell one of its webs. Ultimately it kept the Red network, to be henceforth known as NBC. The Blue network was renamed the American Broadcasting Company (ABC) and was dispatched to an individual buyer. You will find references in this volume to NBC (properly understood as the Red network), NBC Blue, the Columbia Broadcasting System (CBS), the Mutual Broadcasting System (MBS) and, finally, ABC.

I've attempted to give you some idea of the numbers who were listening to the audience participation shows each week or each day, too, as the case might have been. The ratings figures cited in each chapter refer to the practices of determining a program's popularity, which profoundly affected the sale of a program's advertising time. For many years these figures were provided by the firm of C. E. Hooper, Incorporated, which kept tabs on the audience response to radio shows using a method known as "coincidental ratings." Hooper made random telephone calls to people living in 36 metropolitan areas. Respondents were asked to name any program they were listening to at the time of the phone call. The sampling resulted in an estimate of audience size for a given program. Unfortunately, its scope disenfranchised those people living in rural communities and smaller and medium-sized towns.

A "Hooperating" of 13.4 for a series meant that out of every 100 telephone calls placed, 13.4 respondents said they were listening to that specific program at that time. (A rating of 100 would have been impossible, incidentally, for it would have meant that the radios in all households in the nation were on and tuned to a single show. At no time was every set on simultaneously, of course.) A "share" of the total audience was determined by dividing a program's rating by all the sets then in use. A daytime show with a respectable rating of at least 5.0 (which was often enough to keep a series on the air) might net an audience "share" of 22 percent or higher.

When the A. C. Nielsen Company began producing radio audience estimates in the 1940s, it embarked on a different method. Nielsen outfitted thousands of households with audiometers, an electronic device intended to offer a more accurate picture of what Americans were hearing. Using paper tape, the audiometer continuously printed out records of every moment a radio was turned on, graphically depicting the station to which the radio was tuned. The numbers obtained often turned out to be similar to those that the Hooper firm had gained with its method. (In later years Nielsen purchased Hooper, and the firms' efforts were combined to measure the nation's television viewing habits.)

The discerning reader should note that the ratings in this treatise are based on *estimates* derived from such sampling and are never absolute measurements. The figures reflect what Americans were listening to during the winter months (usually mid to late January each year). Ratings may have been a little higher then than in the warmer months for people spent more time indoors in winter and were entertained more often by their radios. (The transistor set had not yet arrived, and portability was generally limited to vehicles that had radios installed, an option that was out of reach for many.) Although this is a rather protracted explanation, it is offered to help the reader understand the audience-measurement data that appears in these pages.

So why produce a book in the first place that is knowingly and admittedly based on a segment of radio's Golden Age that — even with its faithful fans numbering in the millions— pales in comparison to many of the audio comedic, dramatic and mystery offerings?

Is the answer, "Because nobody ever did it before," sufficient?

Hardly.

The fact is, audience participation series have never been given their "just due," and certainly not so in any sustained way. In researching this volume, for instance, only a single work majoring on multiple radio programming in this genre came to the forefront — and it was utterly confined to game shows. To our knowledge — aside from those volumes on single series or performers (e.g., *The Breakfast Club*, Arthur Godfrey, *Information Please* and so on) — no earlier text focused exclusively on the myriad of radio's audience participation shows.

Meanwhile and furthermore, it has been this author's intention to bring this sector out of its obscurity, to enhance an area that made a substantial contribution to our love of the medium of which it was a fundamental part. Hopefully, I have been able to satisfy a quest that other writers have almost overlooked, save for the exception of a few paragraphs in compendiums that emphasize numerous broadcast forms.

One wag mused that in "those" days radio was "America's national indoor pastime."[6] Certainly it was so for yours truly, just as it became for countless millions of radio listeners. It was the first medium to unite us as a people while impressing us with an unlimited capacity for dispensing both information and entertainment.

And a lot of our favorite goodies in those days frequently came packaged as fun and games.

When you dwell on that for a little while, who could ask for anything more?

1

Art Linkletter's House Party

Premise: *House Party* was like a bridge over what could have been troubled water. Competing against NBC's well entrenched soap operas, and the quiz and music shows programmed by ABC and MBS, it appeared each weekday afternoon as CBS was making the transition from multiple serial hours to variety mainstays. Writer Fred MacDonald adroitly observed that soap operas continued as the most popular daytime programming features, except "where a new show was hosted by an attractive and dynamic character." He cited Arthur Godfrey, Jack Bailey (*Queen for a Day*), Tommy Bartlett (*Welcome Travelers*) and Art Linkletter as such magnetic personalities. The latter possessed the charisma to make the concept of such a mishmash work. His ability to talk extemporaneously in any situation with people of all ages and backgrounds was well documented on several earlier audio ventures. His appeal kept the series fresh and spontaneous, helping it set a broadcasting record that lasted a quarter-century. The show combined beauty tips, health hints, contests with odd twists, oc-

casional talent, recurring guests offering sage advice, plus a frothy mixture of interplay with the studio audience and imposing towheaded tykes. It was borne out of a joint effort by Linkletter and producer John Guedel, whose fertile brains dreamed up this little farce over one long night. Guedel's attention was riveted to the need for a concept to plunge him into daytime radio when, in 1944, he learned an advertising agency was seeking a new audio vehicle. He and Linkletter scratched their heads to supply a hodgepodge of human-interest motifs. The next morning Guedel sold the idea, and *House Party* was under contract. For 25 years their efforts paid off—a novelty in good taste—and a rewarding interruption in the midst of milady's typical daily bill of fare.

Producer-Director: John Guedel
Director: Mary Harris
Master of Ceremonies: Art Linkletter
Announcers: Larrie Harper, Jack Slattery
Writers: John Guedel, Walter Guedel, Marty Hill, Jack Stanley

9

Musicians: Muzzy Marcilleno Trio
Sound Effects Technician: Ralph Cummings

Sponsors: The General Electric Corp. was sole sponsor from the series' debut through July 1, 1949, about four-and-a-half years later. When it returned from an 11-week hiatus it was sustained for 14 weeks, then picked up by Pillsbury Mills, Inc., who carried it from Jan. 2, 1950, through May 2, 1952. Lever Brothers underwrote the show from May 5, 1952, through August 24, 1956. At that juncture, participating sponsors serving it included Pillsbury Mills, Lever Brothers, Kellogg Co., Green Giant Co., William J. Wrigley Co., Campbell Soup Co., Better Homes and Gardens magazine, Brachs Candy Co., Dole Pineapple Co., Curad foot pads, Swift and Co., Pharmacraft Corp., Formula 409 cleanser and several other commodities.

Ratings: High: 6.1 (1950–51); Low: 2.7 (1944–45); Median: 4.5 (through 1955–56 season only). During much of its run *House Party* competed with some of NBC's most formidable soap operas, with well entrenched audiences who had followed those story lines for years. Among them were *Life Can Be Beautiful, Ma Perkins, Road of Life, Pepper Young's Family* and *The Right to Happiness*. This undoubtedly impacted *House Party's* numbers, typically holding them to no better than a serialized drama with a mediocre showing.

On the Air: Jan. 15, 1945–Sept. 28, 1945, CBS, Monday–Friday, 4 P.M. ET (25 minutes); Oct. 1, 1945–Jan. 10, 1947, CBS, Monday/Wednesday/Friday, 4 P.M. (25 minutes); Dec. 1, 1947–Dec. 31, 1948, CBS, Monday–Friday, 3:30 P.M. (25 minutes); Jan. 3, 1949–July 1, 1949, ABC, Monday–Friday, 3:30 P.M. (30 minutes); Sept. 26, 1949–Dec. 30, 1949, ABC, Monday–Friday, 3:30 P.M. (25 minutes); Jan. 2, 1950–Jan. 5, 1951, CBS, Monday–Friday, 3:30 P.M.; Jan. 8, 1951–July 1, 1955, CBS, Monday–Friday, 3:15 P.M.; July 4, 1951–Aug. 24, 1956, CBS, Monday–Friday, 3 P.M.; Aug. 27, 1956–Oct. 13, 1957, CBS, varying times, most 25 minutes.

* * *

Arthur Linkletter was born at Moose Jaw, Saskatchewan, on July 17, 1912, to some folks named Kelly who abandoned him. Three decades later — and for three decades following — he would be adopted by every family in America. One observer noted: "He was beloved for his capacity to turn a studio full of strangers into a cozy living room, and then to engage them all in hilarious double-, and sometimes triple-, crosses…. He made the Jolly Green Giant into a household word. He proved that kids say the darndest things. He was the first, and one of the best, game show hosts there ever was."[1]

Arthur Kelly changed his surname to Linkletter after his adoption by an Irish clan whose patriarch, Fulton Linkletter, was a Baptist minister. The Linkletters took off later for evangelical pursuits in California. Young Art's original exposure to crowds and audiences, in fact, came to pass in those devout assemblages.

Before joining the student body at San Diego State College (SDSC) — setting a record in swimming the 50-yard freestyle and captaining the basketball team — Linkletter pursued some diverse occupations: In Chicago he found subsistence as a busboy; in North Dakota, as a reaper; in Minneapolis, a butcher; in Washington state, a lumberjack; in New Orleans, a longshoreman; on Wall Street, a recorder; and in Buenos Aires, a mariner.

While pursuing a degree in English at SDSC on a scholarship, in 1933 young Linkletter broke into radio at that city's KGB. He subsequently turned down a teaching position because he could earn $5 more monthly in radio. He worked fairs, aired expositions and by 1939 was a freelancing San Francisco announcer. Two years earlier he had been radio director for the World's Fair in the city by the bay. He broadcast from battleships, submarines and airplanes, and announced numerous sporting contests. Appearing on 15 shows weekly, he calculated that by 1941 he had worked 9,000 programs and perhaps conducted as many as 45,000 interviews. NBC signed him to its permanent announcing staff in 1942.

"I never considered it work," Linkletter told Tom DeLong in a 1987 interview. "There wasn't any stress involved. It was all ad lib. Besides, it paid amazingly well for something I would have done for practically nothing."[2]

A sincere and abundant capacity for analyzing human nature allowed Linkletter to take advantage of added opportunities. He became the ideal man-in-the-street interviewer. "I wanted to be somebody, but I had no talent," he reflected. "I couldn't sing, I couldn't act. I was about to quit and go into the executive side of the business when the man in the street idea came along, and my whole life changed."[3] He became a veteran of the breed, eventually presiding over 17 man-in-the-street series. Linkletter instantly won the trust of his interviewees; he eclipsed others in surveying people of all walks of life. His baby face often reflected feigned surprise at personal accounts more outlandish than his own, which he handily persuaded his subjects to disclose. One radio historiographer, in fact, labeled him as possibly "the smoothest man in radio."[4]

A gregarious personality and a toothy grin, plus an overly inquisitive instinct and natural ability to talk extemporaneously on almost any subject, opened doors for Linkletter in audience participation arenas. Before long he was hosting remotes from the dingy basement confines of Hale Brothers Department Store in San Francisco. In a series titled *What's Doin', Ladies?*

a wild-eyed Linkletter pawed through housewives' handbags, a technique that was to become one of his hallmark designs. (An announcer for that series was a rising young Mark Goodson, who was to become a kingpin among the game show czars in successive decades.) By late 1943, *What's Doin', Ladies?* — then an NBC Blue audience participation series — originated in Hollywood. Perry Ward became its host in 1945, followed by Jay Stewart, later of TV's *Let's Make a Deal* fame, in 1946. That radio melee survived until 1948.

Another of Linkletter's contributions was an exploit called *Who's Dancing Tonight?* Popular bandleader Horace Heidt had already been airing a similar feature from New York venues. The loquacious Linkletter, meanwhile, attracted West Coast listeners as he gabbed with engaging couples of all ages over KSFO from the ballroom of the Saint Francis Hotel.

Linkletter told on himself as he recalled an interview involving a newly betrothed pair in those days. He proposed that they return a week later and have their ceremony conducted while the show was on the air. He whimsically, though intentionally, declared: "You can consummate your wedding vows right here in the main lobby!"

Recalling the incident years later, he said that remark generated enormous response. "Everyone wanted to hear them consummate their marriage vows. At the time I thought it merely meant to plight one's troth!"

Linkletter also conducted interview features, such as *What Do You Think?* and *Are You a Genius?* These shenanigans couldn't be considered quiz, game or talk shows, one media historian pointed out. They are some "peculiar goulash of the three — a mix of *Truth or Consequences*, *Candid Camera*, and *Family Feud* — in which the host roamed the audience, played pranks, surprised guests, and labored ceaselessly to have a good time."[5] The formula obviously suited Linkletter to a "T."

Producer John Guedel, who was to have a permanent effect on Linkletter's career, claims it was he and *Consequences'* Ralph Edwards who "invented the game show."[6] One day in 1939 Guedel, a former scripter for the Hal Roach Studios, switched on his automobile radio to initially encounter one of Linkletter's charming, witty, seldom-at-a-loss-for-words routines. Impressed by what he heard, he made a mental note to look up the personality behind that animated tongue. A couple of years elapsed before the pair came face-to-face, however, as a result of a prearranged rendezvous by a mutual party. Guedel quickly surmised that Linkletter's gift of gab could be turned into pure gold. And he fully intended to capitalize on the discovery he had made.

While in high school Guedel's rather affluent ancestral clan suffered some financial reverses during the Great Depression, he dropped out of school and sought employment. One of his early assignments was to write then-popular *Our Gang* comedies for Hal Roach Productions. He also worked on *Laurel and Hardy* film shorts. This soon led him into radio as a gag writer. He eventually churned out more sobering substance, however, including a 30-minute dramatic bit for Forest Lawn Memorial Park.

One day, while pursuing some research at the local public library, Guedel encountered a volume titled *Games*. Using it as food for thought, he came up with an idea for an audience stunt show that would be the antithesis of the typical quiz stock. *Pull Over, Neighbor*, created for a Los Angeles station, led him to far greater opportunities. Transferring some of those same concepts to yet another series, he hit the big time when *People Are Funny* gained a national audience and almost overnight ratings success. As a result, Guedel's name

became an instantly identified household word in most American homes; during the decades of the 1940s, 1950s, 1960s and even into the 1970s that moniker would be recognized by virtually anyone owning a radio or television receiver.

On *People Are Funny* he selected Art Baker as the show's debuting master of ceremonies. Baker, a native New Yorker who was born January 7, 1898, is described by an entertainment biographer as "the relatively forgotten host who first introduced the stunt-filled series on human nature."[7] A music student and gospel vocalist, Baker was a veteran of World War I, leading songfests for the Army while overseas. He later harmonized in a barbershop quartet, lectured at Forest Lawn Cemetery and narrated that organization's radio program titled *Tapestries of Life*. Subsequent assignments led him to create *Art Baker's Notebook* and *Hollywood in Person* in 1937. Within two years he was presiding over *The Grouch Club*, and later was at the helm of John Guedel's *Pull Over, Neighbor*.

When Guedel proposed *People Are Funny* to NBC he preferred the extroverted Art Linkletter as emcee over the more pedantic Baker. The network disagreed; Baker would host the show while Linkletter, who actually thought up many of the show's pranks, assisted for a little while. Linkletter, incidentally, had been in on the ground floor of developing *People Are Funny*. Guedel claimed the two men hatched the series in a corner booth of the Brown Derby Restaurant near the famous intersection of Hollywood and Vine. Linkletter later recalled: "The format was unique and simple, an entertaining study of human behavior based on a psychologist's observations and reactions."[8]

The rather avant-garde radio series premiered on April 10, 1942. As time rolled by it became increasingly apparent to many that the show lacked a vital ad-lib quality at the top. A year-and-a-half later

Guedel abruptly replaced Baker with Linkletter. Baker sued him and lost. *People Are Funny* became Linkletter's venue, and the fans quickly forgot there ever had been another host. Baker later went on to emcee television's *You Asked for It*. As for Linkletter, his career rose instantly to national exposure as he displayed a style soon coveted by the industry. For it he netted accolades from such noteworthies as Bing Crosby and Eddie Cantor.

Together, Linkletter and Guedel made a formidable team, and their partnership continued for virtually the remainder of their working lives. (Despite this, Guedel proved that he could successfully pull off grandiose dreams with other partners. One of his most successful achievements occurred when he joined forces with former vaudevillian and screen star Groucho Marx to produce the magnetic comedy-quiz *You Bet Your Life* on radio from 1947 to 1956 and on TV from 1950 to 1961. A chapter is included in this volume focusing on that time-honored series.) Meanwhile, *People Are Funny* prevailed as one of radio's (and video's) most formidable primetime venues. With only minor interruptions, the show continued on radio until June 10, 1960, more than 18 years after it began. On television the original series aired weekly from September 19, 1954 to April 16, 1961, continuing for a few months beyond the radio series' departure.

All of this was preparatory for yet another Guedel-Linkletter collaboration, believed by many industry insiders to be the duo's crowning achievement. Linkletter made no bones about the fact that he personally preferred *House Party* to their earlier successful venture. While *House Party* was a much more laid-back, relaxed show, both it and *People Are Funny* depended upon listener and audience participation for their triumphs. Linkletter confessed that *House Party* "gave me the opportunity to develop a confrontation that elicited

humor from my participants rather than make them the brunt of the joke, as so often happened on *People Are Funny*."[9] The success of *House Party* also made its star a multimillionaire: The series' popularity, sustaining it on the air for a quarter-of-a-century, lined Linkletter's pockets with untold wealth. By developing and splitting ownership of the show with Guedel, the emcee came a long way from his humble origins as a forsaken child. It may be noted, too, that the pair — Guedel and Linkletter — never labored under a contract between them.

How the new program came about is one of the more interesting (and expeditious) developments in the annals of broadcasting. A fan magazine of that epoch recalled the circumstances of *House Party's* conception:

> It seems that John Guedel ... got wind of the news that a certain producer was frantically shopping for a daytime package for a five-a-week broadcast spot. Guedel galloped to a telephone to tell the producer that he, Guedel, had just the thing for him. A red-hot idea. Art Linkletter as emcee ... can't miss. The producer said fine, bring over an outline in the morning.... The only unusual twist to this tale is that John Guedel and sidekick Linkletter stayed up all that night juggling inspirations to find the red-hot idea. Gimlet-eyed and disheveled, they got one. And what's more, the producer took one look at the hasty pudding and said, "I'll buy it."[10]

What they came up with in that all-night marathon was a potpourri of human-interest abstractions that would assure Linkletter of totally unrehearsed exposure before an audience. According to Guedel, the original concept allowed the on-stage action to take place in the various rooms of a house. Hints for the housewives would comprise a major portion of the show — how to dress, how to look one's best, how to cook and how to solve menial but thorny issues at home. Gags would be another aspect of the commotion, with Linkletter's curiosity being checked only within discriminatory limits of acceptable taste. The emcee was perceived as "a master of the double entendre, able to turn an innocent remark into a near-ribald flirtation, without ever running afoul of the censor."[11]

Several sporadic guests may have become celebrities in their own right as a result of their infrequent and casual appearances on *House Party*. Among them, fashion designer Edith Head kept the show's fans apprised of what should be in milady's wardrobe in order to be considered well dressed during the upcoming season. Head often presided over a modeling segment featuring some of Hollywood's best-coiffured debutantes. At one point actor Adolphe Menjou appeared as the program's resident fashion authority.

Dr. James A. Peterson, a marriage counselor at the University of South Carolina, entertained questions from the studio audience from time to time in his area of expertise.

By 1964, an America then gradually turning to health awareness received exercise tips from trainer Bonnie Prudden.

Occasionally, law enforcement agents and social service organization representatives appeared, too, warning listeners about scams that were operating across the nation.

There was something for just about everybody here, in fact. John Guedel and his father, Walter, devised most of the ideas for *House Party*. But Linkletter insisted on performing the show absolutely unrehearsed and scriptless.

There were hints for missing heirs: In its lifetime the show found descendants whose estates exceeded one million dollars.

And there were contests galore! The most frequent, "What's in the House?," included the visual effect (for the studio and television audiences) of a child's doll house physically held by announcer Jack Slattery. A series of clues led players to guess a specific object contained therein.

Meanwhile, there were frequent searches among the studio audience for the oldest and youngest ladies, mothers, grandmothers, fathers and specified individuals. Honorees carried home prizes like mixmasters, waffle irons, toasters, roasters, hand irons and scads of other small appliances. More challenging contests might laden an occasional lucky winner with a kitchen range, refrigerator or laundry machine. Proportionately, there weren't a lot of those given away in the early years, even under General Electric sponsorship. By the final radio broadcast in 1967, nevertheless, the grand prize for identifying the object in "What's in the House?" had soared: a new Oldsmobile Cutlass automobile, commensurate with the fame and fortune that the show had acquired as the years had rolled by.

When Linkletter went "peeking in some lady's purse," he probably provoked more sustained laughter than during any other exchange with members of the studio audience. Jubilantly he'd withdraw a set of dentures from the handbag of an unsuspecting guest, holding them high for everyone to see, then ask a giddy contestant to tell why she had them in her purse. In addition to the "normal fare" he'd encounter in women's handbags—mirrors, eye shadow and lipstick tubes—he would gleefully acknowledge to everybody those rare occasions when he found a small flask of rum or a roll of toilet tissue or a pair of ladies' "unmentionables" tucked into the hidden recesses of a guest's carry-all.

Invariably he'd inquire, "Why on earth would you have such-and-such in there?" as a dumbfounded interviewee stuttered and stammered to offer some plausible-sounding defense. Of course,

He had fun poking in ladies' purses and clued guests who played "What's in the House?" Yet he was even better recalled for the endless hours spent with youngsters. Art Linkletter dwelled on precocious preschoolers and jovial juveniles who frequently said the darndest things! *House Party* audiences ate from the affable emcee's hands while he played good-natured pranks on them for laughs. (Photofest)

that generated still more guffaws from an audience already reeling from the indelicacy of it all. Finally, Linkletter — having picked through several items that could subject an owner to red-faced embarrassment — asked the unsuspecting "victim" if she was carrying a specific object in her purse, such as a pack of chewing gum. If she could produce it she received a nice gift. But if she failed, she was given a "consolation prize" for her good sportsmanship and the humiliation she endured. They were some of the most hilarious moments in *House Party*'s life, and the same gimmick was as well received at the end of the run as it had been at its start more than 25 years earlier.

Linkletter also loved to pick out an audience member at random and engage that individual in extemporaneous banter for a half-minute. If, without looking at a watch or clock, the guest could interrupt their conversation by calling "stop" within five seconds of that time frame, another nice prize — perhaps a lady's jeweled wrist watch or a mink coat — was awarded.

To Linkletter and Guedel, these pranks were "throwaways," fun for the moment, brought out to provide diversion between celebrity guests and kiddie interviews.

Unquestionably, the best remembered feature of the show over its many years was Linkletter's talks with the kids — precocious preschoolers through precipitous preteens. Four or five of them were transported by limousine to the CBS Hollywood studios each day, coming from Los Angeles–area public and private schools for live on-air conversations with the program's host. After years of practice, Linkletter knew how to turn the screw to prompt responses that their mommies and daddies couldn't possibly have wanted to hear on national radio and television: "Who's the most beautiful woman in world?" a rambunctious lad was asked. "My mama used to be," came the reply, "but now that she's thirty-five that's all finished."

Such spontaneous repartee never failed to win vigorous approval of the audiences at home and in the studio. "*Of course* I egged them on," Linkletter admitted. "I was always a straight man for kids or anyone I talked to…. I'd never let on that I thought what a kid said was funny, because they weren't trying to be funny. So I would just listen. I'd play games with kids to get them talking, and I always took my time."[12] Some other typical prompts and rejoinders that occurred:

> To "What does your mommy do?" one dimpled darling sighed: "Oh, she just sits around reading the racing form all day!"

> To "Do you have any siblings?" a five-year-old miss replied: "No, I'm single."

> To "What does your mother do?" a seven-year-old retorted: "She's a housewife." Asked the same question again, he didn't hesitate: "She doesn't do *anything*!"

> Another response to "What does your mommy do?" elicited: "She can't do much of anything for having babies all the time!"

After 23,000 such interrogations with the younger set, Linkletter included some of the better responses he received in a couple of books, *Kids Say the Darndest Things* and *More Kids Say the Darndest Things*. By the late 1990s there was even a television series under that banner, hosted by Bill Cosby, continuing a tradition that John Guedel had initially applied in the early 1940s on radio's *Paging Young America*.

For a long time Guedel weighed which series to bring to television viewers first — *People Are Funny* or *House Party*. When the rival primetime stunt program *Truth or Consequences* suffered a temporary setback following its initial televised performances, Guedel was convinced that it made better sense to put *House Party* before the cameras first. Two years went by, if fact, after that show's assured video success before Guedel and Linkletter attempted to put *People Are Funny* on the tube. In the autumn of 1954 the pair launched a trial run of the latter series on Sunday nights on NBC-TV. *People Are Funny* lasted nearly seven full seasons. While it was well received, it never approached the TV patronage enjoyed by *House Party* across its 18 years on the small screen.

House Party premiered over CBS-TV for 30 minutes on September 1, 1952, at 2:45 P.M. Eastern Time. By February 2, 1953, it shifted to a 2:30 P.M. start, where it remained through September 6, 1968. Losing audience at that hour to NBC-TV's *The Doctors*, the show was transferred to 4 P.M., where it aired in a 25-minute format. But the competition at that hour was NBC's formidable *Match Game*, and it became apparent that the venerable CBS effort was in a fight for its life.

The program was retitled *The Art Linkletter Show*, and the theme altered to provide more talk and less stunt. Diane Linkletter, the emcee's daughter, joined her famous father as co-host. Despite that, the audience continued to evaporate. On February 24, 1969, the show was lengthened to a half-hour at 4 o'clock. Finally, CBS-TV decided to pull the plug, targeting its withdrawal for September 5, 1969. Sadly, on the day before it all came to an end, Diane Linkletter — under the influence of mind-altering drugs—leapt from a tall structure to her death. It caused Linkletter to become a strong anti-drug crusader for the remainder of his career.

The family patriarch had, in the intervening years, hosted his own brief prime-time NBC-TV series titled *The Art Linkletter Show*. It ran from February 18 to September 13, 1963. Its premise was built around pointing a hidden camera at ordinary folks in dubious, often amusing, situations—and asking studio contestants to figure the final outcome. It was kind of like *Candid Camera* inquiring "what happens next?" with prizes for accurate guesses. Within six weeks, however, the format shifted from contestants to a regular cadre of celebrity "judges," Carl Reiner and Jayne Meadows among them. The "Linkletter Players"—thespians Ken Berry, Richard Dawson, Buck Henry, Arte Johnson and Carol Merrill—were also featured. Linkletter's announcer of many years, Jack Slattery, turned up there, too.

In addition to working all of Linkletter's radio and television shows—*The Art Linkletter Show, House Party, Life with Linkletter* and *People Are Funny*—Slattery preceded George Fenneman as announcer on John Guedel's *other* major show, *You Bet Your Life*. Slattery died at age 62 on October 29, 1979.

There are a couple of postscripts to all of this.

Yet another member of the Linkletter family, son Jack, joined his famous father in a revival attempt of the earlier broadcasting efforts. This came just 16 weeks after the daytime TV show's cancellation and Diane Linkletter's death. Ironically labeled *Life with Linkletter*, the 30-minute feature debuted on NBC-TV (weekdays at 1:30 P.M. Eastern Time) on December 29, 1969, with Jack in the role of co-host. The effort—the last of the famous family on a daily network series—ended quickly, on September 25, 1970. This time the family

was unable to compete against CBS-TV's *As the World Turns* and ABC-TV's *Let's Make a Deal*, the latter one of the very programs for which *House Party* had long been a progenitor.

Never say die, however. Steve Doocy revived *House Party* in still another attempt in 1990 as a daily hour-long syndicated show. It lasted all of three months.

Over the years *House Party* was cited by numerous recognized and respected organizations for its contributions to society. The show won the very first Emmy for television's Best Daytime Program in 1955.

Linkletter, in the meantime, co-starred with Ronald Colman, Celeste Holm and Vincent Price in the 1950 motion picture *Champagne for Caesar*. On the occasion of *House Party's* 20th anniversary on the air, the competition — notably Ralph Edwards, who originated *People Are Funny's* major rival, *Truth or Consequences*—paid homage to Linkletter on Edwards' *This Is Your Life*. The date was January 22, 1965. In 1969 Linkletter won a Grammy award for the Best Spoken Word Recording, and in 1980 he published his memoirs in *I Didn't Do It Alone*.

Following his broadcasting career, the effervescent emcee pursued the door-to-door motif he had adopted early in life while working fairs, competitions and other remotes—interviewing the common man and woman for local radio stations. This time Linkletter was traveling the nation as a stimulating speaker on behalf of a diverse range of challenges and opportunities. Looking back, he is appalled by what has transpired in the ensuing years. "We had men-in-the-street [interviews] and now they have men-in-the-gutter.... Everyone then said, 'My God, what's happening to people?,' just as I say it now when I watch a show like Jerry Springer's."[13]

The ebullient master of ceremonies despised the recklessness of TV shows spinning off from *Supermarket Sweepstakes* and *The Price Is Right*. Linkletter put them down for hyping contestants, juicing applause and goosing reactions. In his opinion, there was little to compare between his show, cited for warmth and humanity, and the others. In the 1990s he viewed with disdain such modern video series that required would-be contestants to stand on their seats, wave their arms and scream maniacally. "The reason we had such consistent success is that I was and am truly interested in people," he said, "and that interest communicated itself to millions of listeners across the country."[14]

This author experienced two (actually, four) encounters with Art Linkletter over the years. I distinctly remember in the spring of 1949 — when I was in the fourth grade of elementary school — being dismissed early from class on a trio of consecutive days to accompany my mother to three live broadcasts of *Art Linkletter's House Party*. It was a road show version that was emanating from the Armory Auditorium in our medium-sized city. I recall becoming the envy of every other kid in the fourth grade for that one week only.

As airtime approached I was fascinated by the frenzy of last-minute preparations and instructions given the "studio" audience. I missed none of the congenial banter exchanged between us and Linkletter, nor the director's cues as the clock reached 3:30 P.M. Standing before a floor microphone the host matter-of-factly inquired: "Ladies, who sponsors the next program?" "General Electric!" came the thunderous retort we had been primed to shout. An organist seated upstage left broke into a sprightly rendition of the short, pithy ditty then employed as the program's theme. *House Party's* unpredictable antics would occupy the national airwaves for the next 30 minutes. For an inquisitive kid whose all-consuming passion was radio, it was the fulfillment of a dream. If I couldn't

get to California, then by golly the show would come to me!

I verbalized this recollection some 35 years later as I chatted beside Art Linkletter at a luncheon held in his honor. That morning he had addressed the student body at a private institution of higher learning near my home, distantly removed from the locale where I had encountered him earlier. By then a practicing journalist, I was invited to interview him for my paper. I witnessed the same winsome spirit and gregarious personality that had endeared him to millions across decades long past. I was duly impressed that none of it had escaped him in the intervening years. In fact, I came away from that encounter believing it was *I* who had been interviewed, not he.

The years had been good to him physically, mentally and in every other observable way. Though he was no longer a day-to-day presence in American homes, his ability to discern the key factors in other people's lives was just as apparent as I remembered it from the 1940s, 1950s and 1960s. A truly remarkable individual, Linkletter.

When *House Party* was no longer underwritten by General Electric, it arrived over a burst of chatter from the studio audience, with Jack Slattery inviting: "Come on in ... it's Art Linkletter's House Party."

The then-familiar instrumental theme of "You," featuring Muzzy Marcellino's trio, signaled the start of another half-hour.

Sometimes, as noted, Linkletter took the show on the road, playing to vast audiences across the nation who had only heard it on the radio — broadcasting from whatever city the cast happened to be in. It was a novelty that was genuinely welcomed in the hinterlands across its 22-plus years on radio. For all of that time, *House Party* became a delightfully rewarding interruption in the afternoon melee and humdrum routines that confounded America's typical mid-century homemaker.

2

Arthur Godfrey's Talent Scouts

Premise: Arthur Godfrey was an enigma in broadcasting. He rode the crest of listener popularity, developed lists of prospective advertisers waiting to gain a berth on his shows that were often sold to sponsors for years, and had the CBS network brass eating out of his hand, the result of enormous revenues and audiences he delivered. Godfrey commandeered the airwaves for nearly 15 hours weekly in two mediums, substantially overpowering the competition at all hours while placing multiple programs near the top of the ratings charts. At the pinnacle of his popularity he began a foolhardy, little understood or appreciated dismantling of his vast empire that turned the public from adulation to agitation. Godfrey never won back what he had lost, and it was the start of a downhill slide that continued for the rest of his career. In his heyday one of his most respected venues was *Arthur Godfrey's Talent Scouts*, a weekly showcase of near-professional artists seeking an elusive "one big break" to become established performers. Unlike previous offerings on the air, this show shied away from neophytes seeking an audience for mere amateurish tryouts. The talent on Godfrey's stage was well past that point, auditioning before acquiring an opportunity to perform there. In his typically laid-back, chatty style Godfrey bantered back-and-forth with guests who introduced their talent "finds" before those discoveries were brought on. Winners were determined by an audience applause meter, giving them the chance to appear on Godfrey's daytime show the rest of the week. The series was such a success that CBS-TV soon added a video version of *Talent Scouts*. It was the preeminent series of its breed, and throngs gathered around their radios and televisions on Monday nights to behold who might become the nation's favored minions on Tuesday.

Producers: Irving Mansfield, Jack Carney, Janette Davis (1956–58, TV)

Host: Arthur Godfrey

Announcer: George Bryan

Vocalists: Peggy Marshall and the Holidays

Orchestra Conductor: Archie Bleyer

(1946–54), Jerry Bresler (1954–55), Will Roland and Bert Farber (1955–58, until the television series left the air July 21, 1958).

Writers: Chuck Horner, Ken Lyons, Andy Rooney

Sponsors: In 1946 CBS premiered this feature as a sustaining summer replacement. When it drew large audiences almost overnight, that network found a place for it in its fall lineup. A year later — after the show had aired on different days and in various time periods — it was slotted into a durable half-hour on Monday evenings where it prospered, remaining in place until it left radio in 1956 and TV in 1958. On Mondays it attracted one of Godfrey's major daytime sponsors, Thomas J. Lipton, Inc. The Lipton name (tea, soup mixes and other foodstuffs) and Liggett & Myers Tobacco Co. (who underwrote large portions of Godfrey's daytime show for Chesterfield cigarettes) were to become resolutely identified with "that man himself" during much of Godfrey's broadcast reign. Both would lend their names and deep pockets to still a third Godfrey venture, an hour-long TV variety hour. Beginning Aug. 4, 1947, Lipton carried *Talent Scouts* on radio for eight consecutive seasons. When it bowed out in 1955, The Gillette Co. picked up the series for a final audio season on behalf of its Toni home permanents and related lines of hair care preparations.

Ratings: High: 22.1 (1948–49); Low: 2.0 (1955–56); Median: 12.2 (based on sponsored seasons, 1947–56). By 1952 the audio numbers were tumbling swiftly from double digits that had often topped 20 to single digits — 7.3, 5.2, 3.7 and 2.0 in its final four years. The figures shouldn't suggest a loss of affection for the show, however, even as Godfrey was firing performers with established followings on his other programs. The television ratings for *Talent Scouts* (included in the narrative) suggest that large numbers remained fans to the

end of the run. This plainly suggests that as the 1950s advanced, radio listeners were converting to television viewers. Of a quartet of programs that Godfrey concurrently hosted in the 1950s, *Talent Scouts* invariably drew the largest crowds, on dual mediums.

On the Air: July 2, 1946–Aug. 20, 1946, CBS, Tuesday, 9 P.M. ET; Aug. 27, 1946–Dec. 17, 1946, CBS, Tuesday, 10 P.M.; Dec. 24, 1946–April 22, 1947, CBS, Tuesday, 9:30 P.M.; May 27, 1947–June 17, 1947, CBS, Tuesday, 9 P.M.; July 4, 1947–Aug. 1, 1947, CBS, Friday, 9:30 P.M.; Aug. 4, 1947–June 27, 1949 and Aug. 29, 1949–Oct. 1, 1956, CBS, Monday, 8:30 P.M.

*   *   *

The historians of electronic media have described entertainer Arthur Godfrey via a myriad of picturesque epithets.

Godfrey, "radio's one-man show,"[1] was labeled "as close an approach to a one-man network as radio and television ever produced."[2] Cited as "one of the best-loved men in America,"[3] he was, notwithstanding, variously endorsed as "the most important man in America,"[4] "the most recognized man in America"[5] and "the most powerful man in broadcasting."[6] Possessing "radio's longest continuous career,"[7] Godfrey's plaudits sanctioned the old redhead as "the original and ultimate infotainer."[8]

While he would be "deified and discarded"[9] during an on-air professional life that stretched from the 1920s to the 1970s, he was also recognized as "the greatest salesman who ever stood before a microphone"[10] and "radio's most trusted pitchman."[11] Ultimately, some would consider him "the greatest communicator of the century."[12]

A contemporary biography of his life, however, notes that "most Americans alive today don't know the name Arthur Godfrey."[13] Unlike the same era's Lucille Ball, Milton Berle, Jackie Gleason and Ed Sullivan, whose TV efforts have been recalled again and again, Godfrey's shows weren't transportable. Largely aired live, wandering and scriptless, they — and their star — acquired "no place in the public eye or in the public mind."[14]

In his prime, however, Godfrey — more than any other performer — ruled the broadcasting airwaves, with CBS vice president Jim Seward singularly assigned to that one entertainer. In 1953 Godfrey, by then heard and seen by 80 million Americans weekly, was personally responsible for contributing 12 percent of his web's annual revenues. The total was a tidy $27 million for CBS, while he lined his own pockets with a cool million plus. On the air he often claimed that he paid the network's expenses for the day before CBS chairman William S. Paley awoke every morning. (Paley's biographer hinted that the chairman had little personal respect for Godfrey and the pair was

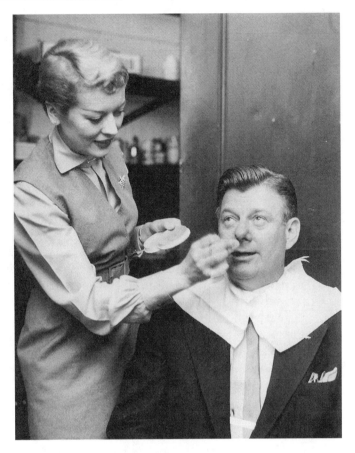

The **Old Redhead**, Arthur Godfrey, spent a lifetime talking to people directly as if they were individuals. Fans and sponsors flocked to his shows and a revolution occurred in the industry as a result. In his prime Godfrey "ruled the broadcasting airwaves," contributing 12 percent in revenues to CBS's bottom line. Here makeup artist Margot Kingsley prepares him for another *Talent Scouts* bender. (Photofest)

never soul-mates.[15]) Actually, no single individual before or since Godfrey has come even close to raising 12 percent of a network's revenues. All the while, Godfrey did it in a contradictory manner to longstanding commercial delivery methods that had been in evidence since radio's incubation: To that time, and addressed to no one in particular, sponsors' messages would be offered in a stuffed-shirt style that frequently began, "Ladies and gentlemen..."

Godfrey dispensed with the formality, a technique he adopted after lying in a hos-

pital bed for four months in late 1931 while recovering from a near-fatal vehicular accident. Returning to the microphone, rather than seeing a vast faceless audience, he recognized a single listener as his challenge: His role was to convince that individual to buy the commodity he advertised. Godfrey chatted as if he was carrying on a conversation in a living room and not over the air. He revolutionized commercial delivery, and scores of sponsors signed on for his programs.

Born in New York City on August 31,

1903, he was the eldest of five siblings in a family headed by a middle-aged Englishman. At the turn of the century young Arthur's father had already been a secretary to several prominent gentlemen. He became a newspaper reporter and photographer of some renown. Eventually he turned his journalistic interests toward publications targeted at horsemen, a popular sport among the wealthy of that period. While that career was at first promising, the advent of the automobile turned men of leisure from horseracing to a different type of horsepower. As a consequence, Arthur's dad received fewer and fewer requests for features on equestrian topics. That put a considerable dent in the Godfrey family budget.

To take up some of the financial slack, Arthur — at the age of 10 — delivered milk and groceries, mowed lawns, shoveled snow and cut firewood for friends and neighbors near their Hasbrouck Heights, New Jersey, home. For a quarter, on Sundays he would pump the church organ. In the summertime he assisted a local carpenter as a full-time helper, adding to the family's meager financial coffers.

Arthur Godfrey's mother, in the meantime, who had earlier aspired to a stage career for herself, played the piano at a local silent movie house. Things grew progressively worse, in spite of combined efforts, and for awhile, out of necessity, the children were partialed out to live with relatives and friends.

At 15, while working at a bakery before and after school, Arthur felt he could take no more of it. He dropped out of school and departed on a cross-country adventure that was to widen his horizons while shaping some of the ideas he would espouse for the rest of his life.

Over the next few years, largely given to nomadic pursuits, the young lad experimented with an infinite array of occupations. While on his journeys he became conversant with bums, degenerates of multiple persuasions, pickpockets and prostitutes. He sought income as a newspaper salesboy, an architectural firm's office boy, as a shoeshine boy, typist for the U. S. Army, coal miner, lumberjack, farmer, tire finisher, dishwasher, radio operator in a four-year stint with the U. S. Navy, insurance audit correspondent, advertising copywriter, automobile body finisher, restaurant counterman, hotel desk clerk, cemetery lot salesman, investor in a traveling vaudeville troupe (he lost $10,000 he earned selling cemetery lots), cab driver and U.S. Coast Guardsman.

During the last assignment, some beer-drinking buddies put him up to trying out as an amateur talent on the radio. That experience was a prelude to what would ultimately become one of the most rewarding aspects of his professional career. Godfrey could play the banjo and ukulele, having acquired skills with both instruments while in the Navy, and was up for the challenge. He won a second and third appearance on Baltimore's WFBR, gaining a permanent job for three quarter-hour shows weekly. At $5 per broadcast, the youthful, freckle-faced redhead was billed as "Red Godfrey, the Warbling Banjoist." (Radio made ample use of descriptive sobriquets in those days. Popular among them was Jan Garber, "the Idol of the Airwaves"; Wendell Hall, "the Red-Headed Music Maker"; Wayne King, "the Waltz King"; Kate Smith, "the Songbird of the South"; Arthur Tracy, "the Street Singer"; Rudy Vallee, "the Vagabond Lover"; Joe White, "the Silver-Masked Tenor"; and Ed Wynn, "the Fire Chief.") Godfrey had at last located the occupation that he had been seeking through years of search. It was 1929 and he was then 26.

His career spiraled upward. For a year he learned the ropes of his profession at the small independent station WFBR. In November 1930 he received an offer, for less money than he was then making, from the more prestigious NBC Red affiliate (WRC) at nearby Washington, D.C. He accepted. Yet on September 16, 1931, an automobile crash nearly claimed his life, leaving him partially paralyzed for two decades, until a hip replacement operation corrected the mishap. The accident sidelined him until 1932, as he recuperated for months in traction while lying in a hospital bed. But that event turned into the watershed experience of his life.

Having nothing better to do with his time, Godfrey listened to the radio. As he listened, the general tone of addressing mass audiences rather than individuals became absolutely abhorrent to him. Thus, when he returned to the airwaves he decided to make a radical departure from the prevailing formality then existing virtually everywhere. He began talking to listeners one-on-one and shook up the conventional practices in advertising delivery. This became a hallmark characteristic that would remain with him for the rest of his career and would also have a profound effect on thousands of others in the industry.

Godfrey later shifted to Washington's WMAL, WRC's companion NBC Blue Network affiliate. But on January 2, 1934, he abruptly quit his job in a dispute with management. He was back on the air in the nation's capital before long, nonetheless, this time at WJSV, the CBS affiliate. Four-fifths of the advertisers for his recently vacated early morning WMAL disk jockey show then left that station and shifted their commercial messages to WJSV. Godfrey was sitting high in the saddle as he harbored a long-held personal objective of gaining a berth on a daily network series.

Soon he was airing on the web in stints on *The Fred Allen Show, Manhattan Parade, Professor Quiz, Singin' Sam* and *Texaco Star Theater*. But not until 1941 did he appear to be going anywhere. That year he convinced the CBS brass to let him try

a dual-station wake-up program. (Actually, the popular newscaster-columnist Walter Winchell, who had heard Godfrey while in Washington, put in a good word for him with CBS officials.) Godfrey would broadcast from Washington over New York's WABC, then the flagship affiliate of the Columbia Broadcasting System. In so doing he was on the air in his native New York from 6 to 7:45 A.M. Eastern Time, Monday through Saturday. That show was then followed by *Sundial* from 7:45 to 9:15 A.M., the disc jockey marathon he had been broadcasting all along on WJSV in the nation's capital.

His ratings were so significant that by 1945 CBS's programming moguls caved in to his consistent harping for a nationwide morning show. He was given the 9:15 to 10 A.M. CBS slot being vacated for the summer by *School of the Air*. A network ban on airing phonograph recordings resulted in its hiring a small orchestra, a couple of vocalists and a trio of ensembles for the untried show.

A fortnight before the new broadcasting venture hit the air, Godfrey was introduced fortuitously — even propitiously — to hordes of Americans who weren't familiar with his name and had never heard his adenoidal, briary, instantly recognizable timbre. He is still remembered as the man who emitted a highly emotional eyewitness account of the funeral of the late President Franklin D. Roosevelt. Two weeks hence, on April 30, 1945, *Arthur Godfrey Time* premiered. It was an instant success and continued without interruption on CBS Radio for 27 years, long after the medium's Golden Age ended.

Godfrey's achievements led the CBS command to seek a primetime vehicle that would capitalize on his ability to draw listeners and revenue to the network. In short order it affirmed an idea that producer Irving Mansfield pitched to comedian Georgie Jessel, which Jessel then rejected. Mansfield was a veteran radio man who earlier worked with Fred Allen and Eddie Cantor and other "immortals." His plan called for showcasing some aspiring performers yet undiscovered by a national audience. Unlike the well known *Major Bowes' Original Amateur Hour*— from 1935 to 1945, and revived after Bowes' death by Ted Mack in 1948–52— Mansfield's concept cautioned against a hokey format that let anyone with "busfare and a harmonica" get on the air. No neophytes would be welcome; the idea offered a refreshingly modified form that could attract mass listening audiences.

Godfrey would host a series featuring near-professional talent seeking the proverbial "one big break." Aspirants would be introduced by a relative, friend or acquaintance whose primary task was to recite the achievements of their "discoveries." A performer would then take the stage and sing, play an instrument, offer a comedy routine, impersonation or ventriloquism act, or demonstrate some other audible talent. An applause meter would determine the winners, based on studio audience response.

CBS liked the idea and so did Godfrey. On Tuesday, July 2, 1946, at 9 o'clock P.M. Eastern Time, *Arthur Godfrey's Talent Scouts* debuted as a summer replacement. Like its companion morning series that featured the same host, it became an immediate success.

Godfrey bantered back and forth with his guests, those namesake "scouts" who had brought their discoveries before the radio audience. Again the emcee was in his element, for the laid-back, easy going environment of this show allowed him to converse just as naturally as he did in the mornings. It was a technique he had been perfecting since 1932.

After they gabbed awhile, Godfrey was fond of prompting his visitors: "Tell us, whom have you brought us?" Listeners heard a recital of the clubs and stage appearances where the entertainers had performed. Godfrey offered a nice build-up, then said something like: "Well, let's see if she (or he) is any good. And now the Lipton spotlight falls on your discovery..." and he repeated the name of the individual or group to be featured.

Unfortunately, Godfrey often carried on so long with the unscripted dialog that there was little time left to determine the winners after the performers' routines. It was only a half-hour show and it was always "tight." When things worked right Godfrey brought the performers back to the microphones near the end of the program for a 20-second reprise of each one's talent. By its applause the studio audience obligingly indicated how well they liked each act. But when there was no time for that Godfrey merely called out the performers' names and the studio patrons clapped.

At least once, when a transcribed 30-second commercial was to air at the close of the show, the engineers cut away from the live program during the reprise to get in the sponsor's message. After all, it was Lipton making the whole thing possible. Following that transcription, announcer George Bryan signed off with: "Tonight's winner was... (and gave the name). This is CBS, the Columbia Broadcasting System." On several occasions the show ran so long that the victor's name had to be held until the following morning, when it was revealed on *Arthur Godfrey Time*. Of course, listeners who were at work and had no radio with them missed hearing the outcome that they had waited for 30 minutes to discover the night before!

While winning the *Talent Scouts* show might open doors to a spawning career without further assistance, the *real* prize— according to singer Phyllis McGuire, who, with her sisters Christine and Dorothy, became champions on December 1, 1952—

was that one could perform with Godfrey the following four weekdays on his 90-minute morning show. He brought the potential stars before his daytime audience, wishing them well at the end of their brief runs. For a few, however — including the McGuire Sisters, Carmel Quinn, the Chordettes, Lu Anne Simms and Pat Boone — fame and fortune began there as Godfrey hand-picked them to add to his stable of permanent performers. They joined Janette Davis, Bill Lawrence, Tony Marvin, Frank Parker, Marion Marlowe, the Mariners, Julius La Rosa, Haleloke, and Archie Bleyer and his orchestra, collectively and affectionately called "the little Godfreys," on his various programs.

There were other names that went up in lights after winning the *Talent Scouts* auditions. Destined to achieve such notoriety were future luminaries Tony Bennett, Lenny Bruce, Roy Clark, Van Cliburn, Patsy Cline, Rosemary Clooney, Wally Cox, Vic Damone, the Diamonds, Connie Francis, Robert Goulet, Steve Lawrence, Ann-Margaret, Al Martino, Marian McPartland, Jose Melis, Shari Lewis and Leslie Uggams. A contemporary Godfrey biographer clarified: "Each musical performer was given a special orchestration, prepared by conductor Archie Bleyer. The orchestra was made up of top CBS staff musicians. This was hardly an amateur hour."[16]

At least two names of subsequent prominence failed to make the cut, however. When previewed before air time by a panel charged with weeding out the novices, neither Elvis Presley (in 1955) nor Buddy Holly (in 1956) was given a green light to appear. The situation suggested that no mortals could be right 100 percent of the time. Or possibly, that Buddy and Elvis might both be having bad hair days!

During its first 14 months on the air (initially on Tuesdays but shifting to Fridays in mid–1947), *Arthur Godfrey's Talent Scouts* was sustained by the network. By August 1947, however, when the series found a permanent timeslot at 8:30 P.M. on Mondays, Thomas J. Lipton, Incorporated — the makers of Lipton tea, soups and other food dishes — bought the program. It would be one of the most profitable commercial ventures in broadcasting. Lipton was already sponsoring a portion of the morning *Arthur Godfrey Time* on CBS. Adding the nighttime show definitely fortified its name before the average listener. That pact became a godsend to Godfrey and the network, too.

Announcer George Bryan linked the superstar and his sponsor at the program's inception: "Lipton Tea and Lipton Soup present *Arthur Godfrey's Talent Scouts!*" To the tune of "Sing a Song of Sixpence," vocalist Peggy Marshall and an ensemble known as the Holidays burst into the opening jingle …

> *Here comes Arthur Godfrey,*
> *Your talent scout emcee,*
> *Brought to you by Lip-ton …*
> *Brisk Lipton tea.*
> *You know it's Lipton tea*
> *If it's B-R-I-S-K …*
> *You know it's Arthur Godfrey,*
> *When you hear them play …*

Trombonist Lou McGarity then segued into the theme music employed on all of Godfrey's shows, "Seems Like Old Times." (More recently, that melody, written by Carmen Lombardo, brother of venerable bandleader Guy Lombardo, has become a symbol of vintage radio.) Even the theme underscored the indisputable link between the host and his longstanding sponsor, based on Lipton's connection with *Arthur Godfrey Time*. (Instrumentalist McGarity, incidentally, lasted 26 years with Godfrey, from the first network broadcast until McGarity's death in 1971, a year shy of the daytime series' demise. Few of "the little Godfreys" achieved anywhere near that level of durability.)

Godfrey was fond of double entendres and often lapsed into monologues bordering on the risqué. (Comedian Fred Allen once referred to the old redhead as "Peck's Bad Boy of Radio.") In one of his typical ribald digressions, on the *Talent Scouts* broadcast of April 18, 1949, Godfrey claimed he had spent the afternoon trying to obtain tickets to two Broadway productions, *South Pacific* and *Kiss Me Kate*. The earliest he could get seats was several months away. "You know what I told 'em, don't ya?" he said to a convulsing studio audience. [*Pause*] "I didn't tell 'em *that* at all," Godfrey exclaimed. "You folks are way ahead of me. Now tomorrow I'll get seven letters from the vice president ... I didn't say it ... I want to get that on the record ... I didn't say it ... I didn't say it." (Godfrey had a penchant for favoring debatable tastes that went back to his days of broadcasting on the New York–Washington dual hookup. One of his sponsors then was Sterling Drugs, the makers of Bayer aspirin. Somehow, when Godfrey pronounced it, the product came out sounding much like *bare ass prin*.[17])

Talent Scouts was soon boasting legions of listeners. This bode well for Lipton and also some of whose executives took exception when Godfrey poked fun at the commercials. Fans loved hearing him give the needle to the client; this was something new. But the Lipton decision-makers couldn't argue with the rapidly increasing sales of Lipton tea and soup mixes. Godfrey was credited with being responsible for most of it.

A radio historiographer observed: "Sponsors were better sports then, and endured kidding by [Jack] Benny, Fred Allen, Henry Morgan, Arthur Godfrey, and others. Perhaps they also just liked being in on the fun, a guest at the party, not the bullying intruders they seem today."[18]

Godfrey's nonchalantness allowed him to turn "the act of brewing a cup of tea into an orgasmic experience."[19] A biographer capitalized on it by recalling a descriptive commercial from one show:

It's a very simple matter to make one if you have the tea bags and the hot water nearby. I think I'll try one. [*Pause*] I always try to get the tag out of it if I can ... Doesn't add much to the taste. [*Pause*] Notice the finger. When handling tea you must always keep one finger in the air. I don't know why. [*Pause*] I pour the boiling water on it ... and let it sit there and stew ... and it's amazing what comes out of there! Amazing! You see how droopy I am now. [*Audience laughs*] Just wait till I have a shot of that tea — that Lipton tea ... Hey, while we're waiting for it to stew did yuh hear about the lady who hid two hundred thousand dollars' worth of diamonds in her bathroom? ... Did yuh? ... [*He pursues the story, then stops and pauses*] Hey, I think we must have a member of the board of directors of the Lipton company down here tonight. He's not enjoying this very much. [*Chuckles*] We better get back to the commercial for a minute, huh?[20]

Godfrey was fond of saying: "Fix yourself a cuppa Lipton tea. It's the cheapest thing you can drink next to water."

On May 13, 1949, he admonished his listeners to "buy anybody's tea ... I don't care what brand you buy because you'll eventually get to Lipton's."

He could be equally animated with the sponsors' other products:

I have here a piece of script from the client. Hey Arch — better give me some soft music. This is a poem ...

In olden days each housewife had a pot ... [*Long pause, accompanied by audience laughter*]

Of soup ... upon the stove ... [*Reads rest of the poem*]

I'll translate it. Lipton noodle soup and Lipton tomato vegetable soup is the doggondest soup you ever had in your life. Ever see it in the box? Here, I'll put them up here ... This is the chicken noodle soup. [*Pause*]

A chicken once sat in a nest near the pot. [*Pause*] It has a decided chickeny flavor. In fact a delightful flavor. In fact, I think there's some chicken in it. [*Pause*] One moment. I will have a look. [*Opens the package, followed by long pause*] No chicken been in here! [*Uproarious laughter during pause*] But it's full of noodles....[21]

Godfrey loved to pick up the commercial copy and hold it in the air for the audience's view. Then he'd toss it onto the floor or wad it into a ball and pitch it on the floor while ad-libbing for the sponsor, irritating the advertising agency no end. He never poked fun at the commodities he espoused, however; he could get bigger laughs ridiculing those responsible for the formality he abhorred.

He was convincing, too. In a 1996 Arts & Entertainment cable network interview, TV personality Larry King recalled:

I guess I was nine or ten years old. And I was home from school, sick. And Arthur Godfrey was doing a commercial for Peter Pan peanut butter. And he said, "I know you're not supposed to do this, but I'm gonna eat this peanut butter on the air" ... He put it in his mouth, and naturally when you put peanut butter in your mouth, you can't talk very good, so he was saying [*King imitates Godfrey trying to speak with peanut butter in his mouth*], "Aw, this is good!" Well, I went nuts. I ran to the cupboard. We had no peanut butter. And with a fever I got dressed ... no one was home ... went to the store and bought a jar of Peter Pan peanut butter and brought it home. I could *taste* that peanut butter. I had to *have* that peanut butter. Arthur Godfrey *sold* me that peanut butter!

On another show Godfrey was pushing a shampoo with an egg-and-milk formula. "If your hair is clean," he countered, "you can always use the stuff to make an omelet."

"Send in the boxtop from Post Bran Flakes for your free coupon," he once told his audience. "The Post folks need those boxtops. They ran out at the factory and if they don't get some tops for the boxes they'll have to send out their flakes loose. And you know those Bran Flakes people hate anything loose."

Godfrey's commercials weren't interruptions in his programs but were integrated parts of the whole. They were original and provoked spontaneous humor. On every show he personally delivered nearly all of the sponsors' messages. Meanwhile, he turned down potential clients that he objected to or whose products he couldn't conscientiously endorse as good buys for consumers. It was a radical departure from the way others were doing it.

Lipton carried *Talent Scouts* until the ratings no longer justified it, and remained with him until his last daily radio broadcast in 1972. In the meantime, Godfrey's other shows maintained a long list of would-be sponsors just waiting for commercial slots to open up. (Radio chronicler Gerald Nachman is convinced that Godfrey was "the second most successful salesperson on the air, after hostess and interviewer Mary Margaret McBride."[22])

His earthy colloquialisms didn't apply merely to the commercials, of course. His tales were purely homespun and delivered in a quasi-hayseed manner that endeared him to his listeners, essentially making him one of them. Steeped in a greeting-card passion, he reverently sprinkled his shows with Hallmark homilies. One of his choicest, repeated at the close of each broadcast, went like this: "May the good Lord willin', we'll see you at the same time tomorrow (or next week)."

If radio made Godfrey a household word in nearly every American home in the 1940s, television portrayed images of this redheaded broadcasting giant in the 1950s. Godfrey's morning show surfaced for a one-time outing on those black-and-white screens on November 23, 1948. The show wouldn't become a daytime staple on the tube until 1952, however, as a simulcast. (The televised *Arthur Godfrey Time* appeared variously between 10:00 and 11:30 A.M. in varying lengths, without interruption, on CBS-TV from January 7, 1952, through April 24, 1959.) Just a fortnight after the morning series' initial one-time trial, on December 6, 1948, CBS-TV began simulcasting the radio broadcast of *Arthur Godfrey's Talent Scouts*. It continued on TV at 8:30 P.M. Mondays through July 21, 1958, about 22 months after the radio series was withdrawn.

Five weeks following that launch, a televised Wednesday night hour-long musical variety show, *Arthur Godfrey and His Friends*, debuted on January 12, 1949. It included all "the little Godfreys" from the daytime show. From its start it was a smashing success. The show's format changed little before it went off the air in June 1957. Revived in a half-hour format on Tuesday nights in September 1958, it included daytime announcer Tony Marvin as the only "little Godfrey" and was simply called *The Arthur Godfrey Show*. It departed from the screens forever on April 28, 1959.

For 13 weeks in the spring of 1950 there was *Arthur Godfrey and His Ukulele*, a Tuesday/Thursday quarter-hour at 7:45 P.M. The old redhead offered live instruction in playing that instrument.

There would also be an extension of the morning show under the moniker *Arthur Godfrey's Digest*. This potpourri of taped repeats featured highlights of *Arthur Godfrey Time* that had aired during the previous week. *Digest* appeared over CBS Radio stations on weekends for several years in the early 1950s.

By October 1950 the video version of *Talent Scouts* was the eighth-highest rated TV show in the nation. A year later it captured first place from comedian Milton

Berle. In 1952-53 *Talent Scouts* and *Friends* ranked numbers two and three, respectively, immediately behind *I Love Lucy*. The following season *Talent Scouts* was third and *Friends* fifth. With dual weekly shows in radio's and television's top ten, Godfrey can lay claim to a record that has never been broken. And it certainly may never be.

Interestingly, after *Arthur Godfrey's Talent Scouts* folded, a serious attempt was made to exploit its success by returning it to TV under an altered format as a summer replacement. Merely titled *Talent Scouts*, the new show debuted July 3, 1962, over CBS-TV. Established celebrities introduced youthful professional performers for their initial network exposure. Among newcomers "discovered" there were Vic Dana, Louise Lasser, Vaughn Meader and Charles Nelson Reilly. The show went off at the end of the summer but reappeared in 1963, again as a seasonal replacement. Its final telecast was on September 17, 1963. Jim Backus was emcee in 1962, and Merv Griffin followed in 1963.

Comedians Bob and Ray frequently parodied Arthur Godfrey on their own national radio series. Their character was called Arthur Sturdley and was portrayed as being as dull as dishwater. Yet there was never any doubt who was the intended subject of their hilarious vignettes in which Sturdley dialogued with a stand-in for daytime announcer Tony Marvin.

Despite all the positive things that can be said about Arthur Godfrey and his momentous contributions to radio and television at mid–twentieth century, his idle backfence chitchat belied a ferocious ego. Make no mistake: He wielded supreme authority over everything at his command. When his wishes weren't precisely followed he became angry, made snap decisions (some of which he later regretted) and sometimes reacted in impish ways that accentuated his unbridled power. His clout and ego together eventually alienated many within the broadcasting industry.

At the outset, he claimed his shows had no stars beyond himself, suggesting little need then for his employees to sign contracts or acquire agents. All "the little Godfreys" worked at the pleasure of their mentor and could be summarily dismissed at will. When he perceived that one had gotten out of line he might totally ignore that individual on a given day, not calling upon him or her for a scheduled vocal number. Working without a script he'd conveniently drain all the airtime with jousting or allow others to perform extra vocals. To add insult to injury, he'd dock a miscreant's pay for failing to appear on the show.

Such a mean streak became even more pronounced as time continued. While most of it stayed beneath the surface and the public knew none of it, the seething burst to the forefront on October 19, 1953, when Godfrey — disturbed over a perceived lack of humility in singer Julius La Rosa — fired him while on the air during *Arthur Godfrey Time*. It was the start of a long good-bye for Godfrey, for the public reacted swiftly, audibly and overwhelmingly negatively. His popularity fell dramatically, and he was never able to recover from it. CBS was at that very juncture considering adding a Saturday morning show to Godfrey's impressive cache, but nixed that idea at once.

In some misguided, unbridled manner Godfrey persisted in dismantling what had been one of the greatest performing triumphs in the history of broadcasting. La Rosa's abrupt departure was followed by the most amazing string of self-defeating acts ever witnessed in the profession. Longtime bandleader Archie Bleyer was fired a short time afterward. In due time Godfrey dismissed the Mariners quartet, Haleloke, a trio of writers (Charles Horner, Preston H. Miles and Charles Slocum),

Marion Marlowe, producer Larry Puck, the Chordettes and Lu Ann Simms. Exclaimed a radio biographer: "What might have been an isolated incident stretched into six years of bitchy, bickering strife."[23]

A few months following La Rosa's dismissal, *Radio–TV Mirror* reported an incident that appeared indicative of Godfrey's style, previously kept from the public. Arriving at the studio before a *Talent Scouts* broadcast, he was appalled by what he saw on closed circuit TV as the talent for that night's show. As a result, he canceled the entire docket and beckoned his morning show regulars to perform as impromptu replacements instead.

Godfrey biographer Arthur Singer reports: "It was common knowledge that Godfrey and [producer Irving] Mansfield hated each other…. It's said that Godfrey would purposefully fill the half-hour of his *Talent Scouts* show till the very last seconds so that there wouldn't be time to run Mansfield's credit."[24]

Years later Julius La Rosa acknowledged that, while he never hated Godfrey for firing him and would always be grateful for the help his career received, his former tutor simply "wasn't a nice man."[25]

Godfrey's temper flared in other ways, adding to his deteriorating relations with the press. On January 7, 1954, he got into trouble for buzzing the tower at the airfield at Teterboro, New Jersey, when he was denied access to a runway he preferred. For six months his pilot's license was lifted as a result of that infringement.

Incredulously, he also cheated death for the second time since his crash in 1959 when cancer was removed from his aorta and he was declared completely cured of the disease. For years he had been a heavy smoker, but he turned his back on tobacco then and confessed to his audience: "I was wrong." Emphysema, sometimes linked to a heavy smoking addiction, would ultimately claim his life more than two decades later.

Godfrey nurtured other talents in addition to radio and television.

In 1946 he acquired a part in *Three to Make Ready*. But he collapsed in rehearsals and was hospitalized for exhaustion, dropping out of the show before it reached Broadway.

The following year, at the urging of Archie Bleyer, he recorded a novelty tune titled the *Too Fat Polka* ("I don't want her, you can have her, she's too fat for me!") and thought little of it. The record — like much of everything else Godfrey touched — nevertheless became a smashing success, selling three-and-a-half million copies. He was stupefied by it. Over a four-year period the poorly trained vocalist recorded six tunes that managed to land in the top 20 charts.

Godfrey maintained his daily radio program until he voluntarily withdrew it on April 30, 1972, precisely 27 years to the day after it had begun. In the late 1950s he dispensed with the large orchestra and several vocalists and ensembles, plus announcer Tony Marvin. By then Richard Hayes, a *Talent Scouts* winner, was the only crooner still featured almost daily. Occasionally Carmel Quinn would come by his microphone. It was a substantially different show in its final 13 or 14 years, but still drew a faithful corps of listeners, some of whom heard it seven days weekly. By then the show was pre-taped in 30-minute installments.

Meanwhile, Godfrey's passions included a strong emphasis on ecology. He was appointed by President Nixon to a Citizens' Advisory Committee on Environmental Quality. In 1966 he ventured into celluloid, playing Doris Day's dad in *The Glass Bottom Boat* on the big screen. For a few months in the early 1960s he co-hosted TV's *Candid Camera* with its creator, Allen Funt. Their egos clashed frequently, however, and Godfrey soon departed. He guest-hosted TV's *I've Got a Secret* once in the absence of panel moderator Garry Moore. In 1964 he was cast in Thornton Wilder's *Our Town* for a two-week summer run at a Pennsylvania theater. The following year he premiered on Broadway in a limited run of *Never Too Late*, opposite Maureen O'Sullivan. He performed in summer stock with roles in *Take Me Along* and *Show Boat*. He also traveled the country starring in horse shows and at rodeos throughout the 1960s.

In private life, meanwhile, Godfrey was married and divorced twice. Like Groucho Marx, he too fathered three children and late in life took up with a Manhattan woman who became his frequent companion in public. It was the aging redhead's intention to marry this young lady, his junior by many years, but that never transpired. In his final years he became resentful of his life and the way it was drawing to a close. After decades of power, prestige and popularity afforded by the national spotlight, he was by then a "forgotten" man by most former admirers. Coincidentally, the parallels with Marx during roughly this same time period are simply uncanny and not to be missed.

Godfrey died March 16, 1983, in New York City. He was 79.

There were others, of course, helping make *Talent Scouts* a driving force in offering new "discoveries" who were loaded with panache. Producer Irving Mansfield was at the forefront. As already noted, Mansfield worked with some of the biggest names in the industry before pitching his concept for a talent entry to Georgie Jessel and then to Godfrey. Mansfield later produced two short-run series for CBS: *It's Always Albert*, starring comedian Arnold Stang, and *The Morey Amsterdam Show*, with that comic playing himself. The latter show also appeared on CBS-TV and then on Dumont TV. Mansfield was married to one of that series' supporting players, Jacqueline Susann. He died on August 25, 1988, at the age of 80.

Succeeding Mansfield as *Talent Scouts* producer was Jack Carney, who also directed radio's *Give and Take* quiz show. He died of a heart attack in 1955 and was replaced the following year by Godfrey's old daytime singing star Janette Davis. By then *Talent Scouts* had left radio altogether.

Announcer George Bryan, meanwhile, introduced a myriad of other audio series: *The Aldrich Family, The Armstrong Theater of Today, Catch Me If You Can, CBS Weekly News Review, The Helen Hayes Theater, Hit the Jackpot, It's Always Albert, Let's Pretend, The Life of Riley, Mr. Chameleon, The Peter Lind Hayes Show, Road of Life* and *We, the People.* In 1946 the composer-vocalist hosted a quarter-hour syndicated show, *Songs by George Bryan.* Born in New York City on June 9, 1910, at age 26 he won first prize in a competition for neophyte narrators: the chance to announce for the *National Amateur Hour* for 20 weeks. Gaining subsequent training at Buffalo's WGAR and WKBW, he returned to New York to join CBS in 1940 where he became a staff announcer for 28 years. Bryan died at Stamford, Connecticut, on June 27, 1969.

In the 1940s songstress Peggy Marshall also prepared vocal arrangements for the children's fantasy program *The Land of the Lost.* She acquired no other major broadcasting credits.

In addition to Godfrey's trio of programs, Archie Bleyer conducted music for *Casey, Crime Photographer; The Charlie Ruggles Show; The Danny O'Neill Show; Fifty-One East 51st; The Gordon MacRae Show; The Janette Davis Show; The Joan Brooks Show; The Patti Clayton Show; Skyline Roof;* and *Stoopnagle and Budd.* In 1934 he turned up on Philadelphia's WIP and on NBC with the *Archie Bleyer Orchestra,* and that same year with *Archie Bleyer and His Commodore Hotel Orchestra* on New York's WMCA. He joined the CBS staff in 1939. Bleyer died March 20, 1989, at age 79.

Outside their stints with Godfrey, subsequent bandleaders Jerry Bresler, Will Roland and Bert Farber left almost no further legacies in professional entertainment. Roland got his start on radio with Pittsburgh's KDKA in 1935 and moved over to that city's WCAE the following year, conducting the *Will Roland Orchestra* at both stations. Farber was a singer on the MBS game show *Title Tales* in 1940, and handled music late in that decade for the NBC romantic drama *Curtain Time.* Otherwise, details of this threesome's careers have been lost to history.

The same applies to *Talent Scouts* writers Chuck Horner, Ken Lyons and Andy Rooney. Yes, it's the same Andy Rooney who for years appeared weekly as the combative and ornery member of CBS-TV's *60 Minutes.*

Godfrey's talent series wasn't the only one airing during the 1940s and 1950s, of course. In addition to *Major Bowes' Original Amateur Hour,* previously mentioned, there was *The Youth Opportunity Program, Live Like a Millionaire* and many more.

Bandleader Horace Heidt had been prominent on the radio entertainment scene since the early 1930s. He pursued a multitude of formats dealing with music, dance and variety, and he occasionally inserted a quiz into the mix. Of his multiple efforts, none is likely better remembered than *Pot o' Gold* (1939–41), the first big-money giveaway to hit the air. Several successor series bore a strong resemblance to the substance of that show.

Heidt is also recalled for an amateur talent series: *The Youth Opportunity Program,* which aired from December 7, 1947, through December 16, 1951. Offered in the same vein as Major Bowes' *Hour,* its distinguishing mark was that Heidt's entourage traveled the USA seeking unskilled talent. Every Sunday night Heidt turned up in a new city where legions of local harmonica players, accordionists and pianists were given a few minutes of airtime on a national hookup. It wasn't radio's finest hour, unless one was related to the aspiring yodelers and hoofers who gained a fleeting moment of fame on the airwaves.

In some ways, *Live Like a Millionaire* came across as a weekday version of *Arthur Godfrey's Talent Scouts*, though its "finds" were strictly amateurish. Some winners obviously hadn't sung previously outside their home showers. The "scouts" who brought these greenhorns before emcee Jack McCoy each afternoon were the offspring or siblings of the "contestants." On Godfrey's show, recall, children frequently introduced their parents/performers, but so did business associates, other relatives, friends, neighbors and passing acquaintances.

Millionaire was definitely a family-oriented series. Some days listeners heard from juveniles who were obviously too young to speak coherently before a live studio audience. Like *Talent Scouts*, the show relied on an applause meter to determine the winners. It ran five days a week, from June 5, 1950, through August 28, 1953.

In any given week, *Millionaire* fans were almost certain to hear a father sing "Million Dollar Baby" ("If you should ever run into a storm, just step inside my cottage door, and meet my million dollar baby, from the five- and ten-cent store"). A mother, father, sister or brother was likely to play a spirited violin rendition of "Hot Canary" or a piano arrangement of "'Till the End of Time." In fact, one might expect to hear those contemporary numbers twice or more in a given week. They were obviously favorites of the bathtub

brigade. Winners were awarded a week's interest on a million dollars, from which the show's name was derived. From 1951 to 1953, though not continuously, an evening video version of *Millionaire* appeared on various networks, days and at altering times.

In all there were two dozen or more talent series on radio, including *The Atwater Kent Auditions* (1927–32), *Budding Talent* (1938–39), *Fame and Fortune* (1940–41), *Lucky Stars* (1946), *Scout About Town* (1946), *Talent Search Country Style* (1951) and *Your Lucky Strike* (1948–49). Most were short-lived. Virtually all featured nobodies from nowhere who appeared to have skipped their music lessons. Not surprisingly, nearly all contestants failed in their quests for lasting notoriety and stardom.

Arthur Godfrey's Talent Scouts was several cuts above such amateurish tryouts. Without equivocation, it was the best showcase for up-and-coming talent aired. Across a dozen years in two mediums it set the pace for others to follow while introducing more than 2,000 near-professionals to the world's stage.

John Dunning summed it up: "*Talent Scouts* is Godfrey at his best — wise-cracking, rambling, then rushing through the spot to get the last act in. The temptation is strong, listening to these [shows], to think of Godfrey as a decent man who lost his way."[26]

In his prime, Arthur Godfrey doubtlessly commanded the most imposing following of anyone in radio and television. Given the era in which he lived, no celebrity in either medium accomplished more.

3

Break the Bank

Premise: This series can deservedly be labeled a forerunner among its peers. It was the first major audience participation program to be identified as a big money giveaway, thereby launching a quest that successor game shows would pursue, resulting in inevitable comparisons. *Break the Bank* was responsible for turning legions of loyal listeners into quiz show fanatics, awestruck by the opportunity of observing their countrymen gaining hefty recompense for possessing mere factual knowledge. Such enlightenment was a prerequisite to the players' success. In the meantime, the questions substantially intensified as the contestants advanced through the game. *Bank* had more going for it than simply giving away significant rewards, however. Its greatest fortune may have been in those who were picked to interrogate the players and dispense those large cash sums. Unequivocally, the most sparkling and satisfying of the several emcees to headline the show was the perpetually upbeat Bert Parks. His effervescence was contagious and effectively overshadowed everything else that transpired during the half-hour. Other superstars who supplanted him brought an array of gifts to the microphone, too. One talent possessed by all of them was an indigenous ability to place their guests and audiences at ease. The series enjoyed a successful run on radio and TV while airing in both daytime and nighttime versions. Long after its original decade-long run had ended, the series was resurrected several times in a variety of formats. The TV quiz scandals had tainted the minds of viewers by then, of course, which reached out to any program that granted thousands of dollars in return for a few simple facts. To their credit, *Bank*'s creators took sensitive precautions to maintain the utmost integrity that had long characterized their series, inspiring large numbers of Americans to tune in routinely during its halcyon days.

Producers: Walt Framer, Edwin Wolfe

Director: Jack Rubin

Writers: Walt Framer, Joseph Nathan Kane, Jack Rubin

Musicians: Henry (Hank) Sylvern (organist), Peter Van Steeden (orchestra), Lew White (organist)

Announcers (Hosts): Clayton (Bud) Collyer, Win Elliot, John Reed King, Johnny Olsen, Bert Parks, Bob Shepherd

Quizmasters (Masters of Ceremonies): Clayton (Bud) Collyer (daytime), Bert Parks (primetime)

Theme Songs: "The Golddigger's Song," "We're in the Money"

Sponsors: Vick Chemical Co. underwrote this series in its first season on behalf of a line of cough and cold suppressants (drops, inhalers, rubs, liquids, etc.). The following year Bristol-Myers, Inc. bought the show for its personal care commodities (Vitalis hair preparation, Trushay hand lotion, Sal-Hapetica antacid laxative, Ipana toothpaste, Resistab antihistamine, Bufferin pain reliever, Mum deodorant and others), carrying it for six seasons during the program's summit years. Multiple sponsors paid the bills in 1952–53. Miles Laboratories, Inc. (Alka-Seltzer stomach-distress reliever, Bactine antiseptic, One-a-Day Brand multiple vitamins, Tabcin heartburn antidote, Miles Nervine anxiety calmative, Chooz antacid gum) picked up the series for its final two seasons, including dual broadcasts in 1954–55, the show's last year on the air.

Ratings: High: 14.7 (primetime 1947–48); Low: 3.4 (daytime 1953–54); Primetime median: 11.6; Daytime median: 4.2

On the Air: Oct. 20, 1945–Apr. 13, 1946, MBS, Saturday, 9:30 P.M. ET; July 5, 1946–Sept. 23, 1949, ABC, Friday, 9 P.M.; Oct. 5, 1949–Sept. 13, 1950, NBC, Wednesday, 9 P.M.; Sept. 25, 1950–Sept. 21, 1951, NBC, Monday–Friday, 11:30 A.M.; Sept. 24, 1951–Mar. 27, 1953, ABC, Monday–Friday, 11:30 A.M.; Sept. 28, 1953–July 15, 1955, NBC, Monday–Friday, 10:45 A.M. (15 minutes); Sept. 27, 1954–Mar. 25, 1955, MBS, Monday–Friday, 12 noon (15 minutes).

* * *

Spawned during the postwar quiz surge, when big-moneyed handouts became the hottest thing on the air, *Break the Bank* was the progenitor of a vast empire of super giveaways. With *Bank's* cash jackpots habitually reaching four figures, the show fed the voracious appetites of mainstream Americans for contests with bigger and bigger payoffs. Ultimately, the frenzy's zenith was attained in the late 1950s in a series of lingering quiz show scandals involving several of its TV contemporaries.

Yet *Break the Bank* was the first of an untainted breed, "designed for intelligent people"[1] who read widely and had "good retentive power."[2] The entertainment industry's insider publication *Variety* suggested that "the idea of winning $1,000 or more on a single program staggered listeners," while calling those earnings "awe-inspiring sums" and sanctioning the series because it "stimulated one's mental prowess."[3] Gaining instant status, the show was espied in 1948 by the fan magazine *Radio Mirror* as "the highest-paying quiz program in the world."[4]

Exposure like that didn't sit well with the critics, however, who derided the fact that paupers could be put onto pedestals in 30 minutes, attracting scores more to tempt their fate. In later years one analyst claimed that these programs turned Americans into "a nation of moneygrubbing Scrooge McDucks."[5] Despite such discourse, the idea of immediate cash payment, coupled with at least a measure of limited fame within one's own community, drew widespread appeal.

The show's origins were of a modest fashion—as a simple quiz broadcast over the nation's smallest aural network. As it gained in stature and acquired hordes of fans, a growing bankroll commensurate with that ascendance propelled it to larger webs offering greater visibility and prestige.

At its inception, nonetheless, the fledgling *Break the Bank* couldn't even agree on a permanent master of ceremonies. Instead, it drew upon a quartet of veteran radio interlocutors whose flamboyant styles and affable repartee with audiences marked them as charming and effervescent entertainers. They included a male foursome who were absolutely adored by their fans—Clayton (Bud) Collyer, John Reed King, Johnny Olsen and Bert Parks, each of them a veteran of multiple audience participation series drawn from lengthy professional careers. Employing a weekly rotational system, *Bank* ascribed the master of ceremonies' duties to them during the initial months it aired over the Mutual Broadcasting System.

To producer Edwin Wolfe—a talented individual who brought impressive credentials to his position, earned across a disparate career as a radio executive—one of this tetrad (Parks) offered unbridled and unrivaled energy. Picked as the sole master of ceremonies when the big-moneyed giveaway moved to ABC a few months beyond its inception, Parks proved an excellent choice. Naming him as quizmaster provided an impetus for attracting and sustaining millions who were to become faithful listeners.

Parks wasn't new to network radio by any means, having arrived at the CBS studios a dozen years earlier. An Atlantan, born December 30, 1914, his radio career began on his hometown's WGST when he was only 16. Hired for the dual roles of announcer and singer, he performed suitably and moved up to the big time in New York a couple of years later. The year was 1933 and he was earning $50 weekly as a CBS staff announcer, substantial capital in that Depression era.

Parks' effusive personality soon caught the attention of comedian Eddie Cantor, who put him on his show as announcer, vocalist and foil to himself. Before long the gregarious Georgian was emceeing shows for bandleaders Xavier Cugat and Benny Goodman, too. His vocational direction appeared set.

Parks gained announcing assignments on several more series: *The Adventures of Ellery Queen, Camel Caravan, Columbia Workshop, Forty-Five Minutes in Hollywood, How'm I Doin?* (an early game show), *The Kate Smith Show, Luncheon at the Waldorf, Matinee at Meadowbrook, Our Gal Sunday* and *Renfrew of the Mounted.*

When summoned in the early 1940s by Uncle Sam, the budding showman interrupted his career to serve his country. Upon returning, he picked up new radio stints, introducing *Judy, Jill and Johnny* and *McGarry and His Mouse.* By that time he could hardly be contained as a mere behind-the-mike narrator. Bursting upon the scene as a rotating emcee—a fresh shot of adrenaline to *Break the Bank*'s audience—Parks unveiled his manifold talents to public scrutiny. And people liked what they found. He'd never be comfortable in the shadows again, even once attesting, "I created a whole era. I started the pattern."[6]

A couple of years after *Bank*'s premiere, he was instrumental in launching another audience participation show on a local New Jersey station. *Second Honeymoon* aired weekdays in 1947 over WAAT as a remote from Bamberger's department store in Newark. It was a human-interest series of the *Queen for a Day* archetype. Housewives selected to appear on the show fathomed why they merited subsequent wedding trips. A panel of judges picked winners, showering them with merchandise prizes and sending them on dream vacations. As its master of ceremonies, Parks moved with the program to the ABC network in 1948. A year later the series transferred to MBS for an ephemeral final run.

The year 1948 was, incidentally, a banner one for Parks. He was selected to host yet a *third* concurrent ABC audience participation show: *Stop the Music!* It would be his crowning achievement as an audio performer. By then he had been resolutely placed among radio's top five or six game-show emcees.[7]

Most memorably, of course, Parks is

recalled by nearly everybody in the country who lived through that era as the vocalist with the leaping eyebrows who bellowed "There She Is! Miss America!" From 1954 to 1979 he presided over the televised Miss America Pageant, requesting the envelope from the judges containing the name of the winner. Withdrawing the name of the lucky lady who would be crowned, he read her state's name aloud, then crooned to her. Parks had arrived in that spot from a long career as a radio and television celebrity, backed with Broadway appearances that included the title role in *The Music Man*.

During the mid–1950s he presided over a two-hour daily radio series titled *NBC Bandstand*, a half-hour of which was simulcast on TV in 1956. Earlier (from 1950 to 1952) he hosted a tri-weekly daytime TV variety outing, *The Bert Parks Show*, initially on NBC, then CBS. By that time he had long been established in the public's mind as a game show host. His additional television credits in the field included *Double or Nothing* (1952–54), *County Fair* (1958–59), *The Big Payoff* (1959) and *Yours for a Song* (1961–63).

Parks was nothing less than a superstar, and to state anything less would be to cast aspersion on a career and personality that was genuinely admired by multitudes of adoring fans. He died on February 2, 1992, at La Jolla, California, at the age of 77.

It was *Break the Bank* that initially thrust Parks before the American public and in due time led him to successively greater ventures. Only 33 when he signed on with the series, he possessed unflagging vigor and bursting enthusiasm that did not escape the notice of Edwin Wolfe, *Bank*'s producer. Characterized as "young, hungry, hyperkinetic ... the most excitable man on radio,"[8] the handsome, virile, supercharged Parks with the contagious smile liked people and wanted them to like him.

He was everything *Bank* required, and he would be its matchless star throughout its years of primetime broadcasting.

Before each show went on the air, about 15 couples or duos (spouses, mixed relatives, same gender teams or other diverse pairs) were selected from the studio audience. Assistants bearing portable microphones roved among the patrons while conducting impromptu interviews as the potential contestants remained in their seats. A handful were brought on-stage for more intensive questioning by Wolfe. Not only did Wolfe pick those who would go on the air, but he also decided the order of their appearance. Candidates who failed to make the final cut received five-dollar checks for their trouble.

When the show went on, each couple or team met the master of ceremonies, who animatedly bantered with them briefly before launching into the game. The proceedings maintained an aspect of formality, definitely reflecting the epoch in which they transpired. On one show, for instance, Parks announced: "Here are our first two contestants coming up to the microphone, and may I have your name please?"

Feminine voice: "Mrs. Alton Blaine."

Parks: "And you, sir?"

Masculine voice: "Mr. Alton Blaine."

From that point on, every direct reference from the emcee to the contestants was addressed to either "Mr. Blaine" (never "Alton") or "Mrs. Blaine" (presumably, he never knew her first name; it wouldn't have been considered proper to ask for it). The show's announcer, however, frequently called Parks "Bert"—showmen weren't afforded the same charity as were contestants.

The game itself was simple. Before the show the pre-selected contestants chose a category from which they were to be asked a round of questions on the air. Responding to eight questions with correct answers broke the bank. Each couple or team was allowed to miss one question. Two misses meant immediate departure, at which point they forfeited whatever monetary sum was tied to the second question missed. That amount was deposited into the bank. The questions — increasing in difficulty — offered cash values of $10, $20, $50, $100, $200, $300, $500 and the bank's contents. The assets there were invariably a minimum of $1,000 and frequently included thousands more. Parks and his peers noted that players were "reaching" for whatever amount was next on their journey to breaking the bank. When they missed a question, the first time he'd mention to what level the misstep had dropped them in the proceedings, saying "You're reaching once again" for such-and-such cash number level.

Parks registered a kind of melancholy behavior that appeared to border on despair when a contestant couldn't instantly recall the answer to a contest question he posed. (A contemporary, meanwhile, Dr. I.Q., was seemingly disgusted on that show when guests couldn't think of an appropriate answer to the questions.) No less than *The New York Times* noted that Parks' physical responses at such intervals were "terpsichorean." A reporter perceived: "He rolls his eyes, his feet stamp rhythmically, he anxiously eyes the clock, gently whispers: 'Think hard.'"[9] The quintessential Parks couldn't stand still very long under *any* circumstance. He once offered this assessment of himself: "I never walk when I can run; I never sit when I can stand; I never talk when I can shout."[10]

His show found a way to retain its audience from week to week by employing a technique familiar to soap opera partisans: If players didn't complete their game by the end of the half-hour, they were invited to return and continue it the following week. Thus, there was impetus to "tune in at this same time next week" to hear the finale of a game in progress.

Break the Bank's creative minds soon developed a method of involving the home audience, too, as did many other quiz shows. Employing a feature called the "wishbowl," *Bank* solicited post cards from listeners aged 16 and older living in the "48 states" or District of Columbia. The cards bore senders' names, addresses and telephone numbers. A card was drawn from a bowl on every show, and the sender was invited to bring someone to the following week's broadcast with all expenses paid. In another version, contestants in the "wishbowl" segment drew three cards. The sender of the first was invited to participate the next week; if that individual wasn't available, the second name was telephoned, and so on. The effect was that it directly involved the listeners at home in the prize-feeding frenzy that *Bank* was helping create on the nation's airwaves.

On August 30, 1946, a U.S. Navy commander and his bride, Mr. and Mrs. Jack A. Weiss, were *Bank* contestants, drawn from the studio audience. Due to his mental prowess in regard to subjects covered by many quiz shows, Weiss was privately tagged by his family as "Uncle Information Please," alluding to another popular Q-and-A series. On *Bank* he pursued the category of geography and answered all eight questions correctly, netting the newlyweds $5,220. In broadcasting's first quarter-century it was the largest jackpot that had ever been won.

When a quiz program offered participants eight substantive questions before they could receive its top prize, not much out of the ordinary could be expected to occur. But occasionally something didn't go quite as expected.

Such was the case on December 24, 1948, when three-year-old Michael Powers broke from his mother's lap while she was seated in *Bank*'s audience. Just as the show was going on the air, the capricious child tore up a couple of steps and burst on-stage. Quizmaster Parks surprised the boy's parents, Mr. and Mrs. Clifton Powers, by inviting them to be contestants. When the show ended, the Powers family had broken the bank for $9,020, easily the largest cash prize earned on a radio quiz program at that time.

One of the eccentricities stemming from *Bank* that other quizzes of that era picked up on was a tendency toward producing an ongoing deceptive stir. Conversation was clearly accelerated via quizmasters who willfully responded to statements before their guests could finish speaking. Further enhancing the rush were musical bridges that seemed to gallop across space. As a result, an atmosphere of breathless excitement and anticipation hung in the balance for much of the time.

Another peculiarity edging its way onto quiz shows of that period was an incessant mention of a sponsor's products, going well beyond the designated commercials. Parks repeatedly updated the fans with precisely how much cash was in "the Vitalis-Trushay bank" at any given moment, for instance. When a reference to one of the sponsor's commodities could be inserted into any neighborly exchange, it was. There may not have been a five-minute lapse in any show when the radio listeners were not reminded who was underwriting it. It must have been the nature of the beast, for several of its protégés were doing the same thing.

Bank was initially brought to the air by the Vick Chemical Company, using it as a marketing vehicle for its line of health care wares. When the show left MBS for ABC a few months later, one of the most prominent names then in broadcast advertising, Bristol-Myers, Inc. bought it. The firm carried the series for a half-dozen years on separate networks—ABC and NBC—initially in primetime, later in daytime. Bristol-Myers also sponsored a televised version of the show. While Vitalis

hair preparations for men, and Trushay hand lotion for women, were the principal beneficiaries of the company's commercials, several of its other well-recognized personal care brands were plugged, too. When Bristol-Myers pulled out in 1952, multiple sponsors stepped in to carry the show for another season. The following year Miles Laboratories, Inc. accepted it, underwriting the series until the end of the run in 1955 on behalf of its extensive array of health-oriented consumer brands.

Shortly after the show's inception each week, an ebullient Parks yelled to the studio audience: "Tell me, does anyone want to break the bank?" That cue was invariably met with as wildly an enthusiastic affirmation as his question was designed to provoke.

In addition to the draw of the big money game (which greatly enhanced its success), *Bank* had more going for it by way of a blended staff of gifted and committed artists who worked tirelessly behind the scenes.

Producer Edwin Wolfe, for instance, was well recognized by that time as one of the better program chiefs in the industry. He brought a range of experience to the show, plus an obvious empathy for people. He had earlier produced the serial drama *Hilltop House*, promoting lofty standards in both writing and acting there. In addition, he directed a quartet of other popular soap operas—*The Brighter Day, Ma Perkins, Pepper Young's Family* and *Road of Life*—and a situation comedy, *The Parker Family*. He also performed in the casts of two of those serials, *Ma Perkins* and *Pepper Young's Family*.

His reputation for firmness but fairness was well received. He had a penchant for introducing aspiring young actors and actresses to their first encounters in radio. When the sponsor of *Hilltop House* shifted its account from one advertising agency to another, Wolfe was deeply distressed by some announced plans to trim the costs by reducing the literary quality of the series. To dispel any attempt to modify the program's high standards, he withdrew *Hilltop House* from the air altogether. Such principles, he believed, were greater than the bottom line. Wolfe lived to the age of 90 and died on September 22, 1983.

Wisely recognizing the artistry and creativity surrounding his fledgling giveaway show, *Break the Bank*, Wolfe determined not to let that staff get away if he could hold it intact. Years later an appraiser of such contests would acknowledge that the "creative team for *Bank* stood together as one of the best ever assembled for a radio quiz."[11] A more fitting tribute could hardly have been conferred.

Walt Framer, for instance, supplied some of the brainpower that Wolfe drew upon during *Bank*'s crucial formative stages and over its first two years on the air. Not until Framer's own giveaway show, *Strike It Rich*, went into production in 1947 did his role with *Bank* diminish. Wolfe relied upon Framer as an executive advisor. Actually, Framer carried the combined roles of co-producer, promoter and writer for *Bank*. As a team player, he obviously gained whatever experience he may have lacked to help him become a successful producer himself. *Strike It Rich* would last for more than a decade, including joined radio and television runs.

It was Framer, incidentally, who suggested that Wolfe name the series *Break the Bank*. Those words were first written on a thick binder that an acquaintance toted into Wolfe's office one day. The gentleman claimed he had gathered "a compendium of every quiz game ever done on radio," and thereby presented it to Wolfe. Wolfe paid the man a royalty every week the show was on the air for the use of that ingenious phrase.

From its inception, *Bank* corralled several of the most congenial crowd-pleasers in radio history as its rotational quizmasters.

John Reed King was one, a celebrated host who "ran game shows in wholesale lots."[12] Across his career, King emceed *Chance of a Lifetime, Double or Nothing, Give and Take, Go for the House, The Great Day* and *The Missus Goes a-Shopping.*

He announced for scads of other shows, too, including, *Americans at Work, The American School of the Air, Bobby Benson and the B-Bar-B Riders, Carol Kennedy's Romance, The Chrysler Air Show, Death Valley Days, Death Valley Sheriff, Duffy's Tavern, Gay Nineties Revue, Grand Central Station, The Heinz Magazine of the Air, The Mel Torme Show, Our Gal Sunday, So You Think You Know Music, The Stuart Erwin Show, Texaco Star Theater, The Victor Borge Show, What's My Name?, The Woman* and *Ziegfeld Follies of the Air.* For a short while he also appeared in the title role of the juvenile serial *Sky King.*

An Atlantic City, New Jersey, native, King was born October 25, 1914. In the early 1930s, still in his teens, he was the voice of the Paramount motion picture newsreels shown in theaters everywhere. He announced big band radio remotes that were broadcast from his hometown, before becoming a student at Princeton University. While a collegian he regularly fed news reports to CBS, apprenticing with leading CBS newsmen Edward R. Murrow and Robert Trout. During World War II he aired a weekly news program in French that was transmitted to occupied France. And after the Golden Age of radio ended, he supplied voice-overs for radio and television commercials until his retirement in the early 1970s. King died at Woodstown, New Jersey, on July 8, 1979. He was 64.

Yet another prominent member of the early roving *Break the Bank* emcees was Johnny Olsen. Born at Windom, Minnesota, in 1910, his initial audio assignment was as the Buttermilk Kid on a Madison,

Wisconsin, station. He advanced to KGDA in Mitchell, South Dakota, not only managing, selling, announcing and singing, but preaching, too, on a daily devotional series. Olsen became chief announcer at Milwaukee's WTMJ next, and then went off to Hollywood for a year. When he returned to Milwaukee he hosted an audience participation show that quickly became an early trademark, *Johnny Olsen's Rumpus Room*.

In 1944 he left Milwaukee permanently to join ABC in New York as a staff announcer. Over the years he warmed up audiences prior to introducing *Beat the Clock, Get Together, On Stage Everybody, Prince Charming, Swingshift Frolics* and *True or False*. Olsen was master of ceremonies on several game shows, too: *Get Rich Quick* and *Whiz Quiz*, plus two more for which he is better remembered in radio—*The Johnny Olsen Show*, running at various times between 1946 and 1957 on ABC and MBS under the added monikers of *Johnny Olsen's Luncheon Club* and *The Johnny Olsen Rumpus Room* (also appearing on Dumont Television, 1949–52); plus *Ladies Be Seated*, co-hosted with his spouse Penny Olsen on ABC from 1946 to 1949. In early 1945 the couple starred in a five-week televised trial run of *Ladies Be Seated* on the Dumont network. It was one of the earliest attempts by anybody to videocase an audience participation program.

Olsen emceed ABC-TV's *Fun for the Money*, and from 1951 to 1953 he was a principal in the cast of *Kids and Company*, a Saturday morning children's show on Dumont TV. His most prominent role, however—the one for which he is still recalled by millions—was as the announcer who originated the national catchphrase "Come on down!" on CBS-TV's *The Price Is Right*. Olsen appeared there from the show's inception on November 26, 1956, throughout its first run, ending September 3, 1965. He returned for a second run

from September 4, 1972, until his death at age 75 on October 12, 1985, in Santa Monica, California.

When Bert Parks was chosen as *Bank's* permanent master of ceremonies, another rising young star, who could boast of a favorable track record with audiences, was retained and appeared destined to go further. Clayton (Bud) Collyer, veteran announcer, actor and audience participation emcee, was designated "host" of the show. It was a kind of glorified title for handling the traditional announcer's duties, including helping to select and welcome contestants on the air and reading some of the sponsor's commercials. His gracious acceptance of the role as "second banana" held him in good stead. When the series left primetime five years later—and Parks with it, having his fingers in more enterprises than he could comfortably handle by then—Collyer got the nod as permanent master of ceremonies on the five-day-a-week series.

Born June 18, 1908, in New York City, Collyer trained to become an attorney, studying at Williams College and Fordham University. When he found clerking for a law firm "dull," he began looking elsewhere. He sang on New York's WABC (now WCBS) while an undergraduate. The actors and announcers Collyer met there were earning as much in a month as he would in a year as a lawyer, he acknowledged later. When he auditioned for NBC in 1935 and won a role in a show, young Collyer abandoned his legal intentions altogether to concentrate on radio. Soon he was earning $85 a week as a CBS vocalist. Before long he appeared on as many as 30 shows every week and carried home seven grand annually, "big dough at that time," he recalled.

Collyer's shows are legion. He announced for *The Benny Goodman Show, Big Sister, The Cavalcade of America, The Guiding Light, The Goldbergs, House in the*

Country, Mary Small, The Philip Morris Playhouse, The Raleigh Room, Road of Life, The Sheaffer Review, Silver Theater, Stage Door Canteen, The Story of Mary Marlin, Truth or Consequences and *Quiz of Two Cities.* He hosted a variety series, *By Popular Demand,* and *Listening Post,* a dramatic anthology.

Unlike most announcers, he could also act. He appeared in the cast of *Hillbilly Heart Throbs* while maintaining long-running roles in *Chick Carter, Boy Detective; Joyce Jordan, M.D.; Just Plain Bill; Life Can Be Beautiful; Terry and the Pirates;* and *Young Widder Brown.*

He won leading parts, too, including the title role in *The Adventures of Superman.* He was imposing while speaking in a high-pitched voice as journalist Clark Kent, then altering his tone to maximum power and depth as Superman. The difference in the dual speech patterns was curiously distinct. He also played the title role in *Chips Davis, Commando (sic).* In addition, he played leads in *Abie's Irish Rose; High Places; Kate Hopkins, Angel of Mercy; Kitty Foyle; The Man I Married;* and *Pretty Kitty Kelly.*

Despite an affiliation with more than two dozen predominantly dramatic series—about half of them soap operas—in the 1940s, Collyer moved to a "new career" as a major audience participation show emcee-host-quizmaster. On *Bride and Groom* of that genre, he married radio dramatic actress Marion Shockley (of *Abie's Irish Rose, The Adventures of Ellery Queen, Mystery Theater* and *Road of Life*). In addition to radio's *Break the Bank,* he presided over *On Your Mark, Three for the Money, Times a-Wastin'* (a.k.a. *Beat the Clock*) and *Winner Take All.* On TV he welcomed contestants to *Beat the Clock* (1957–61), *Break the Bank* (1948–53), *Feather Your Nest* (1954–56), *Masquerade Party* (1952), *Number Please* (1961), *This Is the Missus* (1948) and *To Tell the Truth* (1962–68). From 1966 to 1969 he also reprised an old radio role by providing voice-overs for *Superman,* a Saturday morning children's cartoon on TV. Possibly setting a record among all broadcast performers, Collyer appeared on about four dozen combined radio and television series.

A firm believer in the influence of worshipping the Deity, he consistently took his children every week to High Ridge (Connecticut) Methodist Church. For years he was the parish's Sunday school superintendent. In the years he emceed shows like *Break the Bank,* Collyer frequently bade farewell to parting contestants with a cheery "God bless you!"

At one time he was chosen to head the New York chapter of the American Federation of Radio Artists. In 1948, and again in 1949, he was elected president by the AFRA national electorate. He became a central figure in that group's legendary blacklisting of entertainers suspected of sympathizing with Nazi and Communist causes during the late 1940s and 1950s. Collyer often pursued the role of peacemaker and mediator, while making no apologies for his personal stance: that of exposing any who might threaten America, ultimately denying them work in the performing arts. It was a popular cause in some quarters but resulted in bitter disputes and loss of friendships in others. His death occurred September 8, 1969, at Greenwich, Connecticut.

When Collyer took over *Bank* as permanent master of ceremonies, another member of broadcasting's growing stable of audience participation notables, Win Elliot, replaced him as host-announcer of the daytime series. Elliot, who is better recalled as a sportscaster, was born May 7, 1915, at Chelsea, Massachusetts. He took a job at Detroit's WJR while pursuing studies in radio announcing and writing at the University of Michigan. Following a three-year stint at WMEX, a low-powered Boston outlet, he transferred to Washington as a staff announcer. Soon gaining a berth as host of his own daytime variety show, *Club 1300*, on Baltimore's WFBR, he was additionally the series' producer and writer.

Elliot was informed that had he been known outside that regional market, he would have been signed to replace Ralph Edwards on *Truth or Consequences* when Edwards received wartime greetings from Uncle Sam. "You're the best we've auditioned to replace me," Edwards advised, while assuring Elliot he would "do something" for him "as soon as I can."[13]

Those words weren't hollow. Deferred by the draft board a short time later, Edwards made good on his promise, giving Elliot's name to the NBC Blue network. As a result, Elliot was soon hosting *Musical Mysteries*, a quiz program originating in New York. By 1944 he was also emceeing *Fish Pond*, a short-lived ABC amateur talent series.

In the mid-to-late 1940s, following his own brief stint in the Merchant Marines, Elliot returned to the microphones as master of ceremonies for a trio of game shows—*County Fair* and *Winner Take All*, both on CBS, and *Quick as a Flash* on MBS. In the 1950s he was emcee of yet another CBS quiz, *Walk a Mile*. He announced *The Betty Crocker Magazine of the Air, The Gillette Cavalcade of Sports* and the comedy series *Willie Piper*.

On TV Elliot became the emcee of *It's in the Bag* (1950–52), *On Your Account* (1953–54) and *Tic Tac Dough* (1956–59), and he created his own horseracing game, *Win with a Winner* (summer 1958). During the televised run of the soap opera *Valiant Lady* between 1953 and 1957, he was the announcer and an occasional actor. He also earned credentials as a well-recognized TV and radio sportscaster during that period. Elliot's sports roundups were ongoing CBS features into the 1980s, with a special accent on hockey and horseracing events.

Break the Bank's producer, Edwin Wolfe, insulated that series with still further success—beyond Walt Framer, Bert Parks, Bud Collyer and Win Elliot — by acquiring a competent radio director, scholarly writer and several versatile musicians to add stability to the big-moneyed giveaway.

Multitalented Jack Rubin, *Bank*'s director, had served an apprenticeship on the daytime serial *The Brighter Day*, which Wolfe produced. Rubin gained experience as an actor and writer, too. He won a running part in *The O'Neills*, an early soap opera that he also directed. He was a contributing writer on the comedy series *Junior Miss*, and provided script adaptations for *Hallmark Playhouse* (1948–52). At the time of his death on October 10, 1952, Rubin was writing *The Hardy Family* in syndication. He was just 42.

Questions for *Break the Bank* were crafted by book author Joseph Nathan Kane. Kane often drew upon an 800-page reference work he titled *Famous First Facts* as the basis for the show's inquisition. In 1956 he also published a manual that was directed at aspiring applicants for such fare, called *How to Win on Quiz Shows*. A newspaper journalist by trade, Kane sold "stumpers" to radio quizzes long before he entered *Bank*'s stable of regulars. His capacity for erudition had been the cornerstone for a couple of earlier minor question-and-answer programs.

Citizen Kane was a perfectionist who took great pains to see that his queries yielded no double meanings. Every week he devoted a full day to shaping about 30 questions that would be asked on a single *Break the Bank* broadcast. Then he'd secure the questions in sealed envelopes that he would personally transport to the studio. The integrity of the series was never compromised as a result.

Kane's method of generating questions was opposite that of many contemporary quiz shows of the period. Some sat bright young intellects— fresh from collegiate incubations— before reference volumes with little more mandate than a simple: "Dig." Those scribes may have viewed what they were doing as an occupation; to Kane, it was an all-consuming passion in creativity. His meticulous efforts aptly landed him among the masters of his art.

The music on *Break the Bank* followed a kind of soldier of fortune formula. In the early days, when the show aired on the smallest network, producer Wolfe signed clavier virtuoso Henry (Hank) Sylvern to render the melodic queries at the studio console organ. But when *Bank* moved to ABC a few months later, its enhanced resources warranted some upgrading. Wolfe hired Bert Parks as permanent master of ceremonies. And the lone organist was replaced by a full orchestra under the direction of popular radio maestro Peter Van Steeden. This arrangement continued as the show shifted to NBC three years later. In 1950, when it transferred from prime-time to daytime programming, Parks, Van Steeden and the orchestra all departed. *Bank*'s music then reverted to organ accompaniment by Lew White. Thus a trio of music makers— Sylvern, Van Steeden and White — were responsible for the melody during *Bank*'s 10-year lifespan.

Sylvern's radio repertoire — sometimes as an instrumentalist, sometimes while conducting an orchestra — included *The Adventures of the Abbotts, Arthur Godfrey Time, The Beatrice Kay Show, Beyond Tomorrow, Boston Blackie, Crooked Square, Foreign Assignment, Here Comes McBride, The Jackie Gleason-Les Tremayne Show, Kelly's Courthouse, The Mysterious Traveler, Nick Carter-Master Detective, Philo Vance, So You Think You Know Music, Sonny Skylar's Serenade, Strike It Rich, There Was a Woman, True Confessions* and *The Woman.* This musical virtuoso died July 4, 1964, at age 56.

Van Steeden's record is just as impressive. He conducted orchestras for *The Abbott and Costello Show, The Adventures of Christopher Wells, The Alan Young Show, The Bob Hawk Show, Camel Presents Harry Savoy, Claudia and David, Duffy's Tavern, The Fred Allen Show, The George Jessel Show, The Jack Pearl Show, McGarry and His Mouse, Mr. District Attorney, Quizzer's Baseball, Stoopnagle and Budd, Tim and Irene, Walk a Mile* and *Your Hit Parade.* His orchestra also provided the music for *Bank*'s televised version.

Born April 3, 1904, in Amsterdam, The Netherlands, Van Steeden put together his first band (Van and His Collegians) while he was an engineering student at New York University. They played club dances, college proms, restaurants and resort hotels, landing a spot on New York's WEAF in 1923. He later conducted music makers on numerous remote broadcasts from hotels in that area. Van Steeden succumbed to death at 85 in New Canaan, Connecticut, on January 3, 1990.

Bank's Lew White was at the console or directing an orchestra for all of these programs: *The Adventures of Dick Cole, The Adventures of Nero Wolfe, Betty Moore, Bulldog Drummond, Casey Crime Photographer, Charlie Chan, Cook's Travelogue, Dr. Christian, Ethel and Albert, Grand Central Station, Inner Sanctum Mysteries, The Lucky Strike Dance Orchestra, The Malcolm LaProde Show, Nick Carter-Master Detective, Portia Faces Life* and *The Story of Mary Marlin.*

Born in Philadelphia, he graduated from that city's Conservatory of Music. He played background melody in numerous motion pictures. Before focusing on the pipe organ (releasing numerous recordings made at the Roxy Theatre console), he accompanied renowned cellist Hans Kindler. White died at age 52 in New York City on March 3, 1955.

And finally, among its personalities,

Bob Shepherd, yet another daytime series announcer on *Break the Bank*, brought more modest experience to his assignment. Shepherd carried similar duties for *Pot o' Gold*, *You Can't Take It with You* and *Your Home Beautiful*. He was in the cast of *Jack Bundy's Carnival* and hosted the quiz show *Take a Number*.

There was a generally accepted opinion among network insiders that once ABC-TV inaugurated a flagship station in New York City, only a brief time would elapse before its foremost dual audience participation series—*Stop the Music!* and *Break the Bank*, with Bert Parks as master of ceremonies of both — would be televised. When that did transpire, *Bank* catered to the viewers at home by providing a TV wishbowl from which names of future contestants were drawn while the show was on the air. It had been done all along on radio, but on video there was the added impetus indicated by the wishbowl's conspicuous presence. Beyond that, a lucre-laden tabletop dominated the TV set, where cash payoffs were dispensed to the winners by Janice Wolfe (1949–53) and Janice Gilbert (1953–57), known simply as "Janice, our paying teller."

Decades later, author Maxene Fabe, in summarizing video contests, offered this fawning but perceptive appraisal:

> To say it [*Bank*] owed its great success on early TV to its former life on radio is not to appreciate how many other popular radio quizzes flopped when they tried to make the transition. *Dr. I.Q.* did, and so did *Information Please, Quick as a Flash* and *Truth or Consequences*, while other shows like *Stop the Music* and *Quiz Kids* were only marginally successful....
>
> Some of the reasons for *Break the Bank's* TV triumph lay in its host Bert Parks....
>
> Even without Bert Parks, however, *Break the Bank* would have been a hit, structured as it was to build maximum suspense with a huge jackpot awaiting its winners.[14]

With Parks as emcee, the program ran at night on ABC-TV from October 22, 1948, through September 23, 1949. It switched to NBC-TV from October 5, 1949, through January 9, 1952. Then it shifted to CBS-TV from January 27, 1952, through February 1, 1953. At that juncture the series reverted to NBC-TV and a weekday format, from March 30, 1953, through September 18, 1953. Clayton 'Bud' Collyer was host of the daytime run. Simultaneously, the show played in primetime as a summer replacement on NBC-TV, beginning June 23, 1953. It was canceled by early September, only to be pulled out of mothballs on January 31, 1954, and placed on ABC-TV's primetime schedule. *Bank* continued through June 20, 1956. NBC-TV gave the program a final shot in primetime from October 9, 1956, through January 15, 1957.

Bank's last network run, with Tom Kennedy presiding over a concept that never closely resembled its classic beginning, ran on ABC-TV in 1976 from April 12 through July 23. There were a couple of syndicated intervals beyond that, each ending in a quick demise, neither embracing the show's original precepts. Jack Barry hosted the first of those in 1976–77, while in 1986 Gene Rayburn and finally Joe Farago presided over the latter series.

In its late-run network video version (1954–57), the show's name was augmented to *Break the $250,000 Bank*. The change reflected the viewing public's almost insatiable fascination with top money prizes in the midst of the high roller giveaway era. By then, winning *Bank's* ultimate jackpot required a player to appear on 20 weekly telecasts, offering precise responses to inquisitions of increasing intensity. An inviolate Hall of Knowledge occupied a prominent spot on the set, a substitute for the isolation booths that had become fixtures on several analogous shows with equally impressive payoffs.

Bank and the other quiz series that

followed it had accomplished what they may have unknowingly set out to do: As it turned out, they fed the nation's ravenous craving for exhibiting winners who were gleaning prizes that previously were considered unthinkable. By the late 1950s, however, it was an aberration that was virtually out of control. All of it assuredly aided and abetted the dark days that altered the big prize giveaways forever during those monumental quiz show scandals.

The delirium began with a simple game that was to spellbound hordes of fans as a result of the amazing mental dexterity of a few of their countrymen. It ended in a debacle that, in retrospect, could hardly have been avoided. Even the handful who saw it coming were themselves likely to have been on such emotional highs that they couldn't have altered the course if they had been given an opportunity to do so.

When the bottom fell out for the quiz shows, it changed the way these games would be played from that day forward. Yet millions of *Bank*'s faithful followers could look back across the years and realize that far more than half the fun they had enjoyed was in simply getting there.

4

The Breakfast Club

Premise: A snooze alarm gently rousing Americans from their slumber every morning between 9 and 10 o'clock Eastern Time (earlier in westward time zones), *The Breakfast Club* supplied the corn that put smiles on the faces of millions of early risers during most of radio's Golden Age, and even beyond. To many non–Midwestern ears, Don McNeill's Chicago-based program was an authentic, yet acquired, taste of middle Americana. Throughout its proliferation of silly gags, instrumental and vocal music, inspirational poetry and prose, humorous skits, amusing monologues, contests, assists for common causes, special guests, exchanges with studio audiences and the mail that was regularly supplied by tens of thousands of listeners, the mishmash became a warm-up for the day ahead. An extroverted McNeill, who branded himself "your toastmaster," espoused a conviction that happy stances seldom stem from long faces. Like some of his broadcast peers, McNeill applied a vast arsenal of resources to encourage unified efforts in support of U.S. servicemen, especially during World War II. He also backed copious numbers of additional worthy drives. Fans of the genial master of ceremonies viewed him as principled, clean and wholesome, staunchly standing for love of God and country while espousing classic family values. Most of his audience bought stock in his accepted wisdom. For three-and-a-half decades they carried on a love affair with the emcee and the program he headlined. As McNeill waved good-by each morning at the close of their daily "love-in," he offered his admirers an optimistic "Be good to yourselves!" And while *The Breakfast Club* never became a success on the tube, its audio version acquired a supremely devoted bunch to whom McNeill literally dedicated his career. Early risers from the plains to the mountains, the beaches and the valleys beyond, in the big cities and rural hamlets, soon discovered that, at that hour, his show was without a doubt the best radio had to offer.

Producers: Lou Green, Cliff Petersen
Director: Cliff Petersen
Master of Ceremonies: Don McNeill
Cast Regulars: Fran Allison (Aunt Fanny), Sam Cowling, Jim and Marian Jordan (Toots and Chickie), Bill Thompson

Vocalists: Eugene Baird, Jack Baker, Helen Jane Behlke, Bernie Christianson,

Janette Davis, Clark Dennis, Johnny Desmond, Betty Johnson, Johnny Johnston, Annette King, Patsy Lee, Evelyn Lynne, Marion Mann, Nancy Martin, Dick Noel, Edna O'Dell, Jack Owens, Gale Page, Eileen Parker, Russell Pratt, Mildred Stanley, Peggy Taylor, Dick Teela, Johnny Thompson, Ilene Woods

Vocal Ensembles: The Cadets (Bob Childe, Reo Fletcher, Jack Halloran, Arnold Isolany, Ken Morrow, Cal Scheibe, Homer Snodgrass, Al Stracke, Sam Thompson), The Dinning Sisters (Ginger, Jean and Lou), The Doring Sisters, The Escorts and Betty (Ted Claire, Douglas Craig, Floyd Holm, Cliff Petersen and Betty Olson), The Hollywood Hi-Hatters, Homer and Jethro, The King's Jesters, The Merry Macs (Cheri McKay and Joe, Judd and Ted McMichael), The Morin Sisters (Evelyn, Marge and Pauline), The Originalities (Jean Cafarelli, Bill Giese, Bill Short, Jack Rose), The Ranch Boys (Joe "Curley" Bradley, Hubert "Shorty" Carson, Jack Ross), The Rangers, The Three Romeos (Sam Cowling, Gill Jones, Lou Perkins, Boyce Smith), The Songfellows, The Three C's, The Vagabonds (Ray "Pappy" Grant, John Jordan, Robert O'Neil, Norval Toborn), The Vass Family (Emily, Jitchey and Sally Vass, and Frank Weezy)

Orchestra Leaders: Eddie Ballantine, Walter Blaufuss, Joseph Gallicchio, Harry Kogen, Rex Maupin

Writer: Bo Kreer

Announcers: Jay Arlen, Bob Brown, Jack Callaghan, Don Dowd, Franklyn Ferguson, Charles Irving, Fred Kasper, Bill Kephart, Durward Kirby, Bob McKee, Robert Murphy, Ken Nordine, Louis Roen

Sponsors: The network sustained the show until 1939, having nothing better to place in that early-morning time period. When Swift and Co. bought first one and then a second quarter-hour to advertise its meat products, other sponsors were quick to purchase the remaining quarter hours.

Philco Corp. (for a line of home appliances) and the Kellogg Co. (for its breakfast cereals) were among its most durable sponsors. Others included Cream of Wheat breakfast cereal, O'Cedar mops, the Gillette Co. (for its Toni hair care commodities), Sterling Drugs (Bayer aspirin), Acme paints, Colgate-Palmolive-Peet Co. (Lustre Crème shampoo), General Mills, Inc. (cereals and baking goods) and General Foods, Inc. (Jell-O gelatin, puddings and pie fillings, and Grape Nuts cereal).

Ratings: High: 6.6 (1949–50); Low: 2.6 (1955–56); Median: 4.6 (records available for 15 seasons only, 1941–56). Compared with other shows airing later in the day, these numbers are dismal. Considering the hour the program aired and the fact that many Americans were either at work already or en-route to it, the figures are commendable. The show appealed to an extremely loyal caste that tuned in consistently for decades.

On the Air: June 23, 1933–Feb. 7, 1941, NBC Blue, Monday–Saturday, 9 A.M. ET (varying from 30 to 60 minutes); Feb. 8, 1941–Dec. 27, 1968, NBC Blue (later ABC), Monday–Friday, 9 A.M. In its latter years the series was shortened from 60 to 50 minutes, airing at 9:05 A.M.

* * *

Good mornin', Breakfast Clubbers,
Good mornin' to yah!
We woke up bright and early
Just to how-day-do-yah!
It's first call to breakfast,
For all of you out there …
America, arise!
The Breakfast Club is on the air!

It began as "an hour that no one wanted."[1] It turned out to be ABC Radio's most valuable daytime commercial property, proving that an ungodly time frame that had been abandoned by almost everybody else could be a prime source of

The Breakfast Club was a 35-year marathon at ABC Radio, for many years the web's largest and most lucrative daytime draw. Aired from Chicago, among its principals were left to right, standing: Sam Cowling, Ed McKean, Mary Anne Luckett, Cliff Petersen, Eddie Ballantine; and seated: Don McNeill (toastmaster, who urged fans to "be good to yourselves"), Fran Allison, Bob Newkirk. (Courtesy of Tom McNeill)

network revenue. From its inception on June 23, 1933, on 56 stations until *The Breakfast Club* went off the air for the last time on December 27, 1968 — by then renamed *The Don McNeill Show* for its durable and seemingly unflappable host — it was the longest running early-morning series in radio.

Even at that late date — well after the medium's generally recognized Golden Age had closed — the show continued to be heard on 224 stations. (At its peak in 1953 it aired on 352 stations in the U.S., Canada, Alaska and Hawaii, with a daily listening audience estimated at two million families.)

Considered by some as corny as Kansas in August, for multitudes of others it became an on-the-air equivalent of a warm bowl of oatmeal. In 1938 a radio journalist accounted for its popularity: "Corn and country ham continue to draw more people than caviar. That's why *Breakfast Club*, a show by ordinary people like us, is so successful."[2]

The series was launched when McNeill, who captured his post in an NBC Chicago audition, was allowed to tinker with a little known program then airing on the NBC Blue network (forerunner of ABC) called *The Pepper Pot*. The entry had been running for a few months in the forgotten zone of 8 o'clock in the morning Central Time. *The Pepper Pot* featured an orchestra conducted by Walter Blaufuss, and interspersed melody, with banter supplied by announcers King Bard and Bill Kephart. Given a free hand to enliven the series, McNeill added vocalist Dick Teela and violinist Sleepy Joe Englehart. A halfdozen years after taking it under his wing, the host—calling himself "your toastmaster"—rechristened the whole thing as *The Breakfast Club*. A new tradition was established among American radio listeners that was to impact generations yet unborn.

McNeill subdivided the program into four quarter-hour segments that he designated as the "four calls to breakfast." (When sponsors eventually came along, each quarter hour was assigned the services of a separate announcer, gaining a simple dignity and purity for each commercial message.) In time, the "four calls" would acquire lasting meaning, for each was assigned a specific theme. Blending McNeill's own convivial personality into the mix turned the affair into a lively hour of comedy and variety that obviously caught the attention of the nation's early risers.

Initially relying upon a couple of joke books for most of the show's humorous moments, the host rapidly discarded them. He soon discovered instead that the fans themselves were submitting funnier material than he could reliably manufacture. After a couple of months he also dispensed with the scripts he had been tediously laboring over. From then on he resorted to prepared material for commercials and special presentations only, including prose and poetry that he read aloud during "Memory Time" and "Inspiration Time."

McNeill kept a notebook before him filled with gags, letters from listeners and other ad-lib stuff, and referred to it as often as needed during the broadcasts. His contributions to the rest of the show went un-

rehearsed. Going with his instincts, he proved to be right—the fans *could* produce better material—and the program settled into a long run of music and humorous routines mixed with incidents supplied by the mail. A forerunner of the trade, McNeill unveiled a pattern that was to serve Arthur Godfrey, Robert Q. Lewis, Garry Moore, Tom Breneman and other daytime variety hosts in series that were still to come.

In his memoirs, announcer Durward Kirby, who would rise to larger challenges in the 1950s and 1960s as sidekick to TV comedian Moore, recalls his own experience during 1941–42 on *The Breakfast Club*:

When Don's vacation came along, he asked that I be the man to replace him. Lady Luck was riding with me all the time.

Don had a large, leather bound, indexed portfolio which he brought to the show each day. It was on the table immediately in front of him. Don might say to me, "Well, Durward, what did you do over the weekend?"

"I went fishing with a couple of guys."

"Did you catch any?"

"Nope. We got skunked."

"Well, didn't you get any bites?"

"Not a one."

Now during this give and take, he would open the book to the indexed letter "F" and there would be jokes about fishing. And he would read, "You didn't get any bites, huh? Well, this friend of mine went fishing and he got nothing but bites. His body was covered with mosquito bites when he got home!"

As he hit the punchline, he would raise his arm as a signal to the orchestra, and when he let the arm down, they would play the next tune. That way, no one could top him.

When I subbed for Don, I would ask him to loan me the book, but there was no way he would even consider letting that joke book out of his sight.[3]

McNeill never knew what to anticipate in his informal repartee with members of the studio audience. Risk was always a factor when unknowns were put before live microphones. An ad agency representative aptly confessed: "I get twinges in my ulcer every time I listen to it."[4] Despite that, the spontaneity of such exchanges allowed the program to generate a reputation as "radio's most unrehearsed show,"[5] contributing appreciably to its ultimate euphoria.

For the first few years, *The Breakfast Club* functioned in a rather sterile, placid environment: It had a 12-piece orchestra, a growing company of vocalists, McNeill and an announcer in front of a microphone in a small studio. But in 1937 someone came up with the notion of putting all of it before a live studio audience. From that time forward the show acquired new dimensions of greatness as fans from just about everywhere arrived and reacted to what they had been hearing.

The program drew such big crowds, in fact, that it was forced to move to larger and larger venues.

Across 15 years it broadcast more than 4,000 times from Chicago's Merchandise Mart, the center of NBC activity in the Windy City. For six mornings a week during several of those years 600 people who had requested tickets weeks in advance were lining the hallways outside Studio A when the doors opened at 7:45 A.M. When the program went on the air at 8 o'clock local time, the cast was seated around a table situated on a raised platform about a foot off the floor and perhaps two feet from the nearest spectator rows. A boom mike hung over the center of the table and served all of those seated around the table. Just beyond the cast ranged the orchestra, placing the regular performers and special guests between the audience and the band.

After the years of broadcasting from the Merchandise Mart, the show enjoyed subsequent lengthy runs in the Porterhouse Room of the College Inn at the Sherman Hotel; then the Terrace Casino of the Mor-

rison Hotel; and finally, the Clouds Room of the Allerton Hotel.

Annually, starting in 1950, McNeill would take the show on the road for a month, playing in small towns like Janesville, Wisconsin; Shelbyville, Tennessee; Fargo, North Dakota; and Hot Springs, Arkansas, as well as many larger metropolises—Cleveland, St. Paul, Kansas City, St. Louis, Milwaukee, Oklahoma City, Birmingham, Nashville, Louisville, Atlanta, Jacksonville, Fort Worth, St. Petersburg, Miami, Shreveport, Ottawa, Montreal, Providence, Pittsburgh and Indianapolis among them. Near pandemonium erupted in 1946 when more than 17,000 fans mobbed the tour then appearing at New York's Madison Square Garden. And just as memorably, during the program's first out-of-studio broadcast — a 1934 Florida pickup — baseball player Babe Ruth showed up while entertaining youngsters at a Yankee training camp.

By the 1950s the show was annually drawing in excess of 150,000 spectators to its Chicago-based and remote, sometimes far-flung locales. A listener survey conducted early in that decade indicated that 73 percent of the show's fans resided in urban areas, while the remainder lived in rural territories. At that time women accounted for 65 percent of the home audience, children made up 20 percent and men contributed the remaining 15 percent.

In 1940, and again in 1941, subscribers to *Radio Guide* magazine selected Don McNeill as their favorite master of ceremonies and *The Breakfast Club* as their preferred entertainment series. In its first decade, in fact, *The Breakfast Club* became such a phenomenon that it drew in excess of 100,000 pieces of mail annually. Not long afterward the show received another 250,000 requests for tickets and premiums every year. *The New Yorker* termed its audience "the solid citizens, the churchgoers, the 'squares,' the butcher, the baker and the candlestick maker ... the 'Eds and Ednas' from Maine to California," living in America's heartland.[6]

When, in the spring of 1944, Breakfast Club membership cards were offered, 875,000 requests arrived in *a single week*! With the post office and network staff totally besieged and dismayed, and an unhappy sponsor shelling out $50,000 when it anticipated a demand of no more than 15,000 cards, the stunt that backfired was abruptly halted after only seven days. To its amazement the network discovered that no audience participation program in radio's history had reaped such a tremendous outpouring in both numbers and brevity as *The Breakfast Club* experienced. McNeill literally pled with listeners not to send in any more requests.

As a byproduct of that effort, prizes with a total monetary value of $4,700 were given away to the show's charter members and new listeners. Mrs. Dorothea Harris and Mrs. Frank Whise, both of St. Petersburg, Florida, were major winners in a national "join-up" competition. Each earned a $1,000 war bond, while more than 100 additional recipients reaped lesser sums.

In 1946 McNeill informed his audience about people living in war-ravaged Europe who had lost virtually everything they owned. He invited listeners to "share a meal" with those unfortunates. The response was little short of amazing — no less than 40 *tons* of non-perishable food arrived! Furthermore, the show frequently staged road trips and bond rallies during the war years and urged Americans to contribute toward lofty goals for the common good. McNeill's listeners invariably reacted in positive, thoughtful ways to the massive appeals.

Celebrities such as comedian Fred Allen, whose penchant for downplaying many radio series has been widely documented (e.g., see the chapter on *Stop the Music!*), idolized *The Breakfast Club*. Allen lauded toastmaster McNeill, whom he invited as a guest on his own program, as "a big friendly fellow whose good nature pours through the microphone, and listeners react in the same way anyone reacts meeting him in person."[7]

During each 15 minutes of *The Breakfast Club's* hour there was a distinct "call to breakfast," with hooting, drum roll and trumpet fanfare.

In the first call McNeill interviewed folks in the studio audience who had written intriguing comments on cards they had filled out shortly before the show went on the air.

"Memory Time," appearing in the second quarter-hour, included a poignant piece of prose or verse, often contributed by the listeners at home. Typical among them was a piece titled "The All American Dad," submitted during the World War II era by Margaret Nickerson Martin, a shut-in living in Jackson, Michigan.

In 1938 the show published a book of poems for its listeners and titled it *Memory Time*. (The venture was so successful that several subsequent editions were published. By 1952 more than 750,000 fans had purchased eight different editions of the book, along with *Breakfast Club* yearbooks.) In its same quarter-hour, "Memory Time" was closely followed by "Prayer Time," instituted on October 28, 1944, during the Second World War on behalf of servicemen in harm's way. It immediately clicked with listeners and remained a standard segment through the final broadcast. As the studio lights dimmed, McNeill would instruct the crowd: "All over the nation, each in his own words, each in his own way, for a world united in peace, bow your heads and let us pray." Soft music filtered from the studio organ over the audience (often it was the hymn "Sweet Hour of Prayer") during this brief period of solitude. McNeill concluded it with a verbal "Amen."

"Hymn Time" occasionally followed, in which the whole cast often harmonized on a gospel favorite of the fans. After its introduction in 1948, the "Sunshine Shower" became a popular feature at that juncture, too. Listeners were given the names and addresses of shut-ins at home, in hospitals, in nursing facilities and orphanages who welcomed their greetings through cards and letters. Tens of thousands of communications were mailed over the next two decades. Such sentiment was strongly defended by McNeill, who claimed, "There are too many poker faces in the world today."[8]

The third call began with "March Time." The band struck up a lively processional number as members of the cast and studio audience paraded up and down the narrow aisles. "You envisioned farm wives clumping about big tables," maintained one observer.[9]

The fourth call, "Inspiration Time," included a poem or other message that was often directed at the disconsolate, attempting to provide fresh zeal and vigor. Sometimes it also introduced a humorous message, as in this anonymous submission titled "On Teaching the Wife to Drive":

> First, see your car is out of gear,
> How?— by this gear-shift lever here.
> How can you tell? Why, I feel it. See?
> The thing is simple as can be.
> Now step on that to make it start,
> Great Scott! You'll tear it all apart,
> If you don't take your foot off quick
> The second that it gives a kick.
> Now throw your clutch. For goodness' sake!
> Your clutch! Your clutch! No, not your brake!
> Why? 'Cause I tell you to, that's why,
> There, now, you needn't start to cry.
> Now pull this lever into low.
> Step off the gas and start off slow.
> Look out! You almost hit the fence,
> Here, let me drive! You've got no sense!

The listeners at home didn't supply *all*

of the demonstrative vignettes read aloud on *The Breakfast Club*. The show's staff was constantly scouring media and published sources for stimulating material that would be acceptable to almost everyone. Many of those supplements were sobering thoughts like this one, penned by Chicagoan Burton Schindler. It originally appeared as a letter to the editor of *The Chicago Daily News* under the banner "The Great American Bargain":

> Recently I completed my income tax for 1952 and discovered that it cost my wife and me about $4 a day to be Americans last year. At first, I complained as usual, but on second thought, it seemed that we had gotten quite a bargain.
>
> For our $4 a day we were entitled to free complaint about high taxes, governmental bungling, and the high cost of living for every one of the 365 days of the year. And on Nov. 4th we were given an extra dividend and were permitted to vote to change the things we disliked.
>
> For our $4 a day we bought 24-hour protection at home and abroad, by an Army, Navy, Coast Guard, Air Force and FBI ... through surveillance of the foods and drugs we bought ... National Parks to visit on our vacation ... our mail delivered each day ... the administration of our Social Security Fund ... and daily weather forecasts.
>
> That $4 a day helped pay a debt we owe to a lot of servicemen who died or were wounded to make sure we were safe. It provided food, clothing and shelter to their widows and orphans. It helped pay the wages of the men overseas who are keeping us free....
>
> Our $4 a day bought us the right to live and love and work every day of the year without fear ... and most of all, it gave us 24 hours of hope in the future every day of the year.[10]

Guest stars were used sparingly on *The Breakfast Club* and were seldom allowed to eclipse the show's regular cast. Vocalists who dropped by on occasion included Anita Bryant (whose celebrity status was just beginning), Alice Lon (who was to become Lawrence Welk's initial "champagne lady") and Patti Page (who was soon to be "that singing rage"). Substitutes, while McNeill was on vacation, included such personalities as Don Ameche, Peter Donald, Durward Kirby, Gordon MacRae, Garry Moore and Walter O'Keefe. One morning, as McNeill was reading a commercial, the unpredictable comic Jerry Lewis set fire to the host's script. That resulted in such total distraction that announcers all over the nation missed their station cues!

Once, when diminutive singer Brenda Lee was on the show, following delivery of a commercial for General Foods' Grape Nuts cereal, McNeill remarked: "I'll bet little Brenda wishes she had some Grape Nuts right now." Unhesitatingly, Lee replied, "I don't like Grape Nuts!" For 25 seconds near chaos erupted as the audience broke into raucous, unbridled laughter. Recovering at last, McNeill tried to smooth things over: "Well that's all right, Brenda ... you didn't say anything wrong, because ... the thing is, if everybody liked 'em they wouldn't have me advertising 'em, because then everybody'd eat 'em and there'd be no use trying to get people to try 'em and, naturally, everybody can't like 'em." Sam Cowling retorted: "You're getting out of it, but I'd just let it go!" Added McNeill: "People are always writing in and saying, 'Hey, all that stuff you do—it's all rehearsed, isn't it?' Rehearsed my foot!"

Over the years some other to-be-famous personalities joined *The Breakfast Club's* cluster of on-air talent.

Jim and Marian Jordan, appearing in 1934 as "Toots and Chickie," were among them. Their characters were precursors of the eminently more familiar "Fibber McGee and Molly," whom the Jordans played on their own durable comedy series that was introduced a year later. Natives of Peoria,

Illinois, the Jordans were radio veterans long before *The Breakfast Club's* inception, having transferred from vaudeville to broadcasting in 1924 via WIBO, Chicago. Their professional careers included *Kaltenmeyer's Kindergarten, Monitor, The National Barn Dance, The Sealtest Variety Theater, Smackouts* and *The Smith Family.* They also starred in a trio of motion pictures: *Look Who's Laughing* (1941), *Here We Go Again* and *Heavenly Days* (both 1944). After Marian, who was born April 16, 1898, died at Encino, California, on April 7, 1961, Jim remarried. He subsequently appeared on *The CBS Radio Mystery Theater* and *The Sears Radio Theater.* Jim Jordan, born November 16, 1896, died in Los Angeles on April 1, 1988.

Bill Thompson also joined *The Breakfast Club* cast in 1934. Born July 8, 1913, at Terre Haute, Indiana, he became a dialect comedian, creating memorable characters on the *Fibber McGee and Molly* series: Horatio K. Boomer, Nick DePopolus, The Old Timer ("That ain't the way I 'heerd' it!") and Wallace Wimple ("Hello folks!"). Thompson's other ventures included *The Edgar Bergen and Charlie McCarthy Show, Jamboree, The National Farm and Home Hour, The NBC Night Club, The Ransom Sherman Show, The Sinclair Minstrels, The Story of Mary Marlin* and *The Sunbrite Smile Parade.* In 1957, when the McGees left 79 Wistful Vista, Thompson became a manager for Union Oil Company. He died in Los Angeles on July 15, 1971.

Joe "Curley" Bradley, a member of the singing Ranch Boys trio, evolved into the dramatic lead of the long-running juvenile radio adventure series *Tom Mix and the Ralston Straightshooters* (1936–42, 1944–50). Born September 18, 1910, at Colgate, Oklahoma, he died June 3, 1985, at Long Beach, California. In between, Bradley earned radio credits on *Amazing America, Author's Playhouse, Club Matinee, The Curley Bradley Show, Headin' South, The Ranch*

Boys, The Road to Danger and *The Singing Marshal.* In a 1938 publicity stunt he rode a horse 2,875 miles, from Hollywood to Chicago, then appeared on *The National Barn Dance* that was aired from the Windy City. Bradley played rodeos and was featured in several movies with The Ranch Boys trio. In 1949 the trade paper *Variety* cited him for his "good range and timber somewhat similar to Gene Autry."

There were lots of vocalists and recording artists *The Breakfast Club* initially introduced to America, too. In an unusual turn of events, in 1941 more than 100,000 of the show's fans mailed their own autographs to crooner Jack Baker. These were solicited for his personal scrapbook, another indication of how well the show and its artists were received. Down the road, Baker moved to Nashville, where he regularly appeared on the (Grand Ole) *Opry House Matinee.*

At least two members of *The Breakfast Club* cast later sang for Arthur Godfrey—Janette Davis and Ilene Woods.

Davis, who became one of the most popular members of *Arthur Godfrey Time* on radio and TV, and TV's *Arthur Godfrey and His Friends*, hosted *The Janette Davis Show* on radio. She sang on *Avalon Time, Danny O'Neil and His Guests, Moon River* and *The Red Skelton Show.* From 1956 to 1958 she produced the simulcasted *Arthur Godfrey's Talent Scouts.* Davis later married and retired to Florida.

Meanwhile, recording artist Ilene Woods sang on Godfrey's shows, plus TV's *Of All Things* (1956) and radio's *The Garry Moore Show, Packham Inn* and *The Steve Allen Show.*

Others with distinguished careers in the music industry included Clark Dennis, Johnny Desmond, Joseph Gallicchio, Johnny Johnston, Harry Kogen and Rex Maupin. Comics Homer and Jethro—featured artists with the *Grand Ole Opry*—took a turn on *The Breakfast Club* in the early 1950s.

Dennis, born December 19, 1911, at Roscommon, Michigan, gained tremendous success as an on-air tenor. He performed on *The Bob Smith Show* on both radio and television, and *The Jack Paar Show* on TV. His other radio credits included *Chesterfield Presents, Dial Dave Garroway, Fibber McGee and Molly, The Jo Stafford Show, Name the Movie, The Night Club of the Air, The NBC Minstrels, The Song of Your Life* and *There's Music in the Air. Variety's* assessment of Dennis' ability in 1939 was: "He has one of those voices that runs off the top end of the keyboard and he knows how to sell it."

Johnny Desmond hailed from Detroit, born on November 14, 1920. By the age of 11 he was on local radio in *Uncle Nick's Children's Hour.* As a teen he appeared as a vocalist with the bands of Gene Krupa and Bob Crosby. He sang with the Glenn Miller orchestra over the Armed Forces Radio Network during his time in the U.S. Air Force. Following the war, along with conductor Jerry Gray, he hosted radio's *The Teen-Timers Club.* His career took off with recordings, nightclubs and Broadway musicals. Desmond hosted a decent lot of radio variety series: *The Johnny Desmond Follies; Johnny Desmond Goes to College; The Johnny Desmond Show; Judy, Jill and Johnny; Musicomedy; Phonearama; The Philip Morris Follies of 1946;* and *The Sparkling Silver Summer Review.* On television the baritone vocalized on *The Don McNeill TV Club* (1950–51), *Face the Music* (1948), *Glenn Miller Time* (co-hosting it in summer 1961), *The Jack Paar Show* (1954), *Music on Ice* (hosting in summer 1960), *Tin Pan Alley TV* (1950) and *Your Hit Parade* (1958–59). He also acted in a couple of short-run situation comedies, *Sally* (1958) and *Blansky's Beauties* (1977). Classified by *Time* magazine as "The Creamer," Desmond offset Bing Crosby's "The Groaner" and Frank Sinatra's "The Swooner." He died in Los Angeles on September 6, 1985.

Bandleader Joseph Gallicchio conducted the *Hotel Stevens Symphony Orchestra* over Chicago's WMAQ in 1928. He had his own NBC show from 1936 to 1940, the *Joseph Gallicchio Orchestra*. He was maestro for *Author's Playhouse, Big City Serenade, Curtain Time, The Dave Garroway Show, Edgar A. Guest, Grand Marquee, Hello, Surprise Serenade* and *Tea Time at Morrell's*.

St. Louis native Johnny Johnston, born December 1, 1914, became one of the first artists to be signed by Capitol Records, in 1942. His hit recording of "Laura" sold over a million copies; he introduced the durable classic "That Old Black Magic" in Paramount films' *Star Spangled Rhythm*. Johnston's foray into radio saw the baritone singing on *The Chesterfield Supper Club, Club Matinee, Duffy's Tavern, Rhapsody in Rhythm* and *Songs for Sale*. He conducted on his own 1939 program, *Johnny Johnston Orchestra*, on NBC. He died at Cape Coral, Florida, on January 6, 1996.

In 1929 bandleader Harry Kogen was selected as musical director for NBC's *Yeast Foamers* broadcasts from New York. He, too, acquired his own NBC show — *Harry Kogen Orchestra* — from 1934 to 1938. He conducted music for the following series: *The Bobby Doyle Show, Kaltenmeyer's Kindergarten, The National Farm and Home Hour, The Night Club of the Air, The Sinclair Minstrels, Sunday Dinner at Aunt Fanny's* and *What's Cooking?*

One of the busiest *Breakfast Club* maestros, Rex Maupin, launched his professional career a decade before the show went on the air. In 1923 he led *Rex Maupin's Original Texas Hotel Orchestra*, airing on Fort Worth's WBAP. In 1934 he conducted the *Rex Maupin Orchestra* on NBC. Other radio series featuring him as bandleader included *Author's Playhouse, The Benny Rubin Show, The Big Hand, Black Night, Club Matinee, The Danny Thomas Show, Dreamboat, I Fly Anything, Johnny Desmond Goes to College, Packham Inn, The Ransom Sherman Show, The Sunbrite Smile Parade, Those Sensational Years* and *Wake Up and Smile*. He led orchestras in video's earliest days on *The Benny Rubin Show, The Little People, Music in Velvet* and *Tin Pan Alley TV*.

Numerous other musicians were associated with *The Breakfast Club*. A condensed list of those with other network shows follows:

- Eugene Baird ... *The Paul Whiteman Hour, The Robert Q. Lewis Show, Sing It Again*
- Eddie Ballantine ... *The Russ Brown Show*
- Walter Blaufuss ... *The National Farm and Home Hour, Refreshment Club, Vic and Sade, Walter Blaufuss Orchestra*
- Betty Johnson ... *The Jack Paar Show* (on TV)
- Evelyn Lynne ... *Club Matinee*
- Dick Noel ... *It's a Small World, Ruth Lyons' 50 Club, The Tennessee Ernie Ford Show* (all on TV)
- Edna O'Dell ... *The Affairs of Tom, Dick and Harry; Alec Templeton Time; Hap Hazard; Edna O'Dell*
- Gale Page ... *Dreft Star Playhouse, Fibber McGee and Molly, Hollywood Playhouse, Masquerade, The Story of Holly Sloan* (in which she played the lead), *Tea Time at Morrell's, Today's Children* (with a running dramatic part)
- Russell Pratt ... *Laugh Doctors* (co-star)
- Peggy Taylor ... *The Stan Freberg Show*
- Johnny Thompson ... *Betty Moore's Triangle Club, The Paul Whiteman Hour, Your Home Beautiful*
- And producer-director Cliff Petersen, who had been a member of one of *The Breakfast Club*'s singing ensembles (The Escorts and Betty), appeared in the cast of *Kaltenmeyer's Kindergarten*.

The names of a quartet of *The Break-fast Club* announcers were commonplace in American homes: Bob Brown, Charles Irving, Durward Kirby and Ken Nordine.

Native New Yorker Bob Brown was born December 7, 1904, and eight years later was singing in the choir of evangelist Billy Sunday. Having enrolled at the Cincinnati College of Music, following a 1925 audition he was on the air at Buffalo's WGR. From 1928 to 1932 Brown handled production, penned dramas and supervised announcers at Cincinnati's WLW while narrating *Moon River*. Joining NBC's Chicago staff, his network announcing tasks multiplied: *American Women, Auction Quiz, Backstage Wife, The Ben Bernie Show, Girl Alone, Ma Perkins, The Night Club of the Air, Quicksilver, The Singing Lady, The Story of Mary Marlin, This Amazing America* and *Vic and Sade*. He produced and directed *The First Line, Myrt and Marge,* and *Service to the Front* while hosting an early TV series, *Science Circus*. Brown died in 1980.

Charles Irving's announcing duties were copious, too: *Exploring the Unknown, The Fat Man, The Henry Morgan Show, Heritage, Those Websters,* and *Vic and Sade*. He hosted *Coronet Quick Quiz,* directed *This Is Nora Drake,* and appeared in dramatic roles on *Bobby Benson and the B-Bar-B Riders, The Joe DiMaggio Show, Tales of Willie Piper* and *The Texaco Star Theater*. For a while he played the lead in *Young Doctor Malone*. Irving died February 15, 1981, at the age of 68.

Covington, Kentucky, native Durward Kirby, born on August 24, 1912, got a first taste of radio on the campus station at Purdue University. Liking it, he pursued a succession of upward steps. Beginning in 1931 with WBAA in West Lafayette, Indiana, he moved to WFBM in Indianapolis and was on the air in 1935 at Cincinnati's WLW. By 1937 he was delivering NBC's *Press Radio News* from Chicago, moving to New York City in the early 1940s. As an announcer,

Kirby could be heard on *Alka-Seltzer Time, Break the Bank, Club Matinee, Crime Fighters, The Fred Waring Show, The Garry Moore Show, Hap Hazard, The Henry Morgan Show, Here's to Romance, Hilltop House, Li'l Abner, Lone Journey, Meet Your Navy, Quiz Kids, Sunday Dinner at Aunt Fanny's* and *Two for the Money*. He hosted radio's *Honeymoon in New York*. Turning to TV, he announced, co-hosted or emceed *Auctionaire* (1949–50), *Candid Camera* (1961–66), *The Garry Moore Show* (1950–67), *GE Guest House* (1951) and *Sunday at the Zoo* (1950). Kirby died on March 15, 2000, at Fort Myers, Florida.

Ken Nordine's announcing opportunities included *A Life in Your Hands; Armstrong of the SBI; Jack Armstrong, the All-American Boy;* and *Silver Eagle, Mountie*. He was in the cast of *The World's Great Novels,* and hosted *Night Life* and *The World Adventurer's Club*. In 1951–52 he introduced *The Chicago Symphony Chamber Orchestra* on TV.

Still more *Breakfast Club* announcers, and their roles on other shows, follow:

- Jay Arlen … *I Fly Anything* (announcer)
- Don Dowd … *Black Night* (host), *In Care of Aggie Horn* (announcer), *Moon River* (narrator)
- Franklyn Ferguson … *Faultless Starch Time, The Tom Mix Ralston Straightshooters* (announcer on both)
- Bill Kephart … *Thurston the Magician* (announcer)
- Bob McKee … *A Life in Your Hands* (writer); *Jack Armstrong, the All-American Boy* (announcer)
- Louis Roen … *Today's Children* (announcer)

Undoubtedly, however, *The Breakfast Club*'s most durable supporting players were added in 1937 — Sam Cowling and Fran Allison — who each remained with the show until its finale in 1968. Both began their stints as singers but hit their strides while sprouting into comedians.

Cowling initially appeared as a member of The Romeos, a musical ensemble composed of Gill Jones, Lou Perkins and Boyce Smith, with conductor Eddie Ballantine directing. Over time, Cowling's contributions were channeled into a stream of one-line gags, turning him into Don McNeill's prime foil. In 1943, when he introduced the almost daily feature "Fiction and Fact from Sam's Almanac," Cowling's history as a singer was soon forgotten. Relying on a barrage of inane riddles, he asked McNeill something like: "What's the difference between a tiger and a panther?" When McNeill and other cast members folded, Cowling retorted: "A tiger is a big cat but panther what you wear."

One critic noted that the portly Cowling recited "lousy jokes, worse verse, folklore, nostalgia, and letters from his mailbag."[11] Among them:

• Courtship makes a man spoon, but marriage makes him fork over.
• The distance between the head of a fox to its tail is a fur piece.
• (*Recited during the period Harry Kogen was the show's bandleader*): In spite of the shortage of tropical foods, just by glaring at our orchestra leader you can get Kogen-nuts.
• Fifty percent of the married people in Denver, Colorado, are women.
• Take a forest fire, for instance — now there's a hot one!
• In Arkansas … most of the soil consists of dirt.

On and on the barrage of "unabashedly bad jokes" went. In spite of the fact "the show was hopelessly hokey and often downright silly … there was something unsynthetic about it …. *The Breakfast Club* proved you didn't necessarily have to love a show to listen to it. You listened to it because it somehow connected and, quite literally, spoke to you."[12]

Cowling, incidentally, appeared regularly on only a couple of supplementary broadcast series — radio's *Club Matinee*, from 1937 to 1943, and *The Don McNeill TV Club*, from 1950 to 1951.

The other durable personality debuting in 1937, Fran Allison, was a contralto who developed the character of gossiping Aunt Fanny into a big city version of the *Grand Ole Opry*'s Minnie Pearl of rural Grinder's Switch, Tennessee. Prefaced by the theme "She's Only a Bird in a Gilded Cage," Aunt Fanny was dubbed the "lovable chatterbox." To *Breakfast Club* audiences, Allison — a former schoolmarm — introduced a collection of fictional characters with whom they quickly identified. In countrified vernacular she recounted implausible tales about the antics of the Smelsers, Ott Ort, and Bert and Bertie Beerbower. Her convoluted monologues kept her listeners utterly in stitches.

Allison would acquire yet additional fame with children and adults alike by simultaneously co-starring on Burr Tillstrom's live early evening TV puppet show *Kukla, Fran and Ollie*. The series ran from 1948 to 1952 and from 1954 to 1957. Allison also figured prominently in the casts of numerous other shows. On radio: *Clara, Lu and Em; Kukla, Fran and Ollie* (a 1952–53 audio series); *Meet the Meeks; The National Barn Dance; The National Farm and Home Hour; The Peabodys; The Ransom Sherman Show; The Sunbrite Smile Parade; Sunday Dinner at Aunt Fanny's;* and *Uncle Ezra's Radio Station* (she reprised her role as Aunt Fanny in the latter two series). On TV: *The Don McNeill TV Club, Down You Go, It's About Time* and *Let's Dance* (the latter trio were all short-run series appearing in 1954). Allison was born at La Porte City, Iowa, on November 20, 1907; she died on June 13, 1989, at Sherman Oaks, California.

McNeill, himself, was something of a puzzle in the midst of this daily melee. Told in 1929 by radio station WISN Milwaukee that there was "no future for you in the radio business," he lost his first job as an announcer and scriptwriter. But his determination to succeed wouldn't allow him to become discouraged over what he considered a minuscule setback. That same year (1929), the Galena, Illinois, native, born on December 23, 1907 — who grew up in Sheboygan, Wisconsin — was graduated valedictorian of his journalism class at Marquette University. (In 1942, by then a nationally recognized celebrity, McNeill was awarded an honorary Doctor of Letters degree from St. Bonaventure College.)

His initial intent was to become an editorial caricature artist. He landed a spot as radio editor and cartoonist for *The Milwaukee Journal*, and simultaneously announced for that paper's station, WTMJ. A year later, in 1930, when Louisville's *Courier-Journal* and *The Louisville Times* offered him more money, McNeill sketched for them while announcing on those papers' superpower 50,000-watt radio voice, WHAS.

Meanwhile, he was smitten with the secretary to the journalism school dean at Marquette. Kay Bennett grew up in Milwaukee and was attracted to the strapping 6' 2" McNeill. During his first Christmas in Louisville, he invited her to visit. One day, while driving through the city's Cherokee Park, he proposed marriage. She readily accepted.

A short time later he resigned his posts to pursue a comedy-acting career on the West Coast. With a chum, billed as "Don and Van, the Two Professors," McNeill played venues in and around San Francisco. But a sluggish economy forced the pair to disband their act, and the McNeills decided to chase their dreams in radio. Returning to the Midwest, he auditioned for *The Pepper Pot*. The rest is history. McNeill's

initial weekly salary of $50 for six hour-long shows was eventually parlayed into an annual $200,000 plus for five weekly performances. (Simultaneously, he hosted several more radio series: *Avalon Time*, *Holland Housewarming*, *Refreshment Club* and *Tea Time at Morrell's*.)

Within a few years the McNeills became parents of three sons— Tom was born in 1934, Donald Paul Jr. in 1936 and Bob in 1941. The whole family appeared frequently on *The Breakfast Club*, becoming familiar to its regular listeners. An annual family Christmas show was a highlight with fans across the program's long run. When the boys were in school, Kay McNeill often pulled up a chair to the coast-to-coast breakfast table and dialogued with her famous husband on a surplus of topics. She wrote a 64-page hardback photo-filled volume in 1944 titled *Don's Other Life* that the show issued as a listener premium. In it she revealed what she termed "the private life of a radio wife."

In her book, Kay McNeill took readers through a typical workday for Don, offering some intriguing behind-the-scenes insights into a radio performer's private moments. Beginning at 5:40 A.M. Central Time each weekday, she and the three boys and their dog attempted to roust the family patriarch from his bed, she reported. (In 1938 McNeill realized a long-held aspiration by conducting the show for one day while pajama-clad at home and from his own bed, while the remainder of the crew appeared at the studio.) Each morning the family spent time together around their own breakfast table before McNeill drove his own car from their suburban Winnetka, Illinois, home to the Merchandise Mart in downtown Chicago. He'd arrive in the studio 15 to 30 minutes before airtime, 8 o'clock local time.

Following the show, McNeill and the cast traditionally spent awhile personally greeting the studio audience, shaking hands, answering questions and signing auto-graphs. At about 9:30 the host invited ser-vicemen and women in the crowd to join him as guests for a second breakfast before he returned to his office in the Merchan-dise Mart. There he answered correspon-dence and handled a myriad of details pur-suant to the show. Meanwhile, the rest of the cast — including orchestra, vocalists and ensembles — hung around the studio for a 45- to 60-minute rehearsal (usually between 10 and 11 A.M. local time) for the following day's show.

Unless McNeill had an evening ap-pointment in the city, he normally drove home to Winnetka in mid to late after-noon every weekday. "We seldom spend the evening with celebrities, and you could count on the fingers of one hand the times we have visited a nightclub," Kay McNeill confessed in the early 1940s. "I think maybe we're just a too-typical American family." Their sons were in bed by 8:30 P.M., and most nights Don turned in within an hour after that.

McNeill's personal philosophy not only permeated *The Breakfast Club* but was also a strong bond in creating and main-taining a loyal following. He frequently and joyously exclaimed that the show was "a get together time for all of us who smile before breakfast and then can't break the habit all day long — the place to come when a feller needs a friend."[13] Part of his atti-tude was expressed in a Breakfast Club Family Album issued by the show in 1942 and titled *Keep 'em Smiling*, in which he expressed some of his precepts:

• America's homes are America's fu-ture.

• Our American people have the wholesome courage, the fearless spirit to overcome any brutal force that would men-ace the security, the families, the homes of which we're so justly proud.

• The American mixture of faith in the Almighty, ingenuity, and love of free-dom for all, spell Victory!

• All our combined efforts are needed to insure this Victory, and for it we must be prepared to sacrifice everything.

• A spicy dash of humor and a sooth-ing draught of inspiration are as essentially a part of our daily diets as food itself.

• It is the function of the Breakfast Club as an American institution to boost our morale in the morning when it tends to ebb lowest.

• Therefore, in peace or war, we of the Breakfast Club must "Keep 'em Smil-ing!"

Interestingly, in its first six years on the air *The Breakfast Club* was broadcast commercial-free. It was actually a virtual no-man's land that no sponsor dared touch. But when Swift and Company bought first one and then a second quarter-hour seg-ment, other advertisers were quick to climb aboard. For many years Philco Corpora-tion and the Kellogg Company underwrote it. Some others included the Toni Division of the Gillette Company, Cream of Wheat, Acme Paints and Sterling Drugs (for its Bayer aspirin). At one point the hour maintained an annual budget of $4 mil-lion, boosting McNeill as ABC's prime money earner in the late 1940s and early 1950s.

The program spawned an idea for a similar West Coast series, *Breakfast at Sardi's*, which was later known as *Break-fast with Breneman, Breakfast in Holly-wood* and *Welcome to Hollywood*. Though never as successful as the original, the California conclave — inaugurated in 1941 as *Breakfast on the Boulevard* over Los Angeles' KFWB — was presided over by Tom Breneman until his unexpected demise in 1948. The show became an 11 A.M. Eastern Time staple for most of its run, on the same network airing *The Break-fast Club*.

This series initially emanated from Sardi's Restaurant on Hollywood Boulevard. There were no vocalists, quizzes or prizes; Breneman simply asked crazy questions of his predominantly feminine audience each day. For that he received "spontaneous, witty, sometimes devilishly clever answers," according to one sage.[14] Upon Breneman's death, Garry Moore stepped in to fill the void for a while, followed by Cliff Arquette, John Nelson and Jack McElroy. It was never the same as in its heyday, however, and the program disappeared in 1951. Jack McCoy starred in a brief NBC Saturday-only reprise of the series from 1952 to 1954.

In the meantime, Don McNeill seemed to ABC decision-makers like a natural for TV. In the tube's embryonic stage, on September 27, 1946, at 8 o'clock in the evening, Chicago's WBKB-TV telecast a one-time experimental *Don McNeill's Dinner Club*. It featured the morning show's host and its principals. Less than two years later, on May 12, 1948, TV stations in Baltimore, New York, Philadelphia and Washington, D. C. offered their viewers a live performance of *The Breakfast Club* radio show. It was the first time a daytime feature had been simultaneously broadcast on radio and television.

During that epoch, ABC-TV moved cautiously in airing any program on weekday evenings before 6 o'clock. Yet it was eager to establish its radio morning mogul in his own weekly variety series. *The Don McNeill TV Club* bowed on Wednesday night, September 13, 1950, at 9 o'clock Eastern Time. This series showcased all of the regulars from the morning program, plus weekly guests who were purposely overshadowed by the cast.

Could this venture have threatened Arthur Godfrey, who with his own company of daytime regulars and special guests appeared on Wednesday evenings in the 8 o'clock hour on CBS-TV in a similar home-spun series? A Godfrey biographer notes that the old redhead viewed McNeill as a competitor, failing badly to hide his personal disdain for his archrival. How so? Their morning shows aired at separate hours. While McNeill had a dozen-year head start on Godfrey, *The Breakfast Club* could be sized up as cornball and barnyard antics, while Godfrey's daily discourse likely appealed to a more sophisticated audience. Not much to intimidate there. Despite that, McNeill personified what Godfrey had honed to perfection, the art of speaking to a single individual, at once demonstrating a gift that few radio hosts were able to adequately exhibit.

Yet when McNeill came along with a televised hour immediately following Godfrey, and patterned after the master's own show, the old redhead may have felt that the sheerest form of flattery *wasn't* imitation at all, as an established adage suggests. Did familiarity, to him, breed contempt? Was it simply infringement upon his (Godfrey's) perceived "turf"? Several media arts scholars have pointed out that an apparently one-sided rift existed between the pair. If McNeill carried any grudge, it was heavily veiled. Apparently, his feelings—if he had any—weren't recorded in the press.

Their basic conflict, as envisioned by Godfrey, may have stemmed from the parallels in the Wednesday night TV programs, though that has never been confirmed. At this distance, one may only conjecture.

McNeill figured in at least one major Godfrey flap, however—one of numerous fiascoes involving the major CBS moneymaker. It occurred as Godfrey fired his longtime bandleader Archie Bleyer. Their association ended abruptly when Bleyer, who had created his own recording label, had the audacity to go to Chicago to tape McNeill reading a sequence of poems. Godfrey was already miffed over Bleyer's dating Janet Ertel, one of The Chordettes, a chic women's quartet then appearing on his shows. That was in direct violation of a Godfrey policy prohibiting courtship within the ranks. (Bleyer later married Ertel.) At last, the McNeill recording was perceived as an intolerable act of treason.

"His [Godfrey's] petulance and arrogance," declared a critic, "were the stuff of legend."[15] While the dispute played out in the tabloids, Bleyer never responded, leaving to Godfrey any explanation for the press. Journalists surmised it as another instance of Godfrey's jealousy. As in the infamous firing of singer Julius La Rosa a short time before, Godfrey apparently believed Bleyer was becoming too successful and was running ahead of the captain's expectations for his team. The result was one of a string of exhibitions in which the mastermind seemed determined to publicly self-destruct.

Godfrey guitarist Remo Palmieri assessed: "I think the show went steadily downhill after Archie left ... because he was the brains behind all that entertainment and what made the show successful."[16] By contrast, *The New Yorker* elaborated on McNeill's position, explaining that there was little public discord and no ill-serving behavior like that displayed by Godfrey. "Once they [McNeill's cast members] get on *The Breakfast Club*, they settle down to the most secure job in radio."[17]

Nonetheless, McNeill's Wednesday night television venture never caught fire with the masses, although the network gave it a season-and-a-half to do so. "Perhaps there was only room for one Godfrey," some speculated.[18]

The Breakfast Club's eventual foray into television, a simulcast of the radio show that began on February 22, 1954, was regrettably little short of disaster. McNeill and his entourage came off looking like neophytes. Attempting to cheerily consume breakfast while on the set, they appeared stiff and disoriented, having *never* eaten a meal during the radio-only run. It

didn't look or feel right, to them nor to the home audience, and the series left the tube forever on February 25, 1955.

The ultimate dynamic in the video failure, however, was far more conclusive: The show didn't attract any sponsors during the grace year the network extended it. ABC's lack of sponsorship kept the chain from scheduling *any* weekday series earlier than 1 o'clock Eastern Time until late 1958, with the exception of *The Breakfast Club*, which was a sustaining feature. McNeill may have correctly identified that as the cause of his video misfortunes: "There was no network programming around us, which made it very difficult to come up with the supposed ratings which advertisers and agencies ... insist on," he told the entertainment industry's *Billboard*.[19]

A clear distinction between the visual and audio mediums was extended during one facet of the show's simulcast experiment. Viewers observed that the commercials on TV were presented live, while those heard by the radio listeners were aired on tape.

McNeill attempted a final television comeback when he tried emceeing a Sunday afternoon game show on ABC-TV. *Take Two* premiered on May 5, 1963. It featured dual pairs of players competing to identify a connection between two of four photos placed in front of them. On a special presentation on June 23, 1963, which signified the thirtieth anniversary of *The Breakfast Club* on radio, humorist Peter Donald and Fran Allison (Aunt Fanny) coemceed *Take Two* as McNeill played the game. *Take Two* was doomed from its start, nonetheless, for it never attracted a sizable audience. By August 11 it was gone from the small screen. With the exception of occasional guest shots, McNeill's video days were over. From then on he would concentrate solely on radio once more.

When a listener chastised McNeill for failing to give away valuable prizes as many other radio shows did, he asked his audience what they thought of it. He received more than 50,000 replies, an overwhelming majority of them stating that they didn't want washing machines, furniture or fur coats. Instead, they simply preferred the kind of *Breakfast Club* corn that McNeill and company had dished out for so many years. They were genuinely contented, they confirmed, with a bit of McNeill judgment included in the 1942 family album: *America needs to wake up with a smile, because a day begun happy makes life worthwhile.*

Long after other network shows were dying by the dozens, *The Breakfast Club* continued to sally forth every day in its traditional upbeat style, altering little from its formative years. About its only variance was to move from broadcasting before a daily live studio audience to pre-recording shows one day ahead of broadcasts, while still performing them before a room full of spectators.

In early August 1968 this author, an unrepentant fan of this durable series for more than two decades, at last made a trek to Chicago. *The Breakfast Club* was then only four months shy of airing its final hour, although that had not yet been announced. With great anticipation I had written to the network well in advance to secure a free ticket so that I might witness a lifelong dream.

Arriving at the Allerton Hotel before the appointed day's transcription was made, I was in awe of the trappings that surrounded that audience. I suppose it was about what I had imagined for so long. But I was resolutely dismayed to learn that Don McNeill — whom I had waited for so long to see — was away on vacation. In his spot sat singer Gordon MacRae. MacRae wasn't a bad choice; he simply wasn't Don McNeill!

Imagine my surprise when a comment I made on my audience survey card —

yes, those cards were still being collected that many years later — provoked a live interview by one of the announcers. Even though the show was taped to air the following day, it dawned on me some time later that that was to be my network debut!

It never happened. I listened intently to the ABC affiliate the following morning, anticipating hearing my own voice. Alas, the show ran long and my interview was cut. Without Don McNeill, I finally rationalized, it wouldn't have meant that much anyway.

At the end of each program the cast would jubilantly harmonize: "America is up! The Breakfast Club now leaves the air!" And Don McNeill would admonish listeners — as he had done for decades — to "Be good to yourself!"

In her 1944 book about her husband and his show, Kay McNeill posed the question: "Is it possible for Don to continue as *Breakfast Club* master of ceremonies for many years to come?" Not discerning the future fortunes of radio at that time, of course, she claimed that McNeill hoped to continue at his post "until one of the boys (their three sons) could take over the job."

No one could possibly have dreamed that what they had going would last for more than 35 years! Nor that, when the show signed off for the very last time, network radio — with the exception of news, sports and a few sporadic features — would have virtually been dead for eight years already.

None of that. All of it would have seemed too implausible in the mid–1940s.

McNeill, king of the weekday radio audience participation format, who never experienced those widely publicized tantrums thrown by one of his contemporaries, died on May 7, 1996, at Evanston, Illinois. He was 88. No one had dominated daytime radio for as many years as he, and, undeniably, that made him a legend in his own time.

5

Bride and Groom

Premise: Could matrimony, virtually by itself, develop into the basis for a permanent radio and television series? ABC Radio, CBS-TV and NBC-TV thought so and gave the institution every opportunity to flourish. Large numbers of fans sat enthralled, first listening, then watching, while more than 2,500 couples tied the knot over a dozen-year period. The daily live feature was separated into a trio of segments. In the first, master of ceremonies John Nelson interviewed a lucky couple who had been chosen for the all-expense-paid nuptials and a honeymoon of their dreams. Before a live theater audience in a Los Angeles hotel, Nelson inquired how the twosome met, what attracted them to one another, something of their backgrounds and their future plans. In the second part — while the betrothed pair was ushered offstage and into an adjacent chapel for a private ceremony, beyond hearing range of the crowd — Nelson interviewed various guests drawn from the audience, regularly including honeymooners and couples who were celebrating significant anniversaries. Thirdly, in the closing minutes of the half-hour, the ceremony over, the newlyweds returned to the microphone.

They were showered with an almost unbelievable plethora of gifts, an announcer judiciously listing each prize, describing it ad nauseam while jubilantly naming its manufacturer. At the end, the happy duo departed for a wedding trip with a rousing send-off from the audience. While this program lasted only about five years on radio, it prevailed for another four years on the small screen. And though it could never be classified as one of the most popular programs on the air, it was a tradition that many faithfully enjoyed, centered on one of life's most solemn and meaningful moments. Few series could hardly come as close to being labeled "reality-based" as this show.

Producers: John Masterson, John Nelson, John Reddy

Directors: Marvin Beck, Edward Feldman, John Masterson, John Nelson, John Reddy, Wayne Reeves

Master of Ceremonies: John Nelson

Announcer-Vocalist: Jack McElroy

Organist: Gaylord Carter

Hostess (backstage detail): Roberta Roberts

Writer: John Reddy

Sponsor: Six weeks into the run, on

63

January 7, 1946, Sterling Drugs bought the series, underwriting it the rest of the way for its long line of personal care and drug commodities—Bayer aspirin, Campho Phenique antiseptic, Double Danderine hair preparation, Dr. Lyons' tooth powder, Energine cleaning fluid and Energine Shoe-White polish, Fletcher's Castoria baby laxative, Ironized Yeast supplements, Mulsified Coconut Oil shampoo, Phillips' Milk of Magnesia family of brands (cleansing cream, laxative, toothpaste), and more.

Ratings: High: 4.4 (three seasons, 1947–48, 1948–49, 1949–50); Low: 2.4 (1945–46); Median: 3.8 (five seasons). This show had to compete against greatly beloved soap operas on both CBS and NBC that could boast long-held listening habits among fans. While it, too, acquired a core following, as a result of the serials' enduring popularity, it never really came close to reaching its greatest potential.

On the Air: Nov. 26, 1945–Dec. 28, 1945, ABC, weekdays, 4:15 P.M. ET; Dec. 31, 1945–Feb. 2, 1950, ABC, weekdays, 2:30 P.M.; Feb. 5, 1950–Sept. 15, 1950, ABC, weekdays, 3 P.M.

*   *   *

When people think of the inviolability of marriage, most agree it's an institution sanctified by God. A radio series in the 1940s resulted in nearly 1,000 such unions. A masculine trio, all bearing the appellation *John*, masterminded the program. Does first, second and third John sound biblical enough for you?

John Nelson was master of ceremonies on *Bride and Groom* during its five-year ABC Radio run (1945–50). Later (1951–54) he turned up in the same role on television.

Co-producing the show with Nelson were John Reddy, who wrote it, and John Masterson, who also produced a highly acclaimed ABC weekday series, *Breakfast in Hollywood* (earlier *Breakfast at Sardi's*). This trio produced a couple of other radio series—*Rebuttal*, and *Eleanor and Anna*, the latter featuring Mrs. Franklin D. Roosevelt and her daughter.

Bride and Groom was a most unusual half-hour Monday-through-Friday feature. Announcer-vocalist Jack McElroy brought an engaged couple on-stage with these lyrics, sung to an organ's accompaniment:

> *Here's to the bride and groom,*
> *On their joyous wedding day;*
> *Let's toast the lucky pair,*
> *Start them on their way ...*
> *We wish them every happiness ... today!*

Nelson interviewed the couple, encouraging them to share their love story from their first meeting. Then McElroy sang a romantic number to the couple that they had chosen for that momentous occasion. Then they left the stage of Los Angeles' Chapman Park Hotel (later the Hollywood Knickerbocker) to be married in an adjacent chapel by one of about 30 clergymen who were retained by *Bride and Groom*. The couple returned to the stage about 10 minutes later, following their nuptials.

Meanwhile, host John Nelson proceeded with the live radio program, often inviting a studio guest to describe the bride's attire to the radio audience. Almost daily he would interview members of the studio audience who were celebrating anniversaries that day—many of them for 50 or more years. Each couple was given expensive gifts, often his and her watches. The momentary notoriety and parting handouts were enough to draw a contingent of three or four couples on every show that had reached such milestones.

Then the newlyweds were ushered back into the theater where they were showered with luxurious gifts, including luggage, jewelry, appliances, silver, a reception and a week's expense-paid honeymoon to the destination of their choice. Before the show ended, Nelson invariably reached for the bride to steal a kiss—as if it went with the turf! The bridal pair had earlier received a complimentary wedding, gown, tuxedo, rings and more accouterments for themselves and their attendants, along with a chapel, musicians, flowers, minister, photographer and other amenities. In the 1940s it had to be one of the most extravagant ceremonies available to the middle class.

It was an established fact during that epoch that, for no more than having their commodities named on the air, manufacturers were loading various giveaway shows with oodles of merchandise. In calendar year 1947 alone, *Bride and Groom* netted $500,000 in loot, including Bulova watches, Kaiser-Frazer automobiles, Kelvinator refrigerators, Kimball pianos and Oshkosh luggage. Had those on-air mentions been billed by the network, the web could have reaped a tidy $5,000 per "plug."

And just how did those lucky twosomes qualify for *Bride and Groom*, and thus haul away all that booty?

First-time engaged couples were invited to write the show to introduce themselves. Director John Reddy often made the final selections about who would ultimately appear. Sometimes a panel of judges substituted for him, pouring over the applications while seeking the most captivating candidates they could find. (*Time* magazine reported that when the show went to television, it received more than 70,000 inquiries on behalf of couples wanting to be on it.)

A policy of the show automatically eliminated divorcees from consideration. Roman Catholics were excluded, too, because their faith required them to be married in a church ceremony.

Meanwhile, the human-interest elements were varied but almost always there.

A young woman with the good fortune of winning the "wishing ring" on Tom Breneman's *Breakfast in Hollywood* hoped for a *Bride and Groom* wedding. She got it. *Bride and Groom* director John Masterson was a producer of Breneman's show, and John Nelson, who hosted *Bride and Groom*, was the Breneman series announcer.

One young couple told how they had met on adjacent stools at the fountain counter of a local drug store.

Another pair, both blind, found each other at a school for seeing-eye dogs.

Celebrities, too, tied the knot on the program. Clayton (Bud) Collyer, serial actor-announcer and quizmaster-host-emcee of scads of radio series, married serial actress Marion Shockley in 1948. He went on to host *Break the Bank*, as well as television's *Beat the Clock, To Tell the Truth* and several more game shows. (For a detailed account of Collyer's many activities, see the preceding chapter on *Break the Bank*.)

On occasions, *Bride and Groom* departed from its usual practice of marrying couples—whose ages ranged from the teens to the eighties—to honor a couple then celebrating their golden wedding anniversary, or perhaps newlyweds currently on their honeymoon. These doublets, too, had lavish gifts bestowed upon them.

An organist's rendition of "Here Comes the Bride" was, appropriately, the show's theme. Jack-of-all-trades announcer Jack McElroy, who possessed a superb singing voice, doubled as the series' soloist. When he wasn't crooning "Believe Me, If All Those Endearing Young Charms" or "Together," he was touting one of sponsor Sterling Drugs' multiple remedies—Double Danderine shampoo, Bayer aspirin, Astring-O-Sol mouthwash, Energine cleaning fluid, Haley's M-O mineral oil laxative or some other—commodities that surely must have been on every newlywed's mind at that propitious moment!

The show debuted at 4:15 P.M. Eastern Time on ABC on November 26, 1945, but shifted to 2:30 P.M. on December 31, 1945. It remained in that time period until February 5, 1950, when it moved to 3 o'clock and was entrenched there until the end of the run on September 15 of that year. Sterling Drugs bought it on January 7, 1946, and carried it the rest of the way.

When the radio series was withdrawn, Nelson, Masterson and Reddy merely transferred their creative flair to television. *Bride and Groom*'s video version premiered on CBS on January 25, 1951, about four months after its radio run ended. With minimal disruption, it remained a daytime CBS staple through October 9, 1953, alternating telecasts between two and five days a week. Nelson remained the host as the program moved to NBC on December 7, 1953. The series was canceled on August 27, 1954, yet — after a three-year absence — was given a six-month reprieve on July 1, 1957.

For a month, Frank Parker, a vocalist on *Arthur Godfrey Time*, hosted the show. A singing duo, Robert Paige and Byron Palmer, succeeded him. *Bride and Groom* aired its final video presentation on January 10, 1958.

In July 1951 Masterson, Nelson and Reddy earned the distinction of gaining the largest legal judgment in broadcasting history as of that date. They had gone to court to seek an injunction against a local Hollywood program called *Wedding Bells* that they alleged merely duplicated *Bride and Groom* under another moniker. When a jury awarded them $800,000, the trio announced that all they really wanted was acknowledgment of the fact. They settled for $800, applying it to a cocktail party to which they invited both plaintiffs and defendants. The court, of course, had never seen anything like it!

Bride and Groom's master of ceremonies, John Nelson, was born in 1915. He attended Gonzaga University, then spent three years in the U.S. Navy and later produced radio and TV series for the U.S. Air Force. In addition to announcing *Breakfast at Sardi's* (a.k.a. *Breakfast in Hollywood*), he introduced the weekday radio talent series *Live Like a Millionaire* and hosted a game show called *Add a Line*. With John Masterson and John Reddy, Nelson co-produced *Eleanor and Anna*, and *Rebuttal*. Nelson hosted another TV series: *Know Your NBC's* (1953–54), becoming a program executive for that chain. He later managed KPLM radio at Palm Springs, and died in that city on November 3, 1976.

Jack McElroy, the singing announcer who ballyhooed Sterling Drug products while crooning to the newlyweds, was pressed into service as a replacement for Tom Breneman as host of *Breakfast in Hollywood*. Breneman had died unexpectedly in April 1948. Initially, rising radio (and soon, television) star Garry Moore filled in for a brief spell, but that duty fell McElroy's way shortly thereafter, and he carried it for about a year. He, too, died at an early age, 45, on March 2, 1959.

Bride and Groom organist Gaylord Carter was responsible for the music on radio's *Amos 'n' Andy, Breakfast at Sardi's* (a.k.a. *Breakfast in Hollywood*), *The Jack Kirkwood Show* and *Raffles*. On television he accompanied the game show *Glamour Girl*.

Beyond those named, others associated with *Bride and Groom* in official capacities earned no other recorded industry credits.

Counting the nearly 1,000 marriages performed on radio, the combined radio-TV *Bride and Groom* saw more than 2,500 couples tie the knot. It was a novel treatment of one of life's most meaningful observances; for more than a decade, millions of viewers and listeners sat mesmerized, enthralled to be witnesses to this colossal life-changing event.

6

Can You Top This?

Premise: This show maintained a facile premise, that of tickling the funnybones of Americans of all walks of life. Each week it offered squeaky-clean humor that routinely could be appreciated by every age group as it boldly pursued its hypothesis. The result was a rollicking half-hour of virtually unimpeded mirth combining the interests of listeners with on-the-spot reactions of a live studio assemblage. The audience participation factor allowed the folks at home to submit their best humor — and thousands did so each week — to be recounted before a panel of recognized comedians. These wits were just waiting to tell a taller tale on the same theme than the one they had just heard. If their wisecracks grabbed a higher studio response than the listener's submissions — measured by a mechanical device recording decibel levels — the joke-sender earned little for his or her efforts. But when the panelist-sages failed to surpass an entry, that listener earned a generous cash prize. It was all in fun, and *Can You Top This?* and its quipsters won spots in the hearts of vast numbers of listeners. Their gag-swapping frenzy remained on the air for a dozen years, in fact. There was seldom a cloud of doubt

hanging over the content of the tales told here; they could be shared openly with anyone, generally without fear of personal affront. Only a handful of subjects were considered taboo. As in the cases of some other popular radio features, an attempt to televise this frivolous melee succumbed to a quick death. Few viewers wanted to see a group of mellowing chaps exchanging anecdotes around a bare table. Their barrage of witticisms obviously appealed more to an audio sensibility than to a visual one. On radio, however, this show came into its own, acquiring a sweeping appreciation that some others of the form missed almost altogether.

Creator/Owner/Producer/Director: "Senator" Ed Ford

Producer: Roger Bower

Directors: Roger Bower, Jay Clark, Alan Dingwall

Hosts: Roger Bower, Ward Wilson

Quipmeister: Peter Donald

Panelists: "Senator" Ed Ford, Harry Hershfield, Joe Laurie Jr.

Announcer: Charles Stark

Sponsors: The show was sustained by the Mutual network from its inception until it attracted the Kirkman Soap Co. as sponsor, from Feb. 3, 1943, through Sept. 19, 1945, on that network. A concurrent series bowing on NBC on Oct. 3, 1942, and continuing for six consecutive seasons, through June 25, 1948, was underwritten by Colgate-Palmolive-Peet, Inc. for its extensive family of personal care products: Colgate dental cream, Palmolive shave cream and toilet soap, Lustre Creme shampoo, and others. NBC sustained it in 1948 as a summer replacement for *The Judy Canova Show*. The series was carried by MBS once again from 1948 to 1950 without full sponsorship, although the Ford Motor Co. participated frequently in its commercials. On Jan. 2, 1951—having transitioned to ABC without a sponsor, and vanishing quickly from that web's schedule—the program returned when the Mars Candy Co. bought it for its Milky Way, Forever Yours, Mars and Snickers confections. That arrangement persisted through June 26, 1951. At that juncture the program returned to NBC, first in weeknight and then weekly formats, boasting multiple sponsors or sustained by the network until the end of the run.

Ratings: High: 16.5 (1944–45); Low: 3.1 (1949–50); Median: 10.6 (based on all seasons except 1940–41, 1941–42, 1948–49 and 1953–54).

On the Air: Dec. 9, 1940–May 12, 1941, MBS, Monday, 9:30 P.M. ET; May 20, 1941–Jan. 26, 1943, MBS, Tuesday, 8 P.M.; Feb. 3, 1943–Sept. 19, 1945, MBS, Wednesday, 7:30 P.M.; Oct. 3, 1942–Sept. 27, 1947, NBC, Saturday, 9:30 P.M.; Oct. 3, 1947–June 25, 1948, NBC, Friday, 8:30 P.M.; July 3, 1948–Sept. 25, 1948, NBC, Saturday, 9:30 P.M.; Sept. 29, 1948–May 24, 1950, MBS, Wednesday, 8 P.M.; Sept. 23, 1950–Nov. 25, 1950, ABC, Saturday, 9:30 P.M.; Jan. 2, 1951–June 26, 1951, ABC, Tuesday, 9:30 P.M.; Oct. 5, 1953–Mar. 26, 1954, NBC, Monday–Friday, 10:15 P.M.; April 2, 1954–July 9, 1954, NBC, Friday, 9:35 P.M.

* * *

Pure and simple, this was a radio gagfest.

For a dozen years a trio of maturing vaudevillians appearing on this squeaky-clean joke-telling marathon sought bigger laughs than those guffaws produced by the puns submitted by listeners.

In a prominent trade paper, a show business critic assessed: "It's an engaging half hour that provided that expensive radio luxury—humor—at minimum cost and production headache…. Easy-going, angled for giggles and very listenable."[1]

The panelists included comedians "Senator" Ed Ford ("Good evening"), Harry Hershfield ("Howdy!") and Joe Laurie Jr. ("Hel-low"). Yarns from listeners were delivered by contemporary comic Peter Donald, renowned as a master dialectician who often chose ethnic-sounding vernacularism to gain wider acceptance of ordinary quips. Donald routinely employed an Irish brogue, a throwback to his enormously popular alter ego figure Ajax Cassidy (a permanent 1946–49 resident of "Allen's Alley" on weekly broadcasts of *The Fred Allen Show*).

Ward Wilson moderated *Can You Top This?* for most of the run. He offered a topic on which the next round of jests hinged. He also shared the hosting duties with Roger Bower who, in addition, produced and directed the show at varying intervals. Charles Stark was the announcer for the entire run.

One of the panelists, "Senator" Ford—who wasn't an elected official representing anybody at all, but who called himself by that prefix merely to enhance his status as an orator on the banquet circuit—was creator, owner, producer and executive director of the show. Like the others, he maintained a large repository of wisecracks (believed to exceed 15,000 gags among the panel threesome) that could

Perhaps the funniest assemblage of men on the air listened to comic Peter Donald tell listener-submitted jokes, then tried to derive greater laughter from the studio audience by attempting taller tales. Claiming they had 15,000-plus gags in their combined repertoire, panelists of *Can You Top This?* with Donald at far left included *(left to right)* dour-faced "Senator" Ed Ford, Joe Laurie Jr. and Harry Hershfield. (Photofest)

yield explosive laughter at a moment's notice. A trio of Ford's quips, delivered on the air with basso profundo timbre in a strikingly wry, haltingly staccato style, follows (incidentally, these gags are typical of those rendered by all of the show's panelists):

(1) Two twins were doing their homework. One says to the other: "Who chopped down the cherry tree?" The other kid replies: "Popeye." Startled, the first one questions: "Popeye?" The other says: "Yeah. When George Washington's old man asked him who chopped down the cherry tree, he replied, "Pop ... I did it."

(2) A guy gets into a barber's chair. The barber says: "How do you want your hair cut?" The guy replies: "Off."

(3) A guy drives up to a tollgate. The gatekeeper states: "Fifty cents for your car." The driver says: "Sold."

Each of these jests reached 1,000 on a 'laugh meter,' an electronic apparatus connected to a studio microphone that recorded the level of audience response. An indicator was kept on-stage in full view of those witnesses. Once in awhile a joke gained only a snickering retort, registering 200 or below on the scale. The majority of puns exceeded 500, with most of them hitting 1,000.

A listener's submission that was read over the air earned $10 for the sender ($5 in the earliest days). The contributor gained another $5 every time a panelist told a subsequent joke on the same topic but failed to reach 1,000 on the laugh meter. Consequently, a collapse of the panel would bring the listener $25, a tidy sum in those days of simple radio giveaways.

The *Can You Top This?* staff typically received about 6,000 jokes every week from the folks at home. Screener Betty North pored over the mail before forwarding her picks to the producer, director, host and chief storyteller. Ostensibly, only those gags pertaining to arson, politics and religion were considered off-limits, although North got away with omitting some categories of her own: death, deformities, race and stuttering. Jokes about nationalities were fair game, however, and Peter Donald's dialects could readily convert from Italian to Irish to Jewish to whatever else seemed appropriate and appealing. North claimed she liked "fast jokes, talking stories that don't require anything visual to put them across."[2] A quip's age was of little consequence: Audiences laughed at *Today's Chuckle* from current newspapers just as they did a humorous tale that had been circulated for decades.

Across the show's dozen-year run, Ed Ford claimed that—in one form or another—he had heard every joke that was sent in by a listener. This triad of wits—tabbed the *Knights of the Clown Table*—altered their stories often to fit a myriad of settings. They adroitly interchanged ethnic characters, locales and other circumstances with direct bearing on a quip's environment. Sometimes enough elements were masked that listeners hardly recognized a retelling of the "same old story."

Ford punctuated his tales with a battery of recurring characters who were named in his storytelling. Principals included Ditsy Baumwortle, Ockie Bopp,

Dopey Dillock, Mrs. Fafoofnick, Elmer Smudgegunk and Mr. Snapgirdle. The casual mention of one of these figures unleashed a veritable tittering across an expectant studio audience.

The show's opening, which was adjusted slightly from time to time, captured the imagination of a listening public as the program burst onto the airwaves with uproarious studio laughter—reminiscent of the highly recognized debut heard concurrently each week on *Truth or Consequences*. Beyond the laughter, the opening continued:

> WILSON: *Can You Top This?* Why does a chicken cross the road?
> DONALD: That was no chicken, that was my wife.
> WILSON: Can you top that, Harry Hershfield?
> HERSHFIELD: Sure.
> WILSON: Can you, Senator Ford?
> FORD: I might.
> WILSON: And you, Joe Laurie Jr.?
> LAURIE: Maybe.
> STARK: Those expedient exclamations introduce the pint-sized author-comedian, Joe Laurie Jr.; the popular after dinner speaker and current topic humorist, Senator Ford; and well-known cartoonist and after dinner speaker, Harry Hershfield. These effervescent entertainers bring you another session of *Can You Top This?* with the best wishes of Kirkman's soap flakes. And now here's your master of ceremonies, Ward Wilson.
> WILSON: Thank you, Charles Stark. *Can You Top This?* is unrehearsed and spontaneous, and our top rule is "keep 'em laughing." Anyone can send in a joke, and if your joke is told by our storytelling genius, Peter Donald, you get ten dollars. Each of the three wits tries to top it with another joke on the same subject. Each time they fail to top you, you get five dollars ... so you have a chance to win as much as twenty-five dollars. But regardless of whether you win ten or twenty-five dollars, you will receive a recording of Peter Donald telling your story

on the air. Laughs are registered on the *Can You Top This?* laugh meter in full view of our studio audience, and in all cases the decision of our judges is final.

Not just the gags but also the ebullient on-air personalities made this show work. A proper examination of the series' success, what permitted it to remain on the air for so long, should start with an introspective look at its principals.

Producer Roger Bower was born in New York City in 1903. In 1927 he broke into radio at his hometown's WMCA, moving to WOR the following year, a flagship station of the future Mutual Broadcasting System. For 24 years he directed one of radio's first terror series, *The Witch's Tale*, and produced and directed a weekly whodunit mystery, *The Crime Club*. He provided live coverage of the inaugural Macy's annual Thanksgiving Day parade, too.

Bower produced *The Adventures of Leonidas Witherall*, *The Paul Winchell-Jerry Mahoney Show* and *The Rookies*. He directed *The Grummits*, *Leave It to Mike*, *Secret Missions* and *Take a Note*. He also produced and directed *Famous Jury Trials* and *It Pays to Be Ignorant*. He was master of ceremonies for the joke-telling panel of radio and television's *Stop Me if You've Heard This One*. Bower died at Sharon, Connecticut, on May 17, 1979.

Bower, Jay Clark and Alan Dingwall all directed *Can You Top This?* Radio historians have offered nothing about Dingwall, raising the possibility that his stint on the show may have been brief. The responsibilities he carried out elsewhere could have been negligible also. Regretfully, all we know of Clark is that he directed *Hop Harrigan*, and produced and wrote *Jungle Jim*, a pair of juvenile adventure series.

The *Can You Top This?* emcee on both radio and TV was Ward Wilson, a native of Trenton, New Jersey, born May 22, 1903. One of the most versatile personalities on

the air, this electrical engineer-turned-broadcaster (after years of testing mikes and lines at program rehearsals) developed a flair for impersonations, character and comedy acting, announcing, emceeing, and sportscasting. His creativity helped him launch a pair of early WHN–New York series, *Gloom Dodgers* and *Itty Bitty Kitty Hour*.

He performed in the casts of *The Aldrich Family*, *The Amazing Mr. Smith*, *Burns and Allen*, *The Cuckoo Hour*, *The Fred Allen Show*, *The Judy Canova Show*, *The Phil Baker Show*, *Philip Morris Playhouse*, *The Royal Vagabonds* and *That's a Good One*. Wilson co-hosted the game show *What's My Name?* and was master of ceremonies of *Winner Take All*. He was also a panelist on *Stop Me if You've Heard This One*.

On their respective newscasts, he introduced Van DeVenter, Raymond Gram Swing and Walter Winchell. And following the Golden Age of radio, he was hired as sports director by WEAT radio and television in West Palm Beach. Wilson died in that Florida city on March 21, 1966.

While no single individual can be considered the "star" of *Can You Top This?*, dialectician and master storyteller Peter Donald probably comes as close as any in filling such a role. Born in Bristol, England, on June 6, 1918, the multitalented lad — already a child radio actor by the age of 10 — went to Broadway, then joined his Scottish parents, vaudevillians Donald and Carson, for Noel Coward's *Bittersweet*. Young Donald was soon playing Tiny Tim in *A Christmas Carol*. By 13 he was emceeing a radio series. In a dramatic production of "The Man Who Was Tomorrow," he played seven different age intervals of the leading figure's life.

Donald's early intro into radio led him to acquire parts in numerous series: *The Benny Goodman Show*, *Coast-to-Coast on a Bus*, *Columbia Presents Corwin*, *The*

Grummits, The Horn and Hardart Children's Hour, Into the Light, The Lady Next Door, Manhattan at Midnight, The March of Times Quiz, Second Husband, Stella Dallas, The Story of Mary Marlin, Talk Your Way Out of It, Terry and the Pirates, Treasury Star Parade, and *Your Family and Mine.* He introduced *Melody Lane with Jerry Wayne.* In 1947 he tried hosting a namesake quarter-hour, *The Peter Donald Show,* which didn't survive long. Undoubtedly, his single best remembered role was as Ajax Cassidy, the crusty old stereotypical Irish loudmouth on *The Fred Allen Show,* who enjoyed a tremendous following every Sunday evening.

Donald became a contributor to the early efforts of television, too. In 1948 he was in the running to become a permanent host of *The Texaco Star Theater* when the sponsor selected Milton Berle, Morey Amsterdam and Henny Youngman for those coveted spots. The rest is history.

He appeared in the videocast of *ABC Showcase* in 1950 while hosting *Ad Libbers* for CBS-TV in 1951 and turning up on panels of four small screen series: *Can You Top This?, Masquerade Party* (which he also moderated from 1954 to 1956), *Prize Performance* and *Where Was I?* As late as 1957 he performed on TV's *Pantomime Quiz.* He was a TV commercial voice-over artist beyond his radio days, and narrated some industrial film documentaries. Donald died April 20, 1979, at Fort Lauderdale, Florida.

The panel on *Can You Top This?* evolved out of a vaudevillian tradition. One radio historiographer suggested that the triumvirate, relying on practiced humor, became "as well-known in their field as the *Information Please* panel was on matters intellectual."[3]

"Senator" Ed Ford, born Edward Hastings Ford in Brooklyn, New York, on June 13, 1887, gained recognition as an illustrator and toastmaster following many years

as a monologist on the vaudeville circuit. He originated and owned *Can You Top This?,* loosely basing the show on joke-swapping sessions at New York's Lamb's Club.

Several critics argued that, among the panelists on both the radio and TV series, Ford was the "toughest" to "make laugh." The digest *Tune In* portrayed him as "dour and sullen offstage as well as on," a depiction recounted by other writers, despite his ability to make the crowds laugh. His dry wit and delivery often resembled some of the characters that comedians Bob and Ray played on their network radio runs. Ford also delivered "pronouncements of plain Yankee common sense," the NBC Artists Service noted.

He was both a writer and cast member of *The Grummits,* an early situation comedy, and a panelist on *Stop Me if You've Heard This One.* Ford died at Greenport, New York, on January 27, 1970.

Harry Hershfield, also a cast member of *Stop Me if You've Heard This One,* was a popular after-dinner speaker, typically delivering 200 speeches annually. He possessed another similarity to Ford: He was a newspaper cartoonist. The author of *Laugh Louder, Live Longer,* Hershfield wrote a weekly journal humor column.

Born in Cedar Rapids, Iowa, on October 13, 1885, early in life he matured into an able comedian and raconteur. His financial and physical resources benefited numerous goodwill efforts. The McCosker-Hershfield Cardiac Home, a benevolence helping indigent heart disease victims that Hershfield and the chairman of the Mutual Broadcasting System launched in 1946, was a prime recipient of his generosity.

The humorist was on both radio and video versions of *Can You Top This?* His death occurred in New York City on December 15, 1974.

Joe Laurie Jr. was born in New York City in 1892. Two of the 80 jobs he claimed he aspired to before drifting into vaudeville and radio were as a gambling hall stickman and a racing stable exercise rider. In between vaudeville shows he honed his talents as a scribe, creating sketches for other performers while penning a *Variety* column and — with Abel Green — a 572-page treatise, *Show Biz: From Vaude to Video*, published in 1952.

In the early 1920s, while appearing in a Chicago production of *The Gingham Girl*, Laurie launched a radio career as a fluke. The stage cast appeared on a KYW radio show, with Laurie being the program's master of ceremonies.

At the invitation of Rudy Vallee, in 1937 he made an extended series of guest appearances on *The Fleischmann Hour*, one of radio's most popular series. In 1941 Laurie turned up in the cast of the soap opera *We Are Always Young.* Just as his panelist peers did, he liked to make talks and infrequently did so before benefit crowds. He was on both the radio and TV panels of *Can You Top This?* Death came to Laurie in New York City on April 29, 1954.

Announcer Charles Stark, the last of the principals of *Can You Top This?*, was a native of Reading, Pennsylvania. He attended the University of Pennsylvania. Entering radio in 1927, he found himself eventually introducing *Claudia and David, Gangbusters, Mother o' Mine, My Son and I, Our Gal Sunday, Scattergood Baines, Strange as It Seems, Sunday Evening Party* and *When a Girl Marries.*

Stark was in the cast of radio's *The Bob Hawk Show.* In 1949 he emceed TV's *The Jacques Fray Music Room,* and announced TV's *The Kraft Television Theatre* in 1955. He offered promotional and spot announcements on video until he retired in the mid–1980s.

Can You Top This? ultimately appeared on three radio networks, and across its 12-year run was broadcast every night of the week except Sunday. In its heyday the se-

ries aired for 30 minutes at varying hours between 8 and 10 o'clock Eastern Time. Following an absence of more than 27 months between 1951 and 1953, the show resurfaced as a quarter-hour weeknight feature at 10:15 P.M. on NBC. That format played almost six months until the series moved to a weekly 25-minute NBC outing, a final gasp that endured for another three months.

While the program was initially sustained on Mutual during its formative years (1940–43), it was underwritten on that network by the Kirkman Soap Company from 1943 to 1945. Colgate-Palmolive-Peet, which sponsored the show longer than any other firm, purchased a concurrent NBC series in 1942. When that association terminated a half-dozen years later, *Can You Top This?* aired sporadic Ford Motor Company commercials on MBS for dual seasons, although the series was often unsponsored. It was sustained by ABC in late 1950 and was picked up for a half-year by the Mars Candy Company in early 1951. The program was sustained or attracted multiple sponsors on returning to NBC in 1953.

In video form, *Can You Top This?* projected crudely. Offering few stage properties for viewers to focus upon, it was virtually the radio show set in front of a camera — with four aging comedians and little more. The jokes were stale and the series was stilted. That attempt didn't last long, the tube version debuted on ABC October 3, 1950, and departed March 26, 1951. Ward Wilson hosted it while Donald, Ford, Hershfield and Laurie swapped wisecracks.

Two decades later, comic Morey Amsterdam purchased the rights and produced a syndicated TV rendition that aired from January to September 1970. Amsterdam, Richard Dawson, Stu Gilliam and Danny Thomas were among the celebrity participants. TV game show emcee Wink

Martindale initially hosted the run and was soon followed by another veteran of that genre, Dennis James.

Can You Top This? was among several radio series to premiere within a few years of each other bearing similar themes.

Stop Me if You've Heard This One debuted on October 7, 1939, about 14 months in advance of *Can You Top This?* It featured a joke-telling panel, too, but departed only four months later — and returned to the air during the autumn of 1947 in a one-year reprise. Listeners supplied the gags but before the punchline was reached the resident wits had to interrupt the storytelling with the rest of the joke. Small prizes were earned by listeners if their quips were read on the air; larger prizes were awarded if the panel couldn't finish the tale. Familiar names associated with this series included Morey Amsterdam, Roger Bower, Ed Ford, Harry Hershfield and Ward Wilson. In retrospect, it appeared to be a warm-up for its much more widely appealing successor, *Can You Top This?*

Ward Wilson also showed up for *That's a Good One*, a 1943 outing featuring some ongoing punsters swapping gags with guest comedians. This series was even less popular than *Stop Me if You've Heard This One* and disappeared within a couple of months.

Another comparable series was *It Pays to Be Ignorant*, which one wag dubbed "radio's lame-brained answer" to such academic fare as *The Quiz Kids* and *Information Please*.[4] Calling it "a feast of the absurd,"[5] the reviewer suggested that its panel of "nitwits" (as opposed to "experts") attempted to respond to "moronic" questions; e.g., Who came first, Henry the Eighth or Henry the First? Rude interruptions and rambling off-topic monologues often intervened, needlessly failing to deal with an answer. When putting this show together, creators Bob Howell and Ruth Howard mustered a panel by assembling "a suitable group of fools."[6] Nobody believed this mishmash with Tom Howard as host (father of Ruth Howard) could survive long. The fact that it did so off-and-on for nine years (1942–51) could be an indictment on how utterly dependent some radio listeners had become on the laugh-lines offered during World War II and post-war years.

At the conclusion of each *Can You Top This?* session, the show departed with a distinctive ending in which everybody in the cast said farewell:

> STARK: And thus ends another laugh session of *Can You Top This?* originated by Senator Ford. Join us again next week ... same station ... same gang ... other jokes ... some new ... some old. Until then we remain yours for bigger and better laughs.
> FORD: Senator Ford.
> HERSHFIELD: Harry Hershfield.
> LAURIE: (high-pitched) Joe Laurie Jr.
> DONALD: Peter Donald.
> WILSON: Ward Wilson.
> BOWER: Roger Bower.
> STARK: So long ... and take care of yourself until we meet again next time.

While this wasn't everybody's favorite series, at its pinnacle *Can You Top This?* garnered strong ratings and for a virtual nonstop half-hour tickled the funnybone of America with clean humor. The show didn't originate the notion of focusing on a joke-telling panel set before a microphone, of course, but it honed the idea and supplied an obvious dimension of affable enthusiasm and brilliance that may have been lacking elsewhere. The fact that the series aired for a dozen years suggests that it may have ultimately perfected the gag-swapping formula — or certainly done it better than everybody else.

7

Dr. Christian

Premise: Imagine rank amateurs— people who had never been published *in their lives*— turning out dialogue for one of the nation's most beloved homespun dramas! Unthinkable? Only in radio! *Dr. Christian* welcomed, and actively solicited, such contributions each week from 1941 to 1954. As a result, the show received well over 100,000 manuscripts while airing about 650 of them. Compensating their authors for the stories it featured, the series entered each wordsmith in a competitive talent pool from which a "best" episode was selected annually. The grand prize was $2,000 cash, enough impetus for many aspiring scribes to "apply." In the meantime, *Dr. Christian* focused upon a beloved old physician who served a small rural hamlet. The drama mustered all of the pathos and heartache that could be squeezed out of the lives of the local citizens, easily exceeding their mere physical ailments. Together with perky nurse Judy Price, the good doctor sought to turn their collective miseries into uplifting opportunities: He dealt with emotional issues as often as he did with matters corporeal. Fans clearly identified with the soft-spoken protagonist, favoring his genteel bedside manner while being decidedly encouraged by his personal bent toward benevolent causes. Overall, the series reached happy endings, especially gladdening the hearts of listeners who heard the dialogue that they themselves had penned. The drama reached two notable feats along the way: for 14 years— without any summer hiatus, incidentally— it occupied a single half-hour time period on one network, something of a record when compared with most others; and the show was underwritten by a single sponsor across a 16-year run. Few primetime series could begin to match superlatives like these.

Producer: Dorothy McCann

Directors: Neil Reagan, John Wilkinson, Florence Ortman

Dr. Christian: Jean Hersholt

Judy Price: Rosemary DeCamp, Helen Claire, Lurene Tuttle, Kathleen Fitz

Mrs. Hastings: Maide Eburne

Announcers: Andre Baruch, Perry King, Art Gilmore

Writers: Ruth Adams Knight, the radio audience

Organists: Ivan Ditmars, Lew White, Milton Charles

Sound Effects Technicians: Ray

Erlenborn, Gus Bayz, Bill Brown, Clark Casey

Theme Song: *Rainbow on the River*

Sponsors: This was one of few prime-time series to go the distance with a single advertiser. The Cheesebrough Manufacturing Co. underwrote the program for its personal care line under the brand name Vaseline. This included petroleum jelly, hair tonic, lip balm and other commodities. Since the show normally took no summer breaks, the commitment by one sponsor became that much greater.

Ratings: High: 17.0 (1949–50); Low: 3.1 (1937–38); Median: 12.1 (for 16 seasons). In only four seasons (25 percent of the total) did ratings fall below double digits. The program remained exceptionally strong until its final few months on the air.

On the Air: Nov. 7, 1937–April 24, 1938, CBS, Sunday, 2:30 P.M. ET; Oct. 18, 1938–April 11, 1939, CBS, Tuesday, 10 P.M.; Nov. 1, 1939–Dec. 27, 1939, CBS, Wednesday, 10 P.M.; Jan. 3, 1940–Jan. 6, 1954, CBS, Wednesday, 8:30 P.M.

*   *   *

SFX: Phone ringing

JUDY PRICE: (cheerily) Dr. Christian's office!

MUSIC: First few bars of *Rainbow on the River*

ANNOUNCER: (theme under) The Vaseline program — the only show in radio where the audience writes the script! Our twelfth annual competition for the $2,000 Dr. Christian Award is drawing to a close. All scripts must be in the mail by midnight next Wednesday.

Dr. Christian was perhaps "the best-known light drama on the air."[1] It has been portrayed as "the *Marcus Welby* of its day"[2] (referring to a 1970s TV medical drama) and even considered "a beloved nighttime serial"[3] (which it wasn't, since its chapters didn't continuously interlock). But what really made this borderline anthology distinctive, setting it apart from all other homey dramas, was that its audience *did* write the scripts! They contributed around 10,000 of them annually in most years of the program's long run. We'll explore that in greater depth momentarily.

Launched in late 1937, the series (originally *Dr. Christian of River's End*) was specifically created for a soft-spoken, Danish-bred movie actor named Jean Hersholt. The efficacy of his role in *The Country Doctor*, a 1936 motion picture, won him a radio drama that was to replicate a typical rural physician. It would also label him with the part for the remainder of his acting career.

Hersholt's film character was based on the very real Dr. Allan Roy Dafoe. Overnight, Dafoe had become an American icon upon delivering the Dionne quintuplets. Meanwhile, in the mythical hamlet of River's Bend, Minnesota, Dr. Paul Christian was to become the beneficent character Hersholt had played on-screen, yet under a different moniker. When Hersholt was denied the rights to Dafoe's name on radio, he created his own: He took the middle name of Hans Christian Andersen, whose stories he loved as a boy. John Dunning observed: "Christian was a strong name: it had obvious biblical strengths and a long heritage in Hersholt's native Denmark. It would work well with Hersholt's Scandinavian accent and would have strong appeal in middle America, where Dr. Paul Christian's practice ... would be set."[4]

The show was to focus on the rural physician and his nurse, Judy Price, meeting the physical, emotional and social challenges proffered by the citizens of River's End. The series, in fact, would permit Christian to live his life helping others in need — "much like Mayberry with a doctor instead of a sheriff,"[5] attested a contemporary media chronologist.

Paul Christian and the people he

appealed to were viewed as hayseeds by industry insiders, however, most of whom limited their ilk to an attitude of "do-goodism" that allegedly prevailed in the nation's heartland. When he wasn't restoring a patient to physical health (at times this seemed but a mere fraction of his pursuits), Dr. Christian was helping those he encountered to find greater meaning in life. He was the kindly philosophical thinker — sort of a township senior adviser — who could put all things in their proper perspective for those people who held even the most jaundiced views. He loved to play cupid and did so frequently. Often he encountered compromised relationships, romantic or otherwise, for which he was called on to unravel thorny issues that separated diverse parties. He even performed acts of heroism, like saving people from burning buildings. Yet when murder became the focus in a single episode, listeners protested vehemently to the network. They wanted their homespun tales to remain on the lighter side. (Even Hersholt, himself, the show's star, acquired many of the traits that were synonymous with the role he played. He refused acting jobs that could have left him choosing directions that would be contrary to his categorical character. The actor also took part in numerous helping-hand efforts and philanthropical endeavors, just as Paul Christian did. When listeners contacted him for medical advice, however, he wisely referred them to physicians in their own communities.)

Christian, a never-married encourager — he was an active member of the River's End Bachelor's Club — resided and maintained his practice in a big white house at the corner of State Street and River Road. The waiting room could be directly accessed through a side entrance to the home. From time to time Mrs. Hastings, the doctor's housekeeper, appeared before the microphone, although she wasn't heard in most installments. Aside from nurse-secretary Judy Price, Hastings was the only other recurring support player in the drama. Most of the patients and others were heard in only one episode. That allowed greater flexibility in casting the show, drawing upon a large pool of West Coast actors and actresses.

Dr. Christian, also known as *The Vaseline Program* (because it was underwritten by a single sponsor for the duration of its 16-year run, and was introduced weekly by that phrase), began slowly. For the first three years the show doubled its home audience every year to an estimated 15 to 20 million listeners. By January 3, 1940 — when it moved to 8:30 on CBS Wednesday nights, a timeslot it would control for the next 14 years—*Dr. Christian* had become one of the most popular dramatic programs on the air. It continued to dominate its time period for virtually the remainder of the long run.

Ruth Adams Knight and other scribes penned the show in its early years, and obviously did so successfully, as the growing audience demonstrated. Somewhere along the path, however, the producer, director, advertising agency, sponsor and network became enamored with a new notion: The audience might be swayed to take an even greater interest in the drama if they could directly participate in some meaningful way. How about inviting them to submit manuscripts that would become the basis for future broadcast stories? It hadn't been done before; at least, not with any fanfare or documented success. It might be just enough novelty to generate even greater interest in this little narrative.

In 1941 they unveiled plans for the future of *Dr. Christian*. Manuscripts would be solicited, but they had to adhere to specific guidelines. Authors of any scripts selected for airing would be typically compensated with a check for $500, a rather tidy sum for unpublished writers in the

Rosemary DeCamp answered telephone callers with a sprightly "Dr. Christian's office!" at the start of many broadcasts of this durable drama. Danish-born actor Jean Hersholt played the namesake *Dr. Christian* for the full run, taking on life-long characteristics that personified the benevolent physician of River's Bend. Theirs became the only show in radio where the audience wrote the scripts. (Photofest)

nor the show took summer vacations (though there were rare breaks in continuity in 1938 and 1939). The program racked up more broadcast chapters than almost any other weekly dramatic series.

While *Newsweek* reported that 7,697 submissions for the Dr. Christian Award were received in 1947, in most years that number approached or exceeded 10,000. Over 100,000 manuscripts were collected in the dozen years the competition was held. Meanwhile, those plays that made it to the air espoused traditional values, interpreting Dr. Christian as the typically altruistic, good-natured figure he had been portrayed as since the series debuted in 1937. If his saintly qualities couldn't be discerned by the script readers (and, ultimately, the listeners), there was a strong chance that an entry into the contest would never be aired.

Actress Lurene Tuttle, who had the good fortune of playing nurse Price about the time the competition was launched, remembered that some of those submissions were less than satisfactory: "The real [ghost] writers on the show had to fix them quite often ... because they were really quite amateurish. But they had nice thoughts, they had nice plots. They just needed fixing; the dialogue didn't work too well."[6] (One of the ghost writers then freelancing for *Dr. Christian*, by the way, was a promising novice named Rod Serling, who was eventually destined for greater elevation.)

1940s and 1950s. Furthermore, each manuscript would compete against all the others aired in a given year. A panel of judges would select the story that they deemed the best submission of the year. The grand prize–winner would receive an additional $2,000 for his or her literary efforts. The cash and that recognition were definitely the *ultimate gain* sought by each author; the endeavor was labeled the Dr. Christian Award.

Was the concept successful? Aspiring wordsmiths came out of the woodwork. The first award was announced on June 17, 1942. Subsequent honors were bestowed annually, even though neither Hersholt

Despite the fact that what audiences heard might not have been precisely what the creatives at home submitted — word for word, at least — some of those so-called "amateurs" were quite good. A few launched professional writing careers as a result of their humble beginnings. One observer allowed that this competition, absent on other dramatic fare, "may have been the most important single factor in the show's long run."[7] It certainly sustained interest, whether an individual listener ever wrote a script for it or not. It was *different*. It surely contributed to the favorable ratings that *Dr. Christian* enjoyed across the final dozen years the program was on the air.

Martin Grams, Jr., created a log of the 788 broadcasts of the *Dr. Christian* series that includes episodic titles and dates they aired.[8] Grams' list begins with "Operation in a Shack" on November 7, 1937, the premier narrative, and ends with the final chapter, "Evenhanded Justice," on January 6, 1954. In between there were such emblematic titles as "Suggestions for Divorce" (June 26, 1940), "Excavation at Midnight" (September 15, 1943), "The Impatient Patient" (March 7, 1945), "A Loose Nut in the Living Machine" (October 9, 1946), "Often a Bridesmaid" (July 7, 1948), "Sorry, Right Number" (December 6, 1950), "The Storm" (January 9, 1952) and "Inheritance" (September 2, 1953).

Dr. Christian originally aired from New York, but after 10 weeks the program moved to Hollywood. Despite that, in weeks 36–41, 58–62, 82–84, 111, 207, 319, 338 and 341–343 the show returned to the Big Apple for its broadcasts. Each program was performed before a live audience, even if it was prerecorded.

Jean Hersholt reportedly never missed more than two of the 788 weekly installments. In the summer of 1945 he traveled to his native Denmark, in part at least to solicit support on behalf of the National War Fund. Skilled thespian Claude Rains stepped into the radio void while Hersholt was away, playing the role of Dr. Alexander Webb. Rains took over the broadcasts of June 6, 13 and 20 that year. Yet the familiar voice of Jean Hersholt returned on the latter show, brought by shortwave from Europe. The following week Hersholt himself was back at his old medical practice.

Hersholt was born in Copenhagen on June 12, 1886, the son of theatrical parents. He was educated in Denmark's Knud School and College, earned a master's degree from Copenhagen Bowdoin College and received two doctorates: in humanities, from Rolling College, and in literature, from California's De Landas University. His initial exposure to the stage came at the Dagmar Theater in Copenhagen, followed by performances with repertoire companies before crowds in the various Scandinavian nations. At 20 he appeared in the first motion picture produced in his native land. By 1913 he arrived in the United States, signing his first film contract within a year. In 1920 he became a naturalized American citizen.

Hersholt's screen credits, though mostly less than memorable, occurred in both silent and sound features. In addition to *The Country Doctor*, the film in which he portrayed the eminent Dr. Dafoe (and the model for launching the *Dr. Christian* radio series), Hersholt played in three dozen other movies, most often for RKO: *Abie's Irish Rose, Alexander's Ragtime Band, Alias the Deacon, Battle of the Sexes, Break of Hearts, The Cat and the Fiddle, The Climax, Dinner at Eight, Emma, Grand Hotel, Greed, Happy Landing, Heidi, His Brother's Wife, I'll Give a Million, Meet Doctor Christian, Melody for Three, Men in White, The Old Soak, One in a Million, The Painted Veil, Remedy for Riches, Run for Cover, Seventh Heaven, The Sin of Madelon Claudet, So Big, Song of the Eagle, Stage Door Canteen, Stella Dallas, The Student Prince, Susan Lenox, They Meet Again, Tough Guy,*

Transatlantic, Viennese Nights and *Younger Generation.*

Occasionally he turned up as a radio guest elsewhere such as on *The Fleischmann Hour.* For a while he was a regular in the cast of *Columbia Presents Corwin.* Aside from his duties as Dr. Christian, and with the exceptions just named, Hersholt had no other ongoing radio assignments. How could he? He was too busy acting in films, a career that rewarded him in 1947 with a two-year turn as president of the Academy of Motion Picture Arts and Sciences.

On the sidelines, he was actively involved with honorary, voluntary and philanthropic efforts. He founded the Motion Picture Relief Fund to aid industry personnel who suffered economic setbacks. When an Oscar panel inaugurated The Jean Hersholt Humanitarian Award, he may have gained his most prestigious recognition. The honor testified to the exemplary life witnessed in its namesake. The distinguished actor died in Hollywood on June 2, 1956, only a couple of years after his radio series left the air. He was 69.

The talented ladies who appeared in the supporting role of Judy Price tendered demonstrable acting credits in a variety of mediums. When the show broadcast from New York in its first few weeks, Rosemary DeCamp was featured as Judy. She was replaced during several maternity leaves in the early years, first by actress Helen Claire (c. 1941), subsequently by Lurene Tuttle (1941–43), then again by Helen Claire (1945–47), before Rosemary DeCamp returned to finish the run. Kathleen Fitz also appeared as Judy Price on sporadic occasions.

Helen Claire was born October 18, 1911, at Union Springs, Alabama. She appeared on Broadway and with touring companies. From 1937 to 1949 she was a fashion commentator for Fox Movietone News. Her radio acclaim included running parts in several soap operas and frequent cast calls for other shows like: *Backstage Wife, Bright Horizon, The Chase, David Harding—Counterspy, Death Valley Days, Echoes of New York, Grand Central Station, Great Plays, Joyce Jordan M. D., The O'Neills, The Parker Family, Roses and Drums, The Sheriff, Stories of the Black Chamber, The Strange Romance of Evelyn Winters* and *The Twin Stars Show.* Claire died at Birmingham, Alabama, on January 12, 1974.

In 1944 Lurene Tuttle was considered "best supporting feminine player on the basis of her all-round capabilities," *Radio Life* reported.[9] She was elected the first distaff president of the Los Angeles local body of the American Federation of Radio Artists. As one of broadcasting's busiest actresses, she was dubbed "First Lady of Radio."[10] Few of her contemporaries, if any, exceeded the sheer volume of shows (at least 50) on which she appeared: *The Adventures of Ozzie and Harriet; The Adventures of Sam Spade; Arch Oboler's Plays; The Bickersons; Blondie; Box 13; Brenthouse; The CBS Radio Workshop; The Cass Daley Show; A Date with Judy; Dr. Christian; Duffy's Tavern; Earplay; Favorite Story; Forever Ernest; The George Burns and Gracie Allen Show; The George O'Hanlon Show; Glamour Manor; The Great Gildersleeve; I Fly Anything; The James and Pamela Mason Show; Lum and Abner; Maisie; Make-Believe Town, Hollywood; Masquerade; Mayor of the Town; Me and Janie; The Mercury Theater on the Air; Mystery in the Air; Nightbeat; One Man's Family; Presenting Charles Boyer; Red Ryder; The Red Skelton Show; Rogue's Gallery; The Saint; The Sears Radio Theater; The Silent Men; Stars Over Hollywood; The Story of Dr. Kildare; Strange Wills; Suspense; Tales of the Texas Rangers; The Theater of Famous Radio Players; Those We Love; Twelve Players; The Unexpected; The Whistler; Yours Truly, Johnny Dollar; The Zero Hour.*

Tuttle, a gifted dialectician, performed in the films of Alfred Hitchcock and Orson

Welles, among them 1960's *Psycho*. She turned up in major television series, too: *Life with Father* (1953–55), *Father of the Bride* (1961–62) and *Julia* (1968–70). She recorded cartoon voice-overs for *NBC Comics* (1950–51), *These Are the Days* (1974–76), *Nutcracker Fantasy* (1979) and *Thanksgiving in the Land of Oz* (1980).

A native of Pleasant Lake, Indiana, she was born August 29, 1907, the daughter of minstrel C.U. Tuttle, who exposed her to the plays he produced. She gained further experience at the Pasadena Playhouse. She died at Encino, California, on May 28, 1986.

Rosemary DeCamp was the best recalled Judy Price by most old time radio fans. She was born at Prescott, Arizona, on November 14, 1910. After majoring in drama and psychology at Mills College, from which she received a master's degree, she joined a touring company. DeCamp, too, performed at the Pasadena Playhouse and on Broadway. Like Jean Hersholt, her career was dominated by the silver screen, although she earned acting credits in both radio (as early as 1933) and television.

One of her initial roles, on *One Man's Family*, didn't last long, her penchant for instructing the director in how to run the show was a "no no," and DeCamp's exodus was imminent. Meanwhile, she turned up on *Atlantic Family, Blondie, The Columbia Workshop, Dot and Will, The Dreft Star Playhouse, Easy Aces, Gangbusters, The Goldbergs, Hollywood ScreenScopes, I Want a Divorce, Plays for Americans* and *Tom Mix*. Her major TV parts came in *The Life of Riley* (1949–50); *Death Valley Days* (1952–75), where she was said to have delivered "homey commercials" for sponsor 20 Mule Team Borax; *The Bob Cummings Show* (1955–59); and *That Girl* (1966–70).

DeCamp failed her first screen test, ironically for the part of Judy Price in a film based on the radio series *Dr. Christian*. Later, when the radio role was about to open up, she auditioned for three days, outlasting every other contender.

Her movie features included *Big Hangover, Blood on the Sun, By the Light of the Silvery Moon, Cheers for Miss Bishop, Danger Signal, Eyes in the Night, Jungle Book, Look for the Silver Lining, Main Street to Broadway, Many Rivers to Cross, The Merry Monahans, Nora Prentiss, On Moonlight Bay, Practically Yours, Pride of the Marines, Rhapsody in Blue, Scandal Sheet, Smith of Minnesota, So This is Love, The Story of Seabiscuit, Strategic Air Command, This is the Army, Too Young to Know, Treasure of Lost Canyon* and *Yankee Doodle Dandy*.

As *Dr. Christian*'s rehearsal and performance was mostly held on Wednesday afternoons (California time), DeCamp departed the movie lot each Wednesday to arrive at CBS by the appointed hour. Leaving the MGM set one week, she discovered that her ride to the studio had not arrived. About that time legendary film star Katherine Hepburn drove up in her convertible. Seeing the consternation on the young actress' face — although the two had never met — she inquired of DeCamp about her troubles. Given an explanation, Hepburn handed her car keys to DeCamp and entered MGM. DeCamp drove over to CBS without further delay.

DeCamp recalled another exasperating incident that happened to her one evening at the start of the *Dr. Christian* broadcast — in front of the live studio audience. When her cue came to move to the microphone to open the show with her time-honored "Dr. Christian's office!," she realized that the sash on her dress was caught in the folding chair she was sitting in onstage. With air time quickly approaching, and having no alternative, DeCamp bound the chair to her buttocks and crossed to the microphone to repeat her famous line. The home audience was oblivious to the action, of course. The studio audience gave them the notion that something was askew, nevertheless, when it responded with thunderous applause!

Kathleen Fitz, who intermittently played the part of Judy Price, had only one other major role in broadcasting — as the lead, Portia Brent, on the radio serial *Brenthouse*.

Maide Eburne, the actress who was heard as Mrs. Hastings, Paul Christian's housekeeper, earned no other radio or television credits.

Andre Baruch was the New York announcer for *Dr. Christian*. Baruch's successor as the show moved west, from 1938 to 1941, was the lesser known Perry King, whom radio biographers have regretfully overlooked. King was followed by the much more recognized Art Gilmore, who remained with the series from 1942 to 1954.

Baruch, a Parisian born August 20, 1906, arrived in the United States 13 years later. He was a pianist; yet when he went to audition at CBS in New York in 1932 he inadvertently fell into the wrong line, being given the printed names of composers from abroad to read aloud. That launched his career as a radio announcer. In some of his early duties he covered baseball games and band remotes.

He may be recalled as the voice of U.S. Steel, and as commercial spokesman (for 22 years) for the American Tobacco Corporation, makers of Lucky Strike cigarettes. As a result of the latter relation, Baruch may be better identified as the announcer for the long-running *Your Hit Parade*, sponsored by Lucky Strike, than for any other radio and television series. Years after it folded, he and his wife, singer Bea Wain, produced a syndicated *Your Hit Parade* radio series that was heard in many markets. The pair launched an early disc jockey program on New York's WMCA, *Mr. & Mrs. Music*, and in the 1970s conducted a talk show on Palm Beach, Florida's WPBR. During World War II Baruch, a major in the U.S. Army Signal Corps stationed in North Africa, was assigned to the Armed Forces Radio Service.

His radio announcing credits were legion, including *The American Album of Familiar Music, The Andrews Sisters Eight-to-the-Bar Ranch, Bobby Benson and the B-Bar-B Riders, Exploring the Unknown, The FBI in Peace and War, Guy Lombardo Time, The Jack Benny Program, Just Plain Bill, The Kate Smith Show, Leave It to the Girls, Linda's First Love, Little Orphan Annie, Marie the Little French Princess, The Mark Warnow Show, Myrt and Marge, My Son and I, Second Husband, The Shadow, Stoopnagle and Budd, Your Hit Parade* and *Your Song and Mine*.

On television Baruch hosted *Masters of Magic* (1949), appeared in the cast of *Shoppers Matinee* (1950) and announced *Your Hit Parade* (1950–57). He also recorded newsreel voice-overs that played in movie theaters. Death came to him in Beverly Hills, California, on September 15, 1991.

Art Gilmore, meanwhile, the best remembered announcer of the *Dr. Christian* series, was born in Tacoma, Washington, on March 18, 1912. In 1934 he interrupted his studies at Washington State College to become a Hollywood reporter, poetry reader and vocalist for a hometown radio station, KVI. He reportedly earned 15 dollars a month for his five-day-a-week stint. In college the same speech teacher who coached Gilmore had instructed the famous Edward R. Murrow before him; both students would become members of broadcasting's elite.

Returning to his alma mater later in 1934, Gilmore announced for campus station KWSC. The following year he transferred to station KOL in Seattle but didn't put down roots. On a vacation in Los Angeles he was hired as a vocalist by KFWB, backed by the likes of Spike Jones on drums and Leonard Slye (later known as Roy Rogers) on guitar. Not long afterward he moved to KNX, and from there was hired as the narrator for *Dr. Christian.*

Like many of his peers, Gilmore could be classified as handsome, tall and imposing. He flaunted tresses of white hair. The potential for radio announcing had hooked him early: "The day I heard the voice of Ted Husing [a popular network announcer and sportscaster of that era] I thought, *That's* what I want to do! I'll work for nothing."[11] Later, when he was thriving, his automobile license plate recapped his success: GAB4PAY.

Gilmore announced *The Adventures of Frank Race, The Amazing Mr. Malone, The Amos 'n' Andy Show, Jonathan Trimble — Esquire, Meet Me at Parky's, Miss Pinkerton Incorporated, Murder and Mr. Malone, O'Hara, Red Ryder* (for which he also whistled the theme song), *Rhapsody in Rhythm, The Sears Radio Theater* and *Stars Over Hollywood.* He also acted on the *Lux Radio Theater* and *Pacific Story.*

On the tube Gilmore played a police captain in *Dragnet.* He provided *Captain Midnight's* opening signature, while announcing for *Alcoa Premiere, Climax!, The Comedy Spot, The George Gobel Show, Highway Patrol* and *The Red Skelton Show.* The Skelton program, he claimed, was his favorite.

Following World War II, at the University of Southern California, he taught announcing to returning GIs. *Television and Radio Announcing* was his text, a volume he co-authored. He narrated hundreds of children's albums, documentaries and travelogues. For more than 30 years he introduced thousands of Paramount Pictures' "coming attractions" movie trailers. He was also the voice of President Franklin D. Roosevelt in a quartet of feature-length films.

Gilmore continued making personal appearances at the turn of the century, often appearing before annual vintage radio club conventions. The Society to Preserve and Encourage Radio Drama, Variety and Comedy (SPERDVAC) honored him in Los Angeles in November 1999 for his lifetime achievements and personal contributions to the industry.

On one memorable occasion, while announcing for *Dr. Christian,* Gilmore was visited by that old malady called hiccups shortly before the live broadcast took to the air. Drawing upon an announcer's time-honored cure, he swallowed a teaspoon of vinegar. The hiccups immediately dissipated.

Gilmore acknowledged: "The announcer's life is a pretty lonely job. You're sort of the Lone Ranger — you do your job and you go home. The announcer isn't part of the show."[12] He confessed that on most shows he usually went out with the crew, not the cast, following performances. Yet author Leonard Maltin recited a tale suggesting that announcers were "the bedrock of radio" and could be counted upon to ride to "the rescue of a broadcast."[13]

> Art Gilmore was drifting into the doldrums during a broadcast of *Dr. Christian* one day when "I heard this snapping of fingers, and I looked over. Jean Hersholt was at a table — later on in the series, he sat at a table rather than be at the same mike with the rest of the cast — and he snapped his fingers. I thought, 'What the heck is going on?' I went over; he had left the last seven pages of his script in the dressing room upstairs. Now, we're on live, coast to coast. Well, talk about luck; normally I'd read my commercial and then I'd turn to the back page and sit there. And fight sleep. Five-thirty in the afternoon is a dull time; you're kind of ready for dinner and you need a little pep. That one particular night, I was following along with him and when I heard the snapping I was able to give him my script.[14]

Announcers, it seemed, could be all things to all people.

Ruth Adams Knight, who penned scripts for *Dr. Christian* in the years before the writing competition opened the show to thousands of aspiring scribes, wasn't limited to that medical practice. She found work dialoguing for a couple of serials—*Brave Tomorrow* and *Those We Love*—and for *Death Valley Days* (which became *Death Valley Sheriff* and later *The Sheriff*). In 1944 *Dr. Christian's Office*, a printed fictional tale that Knight and Jean Hersholt collaborated on, was released by Random House.

Several *Dr. Christian* personnel were connected with the various 20 Mule Team Borax–originated series. Producer Dorothy McCann also produced *Death Valley Days*, although she had no other responsibilities, according to broadcasting annals. *Christian*'s trio of directors also worked elsewhere: Neil Reagan announced for *The Grouch Club*, and produced and directed *Straight Arrow*, yet another western adventure. In the meantime, both John Wilkinson and Florence Ortman directed *The Sheriff*, their only other recorded contributions.

Dr. Christian was a superior, warmhearted drama that maintained a loyal following over its 16-plus years on the air. It was the kind of show that made Americans feel good about themselves. It further encouraged people to share of their own resources with some noble causes, including charitable institutions and the less fortunate, as its star (Hersholt) exemplified in private life.

The program qualifies as a true audience participation series, for it became "the only show in radio where the audience writes the script." Tens of thousands responded to that distinctive opportunity, whether they had previously written anything of significance or not. Unfortunately, most of them didn't turn out material that could be considered acceptable to radio's exacting ear. Yet it was a challenge that some simply could not resist.

In the half-century that has elapsed since that period, such a unique prospect has never been equaled nor repeated. In practice, then, we may ascertain with some degree of authority that in this story line, the fans (i.e., amateur scribes) of *Dr. Christian* had the final say.

Dr. I.Q.,
The Mental Banker

Premise: Doubtlessly one of the most familiar lines ever repeated on the air (again and again, no less!) was: "I have a lady in the balcony, doctor!" Frequently emanating from this show, the line referred to a game player who had been cornered by an aide with a hand-held mike in a movie theater gallery. It was just the sort of gimmick (and catchphrase) that could help the show catch on, and it succeeded very well in its quest. Unlike peer series, *Dr. I.Q.* didn't spend time with idle chitchat; no lengthy interrogations into a contestant's history here. Instead, it used its half-hour to query as many people in the audience as it could, tossing general information questions their way in quick succession. Players were given a chance to claim silver dollars in exchange for their intellect. In fact, only when they succeeded were they identified, never otherwise. That was in line with part of the mystique surrounding Dr. I.Q. himself, whose identity was kept secret from both home and studio audiences. Most would never have believed that at the series' start a mere 26-year-old was filling that schol-

arly post. The show offered a number of weekly features in which participants interacted with the "doctor," some of those segments submitted by listeners at home. Soon after *Dr. I.Q.* bowed from Chicago on the national airwaves in 1939, it went on the road. In so doing, it gave an opportunity to thousands of Americans to participate in its quicksilver competition over an 11-year audio run. The show failed to win a sustained television following in two separate 1950s tries. But on radio, across the previous decade, its legions of fans agreed that this program was "just what the doctor ordered."

Creator-Producer: Lee Segall

Directors: Paul Dumont, Harry Holcomb

Masters of Ceremonies (Dr. I.Q.): Lew Valentine (1939–42, 1946–50), Jimmy McClain (1942–46), Stanley Vainrib (temporarily, in 1947–48)

Announcer: Allan C. Anthony

Theme Song: *You Are My Lucky Star*

Sponsors: A trio of sponsors underwrote this show, although one is singularly and most prominently identified with it — Mars, Inc., whose chocolate candy bars (even one named Dr. I.Q.!) financed the series from its inception through March 30, 1942, and from April 3, 1944, through Oct. 28, 1949. The program continued for Vick Chemical Co. between April 6, 1942, and March 27, 1944. It ran for Embassy cigarettes from Jan. 4, 1950, through Nov. 29, 1950.

Ratings: High: 13.7 (1942–43); Low: 4.4 (1949–50); Median: 10.4. Figures are based on every season except 1943–44.

On the Air: April 10, 1939–July 3, 1939, Blue, Monday, 10:30 P.M. ET; July 10, 1939–March 30, 1942, NBC, Monday, 9 P.M.; April 6, 1942–March 27, 1944, NBC, Monday, 9:30 P.M.; April 3, 1944–1947, NBC, Monday, 10:30 P.M.; 1947–June 20, 1949, NBC, Monday, 9:30 P.M.; July 1, 1949–Oct. 28, 1949, NBC, Friday; Jan. 4, 1950–Nov. 29, 1950, ABC, Wednesday, 8 P.M.

*   *   *

Known as "The Mental Banker," and introduced on the air as "the genial master of wit and information," Dr. I.Q. was tagged "the wise man with the friendly smile and the cash for your correct answers" during the show's opening. The series he fronted — which was considered "the *Jeopardy!* of its day"[1] (*Jeopardy!* being "a photographed radio quiz"[2]) — was a quick-tempo, straight-to-the-point question-and-answer program in which players could win silver dollars for their knowledge of a wide range of general subjects.

An authoritative radio historian considers *Dr. I.Q.* no less than "the first great quiz show on the air…. None before it possessed the style, pace, or longevity of this brisk item."[3]

Unlike its chatty, persona-based contemporaries, *Dr. I.Q.* distinguished itself with a hard-driven, no-nonsense strategy.

"The main attraction was the pace," the sage alleges. "A contestant got one quick shot at the money and the microphone moved on."[4] While other quiz shows spent lots of time building up to the main event by exploring a player's background — finding out why he or she left the hinterlands to pay a visit to Chicago, Los Angeles or New York, for example — that wasn't the case on *Dr. I.Q.* Identities, even that of the master of ceremonies, were closely guarded, except for those answering their queries correctly.

When one of four, five or six assistants with portable microphones who were roving about the studio audience acknowledged, "I have a lady in the balcony, doctor!" that might be all the listeners would ever know about the next participant, other than whether she could answer the question pitched her way.

Coincidentally, at the program's inception, that catchphrase ("I have a lady in the balcony, doctor!") became one of the most memorable and oft-repeated lines of any pre–TV game show, and "perhaps from all of radio."[5] Despite its "slight hint of impropriety,"[6] the phrase was bandied about nationally almost overnight.

Writing his memoirs in the late 1990s, George Ansbro, one of those roving announcers on TV's *Dr. I.Q.*, paid tribute to the phrase, calling it a "fun line." He remembers: "During the years we did the show, the line caught on with the public to the extent that whenever it was used, or quoted, everyone knew it was a good-natured ribbing of *Dr. I.Q.*"[7] (Ansbro himself enjoyed a distinguished 59-year career in broadcasting, including an 18-year run as the announcer for the serial *Young Widder Brown*. He also introduced multitudes of other radio series, including early dance band remotes, before turning his attention to TV. He retired in 1990 at 75, and — at the turn of the century — was still making personal appearances before vintage radio conventions.)

Once Dr. I.Q.'s assistant had introduced the lady in the balcony (or the sailor in the third row, or the gentleman in the right front, or the young lad in the far left corner), the "doctor" might articulate this clarion wail: "Sixteen silver dollars to that young lady for telling me which of the following was *not* one of our famous Revolutionary [War] generals ... Washington, Wayne, Burgoin, Schuyler."

"Schuyler?" the lady answered questioningly on the broadcast of January 26, 1942.

"Oh I'm *soooooo* sorry, I think you'd find it was General Burgoin. He was an *English* general, not one of *our* generals," came the doctor's patronizing reply, feigning pity for the guest. "But a box of Dr. I.Q. candy and two tickets to next week's production to that lady!"

On a typical broadcast, from 35 to 40 questions were asked in rapid-fire succession. The show claimed that while the interrogations were tricky, contestants answered correctly slightly more than half the time. There was a 10-second limit imposed for each query and Dr. I.Q. could be constantly heard *shushing* the audience: "No coaching, please. Let *him* (or *her*) answer it." When a contestant offered absolutely no reply, the emcee would spur him on, urging the faltering contender to respond by inquiring: "Don't you *want* to take a guess?" He appeared exasperated, in fact, when even that didn't motivate some to supply an answer. One wag noted: "Quiz contestants in those days were far more shy and less showbiz savvy than today. Many seemed terribly apologetic when they couldn't deliver the right answer."[8]

The primary sponsor, Mars, Incorporated, "makers of America's most enjoyable candy bars"—which actually *did* manufacture a chocolate bar named Dr. I.Q. (undoubtedly as a marketing ploy for the show), in addition to Forever Yours, Mars, Milky Way, Snickers, Three Musketeers

and more—normally budgeted $700 per week as instant quicksilver prize money for winning players. The sum in silver dollars paid for a right answer was measured by the perceived level of knowledge required by a particular question. (A Denver contestant once won $3,100 for correctly linking a "Famous Quotation" to Lincoln's Gettysburg Address, not an indecent stash in those pre-inflationary years.)

By the television era, the roving assistants with the hand-held mikes were carrying silver dollars in large sacks hanging from their necks, a resolute bow toward the visual medium. When a player satisfactorily answered a question, an assistant doled out the player's winnings with an accompanying flourish that played appropriately to the camera. But in radio, aides grumbled that such heavy burdens burst their tuxedo jackets at the seams, requiring them to have their pockets reinforced. Besides, all those weighty coins made them appear stoop-shouldered, they affirmed.

Dr. I.Q. proffered several special features in its years on the air, some of them supplied by listeners at home, giving those fans opportunities to win prize money, too. In 1939 a *Radio Guide* journalist acknowledged: "There may be more sophisticated quiz shows, but for sheer showmanship and variety, none can beat *Dr. I.Q.*"

For the "Biographical Sketch" portion, someone at home received $250 for supplying a half-dozen clues to the identity of a celebrated mystery figure. The game's initial hint was valued at 75 silver dollars, with the cash prize depleted by five, 10 or 15 dollars as more tips were read aloud. In the end, any sum the studio player failed to earn in the quest to identify the subject was added to the $250 sent to the originator. If the studio contestant was completely stumped, the contributor received $325.

In another weekly match, the "Monument to Memory" (a.k.a. the "Thought

Twister"), a player was required to repeat a phrase verbatim that was read aloud "one time and one time only" by Dr. I.Q. One twister went like this: "*Jim is slim*," said Tim to Kim. "*Jim is slim, Tim*," to him said Kim. On a World War II era broadcast, an actual statement worth 35 silver dollars proceeded: "*We'll slap the Jap off the map*," said Cap to Hap. "*We will slap the Jap off the map, Cap*," to him said Hap. The contestant, faltering halfway through that one, exclaimed to Dr. I.Q.: "Just gimmie the box of candy!"

In the "Right or Wrong" segment, the quizmaster read aloud 12 rapid-fire declarations that had been supplied by listeners (at $50 for each trio of entry statements). The studio audience then branded those assertions as "Right" or "Wrong" on cards they had been given. The cards were collected and tallied by the show's staff following the broadcast. Winners of the "Mastermind Award"—which included getting all one-dozen of the statements right, and was valued at $100—were announced on the subsequent show.

There was also a "Famous Quotation" segment, referred to earlier, in which a contestant could win silver dollars for identifying the source of a popular or well-known expression.

Dr. I.Q. was initially broadcast to a nationwide audience from a Chicago theater. But the Windy City police viewed it as a game of chance, an illegal lottery, and tried to shut it down. Partially as a result, fans in nearly every major American city had an opportunity to play "The Mental Banker's" game. Like a number of its contemporaries, the quiz trekked back and forth across the nation. (One observer referred to it as a "dog and pony show."[9]) Airing weekly for about a month from a single locale, it normally originated from the stages of cinema theaters.

Large crowds of potential contestants often required added performances beyond the weekly radio show. Once, in Portland, Maine, a mob of 2,500 local citizens expressed strong displeasure after learning that the event for which they had paid 75 cents wouldn't be heard by anyone outside the theater walls. Somehow they were under the false impression that they would at least have a modest chance of being quizzed on the air. As a matter of fact, while they *did* have a remote possibility of earning a few silver dollars, or—at a minimum—some candy bars, nobody outside that building ever knew it. That simply didn't sit well with the locals, and they grumbled under their breath.

Frequently the roving announcers with the hand-held mikes who helped Dr. I.Q. ferret out those contestants from the studio audience were well known by native audiences: They were often staff members of the affiliates that broadcast the show, regional celebrities who were ready, willing and anxious to accept network assignments for even minimal notoriety—including those that lasted only a few weeks. (While there were scores of individuals who supplied that role, many names have been lost to history. Some which have been preserved are: Frank Barton, Ward Benton, Jim Doyle, Robert Enoch, Johnny Frazer, Ed Hill, Bert Igou, Gene Kemper, Charles Lewis, Bill Mayhugh, Garry Moore, Ken Powell, Bob Richardson, Ed Rimer, Ralph Rogers, Ed Shaughnessy and Hank Weaver.)

In later years, when the program moved to TV, the traipsing back and forth across the country ceased. During that epoch the show emanated from New York's Ritz Theater on West Forty-Eighth Street, a facility that had been rented by the ABC network. The roving announcers became permanent fixtures then, consisting of George Ansbro, Art Fleming (who would later headline his own daily NBC-TV series, *Jeopardy!*), Dirk Fredericks and Ed Michael. This foursome was displaced in 1958 by a distaff quartet consisting of Carol

Byron, Kay Christopher, Sue England and Mimi Walters. The tele-version's theme song was "We're in the Money."

Dr. I.Q. quickly became a radio staple and a forerunner of the enormous popularity of quiz programs. It aired on the Blue network in its first 13 weeks in 1939, transferred to NBC through 1949, then broadcast for most of 1950 on ABC. Its final show was heard on November 29, 1950.

The television debut occurred three years later. With all of its weekly performances on ABC-TV, its broadcast history included two continuous periods in prime-time, from a premiere on November 4, 1953, through October 17, 1954, originating from New York; then again from December 15, 1958, through March 23, 1959, from Hollywood. During the first few weeks, Jay Owen played the role of Dr. I.Q. on the tube. Jimmy McClain, who had been one of two principals filling that responsibility on radio, followed him on January 18, 1954. Tom Kennedy hosted it during the 1958–59 segment.

Mars, Incorporated underwrote the show for most of its radio run, including 1939 to 1942 and again from 1944 to 1949. Announcer Allan C. Anthony was cited by several reviewers for his ability to deliver marvelously convincing marketing messages on behalf of the sponsor's multiple candy products. He wrapped them in persuasive onomatopoeic-sounding descriptions like "creamy nougat" and "delicious chocolate." Anthony was so convincing at what he did, by the way, that the sponsor assigned him to perform that same duty on other series that Mars underwrote, including *Dr. I.Q. Jr.* and *Inner Sanctum Mysteries.* Anthony died at age 55 on May 11, 1962.

Dr. I.Q. originated in Houston, Texas, under the watchful eye of a local producer, Lee Segall. Conceiving the notion as a somewhat burlesque routine, he packaged it for a sponsor and sold it to several area radio stations. A regionally limited Ted Nabors was Dr. I.Q. on its premiering Lone Star run. He was later supplanted by Lew Valentine, a youthful announcer, actor, vocalist and production manager at San Antonio's WOAI Radio. The popularity of *Professor Quiz*— which offered some similarities to this one, and had been intriguing CBS audiences for three years— helped *Dr. I.Q.* attract a sponsor and a competing network that was willing to bring it before a national audience.

Valentine, then only 26, got the nod as the quizmaster when the show went to a national hookup, although his identity— and age— weren't disclosed to audiences. (His delivery and the inflection of his voice closely paralleled those of another widely recognized announcer-actor-emcee, Clayton 'Bud' Collyer. Many in the home audience probably believed that Collyer was also appearing as the quizmaster on this show, in addition to a myriad of other programs on which he had long performed.)

On occasions, when fans did learn Valentine's real age, some refused to accept it, believing one so young could hardly be such an intellect. The questions he read on the program weren't written or even researched by him, of course. The show's staff and listeners supplied them. Without taking anything away from Valentine, anyone with a gregarious personality who liked to appear before crowds and could read from cards might have also done what he did.

Valentine was born August 5, 1912, at San Benito, Texas, and died at Santa Monica, California, in June 1976. In the summer of 1942 he also hosted the Blue network game show *Sing for Your Dough.* That autumn, when Uncle Sam called, he gave up his radio assignments to devote three years to Army service. Valentine returned as Dr. I.Q. on the program of May 27, 1946, and remained with it to the end of the run.

Could he possibly have been a mere 26-year-old when the erudite *Dr. I. Q.* went on a national hookup? Right you are! Pay that man sixty-four silver dollars! Lew Valentine, who launched his career while the show ran as a regional series in the Lone Star state was even younger *then*! He never really looked his age, and was at least as bright as the show's staff and fans made him out to be! (Photofest)

Subsequently, he was absent for 10 weeks starting December 8, 1947, continuing through February 9, 1948. Stanley Vainrib, who earned no other distinct radio credits, temporarily replaced him. During Valentine's absence from the microphone, he primed himself for an additional series, *Dr. I.Q. Jr.*, on which he would also play Dr. I.Q.

While on his Army hitch, Valentine was succeeded as Dr. I.Q. by Jimmy McClain, a young seminary student who was training for the Episcopalian ministry. In the summer of 1941 he had successfully performed as quizmaster on a preliminary version of *Dr. I.Q. Jr.*

Other notables connected with *Dr.*

I.Q. who had additional radio experience included directors Paul Dumont and Harry Holcomb.

Dumont, who joined the NBC Red network and flagship affiliate WEAF in New York City in 1928, was master of ceremonies for *The Pontiac Varsity Show*. He directed two other series, *Manhattan Merry-Go-Round* and *Peewee and Windy*. Dumont died at 90 on August 24, 1979.

Holcomb, who died September 15, 1987, at 80, pursued several radio assignments. He directed *Curtain Time*, *Judy and Jane*, and *Tena and Tim*; appeared in the supporting cast of *The Joe Penner Show*; and narrated *Moon River*.

The *Dr. I.Q. Jr.* series, a juvenile version of the adult quiz that was also sponsored by Mars on the NBC Radio network, debuted May 11, 1941. Its summer stint ended August 24 of that year. The show didn't return until March 6, 1948, when it was hosted by Lew Valentine, then playing Dr. I.Q. on the simultaneous adult series. *Junior*'s final broadcast aired April 2, 1949.

On the children's version, silver dollars were displaced by silver dimes. While the questions were a little easier, the rapid-fire delivery continued. One of that show's features included announcer Allan C. Anthony's appearances as Bugs Beagle, who shared stories containing factual mistakes. Kids who spotted the errors won prizes.

While it might not be considered one of the most interesting games people played, *Dr. I.Q.* likely raised the national intellect a notch or two. It surely encouraged Americans to gain a broader background of knowledge about a variety of topics. And while *Information Please* and others of its ilk may have been highly competitive, mining the attention of so-called "fact-freaks," no series provided the no-nonsense, in-your-face kind of revelations that *Dr. I.Q.* did, nor did it as well for more than a decade.

Trivia buffs, to be sure, were in their element.

9

Double or Nothing

Premise: It was one of the earliest and most parsimonious giveaway programs on the air. When it debuted in 1940 *Double or Nothing* had few predecessors, *Pot o' Gold* and *Truth or Consequences* were about the only two to maintain any staying power for a while, and both appeared within the previous year. *Double or Nothing* was, therefore, blazing a new trail, becoming the first serious-minded question-and-answer series that would set considerable records in longevity. It ran continuously to 1954, broadcasting on all four national radio networks—for a while airing live shows twice daily. It was spun off into dual television series; just two sponsors entirely underwrote it; and it featured a quartet of enthusiastic young masters of ceremonies who could sway the dourest of audiences. The show's creator, Walter Compton, at 27, was the first of those. His successor, John Reed King, was 28 when he took over. A youthful Todd Russell was next to accept the reins. He was followed by the best-recalled of the quad, Walter O'Keefe, who at 46 moved with the series from primetime to daytime. The quiz also set an example that would be followed by a number of successors, it embraced penny-pinching with a flourish. Its top prize could barely care for an out-of-town guest's hotel bill after a few days in Los Angeles, to say nothing of one's expense in getting there. None seemed to mind, however; least of all those fortunate enough to be extracted from the studio audience and given an opportunity to appear on the live coast-to-coast broadcast. Whether they made any money almost seemed irrelevant; the conquest of getting on that stage mesmerized many, helping them realize their supreme ambition. With such approbation, who could argue that a quiz show — even one doling out diminutive sums like these — wouldn't be a hit?

Producers: Ken Fickett, Lou Crosby, Diana Bourbon

Directors: Harry Spears, Thomas Vietor, John Wellington

Masters of Ceremonies: Walter Compton (1940–43), John Reed King (1943–45), Todd Russell (1945–47), Walter O'-Keefe (1947–54)

Announcers: Alois Havrilla, Fred Cole, Murray Wagner

Writers: Carroll Carroll, Gerald Rice, Harry Bailey

Organists: Elliott Jacoby, Nat Brusiloff, Irv Orton

Vocalist: Frank Forest

Theme Song: *Three Little Words*

Sponsors: Two major manufacturers, one a health goods concern, the other a well-known food processor, completely subscribed the show for its full interval on the air. White Labs (later known as Pharmaco), the makers of Feen-a-Mint chewing gum laxative and Chooz breath mints, underwrote the series for the seven years it was in primetime. When it moved to daytime, the Campbell Soup Company bought it for its extensive line of canned soups, Franco-American spaghetti, macaroni, sauces and other foodstuff commodities.

Ratings: High: 16.1 (1944–45); Low: 3.6 (1947–48); Median: 7.2 (13 full seasons). The show averaged 8.8 as a primetime vehicle, falling back to 5.4 in daytime, hardly a major draw competing against long-entrenched soap operas in the afternoon and *Arthur Godfrey Time* in the morning hours. Let it be noted, however, that this quiz performed admirably while it was an MBS property, harvesting superior numbers to those acquired when it aired on other webs. That could be an anomaly, for MBS series were often considered "also rans" if a show was broadcast elsewhere at any time, in some measure due to having less-powerful stations in its chain.

On the Air: Sept. 29, 1940–May 11, 1941, MBS, Sunday, 6 P.M. ET; May 23, 1941–Sept. 26, 1941, MBS, Friday, 8 P.M.; Sept. 28, 1941–May 10, 1942, MBS, Sunday, 6 P.M.; May 22, 1942–July 13, 1945, MBS, Friday, 9:30 P.M.; July 15, 1945–June 15, 1947, MBS, Sunday, 9:30 P.M.; June 30, 1947–June 25, 1948, CBS, Monday–Friday, 3 P.M.; May 31, 1948–1951, NBC, Monday–Friday, 2 P.M.; 1950–June 19, 1953, NBC, Monday–Friday, 10:30 A.M.; June 22, 1953–Jan. 15, 1954, ABC, Monday–Friday, 11:30 A.M.

*   *   *

On September 28, 1939, a giveaway radio show that was mired in greed debuted on NBC titled *Pot o' Gold*. Anyone at home who was telephoned by the show while it was on the air became the recipient of $1,000 by simply grabbing the phone. There were no questions to answer, no song titles to name — a respondent didn't even have to be listening to the program!

Cinemas all over the nation were soon begging for patrons on the nights *Pot o' Gold* was broadcast. As a consequence, some movie house owners decided to take matters into their own hands. They put on what came to be called "bank nights." If *Pot o' Gold* telephoned a filmgoer while he or she was at the theater, that individual was automatically awarded $1,000 in cash. Both methods for gaining a cool grand seemed hokey to the critics, who recoiled in horror over such pompous and outrageous shenanigans.

Nor did it sit well with a rising young creative talent named Walter Knobeloch (who soon changed his professional name to Walter Compton). He was a dramatics instructor from Dixie — a publicist and a radio talent who was knocking on the door of the big time while staffing at a Washington, D.C. station. Compton hoped to offset those "bank nights" by adding substance to the radio contests that were then in the embryonic stage.

In so doing, he contrived a formula that appealed to a fundamental gambling instinct. In place of a "bank night" at a local movie house, he auditioned his idea on-stage there. With some encouragement, he was soon introducing it to a Mutual Broadcasting System audience in early autumn 1940.

Compton (a.k.a. Knobeloch) was born in Charleston, South Carolina, on October 9, 1912. A Roanoke College alumnus, he stayed on there for a while as publicity manager and drama coach. Returning to Charleston in 1936, he accepted the post of announcing, writing and directing for a hometown radio station, WCSC. He wasn't there long, however; within the year he moved to two other markets in the Palmetto state, Columbia's WIS and Greenville's WFBC. By the age of 25, in 1937, Compton was handling news and special events for station WOL in the District of Columbia. Simultaneously, he reported White House news for the Mutual Broadcasting System. Not long afterward he created the model for a new quiz show. MBS liked it and placed it on the air, with Compton as its master of ceremonies.

In the beginning he asked a contestant a question that awarded five dollars for an appropriate response. A player could earn considerably more, on the other hand. Speaking impromptu for 60 seconds on a given topic — an audible clock ticking off the seconds— the individual had a chance to gain larger sums in increments of two to four dollars by supplying extra facts that could confirm a response.

Finally, the contestant was given yet another chance to increase his take-home cash following the one-minute opportunity. He could double whatever he had previously won by answering one final question. An incorrect response, unfortunately, reduced the poor soul to the five dollars he had initially won. (The same basic theme, in which a contestant could gamble on increasing his winnings twofold — or lose them altogether — had been introduced to radio audiences five months earlier. CBS's *Take It or Leave It* was, by this time, making waves in the industry, quickly finding an audience and breeding new series that tweaked its concept, sometimes only ever so slightly.)

The new series, which Compton appropriately titled *Double or Nothing*, initially appeared as a Sunday evening feature. While it would seldom draw what could be classified as unparalleled audiences (in terms of size), the quiz did attract and maintain an appreciable and loyal following. It suffered no prolonged lapses, in fact, across a broadcasting tenure that exceeded 13 years. It appeared in both primetime and daytime, even airing twice daily for a while. The radio show was spun off into televised derivations, too. And the audio series was wholly underwritten by just a couple of major sponsors for the duration of its lengthy run.

To avoid reading a long list of question categories aloud each time a new contestant came before the microphone, the show placed such data on a large chalkboard in full view of the players and cast. The practice was inaugurated earlier on *Take It or Leave It*, the progenitor of *Double or Nothing* and several other shows with analogous concepts.

The contest's format, nonetheless, was tinkered with incessantly. Somewhere down its long progression, when *Double or Nothing* went to daytime, its initial question was worth only two dollars. A second was valued at four dollars, a third at six dollars, a fourth at 10 dollars and a fifth at 20 dollars. Contestants could then bow out with their 20 dollars or attempt to double the sum with a final question. Subsequently, they wound up with a top prize of 40 dollars or — if they answered incorrectly — they forfeited everything they had already earned.

Each player also had a shot at an 80-dollar grand slam question. On the broadcast of January 2, 1948, for instance, this typical query was posed: "How many large peanuts are required to make a pint of peanut oil?" Contestants offered their estimates, and at the end of the show the master of ceremonies revealed that — according to Planters Peanuts—1,373 large peanuts did the trick. The individual with the guess closest to that number won the grand slam prize.

Finally, still larger sums were awarded in a "sweepstakes" shortly before the program's sign-off. With Walter O'Keefe by then as emcee, and the show sponsored by the Campbell Soup Company (whose color scheme was red and white), contestants finalized their answers as a lively ensemble belted out these lyrics to a spirited tune:

Campbell's brings you the red-and-white sweepstakes ...
Campbell's pays it off again;
Take a try at the red-and-white sweepstakes,
Think about it, think about it, rack your brain!
Come on and join this funny-makin' caper,
If you know the answer, write it on your paper!
Walter, hey Walter, have we got a winner today, today ...
Have we got a winner today?

It appeared that Walter O'Keefe responded more often with "No, I'm sorry, we have no winner today" at the conclusion of that ditty rather than "Yes, we *do* have a winner today." He would identify any winner(s), then read the answer to the question in the sweepstakes. When nobody won, a specified sum would be added to a mounting cash jackpot that would ultimately be claimed by someone triumphant on a future show. The sweepstakes sometimes climbed to several hundred dollars—inflated prize money on such a humble giveaway.

In earlier days, with the program sponsored by Feen-a-Mint, the announcer introduced the series over an organist's rendition of the theme song "Three Little Words":

Feen-a-Mint presents *Double or Nothing.* Yes, just three little words, *Double or Nothing,* the thrilling quiz show with the $100 question, presented by Feen-a-Mint, the modern chewing gum laxative. And here is the man on the asking end of the $100 question, your paymaster of ceremonies, John Reed King.

When *Double or Nothing* made it to

video—in daytime on CBS-TV (October 6, 1952, through July 2, 1954, with telecasts varying from two to three days per week), and briefly on NBC-TV in primetime (June 5 to July 3, 1953)—the format changed again. With Bert Parks as TV's master of ceremonies (and *Strike It Rich*'s Walt Framer as producer), five members of the studio audience tried to answer a trio of eligibility stumpers, qualifying for a jackpot worth double or nothing. Questions in that round were valued at 10, 20 and 40 dollars and—double or nothing—a top prize in the regular game of 140 dollars. Every contestant could participate in the sweepstakes, no matter how he had performed earlier. Players wrote answers to a single question on horse-shaped cards, then whoever offered the correct answer first won the "race."

When Campbell sponsored the series, the show cautioned that there were "no losers." Every contestant, even those forfeiting everything in double or nothing, went home with a gift package of a favorite Campbell soup!

In its earliest years, *Double or Nothing* became a part of its environment, catering to the realities of a war that was absorbing much of the nation's attention. The program's very design allowed it to become an attractive conduit that focused on an escalating GI population. As with many of its contemporaries, the series was outwardly sympathetic to the war effort, from time to time actively saluting such organizations as the American Legion and veterans of World War I. There was a reciprocal arrangement by the government, of course, which often instigated and assisted in carrying out such emphases.

On the broadcast of May 3, 1942, *Double or Nothing* was chosen by the U. S. Naval Aviation Selection Board to announce a major policy change in Navy Air Corps recruiting. For the first time a prerequisite calling for applicants to be college-educated was relaxed. So— with his father, a World War I flying ace, proudly looking on — 20-year-old flight mechanic James B. Taylor III was sworn into the Corps while the show was on the air. The exchange was an impressive exhibition of the Navy's new policy. It was but one example of how *Double or Nothing* and its peer quiz programs cooperated for the good of a greater cause during an era when the nation's collective mind was riveted to the backdrop of international conflict.

Walter Compton, in the meantime, remained with the radio show that he originated through the broadcast of February 7, 1943. He then departed to serve in the U.S. Armed Forces himself. Returning to the workforce just as television was emerging as a major factor in broadcasting, Compton was found on the cutting edge, in front of and behind the cameras. He served on the staffs of a pair of local stations, WAAM-TV in Baltimore and WTTS-TV in Washington, as general manager and news commentator. He was additionally instrumental in launching a Radio and Television Correspondents Association.

The first Dumont Television network newscast, *Walter Compton News*, was also the first to originate, for any network, from Washington. It debuted on a local affiliate in June 1947; two months later a New York outlet was added, creating a unique dual-station hook-up. (This was somewhat reminiscent of a disk jockey show that Arthur Godfrey had broadcast on radio in those two cities just a few years earlier, though not simultaneously.) Capabilities were minimal in those experimental days, however — Compton read from a script while infrequent slides appeared on the small screens. That daily trial feature lasted into May 1948.

In 1957 Compton returned to his first love, radio, becoming a newscaster-commentator for MBS. The catchphrase, "Thank you and thirty," had long been his

recognized trademark. "Thirty" represented a journalist's technique for signaling a story's conclusion. Compton died in Washington at the young age of 47 on December 9, 1959.

His successor as master of ceremonies on *Double or Nothing* was a popular quizmaster whose star was indisputably ascending — John Reed King. Born at Atlantic City, New Jersey, on October 25, 1914, the Princeton-educated King took over the program on February 14, 1943, and carried it through July 13, 1945. He broke into radio during his collegiate days by reading news reports and announcing big band remotes from his hometown. He then worked alongside recognized CBS newsmen Edward R. Murrow and Robert Trout during World War II, supplying a weekly newscast in French that was beamed to occupied France.

But his real destiny for that decade was unequivocal, he ran game shows in wholesale lots. And he did it with great fervor, at one time or another hosting these audience participation series: *Break the Bank, Chance of a Lifetime, Give and Take, Go for the House, The Great Day* and *Missus Goes a-Shopping*. By the 1950s he was emceeing similar competitive fare on TV, only more of it: *Battle of the Ages, Chance of a Lifetime, Give and Take, The John Reed King Show, Let's See, Missus Goes a-Shopping, On Your Way, There's One in Every Family, Tootsie Hippodrome, What's Your Bid?, Where Was I?* and *Why?*

And as if he needed to, King supplemented his income as a master of ceremonies by announcing nearly a score of radio series: *Americans at Work, The American School of the Air, The Columbia Workshop, Death Valley Days, Duffy's Tavern, The Gay Nineties Revue, Grand Central Station, The Heinz Magazine of the Air, The Mel Torme Show, Our Gal Sunday, The Sheriff, So You Think You Know Music, The Stu Erwin Show, The Texaco Star Theater,*

The Victor Borge Show, What's My Name?, The Woman and *Ziegfeld Follies of the Air.*

For a spell this versatile performer appeared on radio as his popular fictional namesake, *Sky King.* John Reed King died on July 8, 1979, at Woodstown, New Jersey. He was 64.

Todd Russell was King's successor as *Double or Nothing*'s master of ceremonies, from July 15, 1945, through June 15, 1947. He remained with the show through its final epoch as a primetime vehicle, before the series' transfer to daytime. During Russell's tenure the program aired exclusively on Sunday evenings at 9:30 P.M., continuing on MBS as it had from its start.

Biographers haven't preserved most of the details of Russell's life. After his stint on *Double or Nothing* he was the original host of *Strike It Rich,* appearing on radio in 1947–48 before Warren Hull's lengthy spell with that series. He also presided over a handful of TV runs like *Pud's Prize Party,* a talent variety hour; *Rootie Kazootie,* a children's feature; and two video game shows, *Wheel of Fortune* and *Who Do You Trust?*

The master of ceremonies for *Double or Nothing* who is indubitably best remembered by audiences today, however, took it over when the program moved to daytime. Walter O'Keefe, a versatile Connecticut-bred entertainer who had been searching for a while for just such a vehicle to properly showcase his talents, assumed the helm on June 30, 1947. The program changed sponsorship at that juncture, for the first time in its history, when Pharmaco (makers of Feen-a-Mint and Chooz) pulled out. Immediately, the Campbell Soup Company signed on, underwriting the series for the remainder of its run. (O'Keefe was buoyantly introduced each day as Campbell Soup's "man of the half-hour," also as "your paymaster of ceremonies." Following the opening billboard, announcer Murray Wagner exuberantly handed the show over to the emcee daily

with "OK O'Keefe!" followed by raucous audience applause.)

The daytime version of *Double or Nothing* was initially broadcast on CBS five days a week at 3 o'clock through June 25, 1948. A month before it ended, on May 31, 1948, Campbell's bought an NBC half-hour at 2 o'clock in which it ran *Double or Nothing* with *different* contestants from those on the 3 o'clock show. When the CBS series expired, the quiz program continued until 1951 at 2 o'clock. Meanwhile, in 1950 it again aired dual broadcasts, this time on *one* network (NBC), which programmed it at 10:30 A.M. and 2 P.M. When the afternoon series lapsed, the chain retained the morning broadcasts for another two years. In its final months on the air, *Double or Nothing* aired at 11:30 A.M. daily on ABC, its fourth web, from June 22, 1953, through January 15, 1954.

Walter O'Keefe was a seasoned, flamboyant comic that had enjoyed earlier opportunities in radio but encountered a dry spell before *Double or Nothing* opened up. Born August 18, 1900, at Hartford, he was almost 47 by the time he took over the quiz show's reigns in 1947. This may have given audiences the perception that he was more experienced and informed than the boyish, thirtyish men who preceded him in that role — on this question-and-answer show and others.

O'Keefe attended prep school in England and college at Notre Dame. Then he went in diverse directions, becoming a stand-up comic and a humorous composer-musician on the vaudeville circuit. He wrote an amusing syndicated newspaper column and even dabbled in politics. In 1940 he directed a portion of candidate Wendell Wilkie's unsuccessful Republican presidential bid.

Following some guest appearances on radio from the mid–1920s forward, O'Keefe mounted a serious foray into broadcasting when he briefly replaced an ailing Walter

The cat that swallowed the canary? If a picture is worth a thousand words, this one says it all for here's a cat who will soon line his pockets with a few shekels earned on *Double or Nothing*. Master of ceremonies Walter O'Keefe may never have encountered a more grateful winner, who obviously risked everything to go for the "big money" (a misnomer for sure, for such never really existed). (Photofest)

for the latter program. In 1938 he presided over *The Walter O'Keefe Show*, a 45-minute weekly variety series. He substituted for five months for Fred Allen on *Town Hall Tonight* while Allen was on the West Coast co-starring in a movie being filmed with Jack Benny. O'Keefe hosted *The Al Jolson Show, The Packard Hour* with Fred Astaire and *Tune-up Time* with Tony Martin.

With Mary Martin, in 1939 he attempted to draw listeners away from the premiering *Pot o' Gold*. That initial telephone giveaway was an alluring novelty for the nation, however, and O'Keefe and Martin were quickly forgotten. Ironically, for a time O'Keefe held an aversion to giveaway programs, just as Fred Allen did across his long career. But just such shows turned out to be the genre that spelled notoriety at last for O'Keefe. In the meantime, he turned to drinking to soothe his pride. He wouldn't have long to languish, nevertheless.

From 1942 to 1944 he co-hosted the game show *Battle of the Sexes*. Then he focused on camp and hospital shows for the Marines, on charity events and radio guest shots. After an absence of three years from a regular radio series, O'Keefe hit his stride as emcee of *The Breakfast Club* during the absence of a vacationing Don McNeill. An

Winchell on an early series, *The Lucky Strike Magic Carpet*. That resulted in his becoming host of a show featuring Don Bestor's band. The still better recognized *Camel Caravan* with Glen Gray and the Casa Loma Orchestra followed. He appeared in the casts of comedy-variety series, including *The Jack Pearl Show, The Saturday Night Party* and *The Tuesday Night Party*, as host agent helped him acquire the role of emcee on *Double or Nothing*, then preparing to shift to daytime. From 1949 to 1954 he concurrently hosted *The Wizard of Odds*, played himself in the short-lived 1952 video series *Mayor of Hollywood* and in 1954 presided over the TV game show *Two for the Money*. From 1957 to 1959 he appeared frequently on NBC's omnibus weekend radio service, *Monitor*.

In 1982, long after O'Keefe's professional career ended, he confessed that his greatest single achievement in life had been conquering alcohol. He credited a movie, *The Lost Weekend*, in helping him start the long journey to sobriety. O'Keefe faced, and often overcame, many other grim afflictions: arthritis, asthma, pneumonia, tuberculosis, two cancer operations, three broken legs, five heart attacks and six kidney stone procedures. He died June 26, 1983, at Torrance, California.

In 1976 author John Dunning labeled *Double or Nothing* "a pretty dull quiz."[1] In that context, he obviously wasn't referring to the dilemma in which Walter O'Keefe once found himself, a situation that no audience participation master of ceremonies before him had ever encountered.

A completely unsuspecting O'Keefe met his greatest on-air challenge on the afternoon of October 15, 1948, as he urged a contestant on *Double or Nothing*—a waitress by profession—to share a few of her experiences with millions in the live radio audience. In a kind of earthy monologue the young woman rambled on about a young man she knew whom she believed to have grave emotional problems. After reciting some of the man's issues for a while, she remarked that a female confidante had suggested that she tell him he could get out of his melancholy state if he would merely "get a good-looking girl like yourself and take her home and just have a big old screwing party!"

The flushed emcee, knowing network censors could cut his show off the air quickly, immediately intervened, changed the subject and accelerated the guest through the contest that followed. While some people in the studio audience apparently missed what the young lady had said, however, it didn't fall on deaf ears regarding those listening at home. The NBC switchboard lit up like a Christmas tree, with irate callers venting their anger in no uncertain terms.

The show had not yet aired on the West Coast, of course, due to the three-hour time gap between the two coasts. Local stations in the far Western region normally transcribed the live show for playback at a later hour. But on that day NBC ordered its affiliates who hadn't yet aired *Double or Nothing* to destroy those tapes, canceling the show for that one day only. Obviously, at least one such transcription survived, however, and subsequent copies of the X-rated episode have been passed from collector to collector across the years.

That incident was so shocking by mid-century standards that, years later — when writer Shirley Gordon recounted it in an article in *Radio Life* magazine — she never precisely revealed what happened. A radio biographer summarized: "After a dozen years of audience-participation programs, this was reputedly the first blatantly suggestive episode to hit the airwaves."[2] It would not be the last.

Radio and Television Mirror, another popular fan magazine of that era, published a story and accompanying color photo of a live production of *Double or Nothing* in its September 1950 issue. The two-page spread noted:

> The scene in the NBC studio looks exactly like this. From the [studio] audience you see the potential contestants seated on the stage, left. Standing at the first microphone is the contestant who is trying to turn the starting two dollars into a forty-dollar jackpot as the stakes mount. At the other

microphone is emcee Walter O'Keefe, flanked by *Double or Nothing*'s staff which includes producer Lou Crosby, director Harry Spears and organist Ervin Orton.[3]

It was a descriptive word-picture that could be "seen" even if the photo hadn't been there!

Over its durable run, *Double or Nothing* required numerous support staff members. Most duties were filled multiple times, just as were those of the program's master of ceremonies.

Three announcers graced that stage — Alois Havrilla, Fred Cole and Murray Wagner.

Born in 1891 at Prague, Czechoslovakia, Havrilla and his family immigrated to this country when he was four. His subsequent command of the English language was so remarkable that he gave no hint of any accent. He held announcing posts for *The Jack Benny Program* and *The Palmolive Hour* while hosting *Strange as It Seems*. His death occurred on December 7, 1952.

Cole, who announced for *Ethel and Albert, Straight Arrow* and *The Strange Dr. Karnac*, died at age 63 on September 20, 1964.

Wagner introduced *Meet Miss Sherlock* and *Tell It Again*.

Double or Nothing was produced by Ken Fickett, Lou Crosby and Diana Bourbon. Historiographers record nothing about Fickett beyond this show.

Crosby was a veteran announcer, speaking for *Gene Autry's Melody Ranch, Lum and Abner, The Rise Stevens Show* and *The Roy Rogers Show* on radio, and *Mayor of Hollywood* on TV. He died at 70 on January 27, 1984.

Bourbon's only other known activity was as director of the series *Life Begins*. She died at age 78 on March 19, 1978.

It also took a trio of directors to air *Double or Nothing* across its durable run, Harry Spears, Thomas Vietor and John Wellington. There is no record of addi-

tional service in the industry for Wellington.

Spears was producer-director of *Take It or Leave It*.

Vietor also directed *Big Sister* and *The Big Story*.

Three writers— Carroll Carroll, Gerald Rice and Harry Bailey—contributed to *Double or Nothing*'s success. Of the trio, only Carroll offered significant writing contributions elsewhere: *The Burns and Allen Show, The Circle, Club Fifteen, The Eddie Cantor Show, The Edgar Bergen and Charlie McCarthy Show, The Frank Sinatra Show, The Kraft Music Hall, Meet Corliss Archer, NTG and His Girls* and *The Rudy Vallee Show*. He also produced *The Al Jolson Show*.

On one occasion, while comparing a player's earnings potential on *Double or Nothing* with that of similar shows, Carroll decreed that the series was a "bargain basement" version of *The $64 Question*. He died at age 88 on February 6, 1990.

Of a quartet of musicians contributing to *Double or Nothing* (Elliott Jacoby, Frank Forest, Nat Brusiloff and Irv Orton), the record of Jacoby alone has been preserved. He also supplied music for *Maudie's Diary, Meet Mr. Meek, Secret Missions* and *Two Thousand Plus*. He died at 75 on March 28, 1977.

With a tenure exceeding 13 years, nearly unprecedented for a game show, *Double or Nothing* became one of radio's hardiest quizzes. The agile ad-libbing of its upbeat hosts, plus its reputation for double entendres and confusion (as in the case of the waitress contestant), undoubtedly contributed to the program's longevity. The series proved that listeners at home were just as intrigued by its question-and-answer format as were the players drawn from the studio audience. And while it may have been a "bargain basement" to better-paying contests, this durable quiz set a pattern that dozens of imitators would follow.

10

Information Please

Premise: It was a series unlike anything else in radio, a quiz with no familiar introductory music. But, even more distinctively, it was an adult-oriented question-and-answer bash for which the queries were posed not by glitzy masters of ceremonies but mainstream Americans who tuned in all over the nation. And get this, to answer those questions, the show didn't rely upon an unsuspecting goon plucked from a studio audience who had absolutely no comprehension of the topical matter to be considered. Instead, this program fielded a corps of cerebral giants who were exceedingly well versed in arts, artists, athletes, archives and almost any subject matter a listener might decree. Far from boring, these scholastic wizards looked upon their assignment not so much as trotting out their mental dexterity, but enjoying the company of one another and reacting to the contributions of its members. Even when they failed to answer a petition, they jousted among themselves, making light of their own ineptness at solving what for them might have been considered "the simplest of riddles." The result was a light-hearted, freewheeling, unrehearsed half-hour of levity, far removed from any high-brow misconceptions. At the same time, regretfully, a high-strung, overbearing owner-producer reserved for himself absolute control over every aspect of the show. That resulted in breached trust with a panelist, several sponsors and a network president. It certainly wasn't the most pleasant way to air a series, and eventually the whole house of cards collapsed around him. To his credit, nevertheless, he was able to place scholarship on a pedestal right alongside sports, entertainment and politics. And in doing so, this series earned the respect of deep-thinkers everywhere.

Creator/Owner/Producer/Director: Dan Golenpaul

Moderator: Clifton Fadiman

Permanent Panelists: Franklin P. Adams, John Kieran, Oscar Levant (twice monthly)

Announcers: Don Baker, Howard Claney, Milton Cross, Ed Herlihy, Ben Grauer, Jay Jackson

Pianist: Joseph Kahn

Sponsors: Sustained by the network for 26 weeks following its inception, the show picked up a sponsor — Canada Dry Bottling Co.— with the broadcast of Nov. 15, 1938. Canada Dry carried the series for its ginger ale beverages through Nov. 5, 1940. On Nov. 15, 1940, the American Tobacco Co. signed on for its Lucky Strike cigarette brand, underwriting the program through Feb. 5, 1943. The series transferred to the H. J. Heinz Co. (ketchup, relishes and other foodstuffs) with the broadcast of Feb. 15, 1943, continuing through Feb. 5, 1945. On Feb. 12, 1945, it became the property of Mobil Oil, lasting through June 24, 1946. The Parker Pen Co. underwrote the series from Oct. 2, 1946, through June 25, 1947. After that, and to the end of the run, the show was sold to multiple (several participating) sponsors.

Ratings: High: 15.0 (1940–41); Low: 7.7 (1946–47); Median: 11.5. (The final two seasons are unreported.)

On the Air: Feb. 17, 1938–Nov. 5, 1940, NBC Blue, Tuesday, 8:30 P.M. ET; Nov. 15, 1940–Feb. 5, 1943, NBC, Friday, 8:30 P.M.; Feb. 15, 1943–July 12, 1943, and Sept. 13, 1943–July 10, 1944, NBC, Monday, 10:30 P.M.; Sept. 11, 1944–June 24, 1946, NBC, Monday, 9:30 P.M.; Oct. 2, 1946–June 25, 1947, CBS, Wednesday, 10:30 P.M.; Sept. 26, 1947–June 25, 1948, MBS, Friday, 9:30 P.M.; Sept. 10, 1950–April 22, 1951, MBS, Sunday, 10 P.M.

*   *   *

ANNOUNCER: It's half-past eight New York time, time to wake up, America, and stump the experts! Each week at this time Lucky Strike sets up a board of four know-it-alls for you to throw questions at. For every question we use, Lucky Strike pays out $10, plus a copy of the new *Information Please Quiz Book*. If your question stumps us, you get $25 more plus a 24-volume set of the current *Encyclopedia Britannica*. Send your questions to *Information Please*, 480 Lexington Avenue, New York City. If our editorial staff edits your question a bit, don't fret over it. In case of duplication, *Information Please* uses the questions that were received first. And now, light up a Lucky Strike

as I present our master of ceremonies, the literary critic of *The New Yorker* magazine, Clifton Fadiman.

FADIMAN: Good evening ladies and gentlemen. Let me remind you again *Information Please* is completely unrehearsed and ad-libbed from beginning to end.
—*Show introduction, 1940–43*

One critic labeled this series "egghead-oriented,"[1] a term of derision used by anti-intellectuals, Webster purports.

But the preponderance of criticism on this one arrived from the other side. And, surprisingly, it was astonishingly favorable.

The show "moved briskly along an intellectual race track that few parallel series could tread upon," one avowed.[2]

A second radio historiographer explained: "On the surface, the show was highbrow, but its earthy humor and the trickiness of the questions appealed to the masses as well."[3]

Said another: "*Information Please* was easily the elite of the genre."[4]

And a panelist on the show itself termed it "the most literate popular entertainment program ever to go out over the air on radio or television."[5]

In its first full season of broadcasting, the nation's newspaper editors—generally some of the harshest critics to be found anywhere—voted *Information Please* "the best radio quiz of 1939 and the fourth best show in all of radio."[6] (It was preceded only by big name stars Jack Benny, Edgar Bergen and Charlie McCarthy, and Bing Crosby.) The following year, the show was given the prestigious "distinguished service to literature" award by the *Saturday Review of Literature*.

While it may have been egghead-oriented to a few, in truth, *Information Please* appealed to the masses, raising the level of inquiry a decided notch, giving an air of respectability to serious inquisition that it had never enjoyed. Reflecting on the series years later, one of its principals allowed:

Perhaps the most intellectual show on radio, yet on a level commoners could appreciate, *Information Please* was a half-hour of levity among principals as listeners sought to "stump the experts!" Clifton Fadiman, moderator, standing before the studio audience, is flanked by a scholarly panel including John Kieran (not shown), two unidentified guests and Franklin P. Adams, seated at far right. (Photofest)

"The program gave the American public new role models beyond those in sports, politics and films. Suddenly, intelligent men and women were looked up to and emulated. And most came across as 'regular guys.' ... Maybe we demonstrated that education is worthwhile and can be fun."[7] On many college campuses, undergraduates voted it their favorite show on radio.

The theory behind *Information Please* stood in opposition to the concept that quiz shows had previously pursued. It was formed in the mind of Dan Golenpaul. With the exception of a couple of short-lived series he produced in the late 1930s, Golenpaul could be characterized as a man bearing a folder of unsuccessful ideas. It wasn't that his motifs weren't feasible or worthy, but simply that he hadn't found a vehicle that clicked. One media critic interprets him as "a controversial personality who knew what he wanted, was relentless in his pursuit of it, and then, having attained it, did battle with everyone, from an equally feisty sponsor to the president of a network, to maintain its integrity and prestige."[8]

Golenpaul was, doubtlessly, one of the

most colorful and contentious characters during the heyday of radio's Golden Age.

A native New Yorker born at the start of the 20th century, Golenpaul was educated at Columbia University. He engineered speakers' forums and political campaigns before being charmed by an opportunity to shape public service programming for independent radio stations. He would further apply his creative abilities by developing some audio efforts in government and education at the behest of both The New School for Social Research and New York University.

He can be credited with introducing the very first magazine-type venture to hit the airwaves in *The Heinz Magazine of the Air*. The omnibus series ran on CBS thrice weekly between September 2, 1936, and April 10, 1938. It included many of the durable elements that would leave a mark on similar potpourri efforts in the decades beyond — music, literature, current events, sports, theater and even a continuing serial drama. (This latter episodic tale, titled *Trouble House*, was written by creative serial author Elaine Sterne Carrington, who was to become widely acclaimed for penning a trio of distinctively durable and compelling soap operas: *Pepper Young's Family*, *Rosemary* and *When a Girl Marries*.)

Also on Saturday mornings in the 1936–37 radio season, Golenpaul was successful in placing the juvenile forum *Raising Your Parents* on NBC Blue as a sustaining feature. Famed interlocutor for the Metropolitan Opera broadcasts Milton Cross moderated an adolescent troupe offering to solve real-life dilemmas faced by some juveniles in the listening audience. A clinical analysis of those suggestions was added at the close of each session by a professional child psychologist.

Golenpaul was openly exasperated when his show and some other unsponsored series were deleted from the schedule im-

mediately after Arturo Toscanini inked a 1937 deal with NBC. Toscanini's contract guaranteed him 40 grand annually. Toscanini would conduct the NBC Symphony Orchestra into the 1950s. "The Maestro put me out of work," Golenpaul claimed in 1964. "But not *Professor Quiz* who was big at the time," he lamented.[9] (Craig Earl, that show's quizmaster and a law school graduate, ex-circus magician and tight rope acrobat, was popularly known as "the King Midas of radio" on the 1936–41 and 1946–48 series. The show is commonly considered the first true radio quiz.)

Golenpaul continued: "I used to get annoyed when he [Earl] made such a great fuss over the fact that a contestant didn't know an answer.... I wish I had these quizmasters and so-called experts in front of me. I'd like to ask *them* some questions. They're probably not much brighter than the average listener."[10]

Golenpaul became obsessed with creating a format that reversed the situation. For most quiz shows, players would be enticed from a studio or listening audience, put on the spot, interrogated and compensated for adequate responses. Golenpaul's rejoinder was to call forth a team of intellectual heavyweights who would answer questions asked by the audience without benefit of advance insight concerning what would be asked. This would turn underdogs into champions, he felt; mere boobs selected from audiences on other shows would come off looking far more scholarly here because they were on the giving rather than the receiving end.

The national webs were dubious, however, convinced that it would all go above the heads of listeners and come across as showy and stifling. It would be up to Golenpaul to persuade them differently.

He made a demonstration tape of the proposed series. For the audition, he drew two names who would ultimately wind up as mainstays of the long-running feature.

(Historian John Dunning attests: "What made it an immortal piece of radio was the mix of personalities who fit the idea so perfectly. The quiz, in fact, was the least important part of the formula."[11])

Golenpaul selected former editor and book critic Clifton Fadiman as panel moderator. For this initial outing of the panel itself, Golenpaul chose longtime newspaper columnist Franklin P. Adams, *New York Herald-Tribune* staffer Marcus Duffield, science writer Bernard Jaffe and Columbia University economics professor Louis M. Hacker.

In April 1938 the audition record fell into the hands of NBC Blue's chief of programming, Bill Karlin. Karlin accepted it as a summer replacement series, offering Golenpaul a bare bones budget of $400 weekly for talent and prizes. Overnight success would change all of that; in six months Golenpaul and the others would be splitting decent compensation as the $400 increased to $2,500. The show bowed as a sustaining feature on May 17 at 8:30 P.M.

Over the next few weeks Golenpaul refined his program themes. He had previously determined that there would be a quartet of erudite panelists. Wisely, he also concluded that they must not be only intellects, but also must possess scintillating personalities. To identify with the listeners, he affirmed a need to establish some continuity among the aggregate. He was to accomplish that by scheduling only two of the four as "regulars" to appear on *every* show. That would create ample diversity in casting the remainder of the panel. It would also allow him to select from a coterie of distinguished guests who could offer fresh and varied perspectives every week.

In her 1986 biography *F.P.A.: The Life and Times of Franklin Pearce Adams*, Sally Ashley details the intense groundwork that went into the initial broadcast of *Informa-tion Please*. No listeners already existed, of course, so the questions for that show had to be cooked up surreptitiously by somebody. Golenpaul, his wife Ann and a high school educator named Gordon Kahn worked at that task. Kahn (no relation to Joe Kahn, the program's musical director) was chosen as editor-in-chief of a permanent editorial board. Meeting in Kahn's backyard, the trio improvised some questions, then set out on a mission of corralling some people to attend the first broadcast, focusing on neighbors and others living nearby whom they already knew. Some of those (Golenpaul's secretary for one) would be assigned mythical names so they could appear on the broadcast to ask the original backyard-instigated questions of the panel.

The program soon switched to listener-submitted queries, of course, resulting in greater control, continuity, participation and listener interest. That gave Golenpaul the added benefit of time to corroborate the answers. The number of questions received from listeners was variously estimated at between 30,000 and 75,000 weekly. Queries pertaining to issues considered debatable, such as politics, race or religion, were flatly rejected — "anything smacking of trouble," *Time* magazine reported.

The show hired a dozen full-time staffers to open, read, sort, file and forward entries to the editorial board. Questions were preserved topically, to be withdrawn when guests with odd areas of enlightenment sat on the panel. That posed another dilemma: When stumpers weren't deployed until years after being received, sometimes senders couldn't be located; their prizes, in such cases, were never awarded.

With the exception of economics professor Louis Hacker, on the first broadcast the panel was the same as the quartet who had appeared on the audition tape. Hacker was replaced by Dr. Harry Overstreet, a

College of the City of New York philosophy professor. Announcer Howard Claney introduced moderator Clifton Fadiman as "an intellectual Simon Legree, the Toscanini of quiz." (Toscanini was obviously a contemporary topic of some import at the time!) Claney delineated the game: "You, the very much quizzed public, will quiz the professors. Yes, the worm turns, and now the experts will have to know the answers to your questions, or else you win five dollars."

In the show's earliest days, when a question was asked on the air, the listener submitting it was awarded a two-dollar cash prize. If the fan's query stumped the panel, the prize was increased to five dollars. In a short while those figures grew to five and ten dollars, respectively. The show became more prosperous as it aged, with the rewards appreciating right along with it. For submitting a question that was asked on the air, a listener would receive the *Encyclopedia Junior*; for stumping the experts, one's prize increased to a 24-volume set of the *Encyclopedia Britannica* and possibly other incentives. (*Britannica* actually forged a stronger identity with the program than the sponsors who underwrote it. For the occasional cost of a set of books, the firm received exposure that money couldn't buy.)

During the era of H.J. Heinz's sponsorship (1943–45), prizes for outwitting the panel included the encyclopedias plus $57 in war bonds and stamps. This was a shrewd promotion for edible goodsmaker Heinz's famous "57 varieties." The top prize in the following year was based on correctly identifying several sections of a multipart question, resulting in a $500 war bond plus the encyclopedia set. The monetary awards were paid out to a cash register's ringing tones, one of the few sound effects on the program apart from a recorded crowing rooster at its opening.

The show's first broadcast was the re-cipient of both bows and arrows in the views of some radio historiographers. One believed it "set the tone and was lauded as a charmer; the dialogue was snappy and brisk."[12] Another countered by panning the panel, describing it as "bright but boring, top-heavy with scholars."[13]

It was crunch time for Golenpaul for sure. If *Information Please* was to become the sterling success that he envisioned, the whole ball of wax would probably hinge on the people he cast to carry it on a regular basis. John Dunning offers no apologies (nor should he) in stating that Golenpaul's "first decision — hiring Fadiman as moderator — was his most important. Fadiman was the spark plug: on those rare occasions when he was absent, the difference was immediately apparent."[14] Others concurred: "Clifton Fadiman remained the fulcrum, bringing to his weekly assignment a measure of liveliness, informality and drollness. His friendly approach made it seem as if the program were being played by family and friends in a living room."[15] In its assessment, *Current Biography* suggested that Fadiman was "the perfect mixture of bright interest and delicate malice that spurs the experts to do their desperate best."[16]

All we know of Fadiman's background seemed to prepare him for the role he would ultimately play at the helm of a pivotal radio series. He was born May 15, 1904, in Brooklyn, New York, the son of a Russian immigrant father who became a pharmacist, with a nurse as his mother. By the time Clifton (nicknamed Kip by his family following a prolonged bout with hiccups) reached age five, his older sibling, Edwin, who would one day manage his (Kip's) business dealings, taught him geography. It was the first of many disciplines Kip would master. In the next five years he acquainted himself with the literary world, exposed to the writings of Dante, Homer, Milton and Sophocles.

An industrious Fadiman didn't expand only his mind as he grew into young manhood, however. He was a soda jerk at his dad's drug store. Courting a new direction, he sold supplies and equipment for boaters, then joined the French-American shipping line as a staff official.

Kip and his brother Edwin were students at the same time at New York's Columbia University. In those years the pair sold rare volumes at a Pennsylvania Station retail bookshop while heavily investing themselves in a community newspaper called *The Forest Hills Reporter*. Edwin was publisher and editor, while Kip delivered the journal to readers. When Kip received his undergraduate degree, Phi Beta Kappa in 1925, his income had reached $1,000 or more annually. Part of it was derived from a stint as book reviewer for *The Nation* magazine.

Following his graduation, Ethical Culture High School beckoned, and Kip responded by teaching English for a couple of years. He joined the publishing firm of Simon & Schuster in 1927 as an assistant editor, and by 1929 was promoted to editor. (*Trader Horn*, a title he recommended that S&S publish that year, became a national bestseller. Metro-Goldwyn-Mayer subsequently purchased the film rights.) By 1931 Kip was reading his criticisms over the air on *The Book Report*, a venture that was short-lived. He became book editor for *The New Yorker* magazine in 1933 and stayed with it for a decade. Concurrently, he was named Simon & Schuster's editor-in-chief, resigning that post in 1935 but remaining an S&S external editorial adviser for a while. In 1945 he became a jurist on the Book of the Month Club selection panel (and later its chairman). He also lent his prestigious influence to the Famous Writers School mail-order course for aspiring authors.

"Few minds have been so admired by middle–America as Clifton Fadiman's," author Richard Lamparski declared three decades ago. "His accomplishments today, however, seem far less impressive than thirty years ago (in 1940) when a college education was still the exception. He had a sharp eye for what the buying public would pay to read and an enormous fund of facts stored in an exceptional memory."[17]

A prodigious reader at 34, who had already cultivated a solid career in letters, Fadiman was about to become one of radio's genuinely rare talents. With a practiced eye for what *Information Please* could be, Golenpaul invited Fadiman to sign on as moderator for his show. While agreeing to participate in the demo tape, Fadiman had serious doubts about the outcome, as did some other participants. "It was a crazy idea, and I told him so," Fadiman mused after the show took off. "No one but Dan had much faith in the program. A shoestring product, it seemed to have no chance of finding an audience or a sponsor."[18]

Fadiman's immediate hit status as a radio personality would open a new career to him on the airwaves. His voice would be instantly recognized by millions over the decades, while his name would become a household word in many homes. In addition to guest stints on *The Pursuit of Happiness* and *The NBC University Theater*, his aural credits would include hosting *Conversation* (his personal favorite, a 1954–57 NBC series of informal chats with guests on almost any topic but politics), *The Human Adventure, Keep 'em Rolling, Mathematics, Monitor, The Piano Playhouse, The Quiz Kids* (on brief occasions when moderator Joe Kelly was away), *RCA Magic Key, This Is Broadway* and *Words at War*. By 1955 he was a roving reporter for the Metropolitan Opera. In addition to emceeing a summertime version of *Information Please* on TV, he presided over brief video outings of *Alumni Fun, The Quiz Kids* and *This Is Show Business*. In the 1950s he also turned up as an infrequent guest panelist on TV's *I've Got a Secret* and *Masquerade Party*.

In later life — no longer teaching, lecturing or broadcasting — Fadiman still contributed sporadic reviews and articles to periodicals like *This Week* and *Holiday* (in 1951 he had become an essayist for the latter). He authored *Party of One* and edited *American Treasury*, and in his 10th decade — in the 1990s — showed few signs of curtailing such prolific literary endeavors. Among them, a rolling tide of prologues to textbooks and anthologies.

Once Golenpaul had enlisted the all-important moderator for his show, he recognized that a key to *Information Please*'s success hinged on fielding an extraordinary panel. Of the original crew, Golenpaul was convinced that only one was a keeper. But what a contributor he turned out to be! Franklin Adams was well versed in poetry, Shakespeare, baseball, and Gilbert and Sullivan, collaborators of many operettas.

Franklin Pearce Adams — infrequently referred to by the initials *FPA* — was a Chicagoan by birth, born November 15, 1881. At 56 his age easily made him the eldest of the *Information Please* tribe as the show premiered. He, too, was unconvinced that Golenpaul had a winning formula. Despite the fact that he had fallen on hard times, Adams discarded Golenpaul's initial invitation, later reconsidering.

Much earlier he had withdrawn from his studies at the University of Michigan to sell insurance, moving on to a hometown daily in Chicago as a cub reporter. Interrupting his career to fight for Uncle Sam overseas during World War I, he returned home to publish several volumes of short prose and poetry while doting on light verse.

In 1913 Adams had moved to the Big Apple to inaugurate an academic column for *The New York Tribune* called "The Conning Tower." It would be his personal

forum of expression for more than 35 years. He is also generally considered the instigator of the Algonquin Hotel's celebrated Round Table discussions. Its lunch partners included the likes of Robert Benchley, Heywood Broun, George S. Kaufman, Dorothy Parker, Deems Taylor and Alexander Woollcott. Adams published some of their writing in his column.

His only other radio attempt, *The Word Game*, ironically debuting on CBS just six nights before *Information Please* did, failed and was withdrawn in four months. Listeners anticipated improvement in word usage and spelling but were dissuaded by the series' slurred words and dead air. On September 17, 1955, Adams was the subject of NBC Radio's *Biography in Sound*. He died at 78 in New York City on March 24, 1960.

Adams became "the expert-in-residence in matters literary" on *Information Please*.[19] "Noted for his urbanity and high wit, the deadpan, innocent-sounding Adams seldom missed on any questions surrounding Shakespeare.... He was once described as a cigar-smoking, pool-playing little gargoyle with a long neck, big nose and bushy mustache — who had a wonderful time each week in one of quizdom's hot seats."[20] Adams' biographer allowed that, "he often captured ideas nobody listening dared express, even though they agreed. His was a special kind of exhibitionism. He didn't display himself in any vulgar sense but loved to show himself as an oddity, a crotchety observer and commentator."[21] No matter. Golenpaul recognized his intense wit, talent, urbanity and intellect. Adams possessed everything the show needed. The first permanent panelist had been located.

Marcus Duffield and Bernard Jaffe — who were on the demo tape with Adams — continued appearing on the show as Golenpaul explored options for the second permanent chair. John Kieran, whom he had met at a Dutch Treat Club luncheon, had favorably impressed him with his insights and the extent of his intellect. Kieran's work as a sports columnist for *The New York Times* earned him the reputation of "sports philosopher." Moreover, he was credited with knowing music, poetry, ornithology (the bird-related branch of zoology), natural history and Shakespeare. He was also fluent in Latin. (In later years he interpreted himself through Latin: *Homo sum, humani nil a me alieum puto* ["I am a man, and nothing pertaining to humanity is alien to me"].) Yet he, too, was apathetic about *Information Please* and had to be persuaded. Kieran's first appearance on the show came in its fourth week, on June 7, 1938.

Born August 2, 1892, at the Bronx, New York, he was the son of a pair of educators. Kieran's father taught classics at Hunter College and later became the institution's president. His mother, a poet, taught in the local public schools. Young John grew up in a home where he was surrounded by books and given exceptional opportunities to learn. He took advantage of them and by the age of 10 had convincingly dazzled his family with extraordinary intellect. While he acquired an early interest in music, he soon found language, literature, ornithology and sports appealing. He matured into an expert diver and swimmer, and was added to his varsity high school basketball squad. He also became the champion of a newspaper-sponsored golf tournament.

In 1912 Kieran graduated cum laude from Fordham University. As did Franklin P. Adams before him, he, too, pursued schoolteaching as his first post beyond college. Kieran wound up in a rural district of New York's Duchess County earning 10 dollars weekly for teaching six pupils. As a sideline, he also operated a poultry business. Within a year he moved to a sewer-construction project where he served as a

time marker. The crew was mostly Italian; Kieran seized the opportunity to study the language, and then to conquer French. By the time he was 23 he was fluent in at least four languages.

In 1915 he launched a professional career as a journalist, for which he would be identified for the rest of his life. Joining *The New York Times* as a sports reporter, by 1927 he was penning the first daily byline column offered by that paper. (Kieran acquired an archival annotation in 1932 by contriving the phrase *brain trust*. In its original use, the expression pertained to a band of sages and techies who put together Franklin D. Roosevelt's initial presidential campaign. Kieran was then covering Governor Roosevelt at the state capital in Albany, New York.)

Kieran left the *Times* for a two-year stint with the Eleventh Engineers in Europe during World War II. Returning to the states, he was picked up by *The New York Herald Tribune*. He soon left that newspaper to join the Hearst syndicate, and in 1943 accepted a post with *The New York Sun* for a year.

During and following his decade-plus assignment on *Information Please*, this prolific writer continued offering literary contributions. Together with other principals involved in the show, Kieran inaugurated the *Information Please Almanac* in 1947, which he edited for many years. As a new millennium began, that volume was still being produced in annual updated installments under the title *Time Almanac: The Ultimate Worldwide Fact and Information Source with Information Please*.

Kieran's further accomplishments included a 1948 NBC-TV series known as *John Kieran's Kaleidoscope* and a subsequent 1951 program on that network called *Treasures of New York*. He also joined the college lecture circuit, wrote features for a myriad of newspapers and authored many books, among them: *The Story of the*

Olympic Games (1936), *Nature Notes* (1941), *American Sporting Scene* (1943), *Footnotes on Nature* (1947), *Natural History of New York City* (1959) and *Books I Love* (1969). By 1969 his literary works had sold over 350,000 volumes. Kieran died at Rockport, Massachusetts, on December 9, 1981, at the age of 89.

"Kieran had a predilection for collecting knowledge and was considered a walking encyclopedia," assessed one reviewer, making him invaluable to *Information Please*. "People were convinced that he knew the answer to every question under the sun."[22] Another witness certified: "He displayed a knowledge of subjects so diverse that ... he was referred to as the man who knows everything. Listeners often addressed their letters containing questions meant to stump him to 'Mr. Know-It-All.' Not only was he familiar with totally unrelated matters, he went beyond reciting facts and figures; his replies to questions usually showed a deep understanding of the considered field."[23] Most would agree that he was "the hardest panelist of all to beat."[24] Yet another author epitomized: "His contribution to *Information Please* was inestimable."[25]

For one broadcast, Kieran's son forwarded a Shakespearean question that none of the panelists could identify. "How sharper than a thankless tooth it is to have a serpent child," Kieran mocked.

Another time, when Fadiman inquired what political sovereign was the son of a bastard, a panelist colleague expressed a belief that Adolf Hitler (ne Schicklgruber) was the proper response. A woman in the studio audience gasped, thinking Hitler was himself the bastard. Prompting the audience to regale in laughter, Kieran observed: "He is if he wasn't!"

In his autobiography, Kieran claimed the show was most gratifying when Golenpaul's initial premise of outwitting the intellects transpired. "It was generally more fun when the answer was wrong," he wrote, "especially if the culprit tried to wriggle out of it. An uproarious error or a brilliant bit of irrelevance was rated far above any dull delivery of truth."[26]

Cohort Clifton Fadiman — asked about Kieran in a late 1960s interview — assessed his old colleague as "the sweetest, most gentle man I've encountered. The only man I know who was not terribly impressed by John's intelligence was John."[27] What a sterling, matchless tribute!

Now with two permanent panel chairs filled for *Information Please*, Golenpaul turned his attention to the third. That would ultimately provide more headaches than either of the others, including the remaining fourth chair, which was to be reserved exclusively for guest use.

Golenpaul turned frantic when a music connoisseur he had selected for the panel abruptly accepted an instructional post in Hawaii. Deems Taylor, composer and music critic, was brought on as a substitute but simply didn't work out, lacking the verbal dexterity and agile wit that made the show gratifying. Irving Kolodin, music critic for *The New York Sun* and a member of the editorial board of *Information Please*, mentioned the name of Oscar Levant at that juncture.

On the broadcast of July 5, 1938, Golenpaul tried out piano composer and virtuoso Levant in the third chair. The audience's response to Levant's droll, though frequently sharp-tongued, retorts was good enough by December 1938 to warrant an invitation to occupy the chair on a semi-permanent basis. Levant's biographers observed that Golenpaul was a difficult man to work with, a fact that shall be explored in-depth later. Reflecting on the selection of Levant, they conjectured: "Curiously, Levant's success on the show didn't endear him to Golenpaul, whose jealousy was aroused by Levant's tremendous popularity. Golenpaul's proprietary feelings about the program led him to resent even those he had handpicked to help make the broadcast a success. But Levant's popularity could not be ignored, so he arranged for the witty composer with the fast comeback to appear every other week on the show, paying him $200 for each half-hour stint."[28] Levant would be free to travel to public appearances for concert gigs and so forth two weeks each month in exchange for being on the panel the other two weeks.

Golenpaul realized that a prime benefit of the sequence was the rotation it offered, providing him with not four but six chairs to diversify the panel's focus each month. It allowed more scintillating intellects to be engaged than if three recurring panelists filled those chairs every single week.

Oscar Levant was born in Pittsburgh, Pennsylvania, on December 27, 1906. Of the trio of familiar *Information Please* panelists, he alone received minimal formal education. From 1935 to 1937 he was fortunate to be a pupil of Arnold Schoenberg, with whom he studied composition in Europe. He practiced music under Sigismund Stojowski; combined, this prepared him to use his natural gifts as a concert pianist and composer. Levant's initial break arrived when he was called in as an eleventh-hour replacement on a recording of "Rhapsody in Blue." That was a turning point, as he developed a strong kinship with the song's composer, George Gershwin. From that humble start he was able to take Gershwin's musical trade stock and launch an artist's career for himself that would carry him on to radio and concert tours. In time, Levant would pen a few popular songs, like "Lady, Play Your Mandolin." He wrote music and lyrics for the film *In Person* and published *The Memoirs of an Amnesiac*, an autobiography.

Levant became an accomplished actor, too, playing in several motion pictures: *An American in Paris, Band Wagon, The Bark-leys of Broadway, The Cobweb, The Dance of Life, Humoresque, The I Don't Care Girl, Kiss the Boys Goodbye, O. Henry's Full House, Orient Express, Rhapsody in Blue, Romance on High Seas* and *You Were Meant for Me.*

His professional life also enveloped radio. Originally "discovered" by orchestra leader Paul Whiteman, he appeared on the latter's show. Levant co-starred in musical variety on *The Al Jolson Show*; was in an ensemble on *Ben Bernie, The Old Maestro*; performed infrequently as a guest artist on *The Bell Telephone Hour*; and appeared as a pianist or comic pianist on *Hildegarde's Radio Room, The Kraft Music Hall* and *The Raleigh Room*.

Levant died on August 14, 1972, in Beverly Hills, California, at age 65. The major achievements of his life were chronicled in *A Talent for Genius*, released a couple of decades beyond his passing.

Aside from the professional dimensions of his career, there was another aspect of Levant that cannot escape notice. He became attractive to the producer of *Information Please* due to a remarkable intellect coupled with an ability to entertain through his delivery. Unfortunately, some of his unbridled, clumsy wit went beyond the bounds of acceptable standards, resulting in caustic and punitive verbalizations.

Author Gerald Nachman considered him "a bad-mannered pianist with a scathing wit whose wisecracks on the show made him a star and boosted his music career."[29] Colleague John Kieran believed that, in Levant, the show "found a positive genius for making off-hand cutting remarks that could not have been sharper if he had honed them a week in his mind. Oscar was always good for a bright response edged with acid."[30] Kieran recalled him as a bundle of nervous energy, repetitiously humming under his breath, whistling, shuffling and drumming his fingers. Levant even dubbed himself "l'enfant terrible" and gained a reputation as the panel's "bad boy," giving the program "difficult moments," according to reviewer Tom DeLong.

When Levant was on the show, musical questions were frequent, sometimes accompanied by pianist Joseph Kahn. Listeners were totally enraptured as the composer-panelist disentangled a hodgepodge of tunes from a melodic smorgasbord and deciphered them correctly. On occasion he would rest his head on the table while slouched in a chair, then without warning he'd look up, raise a hand and — from a rarely heard composition — identify some obscure motif. He was the resident expert in things musical, and was awarded near-genius status by many of the program's fans.

Despite that appraisal, moderator Fadiman allowed: "You never could tell what would come out of his mouth, largely because his conscious mind and subconscious were on the same level. He was unpredictable in his answers."[31] On one occasion, when asked to name the author of an autobiography whose first line read "I was born an ugly duckling," Levant — never batting an eye — shot back: "Eleanor Roosevelt." The network switchboard lit up like a Christmas tree as Democrats across the country telephoned to cry "foul." The correct answer should have been accredited to actress Marie Dressler.

In 1941 Levant signed a new contract with Golenpaul, increasing his salary to $500 per appearance. Insiders had known for a long time that the two men regarded one another with disdain. Golenpaul remained jealous of Levant's popularity, while Levant stewed over Golenpaul's proprietary behavior. Although Levant had made himself irreplaceable on the program, Golenpaul resolved that Levant's budding concert and film pursuits wouldn't flourish at the show's expense. He would shun Levant's requests for extra time away, agitating the panelist by holding him tautly to his contract. There will be more insights into their crossed relationship later in this chapter.

Surprisingly, no women were selected as permanent panelists for *Information Please*. If the show was staged now, could that be possible? Not likely. Because Americans resided in a largely male-dominated society in the 1930s, did that bar at least one feminine sage from their number? Radio historiographers have virtually ignored the matter by not having an answer or perhaps disbelieving the issue even merited consideration. It would be helpful to have known the mind of Golenpaul; nothing in print suggests that he maintained male chauvinist leanings. He may have merely decided to "go with the flow," which was male-oriented, without any thought of bias in choosing the panel's gender.

The only revelation in this arena surfaces from Clifton Fadiman, a man who is generally perceived as keeping abreast of contemporary issues. He appears to have misspoken, nonetheless, at least once in a matter regarding gender. In an interview decades after the last broadcast, he allowed that women were almost never good talkers. If that was his and Golenpaul's perception, one can't help wondering if their exposure to females hadn't been severely limited. Reality (today, at least) might support another conclusion. While *Information Please* was never dull, who knows to what heights it might have climbed had there been at least one bright feminine wit in its midst each week? And what gender barriers from that prestigious perch might have begun to erode even then as a result of such a simple act? We may only speculate about that now.

And what of that fourth chair? It would be the one Golenpaul could play with every week. It offered an opportunity to shift personalities into and out of it who mixed their expertise with a unique delivery, background and humor to complement the panel's "regulars."

One of the oft-repeated tales from the show involved guest John Gunter, who correctly identified the Shah of Iran as Reza Pahlavi. "Are you shah?" moderator Fadiman inquired of Gunter. "Sultanly," came the immediate retort.

Asked to name a quartet of distinguished ladies with the names Elzire, Farida, Hepzibah and Marina, journalist Marcus Duffield expressed familiarity with the name Elzire. Attempting to lend credibility to his answer, he added, "I used to play Indians with her." The audience replied with uproarious laughter, however, as Fadiman delineated: "You must have had a lot of fun. Elzire is Mrs. Dionne," the mom to Canada's then widely renowned quints.

Orson Welles offered prompt and precise answers to nearly every question that came his way. "This is your final time on this show," Fadiman quipped.

Gracie Allen proved that her radio persona as a dimwit was definitely contrived. On request, she recited factual data on aviation, literature, music, pediatrics and politics.

Harpo Marx answered every question with his auto horn while his brother, Groucho, burst into a duet with Franklin Adams, performing a number from a Gilbert and Sullivan operetta.

Prizefighter Gene Tunney awed listeners with a vast storehouse of Shakespearean wisdom.

And Boston Red Sox catcher Moe Berg equally impressed the crowd with his sharp mind and a disparate reservoir of endless knowledge.

Yet some of the visiting stars missed what should have been simple questions.

Elliott Roosevelt couldn't recognize some quotes then only a week old from his mother's newspaper column.

Nor could novelist Rex Stout deliver a recipe for Lobster Newburg, seemingly unaware he had put that very thing in *Too Many Cooks*, one of his Nero Wolfe detective mysteries.

Stuart Chase, an economist, failed to discern *chain stores* by the more common term to Britons, *multiple shops*.

When playwright George S. Kaufman couldn't think of anything peculiar about his drama *Deep Tangled Wildwood*, Fadiman injected: "It bombed, George."

The panelist guest slots turned into coveted affairs for artists seeking to connect with an eminent showcase while plugging their current efforts. Describing the guest roles on another NBC series, *Duffy's Tavern*, one august sage explained: "It was like *Information Please*—the intellectuals loved it, and for guest stars it was like going on the Larry King show—if you got on *Duffy's Tavern*, you were validated as a celebrity."[32] John Kieran claimed that being a guest on *Information Please* was a "badge of distinction."

But it didn't work out for everybody.

Politicians loved to be summoned to the show, yet they possessed the dullest minds, Fadiman averred. Senators James Fulbright and Henry Cabot Lodge, governors Wilbur Cross and Harold E. Stassen, presidential contender Wendell Wilkie, postmaster general James A. Farley, mayors Fiorello LaGuardia of New York and Maury Maverick of San Francisco, and United Nations appointees Ralph Bunche, Sir Gladwyn Jebb and Lester B. Pearson were panelists at least once.

In its earliest days, a rotating crop of visitors appeared semi-regularly on *Information Please*. Besides Oscar Levant, there was Stuart Chase, John Erskine, Lewis E. Lawes (a prison warden) and Hendrick Willem Van Loon. The show later became a revolving door for Fred Allen, Louis Bromfield, Russell Crouse, Lillian Gish, James Mitchener, Christopher Morley, Grantland Rice, Cornelia Otis Skinner, Jan Struther and Deems Taylor. A member of the Adams-inspired Algonquin Round Table, Taylor was on the show no less than 30 times.

Others appearing at least once were Leonard Bernstein, Marc Connelly, Ben Hecht, H. V. Kaltenborn, Boris Karloff, Beatrice Lillie, Alice Roosevelt Longworth, Dorothy Parker, Basil Rathbone, Arthur Rubinstein, Carl Sandburg, Albert Spalding and Dorothy Thompson.

Golenpaul traditionally met each week's guest or guests in his office, where they shared a Scotch whisky before walking to the studio together. He jealously reserved the privilege of selecting the program's guests for himself. This would eventually contribute to his and the show's undoing.

There were others associated with the long-running program who should be recognized, of course, among them a half-dozen who would serve as announcer. A pair of these — Milton Cross and Ed Herlihy — are introduced in the *Truth or Consequences* chapter. The remaining quartet is profiled here.

The multitalented Don Baker sometimes turned up as an announcer on such series as *The Columbia Workshop, Pursuit* and *Strike It Rich*. At other times, this keyboard virtuoso accompanied the comedy *My Best Girls* and the game show *Sing for Your Dough* while at the organ.

Howard Claney, meanwhile, divided his radio time nearly evenly between highbrow opera and soap opera, with a few other tidbits thrown in. On the one hand he announced *The American Album of Familiar Music, The NBC Symphony Orchestra* and *The Metropolitan Opera Auditions of the Air*; on the other, he was a familiar daily voice introducing *Amanda of Honeymoon Hill, Backstage Wife* and *Stella Dallas*. He narrated *America's Town Meeting of the Air, Borden Special Edition, The Jack Benny Program, Mr. Chameleon* and *Waltz Time*.

Born April 17, 1898, at Pittsburgh, Claney launched a stage career in the 1920s, playing in *Cyrano de Bergerac, Juno and the Paycock*, and *Liliom*. A gifted painter and watercolorist, he augmented his income by conducting one-man shows at prestigious art galleries. Taking a job as an announcer at WEAF led Claney to be hired often by radio drama and music series producer Frank Hummert. Ad agencies regularly engaged him for programming that featured Jack Benny, Walter Damrosch, Lawrence Tibbett and Paul Whiteman. He was advertised by NBC Artists Service as "clear-voiced, an expert in selling, psychology, and blessed with an air personality which strikes a note of genuine sincerity into his excellent delivery." One other note on his career, while Claney studied painting abroad in 1938, the European crisis erupted, allowing him to provide eyewitness reports by shortwave radio from London. He died at Charlotte, North Carolina, in April 1980.

The voice of Ben Grauer was christened "the most authoritative in the world" by the National Academy of Vocal Arts. In 1944 that organization voted him "the best NBC announcer." A radio biographer claimed: "He became as much an aural identification mark for NBC as the roar of Leo the Lion for MGM."[33]

Having joined that network's announcing staff in 1930, Grauer appeared on all of the following shows, most of them NBC staples: *The Adventures of Mr. and Mrs. North, American Portraits, America's Town Meeting of the Air, Atlantic Spotlight, The Baker's Broadcast, The Battle of the Sexes, Behind the Mike, Believe It or Not, The Boston Pops Orchestra, The Chesterfield Supper Club, Circus Days, Columbia Presents Corwin, Eleanor Roosevelt, Grand Central Station, The Henry Morgan Show, Home Is What You Make It, Kay Kyser's Kollege of Musical Knowledge, Love Notes, The Magic Key, Meet the Press, Mr. District Attorney, Mr. Keen Tracer of Lost Persons,*

Name the Place, The NBC Symphony Orchestra, Pot o' Gold, Salute to Youth, The Sealtest Sunday Night Party, Service with a Smile, Sleep No More, True Story, Twenty Thousand Years in Sing Sing, Vacation Serenade, Vox Pop, Walter Winchell's Journal, What Would You Have Done?, Your Hit Parade and *Yvette Sings*. In his first 11 years at NBC, Grauer appeared on 70 commercial series. In 1952 he hosted the short-lived daily series *It's a Problem* on NBC-TV.

Born at Staten Island, New York, on June 2, 1908, young Grauer became a child actor in motion pictures and on the stage. Following graduation from City College of New York, he broke into radio and was soon covering some ambitious ventures, the first United Nations conference from San Francisco, horse racing from Aqueduct, New Year's Eve at Times Square, the maiden flight of the blimp *Akron* and the presidential inaugurations.

Grauer kept ties with Hollywood by narrating films, perhaps his best known being 1951's *Kon-Tiki*. Retiring from Radio City in 1974, he continued to take commercial, infrequent TV and Voice of America assignments. He died May 31, 1977, in New York City only two days shy of his 69th birthday.

The remaining *Information Please* announcer, Jay Jackson, was born at Stockdale, Ohio, and educated at two universities in the Buckeye State — Miami and Ohio State. He was announcer for *The Beatrice Kay Show* on radio and master of ceremonies for *Twenty Questions* on both radio and television. His other TV credits include being the quizmaster for daytime and primetime versions of *Tic Tac Dough*, while announcing *Father Knows Best, Masquerade Party* and *The Perry Como Show*.

NBC staff pianist Joseph Kahn provided what music there was during *Information*'s lengthy run. Born in New York City on June 7, 1903, young Kahn gained experience playing alongside his father, a violinist, in silent movies. Later he accompanied concert, opera and pop vocalists while working on 30 radio programs weekly. They included *The Atwater Kent Hour*, where he met his future bride. From 1928 to 1954 Kahn directed both rhythm and serious music ensembles at NBC. One such group appearing on *Vest Pocket Varieties* was known as Joe Kahn and His Kilocycle Kids. He played under Arturo Toscanini on the *NBC Symphony Orchestra* broadcasts and was a regular on *Symphony of the Air*. Ten times weekly he was keyboard artist for *The Story of Mary Marlin* that was aired on dual networks. *The Voice of Firestone* (1928–29) and *Cameos of Music* (1947–50) were among the prominent series that highlighted Kahn's keyboard artistry.

With all of the principals of *Information Please* examined save one, it would be unthinkable to sidestep producer Dan Golenpaul. The show, of course, was a natural expression and extension of the thesis of its creative genius. His unmitigated influence would never abate from the beginning to the finish almost 14 years later. Golenpaul presents a gripping case study, if nothing more than in how *not* to produce a radio program.

While some powers are unable or unwilling to bend their virtual autocratic methods in conducting affairs early in life, many mellow as they age. Not Golenpaul. His techniques crystallized as the years rolled by. Over time he became, in fact, more determined to maintain absolute authority over every consequential decision that affected *his* show. His insistence on controlling each aspect of every broadcast, even the commercials, would alienate a number of sponsors in the process. It would ultimately be the show's downfall, in fact. But it took a long time to get there. Between point A and point B, legions of fans were treated to years of listening pleasure, totally oblivious to what was transpiring in the wings.

Classified as "arrogant" and "aloof" by his biographers, the *real* Golenpaul may surface through a few illustrations. He was approached on one occasion by the editor of *Radio Life* magazine, who requested an interview. In no uncertain terms he told her he wasn't impressed by her periodical nor by her 60,000 readers, and she could put a feature together any way she chose, without his help.

When the American Tobacco Company purchased *Information Please* on behalf of its Lucky Strike cigarette brand in November 1940, an ongoing feud erupted between Golenpaul and the firm's CEO, George Washington Hill. Golenpaul received a list of names from Hill who weren't to be invited to appear on the show. No less a prestigious publication than *The Saturday Evening Post* noted that the producer was "extremely jealous of his prerogative in choosing guests ... there would be no interference from his sponsor, the network, or anybody else." Golenpaul quickly informed the sponsor that there was no way he would abide by such restrictions. (A cigar smoker, Golenpaul was frequently overheard muttering: "Every brand of cigarette is as bad as every other brand."[34])

From the standoff that developed between those two, the situation escalated. In November 1942 Luckies launched an advertising campaign signifying a major change in packaging. Women were smoking more than ever before, company research indicated. Yet the distaff side preferred the white wrapper of Chesterfields from archrival manufacturer Liggett & Myers Tobacco Company instead of Luckies' dark green pack. The new campaign suggested that green was being replaced by white due to a tint scarcity, disguising the marketing issue as a humanitarian act. The ad agency contrived the theme "Lucky Strike green has gone to war." That phrase

became perpetual, bellowed by announcers between questions and any time dead air occurred, totally neglectful of established commercial slots.

Golenpaul went into orbit. "You're lousing up my program and I won't stand for it," he told Hill. The latter pointed out that *he* was paying the bills, it was *his* show and Golenpaul could stew all he liked but he couldn't change a thing. Golenpaul finally won the battle, nevertheless, filing a lawsuit to force the issue, while the journalists had a field day. The petition was dismissed at the hall of justice, but Golenpaul won an enormous triumph in the court of public opinion. American Tobacco Company was perceived as surly and stingy, while Golenpaul was accepted as battling for honesty and excellence. Undoubtedly, the negative tarnish persuaded Hill just three months later to release Golenpaul from his contract with the tobacco conglomerate.

A more somber loss to the show occurred that year (1943) when Oscar Levant departed. Levant biographers Sam Kashner and Nancy Schoenberger described what happened:

> There was trouble in Paradise. To begin with, Dan Golenpaul's suzerainty over *Information, Please!* and his intellectual pretensions were designed to antagonize Levant, who could barely conceal his contempt for the producer. Levant was getting tired of the numerous war bond tours they were booked on. He never did like to be away from his favorite haunts for long, and now he hated to be separated from his wife and daughters....
>
> It had become a custom during the World Series to have "Lefty" Gomez, a pitcher for the New York Yankees and one of the wittiest fellows in baseball, appear as a guest on *Information, Please!....*
>
> After one such appearance, Gomez presented Oscar with a baseball autographed by all the New York Yankees. As he handed

the treasure over to Levant, Golenpaul snatched the ball away. "You don't want this," the producer said.

Angered, Oscar grabbed it back and then hurled it, full force, at Golenpaul, hitting the producer squarely on the chest.

John Kieran and the others quickly stopped a fight breaking out between the two men. But Golenpaul was determined to strike the last blow. He went to the new agency that handled the program, which was now under the sponsorship of the H.J. Heinz Company, and told them Levant had to go.[35]

No one could recall whether Levant quit the series or if Golenpaul found a way to fire him. In any event, it was Levant's dream come true, for he had long tired of the show's rituals. By 1946, however, as the program experienced sagging ratings, he was invited back. Levant returned for an additional year.

Information Please sponsors and networks frequently altered. Golenpaul responded to these perpetual shifts by increasing the rates for his panel and staff.

When Mobil Oil canceled its sponsorship at the end of the 1945–46 season, the Campbell Soup Company was waiting in the wings to underwrite it. At that juncture, NBC decided to yank the series from the web's schedule. Unwilling to carry it on another network, Campbell bowed out. Golenpaul then signed a contract with CBS to carry the series; there he would engage in still more conflicts.

He sometimes invited guests who were anathema in radio's executive suites. Georgia Governor Ellis Arnall and Harold Ickes, for instance, a pair of FDR New Dealers, prompted strong verbal protests. CBS President William S. Paley was indignant over the matter, threatening to cut Golenpaul's show off the air. He countered that he would fight Paley in the press if he dared censor the show. By then Golenpaul was widely perceived as an agitator, and the days of his show were numbered. Previous sponsor

Heinz had been particularly displeased by shenanigans such as these, and the opinions and actions of subsequent sponsor Mobil Oil were even more conservative and inflexible.

Golenpaul clashed with the Parker Pen Company, sponsor in 1946–47, for implanting mentions of its products in questions that the panel was asked. When the show lost Parker at the end of the season, it forfeited its sponsor exclusivity. From that point on the series was jointly underwritten by participating advertisers, similar to a plan other radio programming was starting to follow. Golenpaul expressed strong displeasure of the concept, and again went to court. He smacked his new network, MBS, with a $500,000 suit that time. That act would finally ring down the curtain on the continuity of broadcasts, although there would be a brief reprise three years later, plus a summertime fling on TV.

Despite this, Dunning maintains that "Golenpaul must be forgiven every alleged personal shortcoming, his genius and judgment where *Information Please* was concerned is amply demonstrated."[36] Golenpaul's death came at the age of 73 on February 13, 1974.

The show eventually appeared on all four networks. Initially in 1938 it was on NBC Blue (ABC). At the peak of its popularity in 1940, it shifted to the more prestigious NBC. When NBC canceled in 1946 the program transferred to CBS. A year later it moved to MBS and remained there through the end of the run.

Canada Dry, the first sponsor to underwrite *Information Please*, basked in the show's widespread press coverage (which, some have speculated, could have resulted in part by having acquired so many journalists on the panel). It also benefited from the show's high ratings. In 1939, with sales of the firm's ginger ale products up 20 percent, the sponsor was satisfied that it was receiving a bargain for the $10,000 it was spending on weekly production costs. When sponsorship shifted to Mobil Oil in 1945, production costs had risen only $1,000 per week, an implausible bargain when one considers that 12 million fans were tuning in every week.

After the show ended its radio run, Golenpaul unsuccessfully tried to carry it to television. It ran from June 29 to September 21, 1952, as a summer replacement on CBS-TV. Attempting to play to the newly acquired visual audience, he added accessories of various kinds, plus a bevy of beauties that Fadiman later lamented "only made it a standard show." The truth was, Fadiman interpreted, "We weren't any good." At the time, Franklin P. Adams was in the initial throes of Alzheimer's disease, unable to appear beyond the video premier, casting a long shadow over the effort. "The complex dynamics of television had somehow finally stumped radio's experts," one critic surmised.[37]

In another sense, however, *Information Please* did succeed as a video venture. About 50 programs were developed by Pathe and other filmmakers and shown as short subjects in motion picture theaters, delighting patrons. Go figure.

Then there were the incessant spinoffs and copycat series.

There was *Dr. I.Q.* and *Dr. I.Q. Jr.* (the latter a kids' version of the former), in which an intellect fielded questions in rapid succession to contestants drawn at random from the studio audience. The adult series debuted on a national hookup near the close of the 1938–39 radio season, and the adolescent edition was added in the summer of 1941.

Stop Me if You've Heard This One, a comical throwback to *Information Please* in the 1939–40 season, cast Milton Berle as moderator, and Harry Hershfield, Jay C. Flippen and a guest jester as a "board of experts." Berle would introduce a joke proffered by a listener, tell a portion of it and leave it to a panelist to complete the gag. Most of the show's humor — apart from the jokes themselves — wasn't spontaneous but rehearsed in advance. Berle's penchant toward personal insults offended some fans but may have linked him with Oscar Levant, who had no trouble badmouthing nearly everybody.

In the summer of 1940 *The Quiz Kids*, labeled "radio's juvenile version of *Information Please*,"[38] premiered. *Radio Life* observed that the children on it "would make *Information Please* look as elementary as a Kay Kyser musical questionnaire,"[39] referring to some IQs of 200 and more. The feature was created by Louis G. Cowan, who was instrumental in bringing *Stop the Music!* to the airwaves in the late 1940s.

Can You Top This?, meanwhile, another joke-swapping panel marathon, became an instant success upon its debut on New York's WOR in late 1940. Joining NBC in 1942 (and remaining there for all subsequent seasons but two), its quipsters carried on their frivolity through mid–1954.

It Pays to Be Ignorant, on the other hand, proved to be the antithesis of *Information Please* and elevated joke-swaps such as *Can You Top This?* It was simply inane in its approach to comedy. Bowing in the summer of 1942, the series was classified as "radio's lame-brained answer to such intellectual quizzes as *Information Please* and *The Quiz Kids*."[40] Finding a sillier threesome than its "board of experts" — who had difficulty determining what the questions were — would take awhile.

In the early 1940s a British version of *Information Please* emerged over the BBC titled *Any Questions?* It presented a collection of educators, military tacticians, patriots and scientists who offered profuse explanations of the sum and substance, after dealing with the questions. New York's WNEW rebroadcast the series as *Brains Trust*, but it failed to win Manhattan listeners who, perhaps, preferred a more fulfilling competition.

Transatlantic Quiz, with competing panels on two sides of the Atlantic Ocean, aired in 1944–45. The joint effort was connected by shortwave and broadcast on both NBC Blue and the BBC. Listeners supplied the questions, just as they did for *Information Please*.

Finally, by the early 1950s there was *Answer Me This*, a regional quiz offered by New Haven, Connecticut's WNHC-TV. It reportedly was "as close to the old *Information Please* as was possible to get." Each week moderator Tom Romano of the station staff faced panelists from business, education, entertainment and legal professions, offering "warm, civilized television — not spectacular, not 'bigtime,' just real," a Big Apple reviewer hypothesized.[41] Strong questions, supplemented by animated repartee among the panel members, contributed heavily to the assessment.

In addition to the annual editions of the *Information Please Almanac*, initially issued in 1948, Golenpaul wrote a book titled *Information, Please!* This inside account of the radio show was published by Random House in 1940. He also had a hand in developing several *Information Please* quiz books sold for home consumption.

During its halcyon days, the cast and crew of the program took numerous cross-country tours to encourage Americans to buy U.S. war bonds. Many patriotic-minded programs were conducting similar efforts during World War II. *The Quiz Kids*, for example, sold $120 million in bonds by airing its program from cities across the nation.

In December 1942 — on its first time out — *Information Please* gathered over $4 million in a single performance at Boston's Symphony Hall. Tickets ranged between $25 and $50,000 each. At the Cleveland (Ohio) Music Hall a while later, $50 million in war bonds was sold.

Other locales bid for the show at the urging of the U.S. Treasury Department. On such occasions a half-hour warm-up preliminary usually involved local dignitaries. The live panel program followed, with Adams, Fadiman, Kieran and Levant featured, the latter offering at least one piano selection.

On September 27, 1943, *Information Please* raised an astronomical $277.4 million in war bond sales at a single outing attended by 3,270 fans at Newark's Mosque Theatre. Most of those proceeds were underwritten by several nearby commercial ventures. A big draw on that occasion was the addition to the panel of Vice President Henry A. Wallace and Arkansas Congressman James W. Fulbright.

Following the war, *Information Please* continued touring with a two-hour show, performing for U.S. service personnel at sites of former battlefields. Appearing in the American Zone in Germany, the exhibition featured instrumental music by show pianist Joseph Kahn, recitations and vocals by Beatrice Lillie, a vaudeville routine by Reginald Gardiner and the quiz program itself. A half-million GIs heard the show over the Armed Forces Radio Network. Those lucky enough to be in the audience perhaps never forgot it. *Information Please* bonded with homeward-bound audiences, too, members of whom would confront readjustment anxieties in the not-so-distant future. Audience participation programs were thus exercising a postwar role that hadn't yet been amply exploited.

Information Please also holds the distinction of breaking an inflexible rule at NBC. In 1939 the series became the first permitted to air a single broadcast for both East and West Coast audiences. The show's spontaneity would be diluted, proponents said, if it had to be duplicated via two performances, one to each coast. NBC Blue affiliates in the Pacific Standard Time zone were given the option of carrying the show live from New York at 5:30 P.M. local time, or airing a recording of it later. They chose the recorded version; for the first time, listeners were treated to the message: "This show has been transcribed from an earlier network presentation for release at this more convenient time."

Time magazine inquired if the aberration wouldn't set an objectionable precedent. NBC immediately pooh-poohed the idea, asking: "Would you rather kiss a girl or her picture?" The camel's nose was already under the tent, however, and — given the benefit of time — a large percentage of live programming would evaporate on every network.

Information Please maintained a distinct introduction. There was no identifying musical theme; instead, it opened to a crowing rooster and a sprightly announcer's admonition to "Wake up, America, it's time to stump the experts!" Within two years the audience topped 10 million, and the program was celebrated by such dissimilar digests as *Hobo News* and *Saturday Review.*

Moderator Clifton Fadiman later remembered that he and his colleagues addressed one another in very formal terms during their broadcasts. "For ten years ... we called each other Mister.... People liked it. They wanted to feel a certain distance between themselves and the panel."[42]

He spoke candidly as he offered insights about the show and the genre of conversational programming. A better understanding of the series and the period in which it was produced may result by considering his arguments:

> I was well aware that my own talents were as nothing compared with those of Frank Adams, Oscar Levant, or John Kieran. But I was also well aware that I was so placed as to be able to do one thing better than they could do it themselves. That one thing was to prod them into being Adams, Levant, and Kieran.

No such show could work on TV now because they all have to be mechanically perfect efficient machines to keep things moving. We never worried about time....

In addition to learning something, listeners met three interesting, entertaining people. I knew their characters so well, so I could tease them or set them against one another in a friendly manner.

The questions we asked were not extremely difficult or recondite. A very bright high school graduate could have answered them. It was the way the panel attacked them — the puns, the jokes, the tiny bits of extra information they'd throw in. In getting the answers, the audience got a lot of humor, too; they were all genuinely funny people. It was not a highbrow show. The questions on *Jeopardy!* are much more difficult than the ones we chose.[43]

Fadiman offered further perspectives on interpersonal communications then and now:

> Conversation was in a general state of decline even before 1938. *Information Please* actually helped to revive it....
>
> In the [subsequent] age of TV talk shows, why converse when you can get other people to do it for you? Moreover, there's an absence of a solid, broad-based frame of reference for literature, history, political science and geography. Even the wit and humor of *Information Please* might confuse....
>
> It's impossible for an audience to respect the mind of a F.P.A. and, at the same time, admire the lack of a mind of a John Belushi.
>
> *Information Please* came across as a family show, attracting listeners of all ages, levels of education and degrees of knowledge. It wouldn't have much appeal today.[44]

Something in excess of 200 *Information Please* shows are on tape, preserved for ages yet to come. The run begins with the show's first airing and continues into the mid–1940s. It's extraordinary merriment, in which history, mirth and the delectable, unforeseen turn of an excerpt makes a lasting impression on anyone who admires intellect.

The series may offer future generations invaluable impressions of the people who strongly believed in it — and that includes the listeners — and those who were committed to broadcasting and safeguarding it. In that respect, it could wind up being a priceless, permanent treasure.

11

Queen for a Day

Premise: Silly misery. This perennial competition — which could neither be considered a game nor a quiz — combined facets of both genres. Requests made by more than 25,000 "applicants" (er, "contestants") across two decades were often as witless as they were clad in human suffering. Here ordinary everyday housewives arrived seemingly with one thing on their minds — to get on the show and carry home trainloads of plunder that most would probably never have a need for — and, if so, definitely not all of it right then. To reach that coveted opportunity (at times nearly a thousand competitors had to be tromped over before getting there), one had to devise the cleverest, most curiously absorbing and irresistibly compelling request for a commodity that the show could fulfill. In reality, a wish list of *one*. Writhing before nationwide microphones and TV cameras, its dogged stalwarts exposed some of their innermost secrets, risking all dignity for their aims. To be sure, it was a shameless display! Yet 5,000 of them got just what they asked for — plus a cache of prizes. Tall, balding, mustachioed Jack Bailey singularly and unpretentiously earned his livelihood here while master of ceremonies

in dual mediums across 20 years. His portrayal of the sympathetic, considerate host endeared him to millions, earning a legacy (indisputably his own "crowning achievement") among audience participation shows. When he inquired ebulliently at the top of each weekday's show, "*Would YOU like to be queen for a day?*," women throughout the land swelled with pride, knowing that some poor pining chick was about to have her fantasies fulfilled. Those tuning in were empathetic, rejoicing that one of their number had crawled beyond the dingy discomforts of a meager, often unappreciated, existence. For one day, at least, she'd be treated to the royal trappings that, just maybe, they all deserved.

Producer-Director: Bud Ernst
Directors: James Morgan, Lee Bolen
Masters of Ceremonies: Dud Williamson, Jack Bailey
Announcers: Bob Spence, Mark Houston, Fort Pearson, Gene Baker
Fashion Commentator: Jeanne Cagney
Writer: Jack Bailey
Sound Effects Technician: Arthur Fulton
Sponsors: The show debuted under

multiple sponsorship but within a year was completely underwritten by Miles Laboratories, Inc., largely for its Alka-Seltzer stomach-distress reliever. The firm also promoted Tabcin heartburn antidote, One-A-Day multiple vitamins, Bactine antiseptic, Miles Nervine anxiety calmative and other remedies. When Miles bowed out on Dec. 1, 1950, the series returned to participating sponsors, continuing under that arrangement for much of the run's remainder. During the early years of the 1950s the bills were jointly paid by P. Lorillard, Inc., makers of Old Gold and Embassy brand cigarettes, and the Kraft Foods Co., as a vehicle for its Kraft Dinner and Kraft malted milk commodities.

Ratings: High: 5.0 (1949–50); Low: 1.6 (1955–56); Median: 3.5 (based on 1945 to 1956, inclusive). While the show remained popular with fans, it never attracted the sizable radio audiences that other weekday features drew. We may only conjecture, but had the program aired on CBS or NBC — with their extensive hookups reaching vast numbers of listeners— the figures might have appreciably mounted. By contrast, the series attracted a larger following when it added a weekday television run and the audience could actually view the crowning of the queen before her court.

On the Air: April 30, 1945–1947, MBS, Monday–Friday, 2:30 P.M. ET; 1947–1949, MBS, Monday–Friday, 2 P.M.; 1949–1950, MBS, Monday–Friday, 2:30 P.M.; 1950–June 10, 1957, MBS, Monday–Friday, 11:30 A.M.

*   *   *

There were scores of radio audience participation programs in the 1940s and 1950s featuring three, four, five, six or more masters of ceremonies over protracted runs.

The quiz show genre, in fact, seemed to attract to their helms a mobile clientele. Such programs frequently drew upon the same corps of individuals, invariably male, to spearhead their competitions for a while. Inserting first one, then another, they'd often transfer these noteworthies elsewhere after a brief respite.

But a handful would prove to be exceptions to that norm. Jack Bailey was one. As shows with a competitive premise went, he turned working on *Queen for a Day* into a career. For two decades— including more than a dozen years on radio, and in excess of seven more years on TV after the radio series had ended — he regaled about 5,000 American queens, crowning them on one of the most maudlin broadcast series ever. While Bailey conducted his share of "also ran" contests, his preeminent identity with *Queen* makes it one of the most durable associations of the breed.

An Iowan, Bailey was born at Hampton on September 15, 1907. He grew up to play in a jazz band, to coordinate a tent show and bark for a couple of world's fairs— preliminaries that were to hold him in good stead for what was to become his life's work. An attempted intrusion into radio at San Diego in 1938 didn't go well for him. Not easily discouraged, however, he tried again and broke into the medium as a disc jockey via the Don Lee Network on the West Coast.

In 1939–40 Bailey was paid for voice-overs on Donald Duck cartoons that were then shown in motion picture houses. He provided the voice of Goofy. And on radio he was soon introducing national audiences to such established fare as *Glamour Manor, Silver Theater* and *Duffy's Tavern*. His ability to work a crowd during his pre-radio pursuits helped him derive something new: By 1944 Bailey was presiding over such audio quizzes as *Meet the Missus, Potluck Party* and *Stop That Villain*. Actually, he was then carving out a niche in the industry for which he would be permanently remembered — as a master of ceremonies for audience participation shows.

Appropriately, he would go on to host *County Fair* in 1945 on CBS and preside over the 1949 to 1952 MBS contest *Comedy of Errors*. He became interim host of TV's *Place the Face*, temporarily filling in between Jack Smith and Bill Cullen during the 1953–54 season. And from May 18, 1954, through September 28, 1956, he succeeded creator-host Ralph Edwards as master of ceremonies on a primetime TV revival of Edwards' perennial audience favorite, *Truth or Consequences*.

Bailey died at Santa Monica, California, on February 1, 1980. He was 72.

In spite of his long association with *Queen*, he was the *second* individual to host that venerable series. The first, Dud (Dudley) Williamson, was among its creators. And would you believe the concept for *Queen* was contrived one day over lunch?

In 1945 Williamson was hosting the musical quiz *What's the Name of That Song?* The show had begun two years before on the Don Lee Network. It moved to a nationwide Mutual hookup in 1944. It was to last until its host's untimely death at the age of 45 in Lido Beach, California, in 1948.

Williamson was born in the Klondike region of Alaska, c. 1903, while his dad, a prospector, participated in that state's celebrated gold rush. Growing up in Seattle, the younger Williamson became a vocalist and entered show business on-stage with a local theater chain. At San Francisco, and later in Chicago, he drifted into radio as an announcer. Eventually settling at KOL in Seattle, he became an accomplished radio actor, announcer, director and producer.

The famous power lunch at which *Queen for a Day* was conceived took place after Williamson's *What's the Name of That Song?*—which he also created—caught on among radio's early giveaways. Feted in New York one day by a couple of advertising czars—Robert Raisbeck and Raymond R. Morgan (the latter a brainstormer who in 1931 had helped devise *Chandu, the Ma-*

gician)—the real objective of their repast was to discover another radio vehicle that would allow Williamson to fully apply his interview skills.

On a local remote broadcast a few years before, he had perched himself on a street corner. There he inquired of feminine pedestrians passing by what, at that moment, was the nearest and dearest thing to their hearts. He shared recollections of that experience with his hosts that day. One abstraction led to another, and someone postulated a crazy notion of granting women their most important wishes on the air. The idea seemed plausible enough, yet it had never been tried. Why?

In a little while—on April 30, 1945, initially under multiple sponsorship—the trio's newest weekday matinee feature bowed to the full MBS network under the moniker *Queen for Today*. (Strictly by coincidence, the premiere occurred on the very same day that *Arthur Godfrey Time* debuted on CBS, a legacy that was to continue unabated for 27 years.)

Airing the show from New York, Bob Spence—a Williamson associate on *What's the Name of That Song?*—helped the emcee launch the *Queen* series by interviewing candidates on the air. Nevertheless, in a short while one of the series' major backers—adman Morgan—saw greater potential for their fledgling effort and ordered some changes. He proposed originating the show from the West Coast, then called for an altered title and substituted the jocular Jack Bailey as host. (Morgan's influence was to continue to be felt for years—from 1956 to 1958 the Raymond R. Morgan Company packaged the show for its launch on network television.)

Within eight weeks of the radio debut, Morgan's alterations were instituted. The die was cast for the next two decades; the basic premise and format for the show would remain essentially the same as it then was.

Strikingly, *Queen for a Day* blurred

the hazy line that existed between quiz and game shows. Maxene Fabe, an audience participation series critic, distinguished *Queen* like this: "Not a quiz, and not even close to being a game, nonetheless, this supremely popular show epitomizes the Cinderella fantasy at the core of the best games."[1] On the air the entry deliberately referred to itself as "The Cinderella Show."

Not only granting the wishes of its winners, it also loaded them with merchandise and service gifts that would have mortified a pauper! Simultaneously, it blatantly and interminably enumerated the generosity of the benefactors. Seldom have so many providers and manufacturers been plugged so shamelessly in the history of broadcasting. In a single year, more than three dozen firms supplied it with prize values collectively exceeding a quarter of a million dollars— and did so gratis, unless one counts those as commercials that money couldn't buy.

The bottom line, according to the program's critics, evolved not from making dreams come true, nor from giving away stuff ad nauseum; it was derived, instead, from turning teardrops into addicts who thrived on the foibles of others as the show squeezed out all of the anguish and pathos that could be injected into a half-hour (á la *Strike It Rich*). Some conjectured it was the most insipid tearjerker on radio, packing no less than a "surfeit of human misery."[2] As hard-luck homemakers recounted their tales of woe, tormented contemporaries all over America rejoiced with those who made it out of the abyss of their dismal circumstances, even if they did it only vicariously. (Even the inimitable Fred Allen and his guest one week, comedian Jack Benny, derided the series on Allen's comedy show, acting out a sketch that satirized *Queen*'s hapless victims. When programs of that caliber took such notice, one could be certain that something out of the ordinary was being highlighted on said satirized series.)

Contestants would bare their souls to gain a shot at a few moments of fleeting national exposure on *Queen for a Day*. A wish come true was only the tip of the iceberg, of course; with it came all those stock prizes, plus an Internal Revenue Service investigator clamoring for the taxes on each honoree's winnings. But if a candidate couldn't articulate her simple needs in a tolerable manner to the studio audience, there really wasn't any need to apply anyway; her chances of gaining the crown were perceived as radically diminished.

Furthermore, if a subject stipulated a wish that wasn't merchandise-related, her probability of being picked as a contestant was virtually zilch. Beyond that, some medical or legal needs, for example — while possibly of paramount importance to a potential candidate —carried no sway with the show's producers. Such requests generally offered little gain for manufacturers; therefore, the program acquired nothing by highlighting them. On this show, it appeared, one had to "Be careful what you ask for — you just might *not* get it — because you didn't ask for the proper distress category!"

During *Queen*'s early years in Hollywood, the show originated from several popular venues. Before airtime each day, emcee Bailey would descend from the stage into the studio audience to dialogue with specific ladies. Before he'd return to the stage, he picked out four, five or six contestants (the number varied throughout the run) who had scribbled intriguing aspirations on their note cards. Producer Bud Ernst and announcer Mark Houston assisted him in making the final selections.

On the air, Bailey interviewed each candidate. These women attempted to pry into the hearts of audience members by telling what they wanted, sometimes with all the anguish they could muster.

The Grand Council, a feminine panel that was also plucked from the studio audience, then determined who the finalists

Cries of desperation to the contrary, most contenders for the title of *Queen for a Day* were genuinely smiling, even if simply named a subject in her majesty's court. Gifted emcee Jack Bailey had the ability to elicit candor out of the chaos of their lives, crowning nearly 5,000 who applied. Bailey's ability to lighten even the saddest of tales kept the feature on the air for double decades. (Photofest)

would be. The finalists were put to a vote before the full body, and an applause meter registered the responses. The queen's court was comprised of the also rans, the women not selected as queen.

The selection process was revised after the series advanced to television. The show was attracting larger and larger audiences due to the fact the program had by then become so highly visible. This resulted in bigger pools of applicants desiring to be queen. On a typical morning, as many as 900 women would arrive at the Moulin Rouge studios to complete cards with their fondest wishes on them. (The Moulin Rouge

was a theater-style restaurant located at 6230 Sunset Boulevard near Vine Street in Hollywood. Across a history dating to the early 20th century, the site was known under a half-dozen different labels. Previously, the show had emanated from the El Capitan and then the Hawaii theaters.)

A couple of reviews of those 900 cards by five program staffers netted 400 serious prospects. That number was soon reduced to 21, from whom Bailey picked eight. The total was ultimately narrowed to five for the day's show.

Neither appearance nor age were vital factors in determining the eventual candidates. Personality counted significantly. But the requests themselves made the real difference in a contestant's getting on the show. Celebrating *Queen*'s 15th anniversary on the air, Bailey observed: "It's not so much the wish as the why of the wish. Many women put on their cards that they'd like an ironer to make their work lighter. Who wouldn't! But the woman who wants an ironer so she can take in ironing to help the family finances, that's a different story."[3]

The fantasies of potential candidates ran from the ridiculous to the sublime, and the common to the bizarre. The ladies wanted plastic surgery, false teeth, screen tests and a chance to meet revered dignitaries. Sometimes the zanier a request sounded, the more likely the espouser might land on the show. Some aspirations touched the heartstrings of staff and listener alike. A sampling of a dozen cravings follow, all of them expressed on the show, some of which were translated into reality.

- There was the woman whose brother hadn't been heard from in seven years, whom she hoped could be located through the resources of a capable detective agency.
- One lady, then at a hefty 200 pounds-plus, wanted some professional help in trying to reduce.
- There was the lady who hoped to leave her footprints in fresh cement poured for the sidewalk in front of Grumman's Chinese Theater in Hollywood.
- Another requested a tire for her husband's car so he could travel to and from work; a damaged wheel was currently replaced by a "loaner" from his uncle.
- One family had moved from Detroit to L.A. to gain work; finding nothing, the wife wanted a one-way ticket for her spouse to Detroit, presuming that when he reconnected there he could earn enough income to send for the family.
- There was the minister's wife who gave the cleric's topcoat to charity, figuring she would work and earn enough to replace it

before winter; but she became ill, couldn't work, winter arrived and he had no topcoat.

- One woman who had just moved from Fort Worth to L.A. wanted to locate her misplaced cat in El Paso; it had vanished from Railway Express there as the carrier attempted to transfer the feline from one train to another.
- An enterprising individual hoped to switch places with Jack Bailey — and have him crowned queen!
- Another begged Bailey's services as a manicurist for a day.
- One more requested that a tattoo she acquired during her years in a German prison camp be removed.
- Then there was the woman who wanted a hearing aid for her elderly babysitter, a lady with no other means of gainful employment.
- Yet another contestant, a mother of nine, sought to replace a clothes washer that quit after falling on and disabling her spouse; he also was awaiting heart surgery.

In addition to having their wishes granted — the reason for their being on the show in the first place — the winners were destined to carry away all those tons of loot. Gifts presented to the honoree on the broadcast of May 23, 1952, were typical of that era, and read like this:

A Gray Line limousine to whisk milady and her companion to that day's appointments, including: lunch, supper and a midnight snack at three of Los Angeles' most sophisticated dining spots, each including entertainment and dancing, in addition to dining; afternoon stops at RKO Radio Picture Studios on the sets of various movies then being filmed; along with a complete beauty analysis and makeover at a notable spa.

The following Monday the queen and her companion were to depart Los Angeles by train for a day-long excursion north to San Francisco. In the city by the bay they would be housed at a distinguished hotel; dine in three of the most popular supper clubs in the area; select several western outfits from a fashion boutique; choose new carpeting from the Looms of Mohawk; and have a Yellow Cab at their disposal.

From San Francisco, the pair would be transported to one of northern California's plushest resorts, offering deluxe cabins, meals and superb entertainment while providing unlimited opportunities for casual relaxation, tennis, hiking, fishing, horseback riding, swimming and boating.

Meanwhile, the queen was draped in a bejeweled tiara and sable-trimmed red-velvet robe, presented with four dozen roses, and had her picture taken for the local press. By the time she arrived at home, she was to be greeted by a barrage of additional gifts, including: a wardrobe consisting of an afternoon sundress, a two-piece evening dress, a dozen pairs of nylons, handbag, wristwatch, all-occasion coat, wool jersey, hat and swimsuit; a two-piece luggage set; dual multipiece cookware sets from different manufacturers, provided with cookbook; an electric kitchen pulverizer; a vacuum cleaner; a year's subscription to *TV Times* magazine; a 17-inch Arvin Senator television set; a gas clothes dryer; and a gas range.[4]

And all the winner requested on that fateful day was a pair of dress shoes for each of her five boys so she could take them to Sunday school! What a windfall! Little wonder why hundreds stood in line every day for the chance to fill out a card and have their dreams (and more) instantly materialize!

So much pillage was distributed on the show, in fact, that for a couple of years the network expanded the TV series to 45 minutes daily — acknowledging that the extra quarter-hour allowed sufficient time to pan all those wares with the camera and describe them in glowing detail, leaving enough minutes, of course, to meet the contestants and select the winners! (*Queen for a Day* producers later affirmed that the wishes granted and the shower of merchandise and services distributed topped $5

million by the time the series ran out of gas in 1964.)

As for the runner-up to the queen, on the same day in which the above prizes were awarded to her majesty, number two received an Arvin table model radio and an Arvin automatic iron bearing a five-year guarantee. Comparatively speaking, her story really wasn't worth much.

On that day, every woman on-stage (including the royal court and the Grand Council) was presented with one of the sponsor's products — a package of a Kraft Dinner and a jar of Kraft chocolate-flavored malted milk. The royal court (the contestants who weren't chosen as queen) also went home with a "treasure chest" of Old Gold cigarettes and a Kraft gift basket brimming with several of the food processor's multiple goods.

On rare occasions — human nature being what it is — a winner was forced to return to the show everything that had been awarded to her. Contestants had to sign release forms stating that if they lied about their dire circumstances and such later came to light, they would forfeit their prizes and receive nothing. While this didn't happen often, it occurred more than once. (A couple of critics assessing this show referred to the candidates as "sometimes desperate" women.[5] On reflection, the appraisal may not have been all that illogical.)

In presenting the wardrobes that inevitably became an accepted portion of the merchandise giveaways, a fashion show was added. It consisted of Hollywood debutantes parading across the stage in designer swimsuits, cocktail dresses and furs, all of which might be awarded on any given day. This segment, with its bevy of beauties, soon became a prominent and popular fixture. By the time *Queen for a Day* went to the tube, film actor Jimmy Cagney's sister, Jeanne, offered a running commentary on the models and their clothes.

Several of these belles acquired instant recognition and near-celebrity status. At least one, Marilyn Burtis, moonlighted on Groucho Marx's *You Bet Your Life.* When something went wrong with the duck apparatus, she'd pop out, holding a card bearing the "secret word." *Queen* also acquired an international flavor when it hired several overseas damsels as models.

An "out-of-town queen" was chosen during part of the show's long run. Someone would spin a roulette wheel labeled with the names of the states. A resident from the selected state, who was selected from the studio audience, then pinpointed someone from her home state. A box of stockings was shipped to the honoree of the day.

Occasionally the show introduced other features that involved the home audience. In the spring of 1949, for example, it pushed a Mother-in-Law Queen Contest. Listeners were invited to submit names of those relatives on penny post cards. At the end of the competition, one card was drawn. The winner was brought to Hollywood for a 10-day vacation that included an appearance on *Queen for a Day,* and given loot that closely approximated the stash the daily queens were hauling away.

Another diversion was to present a couple of "jesters" drawn from the studio audience who were encouraged to tell one joke each. The series seemed to evolve into something for everybody as it sauntered along.

Bailey relied upon his announcers to deliver the sponsors' product messages and to describe the wealth that the winners were taking home. These men would also banter back and forth with Bailey on various and sometimes inane topics. Gene Baker, Mark Houston and Fort Pearson took turns filling this bill during the Hollywood audio era.

Baker's voice was familiar to radio listeners for plying his announcing skills on such series as *Houseboat Hannah, Knicker-bocker Playhouse, Lum and Abner,* and *Midstream.* He was there for some of the Bailey-hosted video version of *Queen for a Day,* too. Baker died at the age of 71 on August 14, 1981.

Houston, the first of the trio to introduce *Queen* from the West Coast, was regrettably disregarded by radio historiographers.

Pearson was a veteran of the medium, however, regularly turning up all over the dial. His announcing credits included *Attorney at Law, Beat the Band, Comedy of Errors, The Guiding Light, The Hoosier Hot Shots, Lonely Women* and *The Quiz Kids.*

While nothing is recorded about *Queen* director James Morgan, a smattering is preserved about Lee Bolen and Bud Ernst.

Bolen directed at least two other radio series, *Behind the Story* and *The Casebook of Gregory Hood.*

And Ernst, who not only directed but produced *Queen* for a while, also produced *Heart's Desire.*

Queen had an auspicious launch each day. From its earliest Hollywood epoch, Bailey would almost scream into the microphone: "*Would YOU like to be queen for a day?*" When the show moved to television, he'd shake a bony finger at the camera and offer the same inquisition.

While on radio, announcers introduced him with this rejoinder that was laden with double entendres: "And here's the man who conducts this daily search for Cinderella, your mutual friend, like candied yam and corn-bread, Jack '*What's Cookin'?*' Bailey!" (*What's Cookin'?* was a volume the show published as a premium for its scores of faithful followers.)

Quietly, *Queen for a Day* made several forays onto the tube before it left an indelible imprint there, becoming a national phenomenon to daytime audiences for a while. Its initial exposure on the small screen occurred at 10 A.M. Pacific Time on

May 21, 1947, via an experimental simulcast on what was then designated W6XA0, a Los Angeles outlet. More simulcasts followed, and the show became a regular offering on that channel through July 1, 1948. By 1950, telecasts apart from the radio series resumed on the same outlet, then named KTSL. The series shifted to Los Angeles' KECA-TV the following year. And in 1952 it was simulcast with the radio show on KHJ-TV in Los Angeles. Starting January 24, 1955, ABC-TV fed the show to its six-station regional Pacific Coast Network.

Queen was finally introduced to a national TV audience by NBC on January 3, 1956, at 4:30 P.M. Eastern Time. The show was still originating from the site of its durable radio digs at the Moulin Rouge in Hollywood. (The MBS series continued airing for another 17 months, through June 10, 1957.) The TV version increased to 45 minutes daily on July 2, 1956, at 4 o'clock. It was reduced to a half-hour at 4 o'clock on September 22, 1958. The program shifted to 2 o'clock on March 30, 1959, completing its NBC-TV run on September 2, 1960.

That summer a dispute erupted between NBC and ABC when ABC daytime program chief Jerry Chester revealed that his web was acquiring *Queen for a Day*—written and verbal commitments to the contrary between NBC and the show notwithstanding. An out-of-court settlement allowed the series to debut on ABC-TV September 5, 1960, at 12:30 P.M. It was moved to 3 o'clock on November 14 of that year and settled in until December 30, 1963. Then it shifted to 3:30 P.M. Its final network telecast was on October 2, 1964.

While Jack Bailey continued at the helm of *Queen for a Day* throughout the TV run, during his occasional absences a number of Hollywood notables supplanted him, including Ben Alexander, Dennis Day, Don DeFore, Steve Dunne, Adolphe Menjou, Walter O'Keefe and Jack Smith.

Upon the show's premiere on national television, *New York Times* TV critic Jack Gould primed his readers with this provocation: "What hath Sarnoff wrought?" (Robert Sarnoff was president of NBC's parent company, the Radio Corporation of America.) Sarnoff said not a word in answer to Gould's invective. But years later, *Queen* television producer Howard Blake suggested: "Queen was vulgar and sleazy and filled with bathos and bad taste. That was why it was so successful; it was exactly what the general public wanted."[6] His comments were a throwback to earlier cries from many who saw it as little more than a tear-jerking tale of woe — or, perhaps, *five* tales of woe.

Dick Curtis was master of ceremonies for a Metromedia Producers revival of *Queen for a Day* that originated from the Hollywood Video Center a few years later. Debuting in syndication on September 8, 1969, the series featured Nancy Myers replacing Jeanne Cagney as fashion commentator, with Carl King as announcer. An electronic voting machine tabulated the studio audience's votes in determining the queens. It made little difference, however; viewer tastes and preferences had long since banished revival attempts to the Valhalla of ex-series, and few series were being recalled for permanent residency. On September 18, 1970, *Queen* left the air, apparently never to return.

Writer Gerald Nachman suggested that "people listened to the show the way motorists gape at five-car pileups."[7] Bailey, the same author noted, "had a way of smiling through tears and of jollying sobbing contestants out of their miseries with a chin-up joke before signing off with his jubilant cry, '*I'd like to make EV-ery woman queen for EV-ery day!*'"[8]

Maybe that's why the fans put up with the perceived wretchedness that he delivered for so long.

12

Stop the Music!

Premise: Hard on the heels of *Break the Bank*, this series arrived with the promise of continuing its predecessor's infectious super jackpot mentality and legacy while substituting melodies for verbal queries. The show had "hit" written all over it even before it aired the first time, but its incredible overnight success utterly astonished its creators, producers and the industry (most definitely including host network ABC, then dying for a ratings victory in the show's timeslot). As Americans were swept up in the excitement generated by the prospect of big gain for no pain, millions sat by their radios waiting for their telephones to ring. Many added telephones to their dwellings based solely on the prospect of such calls. Even though the odds were 25 million to one that a given listener *wouldn't* be called by the show, it made little difference. The frenzy continued unabated for nearly two years. Believing, at last, that they might have been victimized by a hoax — or as television siphoned many of them away — and due to the fact that, by then, the giveaway madness could be found on so many other shows, fans turned en masse upon the series that had held such promise of good fortune. Re-

turning to their old comedy and dramatic darlings, they gave *Stop the Music!* short shrift, convinced that their quests for material advantage could be satisfied elsewhere. The series quickly tumbled to the ratings cellar, never again to charm the multitudes nor receive the plaudits it had become accustomed to. At its start, it had knocked off one of radio's most durable comedians, Fred Allen, its most visible casualty. In the end, it met a similar fate, turned on by a flightiness that has long characterized the primary beneficiaries of broadcasting.

Creator: Harry Salter, assisted by Mark Warnow

Producer: Louis G. Cowan

Director: Mark Goodson

Masters of Ceremonies: Bert Parks, Bill Cullen, Happy Felton

Announcers: Don Hancock, Douglas Browning, Hal Simms

Orchestra: Harry Salter, Ray Bloch

Vocalists: Kay Armen, Dick Brown, Jill Corey, Jack Haskell

Theme Song: An original composition

Sponsors: An untried formula was applied from the series' start, selling commercial time in quarter-hour segments. For three years the show was underwritten by participating sponsors, among them Speidel watches and jewelry, Old Gold cigarettes, Anacin pain reliever, Smith Brothers cough drops and others. In its fourth year on the air, Old Gold's parent firm, P. Lorillard, Inc., bought the whole show. When the series returned in 1954 for an abbreviated fifth season, in essence it reappeared on a sustained basis.

Ratings: High: 20.0 (1948–49); Low: 7.6 (1951–52); Median: 11.7 (Figures are unrecorded for the 1954–55 season.)

On the Air: March 21, 1948–Aug. 10, 1952, ABC, Sunday, 8 P.M. ET; Aug. 17, 1954–Feb. 15, 1955, CBS, Tuesday, 8 P.M. (originally 60 minutes but extended to 75 minutes in its final weeks on the air)

*   *   *

Stop the music! Play the game!
We hum the music, you name the same
You can win yourself a bundle of hay …
By naming the tune that we're gonna play.…
Stop the music! Leave that dial
On Stop the Music! *and stay awhile*
We've got fun for everyone and money, too …
Oh Stop the music! It's all to you!
                    — Lyrics to opening chorus

Like the trailblazer series *Pot o' Gold*, which debuted on radio in September 1939, *Stop the Music!* united the same two marvels of the electronic communications age that both embraced — radio and the telephone. Its supposition involved randomly calling Americans from the stage of a New York City studio (with a live audience) and asking them for the name of the melody currently being played on the show. With the desired response, the call's recipient earned a cash or merchandise prize while qualifying for a much tougher subsequent "Mystery Melody." The contents of its jackpot — previously unrivaled in radio's

history — could stagger the imagination of many commoners, persuading legions to break with their habitual listening patterns to tune in to *Music* each week. The fact that the show claimed its stars were "*you, the people of America*" bode well for it, too.

Stop the Music! is well remembered by radio aficionados for sundry reasons. Radio historiographers Tom DeLong and John Dunning, each with multiple radio volumes to their credit, candidly point their readers toward two concepts.

DeLong submits that — certainly in the postwar era — *Music* "created more national excitement than any other game or contest in the country."[1]

Pretty heady stuff.

Dunning advocates that *Music* is primarily remembered as "the show that ended Fred Allen's radio career."[2] (To the uninitiated, comic Fred Allen was an unchallenged entity in the 1930s and 1940s. His Sunday night series dominated the airwaves during its time period. He was finally knocked off the air by the aura encircling this game show.)

For a fair understanding of *Music*, it will probably serve well to explore why these two recollections eclipse others with many who remember the series best. Let's begin with the first and explore the show in depth before turning our focus to the role all of this played in the undoing of Fred Allen.

To begin with, by examining the ratings we can confirm the immense — and immediate — popularity of this show at once. The media hype that prepared radio listeners well before the show went on the air did a good job of whipping them into shape, creating a stir not generally evidenced prior to that date. Beyond that — from the very first broadcast, and essentially overnight — *Stop the Music!* was an unmistakable hit. On the very first outing its jackpot included a $1,000 U.S. savings bond, a 38-day steamship cruise, a diamond ring, a Kabe spinet piano and a Kaiser automobile. War and postwar years of doing without by 1948 had brought Americans to justify: "After half a dozen years of rationing and empty shelves, people just hearing the prizes mentioned gained a certain sense of, 'Well, it's great to be able to have these things again.'"[3]

It should not have come as a total shock, then, that the Hooperatings—the measuring device most wholly favored in that era—touted *Music* as an overnight success. The network carrying it, ABC, confidently anticipated a 4 or 5 Hooperating, twice the aggregate the web had previously attained in that time period with symphony orchestras. To its utter amazement, however, the instant numbers reflected a fivefold increase, ex-

Even though the odds were 25 million to one that a given listener *wouldn't* be telephoned by host Bert Parks on *Stop the Music!*, it made little difference to millions of fans caught in its web. The frenzy continued unabated for nearly two years. Vocalists included Kay Armen and Dick Brown. The show is recalled for putting an end to Fred Allen's comedy farce that had aired nearly two decades. (Photofest)

ceeding 12. By its third week on the air, the show was identified by fan magazine *Radio Life* as "the most talked-about participation show since Ralph Edwards thought up Miss Hush for *Truth or Consequences*." Within eight weeks, *Music* totally swamped all of its competition on the rival networks, surpassing a Hooperating of 20 in a short while. The show vaulted into the top 10 and remained there, ascending the ladder

to second place in the weekly ratings on at least one occasion. A leading journal of the entertainment industry argued that *Music*'s rise might be "the most spectacular climb in rating history."[4]

In the summer of 1948 appeals for tickets to join the show's audience became so great that the program was moved to the capacious Capitol Theatre on Broadway. Thousands had an opportunity to compete there for prizes over a multiple-week run, which included a $5,000 jackpot. In between *Music*'s exhibitions, the new MGM film *On an Island with You*, starring pool princess Esther Williams, was screened. This gave patrons an opportunity to recover from the intense exhilaration they encountered during the *Stop the Music!* exhibitions.

Certainly none of this was anything to be sneered at. The show secured levels of respect for its parent network that the web had been doggedly seeking for years while languishing in the basement at the bottom of the ratings heap. Many of ABC's earlier efforts had ended as dismal failures. But here came *Music* like a coup d'etat. With it, a wake-up call sounded to others in broadcasting. Those networks had little choice but to acknowledge ABC's good fortune and adjust their programming accordingly, especially when numbers alone were weighed. For a change, ABC was doing something very right. That network would bask in the limelight for nearly two years, until its popularity — indubitably tied to a dubious public — would begin to erode.

Music's overnight success appeared to hinge on at least three factors: (a) a penetrating anxiety (or suspense) that resulted from high levels of listener anticipation; (b) a natural penchant among many people to favor an underdog; and (c) a pervasive optimism that perhaps (just perhaps) the next telephone call dialed from the studio might be to the listener's own domicile.

ABC signed the show for an unprecedented full hour. Then it sold commercial time to a diverse cluster of advertisers. It also scheduled the series in one of the most unrelenting timeslots of the broadcast week — Sunday evenings between 8 and 9 o'clock. (*Variety* touted it under an all-caps banner headline that pointed to its fiercest competition: WHO'S AFRAID OF FRED ALLEN?) The resulting hysteria was confirmation enough that Tom DeLong was on the right path in assessing that the nation's entertainment fervor had reached a peak with this show. While the phenomenon lasted, it would meet and even transcend nearly everything else then on the air.

How did it all begin?

Rather strangely, as a matter of fact.

Stop the Music! was the property of producer Louis G. Cowan. It was his first eminently successful venture since he brought a series to the air eight years earlier, known as *The Quiz Kids*, that featured juvenile intellects. (Fred Allen referred to the show as "*Information Please* in short pants.") But Cowan did not conceive *Music*. He wasn't even interested in it initially. Having returned from a post at the U.S. Office of War Information, by 1948 he preferred to assist the Henry Wallace presidential campaign, to develop some documentaries and to seek help in creating broadcasting positions for Negroes.

A little earlier, bandleader Harry Salter had become intrigued with a West Coast–originated musical quiz that had been on the air since 1943 called *What's the Name of That Song?* Contestants attempted to guess the titles of a trio of melodies played in quick succession that netted a top prize of $30 for three correct replies. Now if a telephone could be adapted to increase the pool of players, Salter theorized, the concept could provide all the components needed for a major hit series.

The telephone had already been the catalyst in boosting one quiz show to rapid success. *Pot o' Gold*, with Ben Grauer and later Rush Hughes as hosts, debuted in September 1939. The program offered $1,000 to anyone who was telephoned by the show while it was on the air, merely for answering the phone.

The surge in telephone dependency in the United States in the 1940s is probably worth noting, for it had a profound effect on all similar shows. A demand for new telephone service had risen to record proportions during the Second World War. Home installations were then curbed by military precedence, nonetheless. In the meantime, more and more Americans were becoming accustomed to using existing phones for long distance dialing during the war era, something they had been loathe to do in the epoch leading up to that time.

By the conflict's end, such use had become habitual with many, and showed no visible sign of abating. In 1946 seven billion *more* calls of all types were placed than had been dialed in 1945, a strong indication that demand for telephone service was going to increase in the postwar years. More than four million new telephones were delivered in 1946, raising the number in use beyond 25 million. Within two years nearly every customer who desired a private line had one.

Realizing that most homes were by then equipped with a telephone — which many did not have during the prewar period when *Pot o' Gold* was having its heyday — Harry Salter was to move forward. He initially took his concept for a new show to his friend and fellow bandleader Mark Warnow of *Your Hit Parade*. The pair collaborated, refining Salter's outline, ultimately joining some aspects of Warnow's own show with the giveaway appeal of *Pot o' Gold* and another popular radio musical feature, *Manhattan Merry-Go-Round*.

Salter carried their polished plan to radio producer Mark Goodson. Together they made a demonstration recording, complete with music, telephone calls and sound effects. Then they shopped it to nearly every advertising agency on Madison Avenue. Receiving not a faint glimmer of sunshine, at that point Goodson took the demo tape to fellow producer Louis G. Cowan. Cowan had indicated that he was interested in developing some new ideas to prop up some faltering programming on all the network schedules. This man who had only a short time earlier professed non-interest in new shows played the demo record and within five minutes was exclaiming, "This is a hit show!" as he gushed to his colleagues about it.

"I'll buy it and produce it," Cowan told Goodson, "but only if you do it my way." The two inked a deal that was to be enormously lucrative to Cowan. They also agreed Goodson would direct the show, while Goodson's wife Bluma would procure merchandise prizes to be given away on it.

ABC program supervisor Bud Barry was next to hear the demo recording. For years Barry and his boss, ABC president Robert Kintner, had been searching unsuccessfully for a means of raining on NBC's parade of Sunday night comedy hits. *The Edgar Bergen and Charlie McCarthy Show* on NBC, followed by *The Fred Allen Show*, had dominated the 8 o'clock Eastern Time hour for what seemed like forever. And over at CBS, the dramatic mysteries *Sam Spade* and *The Man Called X* took virtually all of the remaining listeners at that hour who weren't die-hard comedy fans. When ABC attempted to book Rudy Vallee as master of ceremonies for a Sunday evening variety series, the chain was thwarted once again when Vallee chose to act in films instead. Left with an hour of classical chamber music featuring staff and guest symphonies, the third-ranked ABC had all but given up the fray.

Enter Mark Goodson, demo in hand.

Barry fathomed that a quiz show offering lots of music could employ the large aggregate of house musicians, at the very least. To gain even more momentum against the other networks, he would program *Stop the Music!* for a full hour while offering an initial 13-week minimum guarantee, whether the show was sponsored or not. ABC figured that listeners everywhere would be acutely dazzled by the notion of being called by a radio program, even when only the master of ceremonies' side of the dialogue was discernible. That, linked with the possibility of winning a colossal jackpot, would be the ultimate weapon, the network surmised.

At the beginning of 1948 Goodson launched a salvo of promotional puffery that was carefully orchestrated to lure ABC affiliates and potential sponsors onto the *Stop the Music!* bandwagon. Tested before a crowd of typical listeners during a sneak preview performance that was aired over Syracuse, New York's WAGE, *Music* received solid affirmation.

Casting for the show proceeded simultaneously. Salter selected 23 ABC staff musicians for the orchestra while lining up auditions for a vocal duo, one male and one female. An obscure Dick Brown adroitly won the male trial. But the search for a feminine voice that was capable of handling the semi-classics, pops, blues and swing proved more formidable.

Patti Page was one who tested. She was turned down. In the end, Kay Armen was selected, a versatile songstress who had already appeared on varied ABC programs for nearly five years. The Chicago native was selling tickets to movies and working sporadic stints as a dance hall crooner when WSM, Nashville, home of the *Grand Ole Opry*, added her to its personality roster in 1943. Working a dozen programs weekly, Armen sang pop, spirituals and traditional tunes. The station originated a Saturday evening series carried by NBC that featured her as soloist, backed by Beasley Smith's orchestra, a big break for Armen. By January 1944 she was hired away at $75 weekly for a potpourri of singing assignments on ABC in New York. She often appeared on *Philco Hall of Fame* with the web's musical director, Paul Whiteman. Later, Armen was a regular on the Pet Milk and Bob Crosby radio shows. In the 1956–57 season

she joined the NBC-TV musical variety series *Washington Square* on Sunday afternoons.

Armen had been overlooked by *Stop the Music!* under her own name. She attended her audition under the assumed name of "Gwen Hamilton." Her versatility and quick-study skill handily won the day for her, too.

Producer Lou Cowan himself would make the final choice of a master of ceremonies for *Music*, although director Mark Goodson put a bug in his ear — the name of Bert Parks. Parks had been garnering accolades for two years from his extremely successful Friday night ABC quiz series *Break the Bank*. By 1948 the effervescent showman stood at least evenly with — and perhaps ahead of — radio's leading half-dozen game show hosts. His unrelenting vigor allowed him to contribute an upbeat performance every time out on the numerous broadcasts over which he presided. Audiences viewed him as irrepressible and inexhaustible.

"There was something in his voice we liked," said Cowan, as he announced his selection of Parks as emcee. "We thought of him as a version of Li'l Abner because he was young, virile and good-looking. Bert had a warm personality, combined with infinite enthusiasm and solid singing ability."[5] This consummate performer is profiled in-depth in the *Break the Bank* chapter of this volume.

The announcer for *Music*'s initial series, which ran from March 21, 1948, to August 10, 1952, was veteran audio interlocutor Don Hancock. The Anderson, Indiana, native's credits included *Front Page Farrell, The Golden Theater, Grand Central Station, The Horn and Hardart Children's Hour, Just Entertainment, Life Can Be Beautiful, Major Bowes' Original Amateur Hour, Music Box Hour* and *The Romance of Helen Trent*. He would go on to be product spokesman and announcer in the 1950s for the early TV serial *Love of Life* at a time when most televised commercials were performed live each day. Hancock worked as a CBS staff announcer until his retirement in the late 1970s.

In theory and practice, *Stop the Music!*'s procedures were quite simple. Drawing from a huge bank of telephone directories from all over the nation, backstage ABC operators would telephone listeners at random while a musical selection was performed live on-stage. Sometimes the orchestra conducted by Salter played alone; often, either Armen or Brown — or both — vocalized along with the melody. (They would hum the words of a song's title to avoid giving it away.) Typical tunes of the day included "At a Georgia Camp Meeting," "The Hucklebuck," "I'm Looking Over a Four-Leaf Clover," "Isle of Capri," "Golden Earrings," "Ruby," "Someone to Watch Over Me," "Steam Heat" and more. Seldom did any of them get to finish a number, however, which was as frustrating to the audience as it was to themselves. When the studio operators connected with a listener at home, a loud telephone-sounding bell would ring while emcee Parks shouted: "Stop the music!" The melody ground to a halt as a frenetic suspense charged the air. From the telephone operator, Parks requested the name and location of the person on the line, then asked the listener to identify the tune just played or sung.

Interestingly, more times than could hardly be imagined, the listener was often one song behind, naming the tune that had just been featured prior to the one he or she was asked to identify. The listener might have been discussing that particular title with someone else, and possibly had even written it down, then became distracted when the call from ABC arrived. At such times, the emcee punctuated the situation with some good-natured ribbing while the studio audience howled and

jeered. What those in the studio failed to acknowledge, of course, was that offering the right title on cue might not have been as simple as it appeared, and especially if they were at the other end of the telephone line.

A correct response, meanwhile, earned the listener a $50 U.S. savings bond. If the wrong title or no title was given, someone in the studio audience took a shot at the $50 bond. A correct reply on the initial tune qualified a telephone winner for a much greater opportunity. A $1,000 U.S. savings bond and a two-week all-expense-paid trip to Paris were offered at one point for merely naming the "Mystery Melody," an ongoing tune repeated at each qualifying call until a listener could identify it. If no one got it, the jackpot was enlarged with added cash or merchandise. Its prize value persistently topped $20,000 at a given time. At least once during the show's first year the jackpot surpassed $30,000.

Variety assessed: "Even for a listener without a telephone listing the show seems moderately lively and entertaining. Since the many numbers are necessarily short and are interrupted by the telephone question gimmick, the show is jumpy and the otherwise good music suffers…. The phone call gimmick multiplied the old pot of gold climax 12 times."[6]

The man who had started all of this, Harry Salter, found himself selecting and rehearsing at least 15 songs per week with the orchestra. "None of us expected the immediate overwhelming response the program got," he admitted in 1950. "In the beginning I chose the 'Mystery Melody' by simply rifling through my files. It wasn't long before I had to hire three musicologists to assist me."[7]

While the qualifying tunes were usually current hits or standards familiar to just about everyone, the "Mystery Melody" was predictably more difficult. Although listeners might have heard these ditties many times in the past, most couldn't venture a guess as to their identities. The oftheard initial number, for example, "The Vision of Salome," had accompanied many belly dancers. But for weeks no one could name it. Producer Cowan —confident that the show must provide a jackpot winner quite early to remain a huge draw — leaked the title to newspaperman Walter Winchell. Winchell, whose own popular radio series immediately followed *Stop the Music!* on ABC Sunday nights, reported the song's title in his widely syndicated column. From that point forward, Cowan created winners at least monthly by following a similar pattern. (On one show he was surprised when dual jackpots were won back-to-back. The title of the evening's first "Mystery Melody" had appeared in the press for weeks without a winner. After a listener named it, on a subsequent call the orchestra offered a new tune. Without help, the next listener promptly gave the correct response, dumbfounding almost everyone, including the fans and those connected with the show in official capacities.)

Of the trio of bandleaders associated with *Music* (including creators Harry Salter and Mark Warnow, along with Ray Bloch, who supplanted Salter during the show's 1954–55 reprise), none were born on American soil.

Salter entered the world on September 14, 1898, at Bucharest, Romania. After immigrating to the U.S., in 1927 he took to the airwaves playing violin with B.A. Rolfe. A short while later he conducted a six-piece instrumental ensemble each evening on New York's WEAF, airing live from the Rose Room. He also directed the Atlantic Ensemble for Steinway Hall on the Atlantic Broadcasting Company. On his first major network series (*Log Cabin*), Salter accompanied eminently popular soloist Lanny Ross.

Later he led orchestras for several musical quiz ventures besides *Stop the Music!*—

Hobby Lobby, Melody Puzzles and *NTG and His Girls*. He became musical director of such diverse series as *The Amazing Mr. Smith, Mr. District Attorney, What's My Name?, Your Hit Parade* and *Your Unseen Friend*. Salter subsequently produced *Name That Tune,* a *Stop the Music!* spin-off. He remained ABC's musical director well into the 1970s, and died at Mamaroneck, New York, on March 5, 1984.

Warnow, on the other hand, was a native of Monastrischt, Russia, born April 10, 1902. He, too, pursued the violin, becoming staff conductor at CBS in the early 1930s. Warnow alternated between instrumentalist and surrogate bandleader before commanding Broadway *Music Box Revues* and several Brooklyn grand opera companies. At CBS he assisted in introducing radio audiences to vocalist discoveries Morton Downey, Gertrude Neisen and Kate Smith, and the dramatic talents of actress Helen Hayes. Subbing for Downey's musical director in 1941 when no one else was handy to tackle operatic numbers, Warnow allowed: "If it wasn't for radio I'd probably be a starving fiddle player. You go along and then something hits you and you suddenly become box office."

Among his claims to fame were regular performances on the *Chrysler Airshow, Evening in Paris, We the People* and *Your Hit Parade.* He enjoyed the longest run of any conductor on the latter series (from 1939 to 1947), returning to the show in autumn 1949. He died unexpectedly that October 17 in New York City. His brother, Raymond Scott, succeeded him as musical leader of *Your Hit Parade.*

Alsace-Lorraine, France, was the birthplace of Ray Bloch on August 3, 1902. In the 1920s he became a dance band leader after playing piano with several minor combos. He may be best recalled from the 1950s and 1960s as the orchestra conductor–cumfoil on CBS-TV's *The Jackie Gleason Show.* (Comedian Gleason introduced him to a live Saturday night audience every week as "the flower of the musical world.") Yet Bloch earned many other credits between those two eras.

During a radio network career that began in 1930, he directed the music on *Crime Doctor, Gay Nineties Revue, Hollywood Opera House, Johnny Presents, The Milton Berle Show, Model Minstrels, The Philip Morris Playhouse, Pick and Pat, Quick as a Flash, Sing It Again, Songs for Sale, Take It or Leave It* and *What's My Name?* In the 1950s he was musical conductor for Ed Sullivan on that star's early TV series, too. Bloch was a member of the initial board of governors of the Academy of Radio and Television Arts and Sciences. His death in Miami, Florida, occurred on March 29, 1982.

Mark Goodson, who has been variously referred to as producer, co-producer and director of *Stop the Music!*, is—as of this writing—the ultimate game show mogul. Aspiring to become an attorney while pursuing economics at the University of California at Berkeley, by 1938 (at age 23), Goodson first hoped to make a few bucks in radio. When prospects for a legal career faded, he became entrenched in the medium, subsisting as a San Francisco disk jockey. That led him to emcee *Quiz of Two Cities*, a California regional aural effort. A short time later he created his own show, *Pop the Question*. Within three years he was in New York directing several network programs: *Appointment with Life, Portia Faces Life* and dramatic segments of *The Kate Smith Show*, which he also penned. He was announcer for *Battle of the Boroughs*, a local New York series; then he created *Winner Take All*, a blueprint prototype of what turned out to be the remainder of his career.

Goodson linked with William Todman as a salesman for that show. The pair formed a partnership and became to game shows what Frank and Anne Hummert were to radio serials—a major creative production house, the most prolific of their respective genres. Some of the more than 30 games Goodson and Todman collaborated on before Todman's untimely death in 1979 included: *Beat the Clock, Call My Bluff, Card Sharks, Family Feud, Get the Message, Hit the Jackpot, It's News to Me, I've Got a Secret, Judge for Yourself, Match Game, Missing Links, The Name's the Same, Now You See It, Number Please, Password, Play Your Hunch, The Price Is Right, Rate Your Mate, Show-offs, Snap Judgment, Spin to Win, Split Personality, Tattletales, Time's a-Wastin', To Tell the Truth, Treasure Salute, What's Going On?* and *What's My Line?*

Goodson, the busiest and most successful quiz-show producer of all time, defended his occupation, via a 1948 newspaper article, against barbs then being hurled at it: "Most U.S. listeners with their love of sports competition and fascination with games find more drama in contests than in make-believe. But a quiz offers something beyond drama—it permits listeners to 'compete' in the game. While the spectator can only daydream of leaping onto the diamond of Yankee Stadium and saving the day for the home team, quiz contests offer him a chance to join the competition—even though he be thousands of miles from the studio."[8]

Eventually, Goodson would become dismayed with his colleague, producer Lou Cowan, in their joint efforts with *Stop the Music!* We'll deliberate on that momentarily. But let us probe Cowan's offing first.

Louis G. Cowan operated a crystal radio set in the 1920s. From that time forward he was smitten with the notion of sending sound across airwaves. On receiving an unexpected but substantial windfall from a late uncle, he invested in some audio dreams. Years later, Cowan observed: "It seemed to me that if one had any kind of creative talent at all, it might be possible to create something for radio that might become a property."

While still twenty something, he produced a trio of disappointing quizzes: *Musico*, *Play Broadcast* and *Who Said It?* His efforts weren't wasted, however, for that same year (1940) he applied some of the knowledge he gained from those experiences and created the highly successful *Quiz Kids* show. As noted, *Kids* was a pintsized version of the number one game show then on the charts, *Information Please* (which was toppled by upstart *Truth or Consequences* a short time later). *Kids* was later seen on TV, but it never acquired the video draw that it enjoyed on radio.

Cowan would go on to produce other game shows that realized at least modest success, among them early TV's *Down You Go*. The series for which he will always be remembered, however, was the bellwether of an unparalleled tide of quiz programs to follow, leaving a permanent effect on all game series since — *The $64,000 Question*. When that program debuted on June 7, 1955, the complexion of game shows radically changed. The promise offered by this show and some others that copied it (including Cowan's own *The $100,000 Big Surprise* that premiered four months later, and *The $64,000 Challenge* in 1956) deteriorated into the famous quiz show scandals of the late 1950s.

Before anything came to light, however, Cowan was named a CBS vice president, a job he had set his sights on long before. He was soon kicked upstairs to the network presidency, in part at least from the contributions he had made to the web through his own personal ventures. Later, pleading total innocence in the quiz show malaise, he was the sole accused principal in the case who managed to avoid testifying during the legal inquisitions. Denying his involvement, he was still forced to step down in disgrace at CBS and was never employed by the industry again.

His opportunities did not end there, however. Cowan became a professor, teaching for the College of Journalism at Columbia University. He was elected to the boards of directors of Brandeis University and of the national publication *Partisan Review*. He also shared in founding the National Book Awards. On November 16, 1976, in retirement, Cowan and his wife Polly perished in a fire that raced through their penthouse apartment on New York's Park Avenue.

Returning to Mark Goodson, author Maxene Fabe prudently documents that Goodson had not enjoyed his association with *Stop the Music!* Writing in 1979, Fabe allowed:

> Even today, his lip curls at the artificial, now illegal, steps Cowan took to boost his ratings. Each week, to fire up listener interest, the show would plant the answers to that week's mystery tune in Walter Winchell's column. Guest celebrities, seemingly participating spontaneously, were paid fees to appear, their casual chitchat carefully scripted. And during a broadcast, when the telephone calls came pouring in, *Stop the Music* would screen them first, then deliberately stack them in a dramatic order: five, ten incorrect answers first, to build listener suspense before Bert Parks was allowed to shout the correct answer to a white-knuckled, rapt America.[9]

It was also common knowledge — within the business, at least — that *Music* operators routinely spent their Sunday afternoons (the day of the broadcast) dialing potential contestants across the nation in advance. While ABC publicists emphatically denied that such calls were made, one of their number (Richard Osk) claimed in 1985 that this was routine. Those contacted were told to be near their telephones between 8 and 9 o'clock Eastern Time that night, and to anticipate a potential call from Bert Parks.

Was this ethical? Did such warning prime them to listen to their radios and attempt to figure out what songs were being played, giving them an unfair advantage if they were called? What do you think? (Knowing this, comedian Fred Allen alerted millions of listeners to the fact that they were wasting time sitting by their radios expecting a call from Bert Parks. Many poorer Americans had had telephones installed in their homes in hopes of being among the lucky few. But the truth was, as Allen disclosed, most of them would never be called.)

Cowan and his cohorts defended their stance. It saved a whole lot of wasted time while on the air that would have been spent dialing numbers that weren't in working order or at which no one was at home. But did such *lapses* (if that's what they were) make it easier for game show moguls to manipulate established or perceived codes of ethics in order to increase the ratings on their later shows? That is a distinct implication some could have taken from the quiz show scandals. Had any of it been fostered by what could be viewed as a laxity at *Stop the Music!*? We may ponder that, of course, drawing our own particular conclusions.

There was another charge leveled against *Music*, one that raised questions about tradeoffs and kickbacks in regard to merchandise gifts. The swag was doled out to winners after an almost endless laudatory narrative that fawned over each individual prize. Combined, this meant several multiple unpaid commercials on every broadcast. Firms such as VIP Services and Prizes, Incorporated were established to broker the largess, providing it to quiz programs after usurping a generous levy off the top of every "contributed" prize.

Had *Music* and its peers become mere lotteries?

The odds were still 25 million to one that a given listener would be called by the show. The Federal Communications Com-

mission took a deep interest in all of this. It finally concluded that such shows weren't lotteries. All things considered, however, at times it was complex deciding whether radio was in the business of selling or buying time.

Comic Fred Allen was an enigma about whom numerous analytical volumes have been written, some of them during his lifetime and a number following his death at 61 in 1956. A digression to probe his career seems in order because of the colossal impact that *Stop the Music!* had on his professional life.

A vaudevillian who originally hailed from Cambridge, Massachusetts, Allen possessed a witty brilliance that allowed him to host a comedy-variety program, closely followed by millions, for 17 years. At his best he was the cardinal showman, a buffoon who tapped the funnybone of ordinary Americans during the epochs of the Great Depression and the Second World War. Audiences ate from his hand while he parodied virtually everything he found peculiar in the news of the day. His weekly walks in the mid-to-late 1940s down "Allen's Alley," during which he encountered a quartet of farcical residents (Ajax Cassidy, Titus Moody, Mrs. Pansy Nussbaum and Senator Beauregard Claghorn), resulted in some of the brightest and most whimsical connections listeners made with their radios each week.

Some of Allen's renown may be attributed to his unequivocal opinions and blunt outbursts on varied topical issues. If he registered a thought on any subject, the chances were likely that his audience knew what it was. Such fare often crept into the scripting of his program, too—sometimes under a thinly veiled disguise, but more often totally out in the open. His acerbic ad libs separated him from most other comedians whose jabs were more frequently perceived to be offered in jest. At times the undertone of Allen's remarks pointed towards deep-seated, even disturbing thoughts.

Given such a climate, it doesn't take a brain surgeon to discern that Allen could resolutely turn on mainstream citizens' affections with the quiz shows that were sweeping Radioland in the 1940s. In an all-pervasive passion to thwart that momentum, he almost single-handedly launched a largely vocal campaign to annihilate it within the industry. Years after that fixation started, *Stop the Music!*—from the genre that he gave such a Herculean effort to removing—cut Allen down to size and was the ultimate catalyst that banished him from his Sunday night audio stronghold forever.

Respected observers Frank Buxton and Bill Owen, in one of their several texts on the medium, went so far as to allow that, "Radio actually died when *Stop the Music!* got higher ratings than Fred Allen."[10] And humorist Henry Morgan assured everybody that such an aberration drove "the final nail in radio's coffin."[11]

What really brought about the demise of this gifted performer's career? Before pondering that thought, let us review his decade-long agitation with giveaway programs in general. What prompted that?

Allen began satirizing the genre as early as 1939. He soon formulated a devastating, often hilarious critique of giveaway series. Contended Allen biographer Alan Havig: "His dislike of the quiz/giveaway/stunt programs was legendary in the industry."[12]

One of his early targets was the heedless giveaway called *Pot o' Gold*, which debuted on September 26, 1939. While that series lasted only until June 5, 1941, it rebounded for a few final months, from October 2, 1946, to March 26, 1947. Mired in human greed (Dunning's assessment), it offered $1,000 to anyone called by the show while it was on the air.

No musical identification. No ques-

tion. No contest. No need to even listen to the show. One grand for simply answering the phone. No strings attached.

Movie theaters, in the meantime, were emptying out on the nights *Pot o' Gold* aired because their patrons didn't want to miss the prospect of a call. Some owners of these motion picture houses decided to go on the offensive. Individually, they staged ostentatious "bank nights," which offered moviegoers $1,000 if they missed a call from *Pot o' Gold*. (A decade later, *Stop the Music!* and some of its contemporaries would be responsible for reprising the sleazy "bank nights" in some of those theaters. Filmgoers would be indulged with bargain sets of tableware and cheap dishes that were disbursed from movie stages between double bills—the result of a concerted effort by cinema operators to draw people away from their TVs.)

It was too much for Allen; he was incensed. His response was to parody *Pot o' Gold* with an imbecilic skit titled "Tub o' Silver."

What did Allen contemplate in regard to such programming? A few of his comments say it all:

• "Giveaway programs are the buzzards of radio. As buzzards swoop down on carrion, so have giveaway shows descended on the carcass of radio.... Radio started as a medium of entertainment. The giveaway programs have reduced radio to a shoddy gambling device."[13]

• "Contestants are a herd of morons."[14]

• "Many winners are so dumb that they can't find their way out of the building. Months later their bodies are found slumped over their prizes."[15]

• (Advising a youngster who intended to pursue a broadcasting career): "A good way to break into radio would be to shoot a quiz-show MC. A lot of listeners will be grateful to you for killing the MC, and good will is important if you hope to survive in radio."[16]

- "I never thought I'd live to see the day when I'd have to compete with a washing machine. Ice boxes are replacing actors and musicians. The idea seems to be, if you can't entertain people, *give* them something. If that's not a sorry comment on contemporary entertainment, I don't know what is."[17]

- "The millions of listeners who seek entertainment will eventually flee the giveaway programs and radio and turn to television, the theater and leapfrog. Radio City ... will become a *Monte Carlo for morons.*"[18]

- "If I were king for one day, I would make every program a giveaway show; when the studios were filled with the people who encourage these atrocities, I would lock the door. With all the morons of America trapped, the rest of the population could go about its business."[19]

Allen went on the offensive, putting up a $5,000 bounty to anyone who missed a *Stop the Music!* phone call because he was tuned in to *The Fred Allen Show.* He made his offer on October 3, 1948; by November 28 there were no takers and he withdrew it, having consumed its publicity value. The offer, incidentally, had no effect on stemming the tide in the ratings. People sat around their homes on Sunday nights staring at their telephones while waiting for those phones to ring. Despite longshot odds, there was always that chance that they'd be one of those called, something akin to lottery fever in contemporary times.

While Allen depended upon satire to make his case in the past, it failed him then. His comic parody "Cease the Music" on an early outing for new sponsor Ford Motor Company fell on nearly deaf ears. Casting wry comedian Henry Morgan as an ineffective master of ceremonies, the spoof offered listeners prizes that included: a couple of floors of the Empire State Building, a shovel and 20 minutes at Fort Knox, 4,000 yards of used dental floss, a saloon and a bartender, 800 pounds of putty for each family member, the *Queen Mary's* gangplank,

and a dozen miles of railroad track. Unfortunately, people weren't *that* amused.

"Did you folks like the thousand dollar bills you found on your seats when you came in?" Allen caustically petitioned his studio audience before one broadcast. He had clearly lost his sense of humor and gotten mad.

Among all radio fare, Allen's first place ranking, with a Hooperating of 28.7 on February 1, 1948, stumbled from the coveted top 10 to 13th place, with a 16.4 Hooperating on May 7. By season's end, he had plummeted 17.5 points to 38th on the charts, with a Hooperating of 11.2. The show bottomed out at 7.9 in March 1949, its lowest Hooper ever.

Thanks almost singularly to *Stop the Music!*, Fred Allen had tumbled "from the plush pew reserved for Hooper's Top 10 to a camp stool in back of Lum and Abner,"[20] radio critic Harriet Van Horne declared. Coupled with the disappointing ratings, the show's expenses were rapidly escalating. Ford was spending $25,000 weekly in November 1948 (not including air time) to produce the faltering Allen series, while *Stop the Music!*— solidly in the top 10 lineup — maintained production bills that totaled only $12,000 per week. In December 1948 Allen at last ran up the white flag, declaring that he wouldn't be back following the close of the season then in progress. His last show was set for June 26, 1949.

As Gerald Nachman aptly observed: "Allen — suddenly a ghost of radio past — toppled almost instantaneously (with *Stop the Music's* rise), a major victim of the giveaway fad that overtook radio in the late 1940s as a desperate ploy to keep listeners tuned in and deflect their attention from the dreaded tube that had begun creeping into homes like an invasion of one-eyed body-snatchers."[21]

A "general malaise" was epitomized by the fact that a single show could undo "all the work and wit that go to make up the Fred Allen program simply by promising a refrigerator ... and a Persian lamb jacket," one critic proclaimed.[22] Despite that, *Stop the Music!* producer Lou Cowan later admitted: "It was always a matter of considerable regret to me that my show led to diminishing the talent of one of the very great individuals broadcasting ever knew."[23]

Allen inked a contract by which he agreed to appear exclusively in future NBC radio and television features. Since he would never really be at ease nor at his best before the TV cameras—his physical health declining, and his mental state agitated—in many ways the final show of his radio series was his swan song. He met his contractual obligations to NBC from then on, making several appearances on *The Big Show* in the early 1950s. Yet his last major series was, of all things, a quiz program.

In October 1954 Allen signed on as a permanent panelist with CBS-TV's *What's My Line?* Ironically, one of the producers of the earlier adversarial *Stop the Music!* (Mark Goodson) became his employer in TV. By then Allen had come to some terms with his old nemesis. In his last interview, in fact, published in *TV Guide* a month following his death, the comedian defended *Line* as a witty and entertaining game show, not at all like the "numskull" quiz programs he opposed.

Producer Gil Fates recalled that Allen "never really understood how to play the *What's My Line?* game. He never really wanted to or had to. But he understood clearly his function on the program. His baggy-eyed grin, his dry chuckle, and his nasal observations were all we could ask for."[24] (Actually, Allen had made peace with it all even earlier. In the summer of 1953 he emceed a talent evaluation show on NBC-TV for Goodson-Todman called *Judge for Yourself.* Author Maxene Fabe unequivocally dubbed Allen as just plain "terrible" on that series.)

While walking his dog around midnight on March 17, 1956, on New York's West 57th Street, one block from his apartment, Fred Allen dropped dead, the victim of a fatal heart attack. The chair he filled on *What's My Line?* would never be supplied by a permanent panelist again during the program's 11 additional years on the air.

Biographer Alan Havig offered this postscript that assesses Allen's resolve to quell the quiz show insurgents:

> Although he was thoroughly identified with the opposition, ... Fred Allen shared complicity in the rise of the giveaway shows—a fact that he undoubtedly never recognized and would have found difficult to accept. As a pioneer in exploring the uses of amateur performers and average citizens on a network comedy-variety program, Allen helped to invent, and his success sanctioned, the audience-participation device as a source of radio entertainment.... Allen himself helped father the monster he later battled.[25]

There was another NBC powerhouse affected by ABC's *Stop the Music!* which took a different approach to all of this. When Edgar Bergen saw the handwriting on the wall, he wisely announced in December 1948 that *The Edgar Bergen and Charlie McCarthy Show*, on which Bergen played a foil and ventriloquist to a puppet, would take a nine-month sabbatical. In so doing, he departed NBC and—the following autumn—reappeared at his customary 8 o'clock hour on CBS. (Moving the show to CBS was one of the acquisitions CBS executive William Paley made in his famous talent raids on NBC in the late 1940s, netting Jack Benny and several other mainstays for CBS.)

It should be noted that, while Fred Allen found himself virtually alone within the entertainment industry fighting the proliferation of quiz show mania, there were other critics—mainly in the print media—who worked tenaciously to dethrone the king-sized concept. These analysts had a field day with *Stop the Music!*

Music "adopted the press agent's oldest stratagem of strewing coins on the street to attract a crowd"[26] wrote *The New York Times* reviewer. He lamented over the size of the unclaimed jackpot that was steadily increasing while weeks went by without a winner: "Obviously the giveaway trend cannot be stopped now until some master of ceremonies forgets himself and throws in Radio City, too."[27] His opposite at *The New York Daily News* cursed all giveaway programs as "a major calamity,"[28] convinced most took the stance that merchandise was greater than one's own performing ability.

In spite of such zingers, contemporary radio analyst Nachman suggested:

> There was something wholly, if not unholy, American about the quiz show, with its democratic spirit, lucky streak, and rags-to-riches theme: The possibility that any schnook sitting on his stoop in Brooklyn or feeding chickens in Omaha could, with the tinkling of a telephone bell, become a national hero and an overnight tycoon appealed to every red-white-and-blue-blooded Yankee.[29]

And radio quizmaster Bob Hawk defended his profession by exclaiming: "A quiz can't be beat. It can't be touched. It stands by itself. It's a people's program. A good quiz should be called *A Program for the Common People.*"[30]

A year following its debut, *Stop the Music!* surfaced in video form (on May 5, 1949), with millions seeing the prizes they hoped to win while waiting for the phone to ring. Only television set owners were called, so potential contestants were still hearing from the program in advance. With only about eight million homes in the nation equipped with TV by 1949, a listener's chances of being called were materially improved over comparative radio odds.

A trio of appealing vocalists (Jimmy Blaine, Betty Ann Grove and Estelle Loring — succeeded in the 1950s by Marion Morgan, June Valli and Jaye P. Morgan) and a quintet of engaging dancers (Wayne Lamb, Don Little, Marina Palmer, Courtney and Sonja Van Horne) were added on TV. Bert Parks emceed, with the show running on the small screen in three segments, all on ABC: May 1949–April 1952, September 1954–May 1955 and September 1955–June 1956. Guest singers were occasionally featured. Comedy sketches and interviews were interspersed with the musical entertainment for these outings.

Not surprisingly, Fred Allen expressed a thought about video, too: "In the beginning, television drove people out of their homes into saloons [to view it], but now people have sets in their homes and TV is driving people back into the saloons."[31]

Stop the Music! prompted several spin-offs and attempted spin-offs. One of them resulted in *What's My Line?* The game evolved from a concept offered by Bob Bach, an employee of Goodson-Todman Productions. Under the banner *Stop the Camera!*, Bach proposed scattering a few celebrities among a studio audience. An optical take-off of the *Stop the Music!* idea, it required an emcee to telephone someone across the land while a TV camera panned the audience. On recognizing a familiar face in the crowd, the player (*not* the emcee) would shout: "Stop the camera!" It simply didn't work in practice sessions, however.

Bach soon dreamed up another approach — seating several folks with widely diverse occupations on-stage. As the camera panned them, a player at home would be asked to guess their various lines of work. When that notion didn't fly, Mark Goodson stepped in to suggest that one person appear before a quartet of inquisitors who would try to reveal that person's line of work. The rest is history.

There were other spin-offs that could be tied more openly to *Stop the Music!* For one, *Name That Tune* was a direct descendant involving Harry Salter as creator-owner and orchestra conductor. Sprinting a 25-foot route to ring a bell that would make them eligible for a tuneful mystery was a pair of competitive, lissome, sneaker-donned players. Contestants with stage presence who could even entertain a little offered the best exchanges with master of ceremonies Al (Red) Benson. (He was later supplanted by Bill Cullen, George de Witt and Tom Kennedy. A 1970s televised version of the show in syndication, then owned by Ralph Edwards, was retitled *$100,000 Name That Tune*.)

Both children and adults participated on *Tune*. Among the discoveries who turned up, there was Leslie Uggams, then 14, whom Mitch Miller added to his *Sing Along with Mitch* TV series. In 1958 future astronaut and Senator John Glenn was a contestant, too.

Tune vocalist Vicki Mills, only 19 when the series began in the summer of 1953, appeared for a quadrennial, phonetically singing the show's "golden medley" in as many as 30 foreign languages. To spice up the program, in 1956 a top cash prize for identifying the "golden medley" of 10 tunes within 60 seconds was boosted from a mere $1,520 to $25,000.

Another *Stop the Music!* spin-off, radio's *Hit the Jackpot*, also a Goodson-Todman property, featured host Bill Cullen, the Ray Charles Singers and Al Goodman's orchestra. Postcards received from listeners were randomly drawn, determining the contestants on this 1948–49 single-season endeavor. Their writers were telephoned and given an opportunity to answer prize-winning questions.

Stop the Music! continued on radio for four years. But in less than half that time its audience began to drastically fall away, evidencing the same fate that Fred Allen had met when *Music* premiered. The numbers told the story. *Music* was at 20.0 on the Hooper charts in January 1949 and only 10.9 in January 1950, nose-diving from 14th to 66th place. *The Edgar Bergen and Charlie McCarthy Show*, meanwhile — by then on CBS at 8 o'clock in the 1949–50 season — was boasting a 20.4 rating in January 1950, while *The Red Skelton Show* following it commandeered a healthy 19.0. And even NBC's dramatic fare at that hour was ahead of *Music*, *Sam Spade* at 8 o'clock mustered 11.3 and was succeeded by *Theater Guild Dramas* at 12.4.

What had gone wrong?

A primary factor was the magnetic effect that TV was having, which was affecting almost all radio series and genres. (An astute commentator noted that while some of TV's best programs, like *Stop the Music!*, arrived from radio, by 1950 "sight radio" or "radio optics" was beginning to destroy its "hearing-only" competition.[32]) Obviously there was more to it than that, for Bergen, Skelton, *Spade* and those dramas were surviving quite well, thank you. (Bergen, for one, slipped to 15.9 by January 1951 and 14.3 a year later, but *Music* had dropped still further — to 8.3 in 1951 and 7.6 in 1952.)

What really had made the difference?

Some of *Music*'s luster received a tarnishing when widespread reports surfaced involving a handful of disgruntled contestants on similar shows who spoke blatantly to the media. The telephone line to the home of a Cheyenne, Wyoming, woman went dead as she was about to answer a jackpot question on *Sing It Again*, CBS's reply to *Stop the Music!* She threatened a lawsuit against CBS and the telephone company for being disconnected, citing a personal loss of $24,000 in merchandise prizes.

Two Bostonians vied for one $15,000 prize on the same series. Thinking it was a joke when a call arrived from CBS at his pastry shop, owner Rocco Rotondi handed the phone to his buddy William de Marco.

The latter recognized a "phantom voice" and both men subsequently appeared in court claiming the prize as the *legitimate* winner. Rotondi's argument was that he paid the phone bill and that, therefore, entitled him alone.

Even when people won jackpots, trouble often followed. A Cleveland woman, Ola Peth, who acquired $25,000 in merchandise on *Stop the Music!*, learned quickly that she must cough up $6,000 in cash for the tax man. To meet her financial obligations, she sold a slightly used wardrobe, valued at $4,000, and a sewing machine. In her case, as well as in others, the newly rich were reduced to something a little less haughty.

Such negative publicity, and perhaps the years of criticism so frequently reflected by newspaper reviewers, assisted in turning the public tide from shows like *Stop the Music!* By then, too, the novelty effect had worn off, while the duplication of such big-moneyed series had become almost commonplace.

Finally, shows like Bergen's and Skelton's and other familiar radio favorites had been around for years. Once listeners sampled the new fare for a spell, many returned to the audio staples that for so long had made them laugh.

Thus, a combination of factors caused *Music* to fall so far so fast. The show would, nonetheless, continue to air for another couple of years, albeit without the riotous fanfare that had characterized its striking inception.

In the summer of 1954 somebody got the bright notion that *Music*— having been off the air for two years— would face a warm reception if it attempted a comeback. To accomplish that feat, the series switched nights and networks (to Tuesdays at 8 o'clock on CBS), and replaced the entire cast. Rising young audience participation show host Bill Cullen received the nod as the new master of ceremonies. (Cullen was gone before the reprise was canceled six months later, replaced by Happy Felton.) Ray Bloch's orchestra supplanted the earlier band conducted by series originator Harry Salter. The new vocalists were Jill Corey and Jack Haskell. That time around, the show was unsponsored, which undoubtedly contributed to its brevity.

Yet there were some high moments in the short run, just as there were in the original. On the initial reprise show, for instance, Cullen's penchant for wisecracking, as well as his own sparkling humor, brilliantly shone through. At one point the orchestra was playing the "Beer Barrel Polka" and was interrupted by a loud telephone-ringing bell with Cullen shouting: "Stop the music!" The melody instantly ceased, with the exception of the banjo, which continued for several additional strums, tapering off to raucous laughter from the studio audience.

CULLEN: That was Ray Bloch leading our orchestra and Al Caiola, our banjoist, saying "Which way did they go?"

AUDIENCE: *Gales of laughter*

CULLEN: (*Over tittering*) Hello, operator … Who do we have here? We didn't stop the whole band but we got the biggest part of 'em.

AUDIENCE: *Snickering*

CULLEN: Mrs. Norma Young … Kenosha, Wisconsin. (*Speaking into the telephone*) Hello? Mrs. Young? Did you hear that song being played? Did you notice the banjo kept going? … Mrs. Young, I have a question and if you can answer it correctly, I'll send you a $50 savings bond if you'll tell me the name of the polka Ray Bloch and most of the orchestra were playing.

AUDIENCE: *Unrestrained guffaws*

CULLEN: You think *what*? (*chuckles*) … She says she thinks most of them were playing the "Beer Barrel Polka" and that's right.

AUDIENCE: *Thunderous applause*

CULLEN: If you can correctly identify our "Mystery Melody" you will do better … You'll win a $1,000 bond and a trip to Paris.

However, your trip will be on an airplane — you won't bump into Mr. Caiola 'cause he'll be playing on the boat!

AUDIENCE: *Erupts into bedlam*

CULLEN: Al Caiola and his Trio sponsored by Mother Sills, your friend.... (*over snickers*) Listen to this song, Mrs. Young ... Ray, the "Mystery Melody" please.

ORCHESTRA: *Plays a few bars of "Mystery Melody"*

CULLEN: There we are! I'll give you one hint ... The answer isn't "In France They Say 'Oui Oui'" although we know they do. What do you think it is? ... Hunh? What'd you say? ... "In Spain They Say 'Si Si'?"

AUDIENCE: *Pandemonium breaks loose*

CULLEN: That wasn't the right answer, but you'll receive tomorrow by special delivery a $50 bond and a slightly used banjo.

AUDIENCE: *Reeling in raucous giggling*

CULLEN: Thanks for helping us play *Stop the Music!*

During its one-hour sustained (unsponsored) debut, the reprise show offered 23 musical selections, 11 of which were interrupted by telephone calls across America. Five of those listeners who were reached at home were able to identify the tune just played or sung, while two in the studio audience could do so when a caller missed an answer. Nobody named the "Mystery Melody" that night; therefore, at the close of the hour, another $500 savings bond was added to the jackpot. The broadcast featured selections by Bloch's orchestra and singers Corey and Haskell, but also a guest artist, harmonica player Richard Hayman, who offered three instrumental treasures.

Unlike Jack Haskell, the female soloist (Jill Corey) had no discernible credits that distinguished her before her selection for *Music*'s cast.

Haskell, on the other hand, was then appearing on two radio series—*The Dave Garroway Show* (which led to *Garroway at Large* and *Today* on NBC-TV) and the little known *Music from the Heart of Amer-*

ica. In the early 1940s he had been a featured soloist on Chicago's WBBM and WGN. He sang on *Fitch Bandwagon* commercials in that era while a music student at Northwestern University. Returning to radio from Naval flight duty, in 1946 he appeared with Les Brown's band as a baritone soloist on several shows: *Bits of Hits, Design for Listening, Pastels in Rhythm* and a summer replacement series in 1950 and 1951 that bore his own name. Haskell later turned up on *The Jack Paar Show*, plus *Of All Things* (a summer replacement for Garry Moore), as well as *NBC Bandstand*. In 1962 he appeared in the Irving Berlin Broadway musical *Mr. President.*

Announcers for the shortened run of *Stop the Music!* were aural lightweights, Doug Browning and Hal Simms.

Browning was interlocutor for *Go for the House, Music Tent, The Old Gold Paul Whiteman Hour, S.R.O., The Sea Hunt* and *Terry and the Pirates.* He was in the cast of *Ed East and Polly,* too.

Simms announced *Rate Your Mate* and *The Steve Allen Show.*

Bill Cullen, *Music*'s second master of ceremonies, was certified by one media historiographer as the "emcee of more game shows than any entertainer" in the business.[33] Born at Pittsburgh on February 18, 1920, Cullen initially appeared on the air gratis on his hometown's 250-watt WWSW. At the close of the 1930s he was working on games and man-in-the-street interviews with producer Walt Framer (later of *Strike It Rich* fame). Local powerhouse KDKA, with a 50,000-watt projection, hired him away, and before long his ability, talent and winsome personality projected him to network radio in New York.

One of Cullen's early assignments was to announce a debuting soap opera in 1947, *This Is Nora Drake.* But the affable man with the horn-rimmed glasses and elfin grin could not be contained behind a simple microphone. His enthusiasm for work came off as contagious, and he was soon in front of audiences, appearing on such radio series as *Arthur Godfrey Time, Give and Take, Hit the Jackpot, Road Show, Walk a Mile, Winner Take All* and a morning wake-up program over New York's WNBC.

A childhood bout with polio had resulted in a decided limp that kept Cullen from embracing TV for awhile. But by the 1950s he was on the *I've Got a Secret* TV panel. For the rest of his career he routinely appeared on more than a dozen televised series, most of them as a game show master of ceremonies including: *The Bill Cullen Show* (1953), *Blankety Blanks* (1975), *Chain Reaction* (1980), *Child's Play* (1982–83), *Eye Guess* (1966–69), *Give and Take* (1952), *Hot Potato* (1984), *The Joker's Wild* (1984–86), *Matinee in New York* (1952), *Name That Tune* (1954), *NBC Sports in Action* (1966), *Pass the Buck* (1978), *The Price Is Right* (1956–65), *Three on a Match* (1971–74), *Winner Take All* (1952). Cullen died in Los Angeles on July 7, 1990.

The gregarious Happy Felton succeeded him as host of *Stop the Music!* in its final weeks on radio. Felton was primarily a children's performer, presiding over *Happy Felton's Spotlight Gang* Saturday mornings on NBC-TV in 1954–55. Four years earlier the former vaudevillian and bandleader conducted a "Knothole Gang" series airing prior to Brooklyn Dodgers baseball games. He hosted a children's game show (*It's a Hit*) on a New York station until it moved to CBS-TV on Saturday mornings in the summer of 1957.

When it originally went on the air, *Stop the Music!* introduced an innovative method of selling commercial support by radio advertisers. The underwriters were able to purchase time in quarter-hour segments, which they hadn't been able to do previously. As a result, the show was sold to multiple sponsors during its first three seasons, then to one firm — to P. Lorillard, Incorporated for Old Gold cigarettes — in the closing season (1951–52) of the initial four-year run. Interestingly, sponsors who ignored the series when it debuted raced to buy time a few weeks later, Old Gold and Speidel jewelry leading the throng, as *Music* became an overnight sensation.

Stop the Music! was a phenomenon in many ways. It came on like gangbusters, mystified its critics, overwhelmed its competition and instantly attracted millions of the radio-listening faithful. Despite its ability to accomplish the unexpected virtually overnight, it ultimately dwindled to an "also ran" series just as speedily, turned off by many of those who had accepted it so enthusiastically only a short while earlier. Were American tastes that fickle? Not likely. A number of substantial reasons, delineated already, combined to dismantle the show.

Radio had never seen anything like *Music* when it arrived. And when the dust settled, few seemed to miss it. By then the proliferation of big-moneyed giveaways offered far more choices than the typical listener (and viewer) had time to absorb.

Music affixed its mark on a compulsive, even obsessive distraction that wouldn't be extinguished anytime soon, nonetheless. The accelerated growth of the genre benefited from its contributions, exposing it as far more than a mere flash in the pan.

13

Strike It Rich

Premise: By correctly answering a few questions on *Strike It Rich*, a contestant might not walk away with a cash windfall, but instead be supplied with a few merciful necessities: a hearing aid for the hearing impaired, arthritis treatments for those afflicted, a job for someone desperately in need, a van for a choir of blind gospel singers, clothing for a family having lost everything in a trailer fire, and on and on. On radio's "show with a heart," all one had to be was destitute to qualify for the most benevolent broadcasting venture in history. Even screwing up on the quiz didn't eliminate a player from the hope of greater return. There were always philanthropists, businesses, groups and mainstream Americans with generosity written all over them simply waiting to perform some act of mercy. By dialing the show's "Heartline," they assuaged the grief by relieving a hapless victim's misery. The primary reason for the show's existence was, in fact, to help the down-and-out. Given that a staff was feverishly working behind the scenes to see it happen, it was a foregone conclusion that few would leave the stage empty-handed. And just as no good deed goes unpunished, neither did those heroes escape notice by some who would exploit their lofty efforts. *Strike It Rich* was routinely harangued, accused of capitalizing on people in despair. Its wrists were slapped for adding to the welfare roles of New York City. It was ridiculed for allowing at least one fugitive to air a contrived sob story, eliciting empathy from an unsuspecting audience. Yet, as the tears flowed from the many *Rich* helped — and especially from the brimming eyelids of its host, Warren Hull — public reaction sided with it, genuinely impressed by the intent. No audience before it — or since — had witnessed anything like it. The program resulted, perhaps, from an America then endowed with a kinder, gentler generation.

Creator/Owner/Producer/Director/Writer: Walter Framer

Directors: Larry Harding, Jack Tyler

Masters of Ceremonies: Todd Russell, Warren Hull

Announcers: Don Baker, Ralph Paul

Organist: Hank Sylvern

Theme Song: An original composition

Sponsors: The show was sustained by CBS on two occasions, from its inception in June 1947 through October 1947, and again from February 1949 until it left that network in April 1950. Ludens cough drops sponsored it from Nov. 2, 1947 to Feb. 20, 1949. Beginning May 1, 1950 — until the end of the radio run — the program was underwritten by the Colgate-Palmolive-Peet Co. in daytime audio and video series on dual networks, and in a primetime TV version lasting three-and-a-half years. The sponsor's wares included Vel dishwashing liquid ("It's Mar-Vel-ous!"), Fab ("Fabulous") detergent, Palmolive beauty soap and shaving cream, various Colgate dentifrices, Lustre-Creme shampoo, and other personal care and household cleaning goods.

Ratings: High: 7.9 (1947–48); Low: 3.1 (1954–55); Median: 7.0. (Figures don't include the 1949–50, 1950–51, 1955–56, 1956–57 and 1957–58 seasons.)

On the Air: June 29, 1947–1948, CBS, Sunday, 10:30 P.M. ET; 1948–April 30, 1950, CBS, Sunday, 5:30 P.M.; also 1950–April 28, 1950, CBS, weekdays, 4 P.M.; May 1, 1950– Dec. 27, 1957, NBC, weekdays, 11 A.M.

* * *

Reviewers assessing the merits of this series — in the period it was on the air and in the years since — have been less than generous in their appreciation of it for the most part, depicting the show with critical disdain. To wit:

• "*Strike It Rich*, where the lame, the halt, and the blind assembled to plead ... for a few bucks for an operation."[1]

• "... the most notorious show on television" [and, presumably, earlier and simultaneously on radio].[2]

• [*Strike It Rich*] "callously exploits human anxiety to sell the products of a soap manufacturer and does it with a saccharine solicitude that hits the jackpot in bad taste ... a giveaway warped beyond belief ... an instance of commercial television [and radio] gone berserk."[3]

• "*Strike It Rich* was the unfortunate model ... which exploited the destitute as objects for entertainment."[4]

What's wrong with this picture?

We've seen one side of it. But there was — as there always is — another. It is the one that personified the series as radio's "show with a heart."

A sympathetic master of ceremonies was so obviously touched by the impoverished circumstances faced by some of his contestants that it caused him to visibly weep at times. *Strike It Rich* became nothing short of Mecca to millions of beleaguered listeners and viewers in the late 1940s and throughout most of the succeeding decade. Even if they couldn't be included among the coveted handful who were helped by the show, thousands who may have had limited hopes of improving their own meager existences nonetheless gained inspiration from this broadcast endeavor.

The few (estimated at more than 2,000 individuals across a decade) who actually appeared on the air told moving stories of their hardships. Financial need was almost always present. But their situations could just as well involve a single parent attempting to secure a safe environment in which to raise several dependents. Or there was a need for an artificial limb, a replacement for a lost job or furnishings for a family home destroyed by a tornado. Long-term illnesses and travel requests were among the lot. It was an emotional half-hour for just about everybody tuning in. The show's fans were easily caught up in the absorbing melodrama that surrounded a poor wretch's predicament.

Years before, *Strike It Rich* had been born in the heart and soul of its producer, Walt Framer. The son of a Russian immigrant, Framer was imbued early in life with the simple values of working hard, believing in this nation and lending a helping hand to those who could use it. Such lessons set the tone for the ideals he would espouse throughout his lifespan.

Launching a broadcasting career in Pittsburgh — where his father had settled after arriving in America — one of young Framer's earliest diversions was a sidewalk audience participation program known as *Have You Got It?* The show's concept was based on the assumption that — for a few trinkets, a pair of movie tickets or some silver dollars — people would trade virtually anything of little value that they owned.

The announcer for that series, which aired from the sidewalk outside a sponsor's small emporium, was none other than Bill Cullen. Cullen and Framer would both leave indelible footprints upon the national game show genre in the years to come. When Framer left Pittsburgh for New York in the early 1940s, Cullen wasn't too many steps behind him.

One of Framer's initial projects in the Big Apple was to co-produce *Break the Bank*. Producer Edwin Wolfe found him of inestimable value for that impressive jackpot series. Framer went on to produce the CBS-TV daytime game show *For Love or Money* in 1958–59. His versatility allowed him to make notable contributions as a writer, too. In that capacity he toiled over the scripting of a quartet of radio shows — *The Black Hood, Break the Bank, Glamour Manor* and *Ladies Be Seated* — the latter three embracing audience participation formats.

Vigilant until the end about the genre that dominated his professional life, in his twilight years Framer was still thinking up ideas for new shows. After his broadcasting interests folded, he pursued tourism and real estate expansion in Miami. Simultaneously, he unsuccessfully attempted to sell a trio of new game show concepts. In one, globe-trotting excursions would be awarded to couples who could answer a world travel quiz; in another, contestants

would pay homage to the truly "gigantic" individuals who heavily influenced their lives; and in a third, some of *Strike It Rich's* contestants of the 1940s and 1950s would return to the air to reveal what had transpired in their lives in the ensuing years. None of these dreams took root, but the consummate innovator never gave up. Framer died in Miami at 80 on June 21, 1988.

Biographer Tom DeLong, who interviewed Framer in the mid–1980s, recounted: "Walt never forgot his father's words of praise and gratitude over living in the greatest country in the world where people helped each other get ahead. He began devising a quiz show built around the idea of giving a boost to people who were down on their luck and in need of a bit of money to make a go of things."[5]

Framer supplied a working title of "We're in the Money" for his proposed series and ultimately arrived at the "show with the heart" theme. But it was Framer's wife who offhandedly gave the show its permanent moniker. Recounting her perception of its theme to her husband one day, she explained that the players would be telling the listeners why they hoped to *strike it rich*. Those words clicked; Framer was convinced he had found what he had been searching for.

He prepared a demonstration disk in the spring of 1947 and shopped it to CBS, which was then seeking a replacement for *Take It or Leave It*. Network president William Paley bought Framer's idea. Todd Russell, a veteran radio quizmaster then emceeing the popular *Double or Nothing* on MBS, was signed to host the new show. Don Baker was engaged as announcer and Hank Sylvern as organist. Framer and Sylvern had worked together on *Break the Bank*. Baker, who was also an *Information Please* announcer, is covered in that chapter.

Strangely enough, radio biographers

have been silent about the men who assisted Framer in directing *Strike It Rich*. Beyond the names of Larry Harding and Jack Tyler, we have no further clues into their lives.

The show debuted as a sustaining series at 10:30 P.M. Eastern Time on June 29, 1947. Four months later it picked up a sponsor, Ludens cough drops, which underwrote it for nearly 16 months. Reverting to a sustainer in early 1949, *Strike It Rich* was purchased by the Colgate-Palmolive-Peet Company in the spring of 1950, which carried it the rest of the way on both radio and television, including its daytime and primetime performances.

Strike It Rich was variously dissected as a weepy hybrid of several other shows, including *Stop the Music!, Queen for a Day* and *Take It or Leave It*. But, in truth, its premise was plain and simple.

Those aspiring to be on it were asked to summarize their requests for assistance to Framer in writing. ("To get on the program, you had to be in poor shape financially [evictees, widows, and ill or physically challenged people were favorites]," claimed one observer.[6]) From vast numbers of communications received each week, Framer would invite about 20 of the letter writers to the CBS Playhouse every Sunday where the show was aired. They'd casually share their stories in person with him and his staff. Normally, six of them were selected to appear on the show, based upon contrast and audience appeal. Another one or two would be picked from the studio audience.

From the show's earliest days, the master of ceremonies asked the contestants a few easy questions (e.g., "Spell Purple"), for which they were paid in cash. The quiz would progress through several levels, with the ill-fated players betting as much of their money as they dared risk on varied categories.

The reader should keep in mind, nevertheless, that here was a show that sincerely wanted to hand out greenbacks. Nobody would leave it broke, for this was a charity effort that was disguised as a quiz.

To help accomplish its aim, *Rich* had a couple of safety nets built into it which could be readily summoned when some poor soul was losing everything just won — or wasn't doing well with the questions to begin with.

The "Heartline" was the first of those measures, denoted by a large red heart affixed to one of the stage backboards. When help was on the way, the heart reverberated like a beating heart, lighting up on-stage, quickly flashing on and off several times for maximum studio (and, later, television) audience response. The big red heart was linked to a nearby telephone that rang loudly when a rescue was at hand. Listeners hearing the bell (and for the studio audience and TV viewers, seeing the heart light up) meant that somebody tuning in to the show had been moved by the plight of the indigent on-stage. The listener had called the show and offered a donation of cash, merchandise, service, job, artificial limb or whatever was lacking.

Actually, Framer himself was on the line when the emcee picked up the telephone receiver on-stage. Speaking from backstage, he named the individual calling the studio (unless the contributor requested to remain anonymous — some did) and enumerated precisely what had been offered.

The show originally offered up to $800 in cash to a particularly destitute player. That amount was reduced to $300 in 1953 when Framer decided the higher sum attracted an undesirable element that was merely seeking dough, and not because of legitimate impoverished needs.

Sometimes before such funds were dispensed, a "Helping Hand" celebrity appeared, answering the questions for a needy contestant who — for whatever the reason — was unable to play the game. Meanwhile, the celebrity got to plug his latest

"The show with the heart," *Strike It Rich* attracted all sorts of guests and even got into legal squabbles over some of them who were added to the local welfare rolls of New York City. On one occasion a "Helping Hand" celebrity, Gypsy Rose Lee — true to her public persona — offered a smiling Warren Hull, master of ceremonies, her jacket as she answered questions on behalf of a needy guest. (Photofest)

much as days or weeks in advance of air dates. Working behind the scenes, he and his staff placed strategic phone calls to employers and business people that were in positions to greatly diminish contestants' woes. If a widow with several children turned up to plead for a new roof for her house, for example, the show might contact a roofer in her locality to set up a donation. Then the roofer would call the "Heartline" while the show was on the air and make his pledge. The roofer got a plug, the poor widow got a new roof, the show didn't spend a dime beyond the phone calls, and nearly everybody in the audience went away with a sense of emotional exhilaration. *Everybody* came out a winner, Framer hypothesized.

It was the contestants and their dilemmas, of course, which were the catalysts for making the show all that it was.

There was Jackie Mendoza, for instance. A sailor, Mendoza had a six-year-old son who needed a surgical procedure on a clubfoot. A California listener telephoned with an offer of $800, while a Florida hospital agreed to provide free medical services.

To Quinnie Stanley, age 71, went $340. She lived in a Fayetteville, Georgia,

film, recording, stage production, book, charity, TV series, radio show or whatever else he or she might currently be fawning over. Among the elite who turned up for this role were Burt Lancaster, Eddie Cantor, Georgie Jessel, Jackie Gleason, Ronald Reagan and Merle Oberon.

Decades later, Framer acknowledged that considerable assistance for the program was deliberately choreographed as two-room log cabin. She made a trio of simple requests to the show — for electricity, an outlet for a light bulb and a radio. The 340 smackers were expected to fulfill them all.

Strike It Rich presented Helen Root, 69 — living alone in a one-room Manhattan apartment — with a hearing aid because she couldn't afford it.

When a youngster who had been studying violin announced that his instrument had vanished, the Heartline lit up. Walt Framer reported that he had received a call from famed violin virtuoso Fritz Kreisler who was willing to donate a Stradivarius to the youth. (Weren't you warned that all you had to be was *destitute?*)

Then there was Mrs. Anna Kinney of Newark, New Jersey, whose husband had abandoned her and their three sons. By night she sewed aprons, then sold them door-to-door by day in an effort to keep the wolf away from their own door. The family had been living with Mrs. Kinney's mother, but the landlord had evicted grandma, turning them all onto the street.

"The housing authorities have given me four rooms," she wrote the show, "but I haven't any furniture — nothing I could go into housekeeping with. And the children all need new clothes."

She won $200 on *Strike It Rich*. Sensing that that would only be a start, the emcee found a way to multiply her newfound fortune. Taking one of her aprons, he held it before a television camera. "This is worth a lot more than a dollar," he said. "I'll bet a lot of people in our audience would be tickled to have aprons as pretty as this."

Mrs. Kinney received more than a thousand orders from across the nation in the next week. Helping folks in dire circumstances was something that came naturally on the show with the heart.

Yet, where handouts abound there will probably always be someone lurking nearby who tries to be greedy. At least one such incident in *Rich*'s history grabbed the national spotlight.

Completing an audience-participation card one day was an unkempt gentleman who asserted that he needed money to fetch his family from Texas to New York. He had met up with troubles in Texas, which he did not expand upon, but hoped to make a fresh start in the city. The misfortune that his wife and a quartet of kids had been subjected to would make a good story, Framer felt. The young man was chosen to share it on the air.

He won $165 on *Strike It Rich* and departed the studio rapidly. A few days later the program was rebroadcast in Austin, Texas. A local sheriff watching it recognized the man as an ex-con who had fled the state after being indicted for embezzlement and grand theft.

How could a fugitive possibly have gotten on the show in the first place? Framer was red-faced and empty-handed trying to explain it. An alarm went out across the Northeast. The con artist was picked up a fortnight later in upstate New York. And the well-publicized incident provided a field day for some of the show's critics.

Meanwhile, the Travelers Aid Society vehemently protested that *Rich* was beckoning an overabundance of potential show candidates to New York City. People had, as a matter of fact, been asking that bureau for assistance in returning to their homes ever since *Major Bowes' Original Amateur Hour* aired in the 1930s, the agency claimed. Folks were arriving in Gotham from all over the nation and simply winding up on relief. "We don't know if the successes on the show balance off against the human misery caused by it," the society's supervisor allowed. "But from what we see, I'd say they didn't.... Putting human misery on display can hardly be called right."[7]

Another order, the Family Service

Association of America, argued: "Victims of poverty, illness, and everyday misfortune should not be made a public spectacle or seemingly be put in the position of begging for charity."[8]

That's when a stonehearted welfare bureaucrat decided to take the show to court. Commissioner Henry L. McCarthy, calling the series "a disgusting spectacle and a national disgrace," declared that *Strike It Rich* was nothing more than a welfare enterprise due to its "public solicitation of money." Not possessing an official city operating license to solicit funds could cause the show to leave the air. (Years later Framer alleged that McCarthy had hoped to run for mayor and was merely using the publicity enveloping the case to boost his own public profile.)

Framer was livid over the turn of events. The show never gave anybody large sums, he petitioned, which repelled the truly desperate from applying. A sharp debate provided lively reading in the press for an extended period, nevertheless. In the end, McCarthy withdrew his complaint as Framer acceded to a couple of sticking points. From that time forward (a) the audience would be warned not to come to New York unless specifically summoned; and (b) the show would carefully examine every prospective contestant's credentials in advance. An unfortunate byproduct of the latter concession resulted in halting on-air participation by members of the studio audience.

Despite a subsequent clean bill of health that the show received from a New York state congressional review, Representative Katherine St. George of the Empire State was dissatisfied with that turn of events. She presented a measure calling for station licensees to scrutinize individuals or groups for whom funds were actively requested on radio and TV. While on a soapbox, she strongly denounced any attempt that might be made to include U.S. armed services personnel as contestants on *Strike It Rich*. She elaborated: "Our servicemen are well taken care of and do not need the type of help solicited by the show."[9] (Had Ms. St. George considered such audience participation series as *Truth or Consequences*, she could have ignited a bonfire. That show appeared to target at least one or two servicemen on virtually every broadcast. It was a California-based production, however, and may have been of little consequence to her, no pun intended.)

Such negative publicity struck a note of discord with at least one major metropolitan newspaper. *The Providence* (Rhode Island) *Journal-Bulletin* decided to delete references in its radio and television program listings to *Strike It Rich, Welcome Travelers* and *On Your Account*, all three series with similar human-interest themes. The daily publication did so by disavowing "certain radio and television broadcasts which deliberately exploit human want and misery for commercial gain."[10] The newspaper later renounced any suggestion of an attempt to suppress the news, a charge leveled by Walt Framer.

Any discussion of *Strike It Rich* would, of course, be entirely remiss without a meticulous intersect with Warren Hull, who was more visibly identified with the show in the minds of its fans than anyone else. Despite the fact this rising star wasn't the first to emcee *Rich*, the reality that there was someone (Todd Russell) in that role before Hull seems of little meaning. Taking away nothing from Russell's contributions, the fact remains that his tenure is something that the near-cult following this program acquired has virtually dismissed.

Running into Hull on New York's famed Madison Avenue one day, Framer affirmed that he was looking for a replacement for Russell, who was leaving the show. Hull had just completed a brief stint hosting the lackluster Goodson-Todman game show *Spin to Win*. The series appeared on CBS as a Saturday night summer replacement in 1949. Framer inquired if Hull — whom he originally met a few years earlier when Hull, then a Warner Brothers actor, visited Pittsburgh while promoting a film — would have interest in the role of emcee.

(Before continuing, the reader must realize that it would be arduous to separate a number of Hull's business practices from the personal convictions that uniformly characterized his demeanor. This stemmed from his abiding beliefs typifying the Quaker environment in which he was raised. His behavior often evidenced tender, benevolent, supportive traits which were not only obvious to himself but to those around him. In retrospect, it would seem that a show with a premise like that of *Strike It Rich* and the values so strongly espoused by Warren Hull were eminently matched, and possibly preordained.)

Hull viewed *Rich* as one of radio's few public service programs that genuinely attempted to better the conditions of people who were down on their luck and facing almost insurmountable odds. "I'm intrigued with the thought of helping one's neighbor," he told Framer. "I'll agree to perform for you for scale."[11]

Born January 17, 1903, at Gasport, New York, Hull was gifted with a gregarious personality and both singing and acting ability. Deciding to follow his natural talents as a career, young Hull studied voice for a semester at the University of Rochester's Eastman School of Music, not far from his upstate home. He continued his education at New York University.

Musical comedies and operettas provided his initial exposure to the stage. In 1924–25 he appeared in *Follow Through, The Love Song, My Maryland, Rain or Shine* and *The Student Prince*. From there he built a career in "B" movies, the "also ran" second features that were prevalent in an era of twin bills at local motion picture the-

aters. Signed by Warner Brothers, he regularly surfaced in *Spider* and *Green Hornet* serials while turning up in more than 35 less-than-memorable features with titles like: *Bengal Tiger, Bowery Blitzkrieg, Freshman Love, Her Husband's Secretary, The Lone Wolf Meets a Lady, Miss Pacific Fleet, Night Key, Paradise Isle, Personal Maid's Secret, Remedy for Riches, Star Reporter* and *Wagons Westward*.

In the 1930s Hull pursued a broadcasting sideline that would ultimately turn his career in a new direction. While continuing to make films, he increasingly found radio to be a fascinating diversion, gaining employment as a singer, producer and writer there. By 1937 he was known well enough by industry insiders to be elected to the initial officers' roster of the newly established American Federation of Radio Artists.

Hull's earliest permanent network radio assignments included parts on several musical variety series. He was in the casts of *The Gibson Family* (1934–35) and *Log Cabin Jamboree* (1937–38), while hosting *The Vicks Open House* (1934–38), *The Jack Haley Show* (1938–39), and *Melody and Madness* (1939). He announced *The Maxwell House Show Boat* in 1937, *and Good News of 1938, 1939* and *1940* in each of those successive years. On April 20, 1935, he became master of ceremonies of the debuting *Your Hit Parade*. From 1942 to 1948 he was a co-emcee of *Vox Pop*, handling impromptu interviews with passersby on a show that was frequently beamed from far-flung sites. In 1947–48 he hosted the variety series *Mother Knows Best*.

By May 1946 Hull was appearing regularly on TV, too, presiding over one of the first local variety video programs, *Radio City Matinee*. The Monday-Wednesday-Friday hour-long stint emanated from WNBT, New York's NBC affiliate. It was surely a harbinger of things to come.

Hull's television credits extended from

November 1948 to June 1949 with the variety series *Ladies Day* (becoming known as *The Warren Hull Show* in 1949). He also hosted the short-lived *This Is the Missus* in December 1948 and January 1949, an extension of *The Missus Goes a-Shopping* game show.

But his unparalleled claim to TV fame was *Strike It Rich*. When it debuted on CBS-TV at 11:30 A.M. Eastern Time on May 7, 1951, it became that network's inaugural attempt to offer sustained entertainment programming before noon, TV observer Wesley Hyatt recounted. When the tube version transferred at one point to four o'-clock on CBS, an audiotape was made of the live telecast and replayed the following morning for an NBC Radio audience. Both series, plus a third — a weekly primetime effort that was telecast from July 4, 1951, to January 12, 1955, on NBC-TV — were totally underwritten by the Colgate-Palmolive-Peet Company for a variety of packaged goods.

Originally, in 1947, the show had been a CBS Radio Sunday offering until it moved to daily status in 1950, winding up on NBC Radio May 1 of that year. It remained an 11 o'clock NBC staple until it left radio forever on December 27, 1957. The daytime CBS-TV series continued one additional week, until January 3, 1958.

But never say die.

Bert Parks hosted a brief syndicated series of the TV show in 1973, and Tom Kelly did the same in 1978. Under the banner of *Strike It Rich*, a series with a format featuring married couples also joined the NBC-TV weekday schedule in September 1986. That outing, emceed by Joe Garagiola, lasted until June 1987.

Turning back to Hull, in almost daily occurrences it was he who made the show the memorable one it became. The personal agenda he brought transferred him into a visibly demonstrative reactionary to the lamentable situations presented. Hull's eyes frequently moistened, tears stained his cheeks and sometimes his lips quivered at the stories told by some of *Rich*'s contestants.

Producer Walt Framer observed all of this early in Hull's substantial run with the show, and even set up a defense mechanism to deal with it. At such times, tears dimming his eyes, his voice lost in a well of emotion, Hull simply wasn't in any condition to continue until he regained his composure. Sensing that he was breaking down, Framer would signal announcer Ralph Paul to stand by.

"On occasion, he [Paul] has had to walk right onto the stage and take over," Framer advised a magazine reporter.[12]

One example may serve to illustrate the depth of Hull's emotions. There was a youngster who came on the show whose plight was so awful that practically everybody there was thunderstruck. Both of the lad's parents were desperately ill, as well as financially destitute. The youth himself was in the unrelenting throes of leukemia, his very being in constant grave danger.

"I was standing by, as Warren talked to him," Framer remembered. "There were tears in Warren's eyes and I wondered what words he could possibly find. Suddenly, Warren put up his hand and said quietly, 'Let's all bow our heads and pray for this boy.'"[13] How many times have you heard that petition dispensed on a non-religious program?

At the time, Framer contended: "Warren's job is probably one of the most difficult in all of radio and TV. He lives every hardship with contestants, then must turn around and quiz them and, perhaps, deny them money they badly need."[14] He noted that Hull pleaded with contestants to limit their responses to single answers. The rules of the game required him to disqualify any who offered more than one answer.

Hull was personally bruised when the reviewers trashed shows with noble purposes like *Strike It Rich* and *Queen for a Day* by claiming they insulted human suffering. Framer responded that most of the publications that doubted such shows' motives were regularly filling their pages with human distress.

Hull died at the age of 71 on September 14, 1974, at Waterbury, Connecticut.

Announcer Ralph Paul, in a reference to Hull, once claimed: "Those bedroom eyes of his added to the intensity he brought to the show."[15]

(This author recalls attending a public event where Hull was invited to speak during the peak of *Strike It Rich*'s popularity. The aura and magnetism that surrounded him on that occasion was nothing short of stunning. As he pushed through the crowd, his dapper, clean-cut features, flashing eyes and broad grin became overpowering. It was obvious that the assemblage was electrified by his very presence.)

Paul, the best remembered of *Rich*'s interlocutors, served for most of its radio days, and all of its television days and nights. He announced for several more radio series during the late 1940s and early 1950s: *The Aldrich Family, The Mighty Casey, Mother Knows Best* (on which he worked with Hull, who was again emcee), *Scout About Town, Seven Front Street* and *Walk a Mile*.

TV Guide portrayed *Strike It Rich* as "a despicable travesty on the very nature of charity."[16] TV observers Tim Brooks and Earle Marsh, on the other hand, paid the series a high compliment, calling it "the ultimate example of viewer-participation television."[17] Could not a similar statement be applied to radio?

Strike It Rich ran the gamut of positive human emotions. Playing with the heartstrings of millions of Americans who harbored little or no deep-seated skepticism in their own outlooks on life — people who genuinely cared about the sufferings and distress of those less fortunate than they — this show found an abiding place with millions who were moved and at times motivated to respond out of the bounty of their personal resources.

It was an uplifting endeavor unlike any other in broadcasting, and it surely made a significant donation to the moral fiber of the nation. Polemical accounts to the contrary, it provided authentic human interest and empathy, and offered far more admirable qualities than damaging results.

14

Take It or Leave It

Premise: It was one of the simplest ideas for a game show ever derived — fashion a few categories; create some questions; assign a cash value to the first; and double the value with successive queries, escalating the intensity of each one as the rate increases. Allow a player to select a category and risk everything earned thus far by gambling that the next question can be correctly answered. Failure to do so will result in surrendering all prize earnings and dismissal. Finally, allow a player to withdraw from the competition at any time. Simple. Right? Simple to understand. Simple to govern. Simple to win — for anyone with a generous assortment of knowledge. So simple, in fact, that the process was adopted (or adapted) by several other game show creatives who fine-tuned its concept. The basic situation was called *Take It or Leave It* (eventually, *The $64 Question*). The original title referred to a player's option of collecting his winnings and departing, or letting the cash ride, trying for an advanced level — presumably a more difficult question that would net twice the current cash prize. So rudimentary was it that the first question's value was set at a mere $1. (That sum was cherished with far greater esteem

in 1940 than it is today, of course.) Doubling that amount a half-dozen times allowed a lucky contestant to walk away with $64, big money to middle-class Americans having only recently survived the Great Depression. Over a dozen years, the contest was run by five of the most appealing emcees in the radio game show business: Bob Hawk, Phil Baker, Garry Moore, Eddie Cantor and Jack Paar. Each left an indelible imprint on a program that is still fondly remembered by aging audiences. Regrettably, a dark shadow was to emerge from it later — an outgrowth of the series' legacy — that would taint the entire breed for years to come. That was in the future, however. In the meantime, this little farce brought nothing but pleasure to ardent fans.

Producer-Directors: Bruce Dodge, Betty Mandeville, Harry Spears

Masters of Ceremonies: Bob Hawk (1940–41), Phil Baker (1941–47, 1951), Garry Moore (1947–49), Eddie Cantor (1949–50), Jack Paar (1950–51, 1951–52)

Announcers: David Ross, Ken Niles, Jay Stewart, Sandy Becker, Ken Roberts

Researcher-Writer: Edith Oliver

Bandleaders: Jacques Renard, Edgar "Cookie" Fairchild, Ray Bloch

Sponsors: This series may have saved a firm! The Eversharp Pen and Pencil Co., spiraling downward at a rapid clip in 1940, decided to put all of its advertising eggs in one basket, gambling on an untried game show that was itself based on a gambling motif. It turned out to be a fortuitous decision; the firm's annual sales doubled nearly four times in less than six years. Eversharp underwrote the program for a decade, turning it over to RCA Victor in 1950, which carried it for a year before the show was sold to participating sponsors during its final few months on the air.

Ratings: High: 21.3 (1942–43); Low: 9.2 (1950–51); Median: 15.8 (including the series' first 11 seasons). During the Eversharp-sponsored decade, the show never fell out of double digits, being comfortably situated in the low twenties or high teens for six of those 10 seasons.

On the Air: April 21, 1940–July 27, 1947, CBS, Sunday, 10 P.M. ET; Aug. 3, 1947–Sept. 30, 1951, NBC, Sunday, 10 P.M.; Dec. 23, 1951–June 1, 1952, NBC, Sunday, 9:30 P.M.

* * *

Take It or Leave It was the birthplace of the $64 question, a phrase that could be ascribed to the tough and imponderable inquiry. The idiom gained such widespread recognition that it became part of the everyday vernacular of millions and is still in accepted use six decades later. President Franklin D. Roosevelt and British Prime Minister Winston Churchill employed it. John Bartlett acknowledged its popularity by including the phrase in his *Familiar Quotations.*

Hatched as an innocent question-and-answer game, the series from which this axiom stemmed left a sad legacy that launched a media frenzy and ended as a national disgrace. The result? It wrecked its own genre for decades while tainting the formerly prized term *quiz show.* Historiographer John Dunning contrasted the radio series with television's *The $64,000 Question,* its scandal-ridden successor with roots that were deeply embedded in the audio quiz. Incisively observing that the radio series "took itself far less seriously," Dunning noted that while it (the radio show) dealt in dollars and not thousands, "There were no isolation booths for contestants, and all the coaching was done on-stage, in full view of the studio audience."[1] An acute disparity in what was to transpire!

Meanwhile, this audience participation thriller was variously tagged by perceptive raconteur Gerald Nachman as "the father of all quiz shows,"[2] "radio's definitive quiz show"[3] and the "most innocuous of quiz shows."[4] By the mid–1940s, it was—by one respected authority's measure—"the most popular American radio quiz."[5]

During its long reign, *Take It or Leave It* was a lighthearted contest that purposely showcased the on-stage persona of a quintet of convivial quizmasters, plus their facile ad-libbing and interviewing skills. The premise seemed less a quiz and more an opportunity for the game players to become foils for the hosts. In this age of innocence, then, the show thrived, and for a dozen years it manufactured mirth and merriment, turning it into one of radio's most welcomed comic-quiz, tension-relieving half-hours.

In 1946 master of ceremonies Phil Baker confided that gagwriters like Hal Block were preparing three-fourths of the show in advance. The residue consisted of spontaneous remarks. Over their long run, the show's emcees frequently began with hilarious bits of repartee, sometimes akin to Bob Hope's opening monologues, though briefer. Occasionally, this prompted banter with the show's announcer.

Quick, pithy exchanges—some of them unanticipated—tended to bring down the house.

Emcee Garry Moore, while interviewing a contestant in 1948 whose occupation was in real estate, inquired: "How's business?" The alert entrepreneur replied: "Stinks."

That same host encountered a woman who was so nervous that she became totally confused by the game. After giving a right answer to the first question, for the second one she repeated her initial answer. "No," explained Moore, tongue-in-cheek, "that isn't the way we play it, although if you like, I'll ask you the seven questions and you can answer the first question seven times!"

When it became obvious that a sailor-contestant was in over his head, unable to answer any of the questions in the category he had selected, emcee Phil Baker gave the question cards *to him* to read aloud. Then Baker answered the questions *for* the sailor, giving him the winnings.

Such atypical departures regularly distinguished this little quiz from most of its contemporaries and made it a favorite of the fans.

When Baker asked another GI if it was fable or fact that Remus and Romulus had discovered Rome, the war veteran declared that it was "fable." Human error had crept into Baker's answer cards, however, and allowed that "fact" was called for. The contestant was dismissed. Astute listeners who knew the difference didn't let it pass, however — they called and wrote the network in large numbers. As a result, the serviceman returned to the show the following week. Beginning his quest anew, he captured the $64 cash prize and everybody went away happy.

This series was born in the mind of a young Atlanta clinical psychologist who simultaneously pursued some lofty personal goals. At 29, Peter Cranford was research director of the Georgia Education Association, a job that in 1939 required him to provide radio series to advance didactic themes.

Cranford bought into the supposition of one William James, another psychologist and theorist, who espoused the notion that — given adequate thought and effort — virtually anything could be accomplished. Cranford believed James was onto something major, rather easily convincing himself that he could earn a million dollars over his lifetime. Interviewed by author Tom DeLong in 1985, Cranford recalled: "Times were hard in 1939 and I had to make it without any capital."[6]

He continued:

I picked the entertainment field. I had heard that radio networks and advertisers were looking for ideas, so I went to the library and read everything I could about programming. I pondered the question: Why do people listen to one show and not another? I concluded that what an interesting program needed most was audience identification or participation. I studied every game there ever was. The most intriguing centered on a pair of ordinary dice. But how could I put a crap game on radio?[7]

Ultimately he decided that a roulette wheel of the air — a gambling match that would double a player's gain with every correct answer — could lead him to achieve his lifetime ambition if it was properly handled. But when he attempted to sell the idea to Atlanta stations, they balked, fearing listeners wouldn't accept a betting technique.

What then?

Cranford wasn't easily swayed. Informed that a prominent New York radio advertising packager, the Milton Biow Company, was seeking new programming concepts, he decided "nothing ventured, nothing gained." Cranford's "double or nothing" scheme appealed to Biow, which sent him $75 for his idea.

But $75 was a long way from $1 million. Cranford saw far greater possibilities for himself by leasing his game for royalties.

Trying to outsmart him, Biow offered the young capitalist $25 weekly for a half-year, or $625 in all. That didn't float, either. By then Cranford wanted permanent buttressing, having recently joined the ranks of the unemployed. In the meantime, while still deliberating over their impasse, he allowed Biow to put his show — *Take It or Leave It* — on the air. It premiered on CBS April 21, 1940.

A short time later a Washington, D.C. station took Biow to court, alleging that the show's premise had been pirated from a similar model that that station was already using. Cranford helped Biow defend the firm's position and, in return, profited handsomely for his efforts. He negotiated a deal with Biow that paid him $50 per broadcast and a third of anything acquired via licenses of the show's concept for future TV adaptations, movies and/or board games. (With little success, Cranford subsequently tried to create radio and television versions of several other games, including one involving bank nights. He also wrote a few books in the field in which he was trained that sold fairly well. A couple of the more memorable ones are *How to Discipline Children* and *How to Be Your Own Psychologist*.)

Admitting in 1960 that he hadn't reached his million-dollar goal from his transaction with Biow, Cranford noted that he had been well on his way there when the TV scandals broke. While earning only about $225,000 from the radio show and some related licenses, Cranford reaped far greater rewards from *The $64,000 Question* and its spin-off series, *The $64,000 Challenge*, both on TV, occurring in the latter days of radio's Golden Age. Then the bubble burst. Without that unfortunate debacle, who knows but that he might have eventually turned into a *multi*millionaire?

The game itself was based on a series of questions that doubled a contestant's winnings, parlaying cash earnings into a seven-step progression from $1 to $64. Each successive question was purportedly tougher than its predecessor. Sporting an element of risk, the game's rules declared that any question incorrectly answered would cost a player his total winnings. One could quit at any point, however, and take all the winnings home. (That initiative is still popular in modern times, employed on such series as *Who Wants to Be a Millionaire?*)

In the game's early years, such forfeited sums were placed in a jackpot. During that single-question round at the end of the show, all of that week's players were allowed to participate. In the program's latter days, however — with big-moneyed quizzes by then the order of the day — the jackpot question began at 10 times the value of the initial round's final question ($64 × 10 = $640). If no one could answer it correctly, the amount continued doubling in successive weeks until a contestant finally won the jackpot.

Some close observers of the show intimated that — in the qualifying round — the $32 question was often the hardest to supply. This may have been based on sheer numbers, for three-fourths of those reaching that level attempted to go the distance, although only one in five gave a correct response to the $64 question. As the questions increased in value, an exuberant studio audience became unapologetically vocal, even boisterous, while egged on by the show's staff. At times, in a high-pitched frenzy, these witnesses urged a contestant to quit while ahead, shouting: "Take it! Take It!" Yet on other occasions — especially when an audience had lost confidence in a player who had wavered on earlier answers but decided to risk everything by continuing the game — the reactors frequently yelled in concert: "You'll be SOR-eeee!" Just as "the $64 question" — and even the show's name, *Take It or Leave It* — entered many a commoner's dialect, the phrase "You'll be SOR-eeee!" became a widely spoken American colloquialism.

Contestants were drawn at random from the studio audience, though a technique was followed that prevented a single gender or group from dominating the proceedings. During the Second World War epoch, ticket stubs were placed in a trio of glass containers that were separately labeled "Men," "Servicemen" and "Women." Bruce Dodge, producer at the time, drew 10 numbers of ticket holders from the containers and had those individuals accompanied to the stage.

So sensitive was the show to the plight of service personnel, in fact, that — following the war — it routinely selected a hospitalized veteran as a contestant every week. A remote set-up allowed a serviceman to participate from his bedside as the host asked him the questions from the studio. Veterans were given $64 up front for appearing on the show. By answering the questions, they could earn up to $64 more. In addition, the host frequently threw in another $64 when a serviceman appeared to have a special incentive or need. (Emphasizing the show's compassion for veterans still more, a wartime movie included a scene in which a fabricated GI appeared on the program. Actual quiz categories during that period reflected a heightened awareness of military leaders, battle sites and world geography.)

Across the show's long tenure, five entertainers of varying dimensions performed the duties of quizmaster and master of ceremonies on *Take It or Leave It*. While each had had experience before a microphone, the degree was mixed. Four already were established comedians— or would ultimately choose careers that branded them as such, in varying proportions. A fifth was a legitimate quizmaster with a track record to prove it. Most were young and "on the way up"; only one had surpassed the pinnacle of his career.

Milton Biow took more than cursory interest in the selection of these key members of his show's talent. Having auditioned literally hundreds of potential quizmasters, he settled on Bob Hawk, then already under contract to Biow and presiding over a little-known game for Philip Morris on the Mutual network called *Name Three*. Hawk would cram a network career as a game show host — the role in entertainment for which he is best remembered— into less than a couple of decades. He spoke so fluently and smoothly that he coined a term for his task, preferring to be labeled a "glibmaster" rather than a "quizmaster." Long after the radio series ended, *Take It or Leave It* creator Peter Cranford declared that Hawk was his personal favorite among the five individuals who carried the duties of emcee.

Born on December 15, 1907, at Creston, Iowa, while still a teenager Hawk broke into radio in 1926 on a Chicago station. His early assignments included announcing, disc jockeying, reading poetry and impromptu interviewing. Eventually, he was picked to run a couple of network game shows, *Foolish Questions* and *Fun Quiz*, each with brief and less-than-famous runs. But Hawk had discovered his niche and was well on his way to the big time. By late 1938 he was appearing on another quiz, *The People's Rally*, and not long afterward on *Quixie Doodle Quiz*.

To avoid reading a long list of question categories aloud each time a new contestant came before the *Take It or Leave It* microphone, Hawk had that data written on a chalkboard in full view of the players and cast. The procedure was subsequently adopted by other game shows, most notably *Double or Nothing*.

After his first four months on *Take It or Leave It*, Hawk's performance was assessed by an entertainment trade journal: "Hawk is a bit fresh at times, but his al fresco manner, albeit a bit unorthodox in comparison to radio's heretofore circumspect manner of treating the customer always 'right,' is a relief. In fact, this may keynote the humanizing factor in 1940 radio."[8]

Within a year the quiz program had become so popular that the studios and auditoriums hosting it were filled with capacity crowds. Not long afterward, in late 1941, Hawk's contract came up for renewal. Instead of automatically signing a new two-year pact, he held out for a larger share of the financial pie. But Milton Biow retreated. With things at a stalemate, Hawk stalled the outcome until he could acquire yet another game show post, as quizmaster of *How'm I Doin'?* That show debuted on CBS on January 9, 1942, for the R.J. Reynolds Tobacco Company, makers of Camels, a major competitor of his earlier sponsor (Philip Morris). It would be the start of a professional relationship that would carry him for much of the remainder of his career. On December 28, 1941, Hawk was replaced on *Take It or Leave It* by an emcee of recognized star caliber, Phil Baker.

Hawk, meanwhile, had sold himself to an unknown quantity, leaving the security of a top-rated game show to preside over an untested one. *How'm I Doin'?* was, unfortunately, another dismal failure, leaving the air in less than nine months. By then, Hawk had snagged still another CBS quiz for the same sponsor. *Thanks to the Yanks* debuted on October 31, 1942. By July 9, 1943, it was renamed *The Bob Hawk Show* and — with only minimal interruption — lasted for another decade, through July 27, 1953. (Camel cigarettes sponsored all of these shows. As if to signify joining some elite caste, a winner on them was tagged a "Lemac" — "Camel" spelled backwards — while studio audiences sang "You're a Lemac now.")

During his waning years on radio, Hawk was also an NBC disc jockey (1951–54). He died at Laguna Hills, California, on July 4, 1989.

His successor on *Take It or Leave It*, Phil Baker, was a native Philadelphian, born August 24, 1896. At age 14 he ran away from home to Boston, winning first place in an amateur theater competition while there. He had learned to play the accordion and within five years was briefly linked with violinist Ben Bernie on the vaudeville circuit. Baker went on to play in musical revues whenever and wherever he found opportunities. Introduced to radio audiences on *The Rudy Vallee Show*, by 1931 he was given a brief fling on his own NBC show as *The Armour Jester*. He returned to radio in 1933 as *The Gulf Headliner* and headed up *Honolulu Bound* in 1939, each of these ventures for a different sponsor. He was reputedly the first performer to introduce a heckling stooge to the airwaves in his act, centering that intrusion around characters he called "Bottle and Beetle." By 1940 he had grown tired of the routine and he quit radio.

When Milton Biow came calling in late 1941, Baker was ready to jump back into the grind of a weekly show. Biow's offer required little effort and suited his personality and ability. Baker viewed it as "an impelling challenge for a comedian."[9]

Not long after Baker arrived, Biow played a trick on his new star. During the week of Baker's birthday, on the broadcast of August 23, 1942, Biow engaged 750 persons with the surname "Baker" for the studio audience. Thus, every player he called upon was named "Baker."

Baker appeared on *Take It or Leave It* longer than anyone else, thus becoming the most closely identified with the series. He was the program's master of ceremonies until mid–1947, when he tired of it, too, and departed for a round of personal appearances. The next year he tried radio again as the emcee of *Everybody Wins*, yet another giveaway. It lasted six months.

Baker claimed he was paid for learning on *Take It or Leave It*, gaining a liberal arts education by asking factual questions of contestants every Sunday evening. While still the show's master of ceremonies, he confessed:

Before I joined the program, if you asked me anything about anything outside of show business, I would answer you with a brilliant, 'huh?' In the set I traveled, nobody ever gave a straight answer. Either they didn't know, or it was funnier the other way. Don't think for a minute that I know the answers beforehand. I probably wouldn't know more than a very few unless they were neatly typed out and handed to me before each broadcast.[10]

He returned to *Take It or Leave It* on March 18, 1951, then retitled *The $64 Question* (beginning with that show). He remained with it little more than six months, departing when the show left the air on September 30 of that year. On June 25, 1951, Baker put in a single appearance as the host of a new CBS-TV game called *Who's Whose*. It was canceled after only one week; he never again hosted another regular televised series. On December 1, 1963, Baker died at Copenhagen, Denmark.

The third member of *Take It or Leave It*'s quintet of quizmasters had already had broadcasting experience hosting several variety programs. Garry Moore was developing as a full-fledged comic, and 1940s audiences witnessed plenty of that from his varied venues. Born T. Garrison Morfit in Baltimore on January 31, 1915, he got into radio in the mid–1930s at WBAL in his hometown. That soon led him to KWK in St. Louis where he was a sports commentator and news announcer.

Moore had visions of becoming a continuity writer when NBC Blue hired him in 1939 in Chicago to host its *Club Matinee* afternoon variety series. People were laughing at his one-liners, and Moore

reconsidered his direction. He also hosted the *Fitch Summer Bandwagon* that year and conducted a competition for a new stage name for himself. A Pittsburgh lady who suggested "Garry Moore" won $50 for her efforts. Moore subsequently hosted an NBC quiz, *Beat the Band*, and another musical variety show, *Everything Goes*. Using remote pickups from U.S. Army installations, he conducted *Service with a Smile*. In addition, he was a roving announcer on the quiz show *Dr. I.Q.*

One of Moore's biggest breaks came in 1943 when he joined comic Jimmy Durante as co-host of *The Camel Caravan* (soon to be known as *The Camel Comedy Caravan*). That association appealed to four million listeners weekly, lasting into 1947. He assumed the mantel at *Take It or Leave It* on September 14, 1947, and remained through July 24, 1949. When Tom Breneman, host of *Breakfast in Hollywood*, died unexpectedly on April 28, 1948, Moore pitched in, carrying that daily show for 15 weeks in addition to his own.

Undoubtedly his most important radio venture, however, was *The Garry Moore Show*, which ran as a CBS daytime entry from 1949 to 1951 and brought significantly improved name recognition. The show evolved into a daytime CBS-TV series from 1950 to 1958 under the same title, plus a primetime TV series from 1950 to 1951, and again from 1958 to 1967. Moore extended his game show experience, too, by moderating CBS-TV's *I've Got a Secret* (1952–67) and a syndicated version of *To Tell the Truth* (1969–77). His death occurred at Hilton Head, South Carolina, on November 28, 1993.

Biographer Tom DeLong wrote this assessment of the entertainer, typically attired in bow-tie and topped off with a crew-cut: "The likable, unassuming Moore had a reputation for being unfailingly considerate and understanding. Because of his alertness and innate good taste, he always knew what to say in every situation, and whenever necessary, gently got a contestant, panelist or performer off the hook."[11] Typical of those whom Biow selected for this important duty, Moore was openly admired by his audiences.

Emcee number four at *Take It or Leave It* was none other than the established comedian known as "Banjo Eyes," Eddie Cantor, nearing the twilight of a highly successful broadcasting career. His year-long tenure on the show continued from September 11, 1949, through September 3, 1950.

A native New Yorker, Cantor was born January 31, 1892. He began entertaining as a singing waiter at Coney Island and performing in amateur night competitions in the Bowery. By 1920 he was appearing with Will Rogers and W.C. Fields in the *Ziegfeld Follies*. On Broadway he played in *Kid Boots* for years, while his most stimulating success, *Whoopee*, resulted in several Samuel Goldwyn–produced movies.

Cantor was one of Broadway's earliest name stars to appear on radio, initially airing on February 10, 1922, over Roselle Park, New Jersey's WDY. By 1926 he was guesting on *The Eveready Hour*, and in 1931 headlining his own program. Just as he and comedian Ed Wynn had done in musical comedy performances and vaudeville, both demanded a studio audience for their respective programs. This created spontaneity, laughter and applause, they exclaimed. Such "noise" had been banned previously by most shows. Cantor convinced the network and his sponsor, Standard Brands, Incorporated, that a cheering section was absolutely critical for a comic.

Following *The $64 Question*, Cantor regularly appeared in the cast of *The Big Show* on NBC Radio from 1950 to 1952. He frequently hosted *The Colgate Comedy Hour* on NBC-TV between 1950 and 1954, and oversaw a syndicated *Eddie Cantor Comedy Theatre* (1954–55) on video. On June 23, 1956, he made his dramatic debut on *Matinee Theater*, a live, hour-long weekday series on NBC-TV. He also authored two autobiographies, *My Life Is in Your Hands* and *Take My Life*. Cantor died on October 10, 1964, at Beverly Hills, California.

The fifth and final master of ceremonies on *The $64 Question*, Jack Paar, was definitely on the way up. His only real credit at the time he took the reins was in hosting *The Jack Paar Show*, a 1947 summer comedy-variety replacement for Jack Benny that was extended that autumn for another calendar quarter on another network. He, too—like Phil Baker before him—appeared in broken stints on *Take It or Leave It* from September 10, 1950, through March 11, 1951, and again as the last of the show's emcees, then under the moniker *The $64 Question*, from December 23, 1951, until the series went off the air permanently on June 1, 1952.

Paar was born May 1, 1918, at Canton, Ohio. He announced at a half-dozen Midwestern radio stations in the late 1930s. Then he performed for a couple of years before U.S. troops in the South Pacific while serving as a non-combat soldier. Returning from overseas duty, he found work as a temporary fill-in during the absences of Benny, Arthur Godfrey and Don McNeill from their regular radio stints.

Following the cancellation of *The $64 Question*, doors opened quickly for Paar in television. His assignments, invariably as a host, included: *Up to Paar* (summer of 1952), *Bank on the Stars* (1953–54), *The Jack Paar Show* (1957–62, which in 1962 became *The Tonight Show*) and *The Jack Paar Program* (a weekly series from 1962 to 1965). Among his books is 1960's *I Kid You Not*—one of his favorite expressions, which also became a national catchphrase.

No less than five announcers served *Take It or Leave It,* all veterans of other radio series: Sandy Becker, Ken Niles, Ken Roberts, David Ross and Jay Stewart.

Stewart is profiled in the chapter on *Truth or Consequences*.

Resourceful Sandy Becker excelled in multidimensional fields. His announcing duties kept him occupied with *Backstage Wife*, *The Columbia Workshop*, *The Shadow* and *Stepping Out*. He was a gifted actor, too, appearing in the casts of *Life Can Be Beautiful*, *Now Hear This* and *Treasury Agent*, and—for its final 13 years on the air—in the namesake role of the eminent daily serial *Young Doctor Malone*. After a distinguished radio career, Becker provided voice-overs for a trio of weekend TV children's cartoon series: *King Leonardo and His Short Subjects* (1960–63), *The Underdog Show* (1966–68) and *Go Go Gophers* (1968–69). Earlier, in the 1954–55 season, he hosted NBC-TV's *Armstrong Circle Theater*, and emceed a brief summer appearance of the quiz show *Win with a Winner* in 1958. Becker died on April 9, 1996, at the age of 74.

Ken Niles, meanwhile, was born December 9, 1906, at Livingston, Montana, and spent his career almost exclusively as a radio announcer. His brother Wendell is well recalled, too, as a prominent network announcer.

Having begun in the late 1920s at Seattle's KJR, Ken Niles introduced to West Coast audiences one of the first programs offering original dramas that they had ever heard, *Theatre of the Mind*. He later announced scores of network series: *The Abbott and Costello Show*, *The Affairs of Ann Scotland*, *The Amazing Mrs. Danbury*, *The Amazing Mr. Smith*, *Big Town*, *Blue Ribbon Time*, *Blue Ribbon Town*, *The Burns and Allen Show*, *Calamity Jane*, *The Camel Caravan*, *The Camel Comedy Caravan*, *The Campbell's Tomato Juice Program*, *The Danny Kaye Show*, *A Date with Judy*, *Gateway to Hollywood*, *The Grape Nuts Program*, *Hollywood Hotel*, *Hollywood Startime*, *The Judy Canova Show*, *Kay Kyser's Kollege of Musical Knowledge*, *King for a Night*, *Leave It to Joan*, *The Life of Riley*, *Maisie*, *The Marlin Hurt and Beulah Show*, *Mulligan's Travels*, *Phone Again Finnegan*, *Southern Cruise* and *Suspense*. Niles co-produced *Hollywood Hotel* with Louella Parsons, and produced *Southern Cruise*. He died at Santa Monica, California, on October 31, 1988.

If Ken Niles spent his radio career announcing 30 or more network series, Ken Roberts' appearances topped him by no less than 10. Roberts announced for all the venues on which he worked, except for the game show *Quick as a Flash*, which he emceed, and *Easy Aces*, where he both announced and carried a recurring role. Born February 12, 1910, in The Bronx, New York, he performed in summer stock productions, entering radio in 1928 via some of New York's smaller stations. When he gained a berth at CBS, he joined some of broadcasting's most capable announcers.

Over his lifetime he was awarded duties on *The Adventures of Ellery Queen*, *Al Pearce and His Gang*, *Baby Snooks*, *Blind Date*, *Brenda Curtis*, *Candid Microphone*, *Casey Crime Photographer*, *Chance of a Lifetime*, *The Chesterfield Quarter-Hour*, *Crime Doctor*, *Easy Aces*, *Everybody Wins*, *Grand Central Station*, *The Great Gildersleeve*, *Hogan's Daughter*, *The Hour of Charm*, *It Pays to Be Ignorant*, *The Jan August Show*, *Johnny Presents*, *Joyce Jordan M.D.*, *Let Yourself Go*, *Life Begins*, *The Life of Mary Sothern*, *The Linit Bath Club Revue*, *Mercury Summer Theater*, *Mr. Ace and Jane*, *$1,000 Reward*, *The Philip Morris Follies of 1946*, *The Philip Morris Playhouse*, *The Shadow*, *Sing Along*, *This Is Nora Drake*, *Tonight on Broadway*, *Truth or Consequences*, *Vic and Sade*, *The Victor Borge Show*, *What's My Name?* and *You Are There*.

Roberts returned to his roots in 1952 as a local disc jockey on New York's WMGM. For a couple of months that year he was also emcee of Dumont TV's *Where Was I?* He hosted that network's *Ladies*

Before Gentlemen in 1951, and co-hosted *Your Big Moment* on Dumont in 1953.

Announcer David Ross, also a native New Yorker, was born in 1891 and died in that city on November 12, 1975. He got his start on radio in 1926. At the time, he was a drama and book reviewer, and performed a short dramatic reading on New York's WABC, CBS's flagship station. Ross was invited to join the staff as an announcer and was soon affiliated with CBS as a poet-announcer. He made poetry recordings and, in 1932, received a diction award from the American Academy of Arts and Letters.

His announcing tasks encompassed: *Arabesque, The Big Break, The Coke Club, The Columbia Workshop, The Fred Waring Show, The Henry Morgan Show, Lombardo Land U.S.A., Myrt and Marge, The Shadow, The Street Singer,* and *Tommy Riggs and Betty Lou.* In addition, he hosted *Breezing Along,* played the male leads on *Mary and Bob's True Stories* and *The True Story Hour,* narrated and wrote *The Old Curiosity Shop,* and read poetry on *Poet's Gold, A Rendezvous with David Ross* and *Words in the Night.* Ross also read poetry and hosted Dumont TV's 1950 series *Time for Reflection.* Retiring as a freelance announcer at age 81, he continued writing verse for literary periodicals and books until his death.

Take It or Leave It orchestra conductor Jacques Renard had similar duties on *The George Burns and Gracie Allen Show, The Camel Caravan, The Camel Quarter-Hour, The Campbell's Tomato Juice Program, The Eddie Cantor Show, The Joe Penner Show,* and *Stoopnagle and Budd.* He also held the baton before the Abe Lyman Orchestra on recurring occasions. He aired his own series, *The Jacques Renard Orchestra,* over CBS from 1934 to 1937, and on MBS in 1939. Renard conducted the Meyer Davis Orchestra during the inaugural program of station KTHS at Hot Springs National Park in Arkansas on December 20,

1924. The following year he was violinist with that orchestra over New York City's WEAF, the NBC flagship station. In 1928–29 he performed with the Coconut Grove Orchestra on Boston's WEEI, a venue where he had conducted the Mansion Inn Orchestra, his first broadcast experience, in 1924.

Orchestra leader Edgar "Cookie" Fairchild led the music on *The Camel Caravan, The Eddie Cantor Pabst Blue Ribbon Show, The Ginny Simms Show* and *Time to Smile.* He conducted the band on ABC-TV's *The Jerry Colonna Show* in 1951. Fairchild died at age 76 on February 20, 1975.

Producer Betty Mandeville of *Take It or Leave It* also had the distinction of producing and directing radio's long-running *The FBI in Peace and War.*

Still others associated with the game show are mentioned elsewhere, including bandleader Ray Bloch (*Strike It Rich*) and producer Harry Spears (*Double or Nothing*).

Take It or Leave It (a.k.a. *The $64 Question*)— the most innocuous of question-and-answer shows, according to Gerald Nachman — was admittedly manipulated. Yet all of its coaching was done on-stage in full view of the studio audience. The immortal "Who was buried in Grant's tomb?" exploited by Groucho Marx on *You Bet Your Life* originated on *Take It or Leave It,* believe it or not. Host Phil Baker dreamed it up as an obvious-answer question asked of contestants who were about to leave the show empty-handed, having risked their money and lost it all. The query was attributed to Marx for years, but all he did was abscond with it, taking it before 1950s radio and TV audiences and giving it the exposure it never received on 1940s radio. In the pre–*You Bet Your Life* era, Marx was a candidate himself for master of ceremonies of *Take It or Leave It.* He was passed over by Milton Biow, however. Perhaps, in the end, he earned the last laugh by taking the "Grant's tomb" line with him.

In its heyday the show often featured celebrity guests. When comedian Jack Benny appeared under the guise of a Waukegan, Illinois, violinist, he chose the category of music history for his queries. But when the "miserly" Benny — true to his radio character — provided an accurate response to the $1 question, he decided to quit the game, keeping what he had won rather than risk losing it. A dozen years later, while appearing as a guest contestant on television's *The $64,000 Question*, Benny pulled the same stunt, pocketing the $64 he won on the first question and departing.

Take It or Leave It sparked other spin-offs, copies and imitations, in addition to *The $64,000 Question* and *The $64,000 Challenge*. Notable among the clones was the popular 1940s and 1950s quiz *Double or Nothing*. Still others tweaked the same basic formula. Ken Murray hosted a humbly-funded version of it titled *Stop or Go* at Los Angeles' KNX. More derivatives cropped up at several other local stations.

While *Take It or Leave It* allowed Peter Cranford, its creator, a comfortable lifestyle, it provided both the Milton Biow ad agency and the firm for which Biow packaged the show — the Eversharp Pen and Pencil Company — nothing short of a windfall.

In acquiring this business, Biow picked up several new and impressive clients, including such commodities as Anacin pain reliever, Lady Esther cosmetics, Pepsi cola and Ruppert beer beverages. With annual billings of $50 million in the 1940s, Biow joined the coveted list of top 10 advertising agencies in the United States. (Milton Biow himself engaged the services of a young $15-a-week bellhop at the Hotel New Yorker, turning him into a multimillion-dollar marketing icon. At a guaranteed $20,000 annually for life, Johnny Roventini became a living trademark for the Philip Morris Company as he shouted the familiar "Calllll for Philip Mor-raisss!"

on varied radio series that the tobacco company sponsored every week. It was a stroke of genius for Biow, whose agency was then purchasing all of the Morris firm's broadcast advertising.)

Meanwhile, teetering on the brink of bankruptcy at that very juncture, the Eversharp brand had lost significant market share, even though it had invented a "repeating pencil" and a touchless blade-changing injector men's razor. With about $300,000 unspent in its advertising budget for fiscal year 1940, Eversharp — and its president, Martin L. Strauss — were approached by Biow. The ad mogul recommended that the firm spend the balance of its funds on a new radio quiz over the next half-year. "Why wait a whole year to lose money when you can lose it in six months?" Biow opined "Then you have six months left to make back your money. I have a hunch *Take It or Leave It* will make it."[12]

Strauss bought the argument and the show. The fortunes of his company were soon making a stupendous turnaround. Business increased by $28 million in little more than five years, up from $2 million at the show's 1940 debut. In addition, a brigade of new distributors joined the Eversharp bandwagon, increasing that fold from 400 to 5,000 active personnel. With its slogan "Right ... with Eversharp," the company made a conspicuous comeback in its industry. When the series left the air each week, the hosts signed off with the farewell: "Bye, bye ... buy bonds ... and buy Eversharp." Yet before the program's inception, few Americans would have recognized the brand name. *Take It or Leave It* was so successful for Eversharp that the firm single-handedly underwrote the series for the full decade it ran under that moniker.

It should be noted that the scandal that emanated from the legacy left by *Take It or Leave It* in no way impugns the name of a blameless radio quiz. A brief examination of the details that led to that fiasco will illustrate the fact.

Having projected a top cash prize of $64 throughout its existence, after 10 years— in 1950 — with the catchphrase "the $64 question" regularly falling from the lips of scads of Americans, the show's producers decided to retitle their little quiz — what else?— *The $64 Question*. From March 18, 1951, until the program left the air forever on June 1, 1952, it was known under the new appellation, without any format changes.

Sometime after its departure, Milton Biow determined to disperse his advertising agency and retire. In 1955 he sold half his interest in what had been a very profitable *Take It or Leave It*— including the right to use the figure 64 — to a new quiz being readied for television by producer and packager Louis G. Cowan (who is profiled in the chapter on *Stop the Music!*).

Cowan's quiz, an outgrowth of *The $64 Question*, was to be built on the same principle of doubling the starting amount, which was to start with $1,000 instead of $1. The ultimate prize would be $64,000, hence the title *The $64,000 Question*. The show was wildly anticipated even before its debut on CBS-TV on June 7, 1955, with Hal March as emcee. No audiences of any previously broadcast competition had ever witnessed cash prizes at that level; therefore, the national response was euphoric. After a player reached the $4,000 level he was asked only a single question weekly, prolonging the attention span of viewers while adding to the show's mystique. Just as players had done on the radio version, one could quit at any time or risk everything already won by trying for the next level, each time doubling the earnings to a maximum of $64,000.

So successful was the TV venture that other mega-moneyed quizzes began appearing elsewhere, including *The Big Surprise, Twenty-One* and — on April 8, 1956 —

a spin-off of the original video series labeled *The $64,000 Challenge*. The latter involved contenders battling former winners of *The $64,000 Question*, contestants whose prize money totaled at least $8,000. Eventually, in an effort to maintain supremacy among the growing maze of giveaways, *The $64,000 Question* added three new plateaus, boosting its top prize to $256,000.

If it had all stayed clean and honest, who knows where this might have led?

But it didn't.

In their incessant drive to win higher ratings against the competition, the producers of several of these giveaways— among them, *The $64,000 Question*, *The $64,000 Challenge* and *Twenty-One*— tainted their genre by discussing potential questions and answers with *some* (but not all) of the players, driving up the ratings. (Specifically naming those shows two decades later, genre interpreter Maxene Fabe attested: "Three of the best games ever were also the crookedest."[13])

Had not a disgruntled contestant in August 1958 on *Dotto*— a lesser-known TV quiz with daytime and primetime editions— spilled the beans, declaring the show was "fixed," the scandal that erupted and destroyed Americans' confidence in what they had been watching might never have transpired. It turned out that that revelation was but the tip of the iceberg.

In the ensuing investigation and subsequent trials, finger pointing of many persuasions surfaced, involving a widespread number of shows and individuals. When other contestants testified that they had been prompted with answers, deep secrets that had been carefully tucked inside dark corners suddenly appeared in the light; and with those came the virtual banishment of a species for many years. *The $64,000 Challenge* abruptly departed September 7, 1958; *Twenty-One* was gone on October 16 of that year; and *The $64,000 Question* disappeared November 2.

Nearly two decades elapsed, in fact, before a syndicated revival of the original big money quiz that doubled players' winnings surfaced under the title of *The $128,000 Question*. It featured Mike Darrow as originating host, in 1976, and a youthful Alex Trebek the following year. By 1978 it, too, was gone, having lacked both novelty and suspense. Its predecessor had been televised live, with contestants succeeding or failing in front of the whole country. The reprise, on the other hand, pretaped weeks in advance and shown by local stations at varying times and on different dates, missed the tension that the original generated.

It would take *Twenty-One* even longer to make a comeback. In light of the successful *Who Wants to Be a Millionaire?* that debuted on ABC-TV in 1999, NBC-TV reintroduced a modern version of its former famous scandal-ridden show — complete with isolation booths — that autumn. It had been 41 years, and a couple of generations, since the model on which it was based had left the air.

Take It or Leave It may have spawned these shows — but never the disgrace they became. Audience members, emcees and other staffers unhesitatingly supplied answers to the radio contestants, too. Yet none of it was done via the clandestine methods employed by those who later exploited the players in a feverish pitch to hype the ratings.

On the radio series, shouting out hints frequently made the outcome funnier, especially when a contestant didn't connect with the clues. It was done in jest, of course, and seldom resulted in the tense moments that the TV series with their isolation booths netted. Then again, the stakes weren't nearly as high. Garry Moore may have said it all when he inquired of a contestant: "So what are you going to do if you win the $64? Make a down payment on a pork chop?"

15

Truth or Consequences

Premise: Distinguishing this audience participation marathon from nearly all of its contemporaries isn't difficult. This show offered unbridled antics that urged average citizens to poke fun at themselves—even appearing as it did during a global war interval and the aftermath from it. When the series picked up speed, moreover, it encouraged common folk to share from the bounty of their resources with a host of charitable enterprises to which the program developed an affinity. On the way to fulfillment, this boisterous, rollicking Saturday night stomp-and-romp became an instant favored pastime with millions, remaining so throughout the 1940s. It was an attention-gaining, headline-grabbing melee that gave the fans something to chuckle about between shows. Sheer lunacy resulted from its ongoing quests for hilarity by staging sightless gags that appeared as funny to the fans at home as to the studio audience that could witness the antics as they took place. The more bizarre a prank, the more listeners seemed to fall under *Consequences'* spell. Some stunts continued for weeks, allowing new admirers to be drawn into the mystical web, if only to see where all of it would lead. At the helm of the week-end-ing fiasco, host Ralph Edwards set it all into motion with his inventive mind. Taking ample pains to unerringly set up each caper, thus realizing maximum response as an outcome, Edwards' rejoinders netted the effect of turning the high jinks into mere child's play. Yet here were adults having the time of their lives! While some listeners may have wondered about their own addiction to it, the show's squeaky clean demeanor left nearly everybody who tuned in regularly believing it was a half-hour well spent.

Creator-Producer-Host: Ralph Edwards

Directors: Herb Moss, Bill Burch, Bob Seal, Ed Bailey

Production Manager: Alfred Paschall

Production Assistants: Carl Frederick, Fred Carney, Bill Hawes

Announcers: Mel Allen, Ken Carpenter, Clayton (Bud) Collyer, Milton Cross (remotes), Ed Herlihy, Jerry Lawrence (remotes), Ken Roberts, Verne Smith, Jay Stewart, Joe Walters, Harlow Wilcox

Writers: Bill Burch, Phil Davis, Paul Edwards (Ralph's brother), Ralph Edwards, Carl Jampel, George Jeske, Mort Lewis, Carl Manning, Al Simon, Mel Vickland

Musician: Buddy Cole

Sound Effects: Lloyd J. Creekmore, Bob Prescott

Theme Songs: "Merrily We Roll Along"; "Hail, Hail, the Gang's All Here"

Sponsors: Procter and Gamble Co. initially brought this show to the air for Ivory soap (March 23–July 27, 1940). However, it became a smash hit during a durable, better-recalled Duz detergent run for P&G (Aug. 17, 1940–June 24, 1950). Returning to CBS for a season, the series picked up the Philip Morris Co. (for its Philip Morris cigarettes) as sponsor. Back at NBC, the Pet Milk Co. underwrote the program from June 17, 1952 to April 15, 1954. Multiple patrons carried it in its final season.

Ratings: High: 25.7 (1947–48); Low: 5.6 (1952–53); Median: 14.9 (all except the 1951–52 season included).

On the Air: March 23–July 27, 1940, CBS, Saturday, 9:45 P.M. ET; Aug. 17, 1940–June 27, 1942, NBC, Saturday, 8:30 P.M.; Sept. 12, 1942–June 26, 1943, NBC, Saturday, 8:30 P.M.; Sept. 18, 1943–July 15, 1944, NBC, Saturday, 8:30 P.M.; Sept. 9, 1944–July 7, 1945, NBC, Saturday, 8:30 P.M.; Sept. 8, 1945–July 6, 1946, NBC, Saturday, 8:30 P.M.; Sept. 7, 1946–July 5, 1947, NBC, Saturday, 8:30 P.M.; Sept. 6, 1947–June 26, 1948, NBC, Saturday, 8:30 P.M.; Aug. 28, 1948–June 25, 1949, NBC, Saturday, 8:30 P.M.; Aug. 27, 1949–June 24, 1950, NBC, Saturday, 8:30 P.M.; Sept. 5, 1950–May 29, 1951, CBS, Tuesday, 9:30 P.M.; June 17–Sept. 30, 1952, NBC, Tuesday, 9:30 P.M.; Sept. 18, 1952–June 18, 1953, NBC, Thursday, 9 P.M.; June 24, 1953–Sept. 16, 1953, NBC, Wednesday, 9:30 P.M.; Sept. 24, 1953–April 15, 1954, NBC, Thursday; Oct. 26, 1955–Sept. 12, 1956, NBC, Wednesday, 8 P.M.

*   *   *

Imagine yourself seated in a studio audience anticipating the start of a live radio performance of one of America's most electrifying half-hours. The announcer is just completing his warm-ups, having encouraged hundreds of spectators to ebulliently respond to some anticipated zany antics planned for the night's weekly broadcast.

In a final prelude, a couple of gentlemen (most likely servicemen in uniform) are plucked from the studio audience and brought on-stage. Following a brief interview, they're invited to compete against each other for a cash prize. Their instructions are to fetch articles of women's clothing from a nearby trunk and put them on over their uniforms. The object of the exercise is to determine who can complete his outfit first.

The exhibition is precisely timed. Just as one of the contestants begins to wiggle into a girdle — with the studio audience convulsing into gales of laughter approaching near-hysteria — the sweep second hand of a big wall clock reaches the top of the half-hour. At precisely that instant an engineer throws a switch and this undisciplined mayhem bursts onto the national airwaves. The show's announcer gleefully informs millions of radio fans nationwide: "Hello there! We've been waiting for you! It's time to play *Truth ... or Consequences!*" A hasty rendition of "Merrily We Roll Along" in glissando-like form erupts from the studio console, confirmation that — once again — listeners coast to coast have tuned in to the jocularity and bedlam they expect from *Truth or Consequences*.

Now, fast forward to the present.

Media consultant Leonard Maltin refers to this show's opening as "the most memorable — and consistent — audience reaction in the history of radio."[1] While deprived of both audible and visual accounts of what has caused such an explosion in a broadcast studio, the program's legions of fans are, nonetheless, eager to lay aside their cares for a half-hour. No matter how ludicrous it may now seem, *Truth or Consequences* had become a national shrine, one that many U.S. citizens at mid-century could hardly rise beyond.

It became an addiction; virtually every Saturday night in the 1940s, *Truth or Consequences* was an itch that millions of Americans faithfully scratched as an integral part of their weekend agendas. While its merrymaking at times reached epic proportions (*Life* magazine labeled it "the nearest thing to insanity in radio"), the folks at home didn't require a visual medium to plug into the boisterously engaging events rollicking that Hollywood stage. (The show aired from New York in its first five seasons, moving to Hollywood in autumn 1945.) Verbal descriptions by creator-host Ralph Edwards, coupled with the expressive responses of a studio audience, told the story to hordes of unseen patrons at home.

Gerald Nachman purports that if there's a fine line separating quiz and game programs, an even finer line divides game and giveaway shows. He submits that game shows may be isolated from stunt shows by the most minuscule of differences.[2]

Indubitably, *Truth or Consequences* was the catalyst that prompted the launch of several stunt shows to follow. Through numerous reincarnations of this program that continued for five decades, it never lost the original premise of its founder: to show America having fun.

Edwards directly answered the critics who believed that sociologists and psychologists would shudder over those who voluntarily appeared on this show, subjecting themselves to inane indignities. Stating that the participants could in no way be dubbed lunatics, he characterized them as typical attorneys, ministers, sales reps, homemakers and taxi drivers who were merely "out for a little fun, and perhaps a cash prize."[3]

Just what *was* this psychosis that had so much of the country glued to its radio sets during the 1940s and — to a lesser extent — the 1950s? One national magazine observed audiences being led to a sphere where "demented situations" derived "lots of fun" while simultaneously appearing as "the essence of normality."[4]

The mania consisted of stunts such as substituting a trained seal on-stage for a man's wife. The blindfolded husband was to be tested on his ability to climb into bed late at night without waking his "wife." While comforting his bed partner, he snuggled close, soothing "her" skin. During the upheaval, the seal retorted with grunts as the studio audience exploded into raucous pandemonium.

One Halloween Edwards sent an unsuspecting lady on a haunted house venture away from the studio (she was blindfolded, as he so often liked to do to traveling contestants). If she could correctly guess where she was upon her arrival, she'd earn a hundred dollar bill. After the woman departed from the studio, the sly-as-a-fox Edwards joyously affirmed: "Oh, what's gonna happen to her!" He confessed that the show had worked with the lady's husband without her knowledge. Staffers transformed their home into a scary cavern with recorded ghost screams and hideous monster trappings. Then Edwards quipped, a tinge of madness in his exuberance, "Aren't we devils?" (It was a catchphrase he employed at least once on virtually every show, and it quickly became part of the national lexicon. With some regularity, for years the query fell from the lips of millions of fans.)

The contestant, still blindfolded near the end of the program, had no idea where she was but allowed that it "smells like a brewery in here!" The studio audience bellowed ecstatically, and for being a good sport, Edwards gave the contestant the hundred dollars anyway.

These were the types of monkeyshines

that transpired weekly, becoming a Saturday night ritual for much of the country for over a decade. A look at how it all began will be helpful in drawing the uninitiated to an understanding of the series' impact in the annals of broadcasting. Let's begin by focusing on Edwards himself, the show's creator and abiding inspiration, who remained with it as master of ceremonies throughout its radio run.

Born on a ranch in northern Colorado near the little hamlet of Merino on June 13, 1913, as a youngster Edwards milked four cows twice daily. He also made frequent pack trips into the Rockies during boyhood. At age 12, when the Edwardses relocated to California, young Ralph ceded his love of outdoor camping to the Sierra Nevada range. Years later, after becoming a national radio celebrity, he reflected on those days:

> Many were the rainy nights when mother and dad and three of us boys racked our brains over guessing games, dressed up for Charades, spun scary stories for Ghosts, but the best nights of all were with a gang around when we sing-songed "Heavy Heavy Hangs Over Thy Head ... Is it Fine or Superfine? Tell the Truth or pay the consequences."[5]

In those experiences enacting some variation of an old parlor game commonly known as Forfeit, the competition usually called for holding some familiar object over the head of the player who was designated "it." "It" couldn't see the object, of course. Given clues, if "it" was unable to identify the article — or sometimes answer a silly question — he or she had to pay the consequences. It was simplified, of course, like kissing a boy or girl of the opposite gender from a nearby ranch.

Unknown to the Edwardses then was that that little pastime would have a teeming effect upon members of their household for years to come. But lest we get ahead of the story, nearly two decades elapsed before Forfeit was to dazzle Americans coast to coast, catapulting young Ralph into instant stardom.

By 1930 the youth was pursuing radio as a vocation, plying his abilities at a nearby Oakland station as a writer, actor and announcer. There he gained acumen that was to sustain him for the rest of his working life. Honing new skills, he soon became a familiar voice to listeners of that city's station, KROW. Simultaneously, he was working at KPRC in San Francisco and pursuing a bachelor's degree at the University of California, Berkeley, a diploma he was awarded in 1935. At Berkeley Edwards was active in the drama department. During his enrollment he appeared in practically every little theater production produced there.

Single, young Edwards was enamored by the prospects of a lifetime investment in network radio. At age 22, in 1935 he decided to cast his lot in New York City. Thumbing his way across the continent with a few greenbacks in his jeans, he soon reached his destination. There he found sleeping quarters in a Manhattan chapel while often accepting meals from Bowery soup kitchens.

Remaining focused, however, he lined up several radio auditions. In a short while he was appearing on network shows like *Renfrew of the Mounted*, and *Stoopnagle and Budd*. Not much later, CBS put out the word that it was hiring a staff announcer — and 70 aspirants showed up, Edwards among them. He won the spot and in a brief span found himself a rising interlocutor on as many as 45 shows weekly, including: *Against the Storm, Coast to Coast on a Bus, A Dream Comes True, The Gospel Singer, The Gumps, The Horn and Hardart Children's Hour, Life Can Be Beautiful, Major Bowes' Original Amateur Hour, The Phil Baker Show, Town Hall Tonight*, and *Vic and Sade.*

One radio biographer noted that Edwards' cordial approach to commercials on the daytime soap operas "all but revolutionized" announcing in that period.[6] The effusive host inserted "conversational punctuation" into advertising copy, almost as if addressing each feminine listener individually. On one show, for instance, he ad-libbed this discourse:

> You know, when you listen to *Life Can Be Beautiful*, you get the feeling that Chi Chi and Papa David and all the others are sort of like old friends. Don't you think that's the way it is? Friends that you look forward to visiting with every day. Now, I never heard of anybody looking forward to dishwashing, but [*chortle*] just the same, I know a lot of you feel friendly to the soap that helps your hands look nice and gives you speedy suds at the same time. Yes, Ma'am, I mean good old Ivory Flakes....

The shows Edwards appeared on provided him with a quite comfortable living in that Depression-recovery era. He admitted later that his annual salary by that time exceeded $50,000. At one point he suggested that his voice introduced more commercial programs than anybody else on the air. Despite such good fortune, however, he was a malcontent. Years later he would muse: "I didn't want to be just an announcer."

Having probed the successes of those who had risen to the forefront of broadcasting careers, he was persuaded that performers who took a hand in developing unique program styles gained status among radio's well-heeled royalty. The best of all possible worlds, Edwards thought, would be to prove himself as an innovative program producer. Such an opportunity might allow him to concentrate on only one or two primary efforts rather than running from show to show throughout the workday.

Edwards believed that the risk of giving up his secure and lucrative commitments would be the right thing to do in exchange for an opportunity to achieve his dream. Through the grapevine he learned in 1939 that one of radio's most respected underwriters, the Procter and Gamble Company — which was paying the bills for several of the shows on which he was then working — was searching for an innovative concept for a nighttime radio series.

Edwards wracked his brain trying to think of a format that had never been tried on the air. Some years later he recalled the exact time and place that inspiration hit him and *Truth or Consequences* was born. He had just arrived at home from the studios late one Thursday afternoon in November 1939. Having thought for weeks of little else beyond dreaming up a new show, suddenly — in the company of his young bride, Barbara, and her parents, who were in New York on a visit — he remembered the old parlor game his family had played back in Colorado: Forfeit. While the game hadn't been enacted before an audience, Edwards sensed that people watching it in a studio — and millions at home transferring the action in their minds — would love it.

He got on the phone with John MacMillan, the radio kingpin of the Compton Advertising agency, and exuberantly shared his idea. MacMillan questioned: "When can you audition it?" Edwards replied that he could have something together within two or three weeks; MacMillan asked if he could do it by Sunday, three days hence. Edwards gulped, yet readily agreed.

That night he dispatched a buddy (Jack Farnell) from Oakland, who was then in New York, to the public library to search for questions. In the meantime, Barbara, her parents and Ralph began thinking up consequences. The following day — in between his radio stints on *Life Can Be Beautiful*, *Against the Storm* and *The Gospel Singer* — he arranged for the studio audience of *The Horn and Hardart Children's Hour* program, which he was then emceeing, to remain an extra 45 minutes after Sunday morning's show. They would provide the live audience he needed for an audition performance.

He engaged Andre Baruch, with whom he had shared an apartment in their bachelor days, and his wife Bea Wain to make a celebrity appearance on the show. On Saturday night he imposed on some University of California chums who were living in the area. Inviting them to supper, he led them to play *Truth or Consequences* after dinner, a kind of "dress rehearsal" for the next day's trial run.

A transcription disc of the audition, which came off without a hitch, was given to Compton executives on Monday. They responded favorably and shipped it off to Cincinnati for reactions from Procter and Gamble's sensitive ears. A green light wasn't long in arriving. Within four months *Truth or Consequences* hit the airwaves, premiering for Ivory soap on March 23, 1940, for 30 minutes over the Columbia Broadcasting System. It was the start of a broadcasting venture that would entertain American audiences for five decades. And for his efforts, Edwards—the man who had risked career and livelihood for a shot as a program creator, owner, producer, writer and master of ceremonies—would be certified as radio's youngest entrepreneur.

The exhibition itself was to carry quiz programs to an altogether new plateau. Simple in concept, it decreed that contestants would attempt to answer an inquisition for which they were almost never prepared. There were impractical queries like:

"Why is a hunting license just like a marriage license?"
Answer: "It entitles you to one deer and no more."

or

"Why would anybody bring a bottle of milk to a poker game?"
Answer: "To feed the kitty."

For a rare answer that was accepted by the judges, contestants were paid a handsome $15. But as rapidly as a player missed a question, sound effects technician Bob Prescott pressed a button that created a tone that audiences came to anticipate, soon identified as "Beulah the Buzzer." This reverberation indicated that a wrong response had been given and a penalty must be paid. The fun really started then.

Numerous contestants admitted that they missed their questions on purpose in order to carry the exposition to its ultimate conclusion. As a rule they wound up as the dupe of some elaborate practical joke that the show's creative staff had dreamed up.

On a 1948 outing, for instance, Edwards told Mrs. Earl Peterson of Milwaukee, Wisconsin, that a psychic would reveal her future to her that evening. She was sent offstage to retrieve a crystal ball that the clairvoyant was to use. But while she was out of earshot, Edwards quipped: "Oooooooo—what's gonna happen to her!" It was another of his favorite catchphrases that he introduced once or twice on every show. He apprised the studio and radio audiences that, offstage, the contestant was being told that her husband would appear in disguise as the fortune-teller. Each time he correctly answered one of her questions, she was to kiss him. With flippancy in his voice, Edwards chortled: "What she doesn't know is ... we're substituting actor Boris Karloff for her husband!"

Peterson, the husband, had supplied the answers to questions his wife was to ask the medium. Wearing heavy camouflage, Karloff would offer memorized replies to her queries, receiving a kiss for his efforts. The audience expectantly awaited the outcome as Edwards exclaimed with glee: "Aren't we devils?"

The bedevilment transpired and Mrs. Peterson wasn't surprised when the seer responded perfectly to every inquiry. In fact, with each query the studio audience broke into a convulsive, boisterous crescendo. After the final inquisition and smooch, Edwards asked: "Mrs. Peterson, do you think your husband would mind your kissing this total stranger?"

"No," she replied confidently, "I knew it was him all the time.... I know those lips." The audience roared.

During a slight dip in the gales of laughter, Edwards announced, "OK, swami, go ahead and remove your beard and turban; she knew it was you all the time." The contestant nearly passed out as she screamed: "It's Boris Karloff!"

The contagious response of the studio audience must have been enough to satisfy the listeners at home who could only visualize the gag. That was the beauty of radio, of course. In the theater of the mind, everyone was free to imagine precisely how a stunt was being played out in a studio far away.

Complex groundwork for a show sometimes required the use of live animals or piping in segments that originated from sidewalks and depots, as well as remotes that featured players involved in stunts in progress, plus appearances by entertainment luminaries tapped as part of a gag. While the stars weren't paid large sums (as they often appeared plugging something they were then doing), the whole contrivance required an excessively large budget. But the sponsor had deep pockets and was obviously convinced that the return on its investment was well worth it.

Occasionally some of *Truth or Consequences'* stunts backfired.

When Edwards sent Lamonte Tupper from Los Angeles to Minnesota to hook a specific fish that had been tagged, the contestant ran into difficulty in catching his prey. But the governor of Minnesota — sensing that some potentially flattering publicity for the state might be going down the drain — stepped in. Ordering the state's game wardens to catch the fish, he had them place it in a bathtub in front of the state capitol at St. Paul. Tupper reeled in his fish and captured a $500 prize from the show. And the state of Minnesota capitalized on it, as the bathtub photo appeared in newspapers nationwide.

In another jaunt that initially went awry, contestant Rudolph J. Wickel was told on a 1944 broadcast that the show had buried a thousand dollars for him. He would find the money in an abandoned plot in Holyoke, Massachusetts, where Prospect and Walnut streets intersected. The masterminds obviously hadn't thought that one through, however. *Time* magazine reported that, no sooner had that notice reached the ears of eager listeners than a throng of prospectors debarked at that precise Massachusetts corner and started to dig. Long before Wickel arrived by train with a pick and shovel in tow did a pair of foragers unearth 500 silver dollars each. The plot of ground, said *Time*, "looked as if it had been bombed." To save face while calming some ruffled feathers among the locals, Edwards agreed to convert the vacant lot into a public park.

The show would get even more mileage out of the fiasco, however. Initially paying the contestant with $1,000 in Confederate money, Edwards next gave Wickel a 1,500–pound safe containing half of an authentic $1,000 bill. He also burdened him with a parrot, claiming that the bird would reveal the location of the currency's other half. Things got out of hand once more when the parrot failed to deliver.

Edwards informed the determined contestant at last that he'd locate the elusive half-bill between the pages of an unidentified book. Encouraging listeners to contribute texts (which would wind up in due time in the hands of a benevolent Victory

Book Campaign), the request netted 17,000 volumes. In one of them Wickel found the other piece of currency, but not before Edwards had extended the caper — and gained listeners' rapt attention — over several extra weeks.

Most of *Truth or Consequences'* stunts weren't that involved.

A couple sat at a table on the studio stage and attempted to carry on a normal dialogue while feeding each other blueberry pie. Both were blindfolded.

A soldier telephoned his steady sweetheart back home, and he, too, attempted to carry on an even conversation. Hindering him was the curvaceous, well-stacked model who sat on his lap while gurgling sweet nothings in his ear. Throughout his ordeal he sought to maintain composure without divulging the circumstances, while bringing the studio audience to peak hysteria.

Another contestant was asked to sing "Donkey Serenade" while accompanied by a chorus of a score of live donkeys. "Everybody had a big laugh," Edwards recalled. "Except perhaps the NBC custodians."

Such shenanigans soon deposed the reigning *Information Please* as the nation's most-listened-to question-and-answer program. Even though some may have felt a tad foolish for being drawn under its magic spell, the fact that millions of admirers were tuning in to *Truth or Consequences* every Saturday night spoke volumes about how it was received. Wrote one observer: "If nothing else, it made you feel superior to the willing clucks who allowed themselves to be made ninnies of nationally; it probably helped that nobody could be seen."[7]

Comedian Fred Allen, whose distaste for giveaway programs has been well documented, and who — for a decade — conducted a tirade against such fare within the industry, satirized Ralph Edwards' show in 1941. Referring in a sketch to "Truth or Subsequences," Allen featured poorly informed contestants who couldn't even exhibit such common knowledge as the name of the first U.S. president. Silly tricks followed. Barclay Krawl of Poison Pen, Iowa, was outfitted as an infant, while Mrs. Krawl, in a charade as the child's father, blew cigar smoke while reciting "The Village Blacksmith." A repulsive master of ceremonies, meanwhile, giggled uproariously with the guffaws of a studio audience. In retrospect, such parody may have actually enhanced *Truth or Consequences'* favorable acceptance with the public, as did some of Allen's other put-downs.

During World War II — when the nation experienced a shortage of pennies in circulation — a Staten Island housewife, Mrs. Dennis Mullane, was instrumental in doing something about it. Edwards asked listeners to send her, mother of the youngest Marine in uniform (he was 17), copper pennies so she might purchase a war bond for her son. As thousands of envelopes started arriving at her home, the woman frantically appealed to the emcee for help. Edwards dispatched some recruits to assist in opening the mail and counting the receipts. (By the time it tapered off she had acquired 130,000 pieces of mail.)

On the following Saturday night's show, Edwards presented her son with 315,000 pennies ($3,150), plus quarters, half-dollars, dollar bills and extraneous gifts that listeners had sent in. The youth said he would give 20 percent of the proceeds to the Marine base at Camp Lejeune, North Carolina, to purchase sports equipment. U.S. Mint director Nellie Taylor publicly acknowledged *Truth or Consequences'* efforts on behalf of the nation, drawing upon that occasion to remind lethargic Americans: "Every penny hoarded means that another must be made from scarce metals urgently needed for the war."[8]

Helping to improve the plight of someone in need and, in particular, supporting charitable causes became a byword for *Truth or Consequences.*

For a Mother's Day airing, the program flew Mrs. Margaret McGinn, a mother of 16, from Erin, Ireland, to Los Angeles to surprise a son she hadn't seen in two decades. The unsuspecting progeny, who surfaced at the *Truth or Consequences* studios by way of the clandestine efforts of some friends, encountered a heartwarming reunion. Then the program underwrote a two-week vacation for mother and son to several prominent southern California attractions. Speaking of that occasion, Edwards acknowledged in a fan magazine, "Those are the miracles it is fun to make."

In early 1943 a 14-week cross-country jaunt allowed Edwards to entertain military personnel at remote bases while he took the show to audiences beyond the nation's broadcasting centers. When a Denver committee oversold the available seating by 1,500, an extra performance was added. A crowd of 9,000 showed up to view the live broadcast at Topeka, a city of 73,000 residents.

While on tour, the show encouraged local audiences to purchase E bonds in support of the national war effort. More than $500 million was raised for the U.S. treasury as a result of these tours, which exceeded 100,000 miles. Edwards was presented with an Eisenhower Award by the U.S. Treasury Department in recognition of the show's efforts toward the welfare of the nation.

The format for *Truth or Consequences* was usually blocked out a month or so in advance. While Edwards himself thought up many of the stunts, he was abetted by what he labeled the show's "brain trust." In addition to its creator, this compelling assemblage included Phil Davis, who joined the ranks after the initial year on the air, and who became chief idea developer; Al Paschall, the program's production manager, who came aboard only four weeks after the debut; and a quartet of gag writers— Bill Burch, Ralph's brother Paul, Mort Lewis

and Mel Vickland. The brain trust normally met every Tuesday to consider potential consequences.

Beyond all of the zany ideas this bunch proffered over the long run, it unquestionably gained more plaudits for the show via a series of stunts that made utterly good sense. Over several seasons a procession of hidden celebrity identities, in conjunction with a few noble charitable causes, was introduced. Some of the nation's attention was riveted to the show as the sequences grabbed news headlines. One radio historiographer suggested that, through such efforts, the series "electrified the country."[9]

It all began as a gag on the program of December 29, 1945. Edwards tells about it in his own words:

> I had got so fed up with radio programs which asked a contestant some first grade question like what is the capital of the United States and rewarded a correct answer with a gift of a Cadillac, that I decided to run a give-away to end all give-aways.... I felt then, and I still do, that a radio show which cannot hold an audience on the basis of its entertainment value should not be on the air.[10]

He penned a poem that was marinated in clues:

> *Hickory dickory dock,*
> *The hands went round the clock*
> *The clock struck ten*
> *Lights out*
> *Goodnight.*

An unidentified reader (prizefighter Jack Dempsey) offered this jingle every Saturday night for several weeks. Various contestants were given an opportunity to identify the man whom Edwards called "Mr. Hush." A small jackpot of merchandise grew every week as participants failed in their efforts to name the luminary. Eventually, the "crackpot jackpot" reached

$13,500, a hefty sum by mid–1940s standards. At that point a Navy lieutenant, Ensign Richard Bartholomew of Fayetteville, Arkansas, guessed the name of Dempsey and claimed the prizes. Radio jackpots often included automobiles, travel vouchers, airplanes, motorboats, house trailers, mink coats and jewelry among their stashes, incidentally.

By then, *Truth or Consequences* had attracted a horde of new listeners who were clamoring for more guessing games. Edwards recalled a personal inner struggle that such heady success brought him.

> I couldn't let them down. Nor could I, in good conscience, go along with a technique which turned radio into an oversized grab bag.
> The months between the Dempsey contest and our Mrs. Hush game with Clara Bow were an agony of conferences with lawyers, United States government legal experts, and ultimately — for I had found a "right reason" for the contests — with officials of the March of Dimes.[11]

The contests continued, but for worthy endeavors.

The subsequent "Mrs. Hush" competition featuring silent screen star Bow focused on the concern of many Americans who could be motivated to assist in the fight to end the crippling disease known as infantile paralysis, or poliomyelitis, then sweeping the nation. The March of Dimes was a charitable foundation whose sole mission was to raise donations to conquer the dreaded scourge.

By then the emphasis for these mystery celebrity events had shifted from studio participants to the millions who were hearing the show on radio. Listeners could voluntarily submit donations while attempting to identify "Mrs. Hush." All they had to do was to complete the following statement in 25 words or less: "We should all support the March of Dimes because...."

From the mail each week the contest judges drew a select number of "best entries." This qualified their writers to be eligible for a possible telephone call from Edwards while on the air the following Saturday night. If no one who was interviewed could name the mystery celebrity during a show, new clues would be given and more prizes added to the jackpot that the eventual winner would receive. The fans at home were given added opportunities to be called. They could send in new statements each week and could add March of Dimes donations with it if they wished.

There was no rush to reach the outcome, of course. Why would there be? The participants were having fun, while millions of listeners were holding their breath; the March of Dimes was reaping tangible benefits, eventually topping $545,000 directly from this appeal; and the show was once again harvesting favorable treatment in the news media coast to coast.

By the time Mrs. William H. McCormick figured out at last that the hidden identity belonged to Bow, which earned McCormick $17,590 in merchandise, Edwards realized he had a good thing going that couldn't be dismissed. "I have no right to discard an idea which can do this, especially when it gives half the people of the country a wonderful time besides," he announced.[12] More mystery celebrity contests followed.

Dancer Martha Graham was eventually identified as "Miss Hush" by a listener who claimed over $21,000 in prizes. Another $672,000 went into the March of Dimes coffers.

What had been originally intended as a satire of the high stakes competitions on radio had actually become broadcasting's biggest giveaway. The stash secured by Mrs. Florence Hubbard for naming Jack Benny as the "Walking Man," a 1947 contest that transfixed the nation's listeners for weeks, was typical. Her booty would gladden the heart of any Internal Revenue Service official, while at the same time posing the query: What's the beneficiary, the American Heart Association, getting out of all of this? (Actually, the AHA amassed more than $1.5 million from the contest, although anyone toting up the prizes while forgetting they were donated might have had pause to wonder.) The widowed Mrs. Hubbard, age 68, a $30-a-week sales clerk for Chicago's Carson-Pirie-Scott department store, was encumbered with all of the following after her on-air revelation:

Bendix home laundry (including washer, dryer and automatic ironer)

$1,000 diamond and ruby Bulova watch

4-door Cadillac sedan

Tappan gas kitchen range

16mm motion picture sound projector and screen with a print of the Hal Wallis production "I Walk Alone" and delivery of a Motion Picture of the Month for one year

Two-week vacation for two from anyplace in the U.S. to Union Pacific's Sun Valley, Idaho, all expenses paid

$1,000 J. R. Wood and Sons art-carved diamond ring

Electrolux vacuum cleaner and all the attachments

1948 RCA Victor console FM-AM radio and phonograph combination and TV set in a single cabinet

Servel silent gas refrigerator

Art Craft all metal venetian blinds for windows throughout the entire home

Sherwin-Williams agreed to paint the house inside and out, paint included

Complete wardrobe of women's clothes for every season of the year, designed by Faye Foster, consisting of street dresses, beachwear and play clothes

Frigidaire home freezer filled with Bird's Eye frozen foods

Luskum Silvair all metal airplane

Kitchen and bathroom completely installed with ceramic tile by the Pomona Tile Manufacturing Company

Dining room and two bedrooms filled with Idaho Pine furniture

$2,400 deluxe 3-room Normel trailer coach equipped with modern kitchen and sleeping quarters for four

Remington Rand noiseless model 7 typewriter

14-foot Aluma Craft boat complete with Champion outboard motor

$1,000 full-length Persian lamb coat designed by furrier Max Foyer

Two-year supply of Pepperell sheets and pillowcases for every bed in the house

Choice of $500 worth of Westinghouse electric home appliances

Story and Clark piano

Universal electric blankets for every bed in the house

Three Coronada air-cooled summer suits for every man in the immediate family

Roger and Company desk console Sew-Gem electric sewing machine

Even a pauper could have turned into a princess with spoils like these! The generous publicity to the providers was worth far more than the minimal outlay for prizes that they surrendered, while millions reveled in that extensive list as it was read aloud every Saturday night for months.

The winners of such competitions not only received cash and merchandise jackpots, but they turned into luminaries themselves. The aforementioned Mrs. Hubbard acquired 40 marriage proposals from her instant fame and fortune. Still others achieved celebrated status within their own local communities.

(When Jack Benny was identified as the "Walking Man," Edwards explained that the comedian hailed originally from Waukegan, Illinois, meaning 'walk again' "as named by the Indians." As part of her quick rise to luster, Mrs. Hubbard, who unmasked Benny, was invited to appear on the following Saturday night's broadcast of *Truth or Consequences*. Later, speaking on the air with Edwards from his secret hideaway, Benny allowed [to tumultuous studio cackling]: "I'd like to get Mrs. Hubbard as a guest on my show the following Sunday night. And if we can't get her, Ralph, would you see if you can get Carson, Pirie or Scott?")

The American Heart Association gained national acclaim for the first time in its brief history when it received the proceeds from a trio of *Truth or Consequences* mystery celebrity competitions. In excess of $2.5 million was raised from endeavors involving the "Walking Man" (comic Benny), "Whispering Woman" (vocalist Jeanette MacDonald) and "Mr. Heartbeat" (poet Edgar A. Guest). A "Mr. and Mrs. Hush" campaign (featuring musicians Moss Hart and Kitty Carlisle) enriched the coffers of the Arthritis Foundation. By late 1948 the Mental Health Drive was the program's recipient of choice during a "Papa and Mama Hush" competition (involving dancers Yolanda and Velez).

Ralph Edwards Productions in Hollywood reported that *Truth or Consequences'* radio efforts ultimately tallied $22 million for munificent intents.

In addition to the mystery celebrity contests, some of the more eccentric stunts infused heavy doses of notoriety into *Truth or Consequences*. One mid-century venture resulted when Edwards persuaded the rather drowsy pueblo resort of Hot Springs, New Mexico, to change its name to Truth or Consequences. (One of the town's few claims to fame had previously rested on some warm mineral baths below it that annually still draw thousands who seek temporary relief from the discomforts of arthritis and rheumatism.) The citizens voted 1,294 to 295 for the name change as the radio show's tenth anniversary approached. The new moniker took effect on March 31, 1950. That was enough to catapult the obscure village into national prominence for a fleeting moment in time.

On Saturday, April 1, 1950, about 10,000 residents and visitors converged on the little village for an initial fiesta that has been subsequently held every year. On that evening the national radio show was broadcast from the high school in its newly-acquired namesake city. Chamber of Commerce literature now claims it was "the start of a unique relationship between a man and a town." Edwards continued to attend the fiesta every year in the company of several well known celebrities whom he invited.

A half-century later, Truth or Consequences, New Mexico — with about 7,000 inhabitants — prides itself on its unique moniker. In addition to the three-day fiesta, there are other radio program–related reminders. Ralph Edwards Park hosts community picnics and recreational events. There's a street called Ralph Edwards Drive. And at Geronimo Springs Museum, the Ralph Edwards Room flaunts a large collection of photos, awards and other memorabilia from Edwards' life. Ralph's wife, Barbara, was instrumental in furnishing it. Luminaries who have accompanied Edwards on his treks to the Land of Enchantment are chronicled in photos appearing along a wall in that room.

The town was also the impetus for some of the show's stunts. When contestant Al Baker couldn't answer a question that was posed to him, his penalty was to hit a golf ball over "the longest course in the world" — 823 miles from Los Angeles to Truth or Consequences. Such outlandish pranks, with their consummate photographic opportunities, offered still more occasions to enhance the town and the show's affinity for the public limelight.

Interestingly, when the show's audition pilot was done in early 1940 it was recorded on a transcription disc, as there was no

Ralph Edwards, in Hollywood, points contestant Al Baker toward Truth or Consequences, New Mexico, 823 miles distant. Baker's penalty for not correctly answering a question on *Truth or Consequences* is to drive a golf ball over "the longest course in the world," between the two locales. A crowd of spectators gives the golfer a sendoff on his long distance journey. (Courtesy of Ralph Edwards Productions)

tape at that time. Even after the advent of tape NBC didn't allow its use for many years. (Among other reasons, there was a prevailing feeling in the industry that a certain amount of spontaneity would dissolve if a show were taped ahead of time.) Instead, *Truth or Consequences* was performed in New York *twice*: first for the East Coast stations, then three hours later it aired a similar live show for the West Coast. The second performance included the same acts as on the earlier broadcast but with different contestants. In 1945, when the program began originating from Hollywood, a live show was performed for the East Coast as before, with a second live show for the West Coast three hours later. Again, the same acts were aired with different contestants.

Not until October 4, 1947, did NBC permit the show to replay the original live show to the West Coast. And it was June 9, 1949, before such programs were allowed to be taped for broadcast, and then only under extreme circumstances. Even the April 1, 1950, outing from Truth or Consequences, New Mexico, was done live. Beginning with the 1950–51 radio season the series was at last aired live on tape.

Truth or Consequences made several forays into early television that gave it some fleeting notoriety, too. An initial test on

New York's WNBT-TV on July 1, 1941, acknowledged the presence of cameras with gags that offered a visual orientation. One player's consequence, for example, was to wear a grass skirt and dance the hula.

Something of significance in the annals of TV beyond that episode occurred that same day. For the first time the Federal Communications Commission permitted commercialized programming to begin on that day. WNBT's inaugural offering at 7 o'clock in the evening was Lowell Thomas reading the *Sunoco News*. The first sponsored TV quiz appeared a short while later—*Uncle Jim's Question Bee*, with host Bill Slater and announcer Dan Seymour, presented by Lever Brothers' Spry shortening. Within an hour *Truth or Consequences* was on the air as the second commercial quiz telecast, with Procter and Gamble underwriting it for Ivory soap. The times, by then, surely were a-changin'.

In *Truth or Consequences'* second TV outing on May 27, 1944, the radio show was merely simulcast on both mediums with no overt changes in demeanor or content. But in its third trial over Hollywood's KNBH-TV on January 21, 1949, the madcap farce played once more to a visual audience, as some contestants received pies in the face.

Was this a foretaste of things to come? *Truth or Consequences* premiered to a weekly television audience the following year, on September 7, 1950 over CBS. It continued for a single season to June 7, 1951. Two NBC-TV nighttime renditions appeared next, from May 18, 1954 to September 28, 1956, and from December 13, 1957, to June 6, 1958. A weekday NBC-TV version ran at varied hours, from mid-mornings to late afternoons, with only a couple of brief interruptions between December 31, 1956, and September 24, 1965.

Newspaper electronic media critic John Crosby didn't mince any words in his appraisal of the visual *Truth or Consequences*: "The radio version … was the ultimate of silliness, but at least it was decently veiled. Its television counterpart is a monstrosity of vulgarity."

While Ralph Edwards was the only host of the radio show across its 16 years, by the time the program appeared on NBC-TV in 1954, he was fully ensconced on *This Is Your Life*, a spin-off from the radio series. *Truth or Consequences* owner Edwards hired *Queen for a Day* host Jack Bailey as emcee of the video show. When Bailey subsequently departed, Steve Dunne was given the nod for the 1957–58 nighttime version.

In the meantime, in December 1956 Edwards had been charmed by the appealing voice of a Pasadena, California, radio audience participation host whose name and station call letters he failed to get, other than "Bob." He put his telephone operator, Billie Clevinger, on the trail. Working over the weekend, she turned up Bob Barker, then an unknown figure beyond the immediate vicinity. Edwards called him and asked him to drop by "at his convenience." Twenty minutes later Barker turned up and Edwards hired the small-time emcee for a five-day-a-week daytime version of *Truth or Consequences*, which he had just sold to NBC-TV. That series lasted until 1965. Then the show went live on tape via syndication, from 1965 to 1975, with two additional years in reruns. By that time, Barker was also well entrenched on *The Price Is Right*.

At the turn of the century Edwards and Barker were still commemorating the anniversary of their first meeting, celebrating annually over lunch on that December date.

Two attempts to resuscitate *Truth or Consequences* in TV syndication—in 1977–78 with Bob Hilton, and in 1987 with Larry Anderson, the latter assisted by comic Murray Langston—died quick deaths. The halcyon days for stunt shows had obviously passed.

But the entrepreneurial spirit of Ralph Edwards wasn't done yet.

This Is Your Life, the first of the "reality" shows, had its origins in an April 27, 1946, *Truth or Consequences* exhibition. A young ex–Marine, Lawrence Trantor of Murray, Utah, who had been wounded at Luzon and was paralyzed below the waist, was brought face-to-face with people who had touched his life in meaningful ways. One by one he was reunited on-stage with old friends, family and neighbors. But that was only half the story.

Knowing of Edwards' penchant for assisting worthy intents, U.S. General Omar Bradley asked him to do something for returning disabled servicemen, particularly for paraplegics. "Many are without hope," confirmed Bradley, "and are afraid they will be a burden to their family and friends." Edwards decided to devote a segment of *Truth or Consequences* to wounded veterans, with the show featuring Trantor as a result.

Bradley's aim was to help such men return to civilian life, and that meant looking to the future. While hospitalized, Trantor had taken up the hobby of watch repair. Aware of that, Edwards made a proposal to him: Working with the Bulova Watch Company, Edwards arranged for the show to send Trantor to a Bulova School of Watchmaking. When he completed the course, the show would set him up in a jewelry store in his hometown. It was an offer the vet could hardly refuse.

That chapter struck a favorable response with audience and cast alike. During the Christmas season of 1947 the program saluted another veteran, Hubert Smith, a Greeneville, Tennessee, paraplegic, then confined at the Long Beach (California) Naval Hospital. Via a three-way remote, from his hospital bedside the wounded soldier visited scenes of his youth—his high school, a corner drug store, his church and his grandmother's home. He spoke with teachers, his doctor, pastor, a clerk at the Greeneville general store and classmates at the school who sang Christmas carols to him. Culminating this feel-good surprise, the show flew the recruit's mother, father and girlfriend to California to spend the holidays with him.

"This boy's story touched the hearts of America, as it had touched ours—and our country is rich in these stories," Edwards later concluded. "Our country, I have come to believe … is richest of all in its people."[13]

And what of Lawrence Trantor, the vet who was sent to Bulova's school? In 1948, a couple of years after he initially appeared on *Truth or Consequences*, the wheelchair-bound young man, by then accompanied by a charming redhead, returned to the show after completion of his course in watch repair. Edwards presented him with the keys he had been promised to a store in his hometown, plus an inventory and a check to open a bank account.

As these accounts unfolded, Edwards realized that he had stumbled onto an unused programming concept, resulting in *This Is Your Life*. The show was launched on radio later in 1948.

Hosted by Edwards, *This Is Your Life* was on radio from 1948 to 1950 before moving to TV in 1950. It aired on the small screen in primetime from 1950 to 1951, 1954–56, and 1957–58, and in daytime from 1956 to 1959 and late 1959 to 1965. The show was seen in syndication from 1966 to 1975, 1977–78 and 1987–88. It highlighted incidents in the lives of celebrities as well as ordinary citizens. Appearances were secretly and elaborately choreographed in order to realize the ultimate element of surprise when people learned on the air that they were to be featured subjects. Few shows exceeded it in reaching its compelling human-interest levels.

Ralph Edwards wasn't content with only two winners in his stable of "people" programs. He produced the NBC-TV weekday game show *It Could Be You*, which enjoyed a run from June 4, 1956, to December 29, 1961. It also turned up as a nighttime NBC-TV series from July 2, 1958, to September 27, 1961. Bill Leyden was host, and Wendell Niles announced. Leyden surprised unsuspecting audience members with tricks, like presenting a layette to a father, gaining a concert gig for a fiddler or, more often, an unexpected reunion between long lost individuals.

On Edwards' *Place the Face*, successively hosted by Jack Smith, Jack Bailey and Bill Cullen, contestants from the studio audience met obscure people from their pasts whom they tried to identify. The show ran in primetime variously between 1953 and 1955 on NBC-TV and CBS-TV.

Two other Edwards creations — the syndicated game show *Crosswits* (1975–80, 1986–87), in which player teams tried to guess hidden identities, and a syndicated hall of justice drama, *The People's Court*, launched in 1981 — sprang from its producer's hallmark human interest predilection. Each of the shows created by Ralph Edwards Productions has been characterized by similar emphases.

When new stunt shows were offered by other programming innovators, which came close to being carbon copies of *Truth or Consequences*, Edwards admitted: "I used to get angry…. Now I just get to work. There is a real challenge in competing with your imitators — and staying on top."

"Radio creators," he explained in 1949, "have no copyright protection — but it shouldn't be necessary. There is such a thing as creed of showmanship. There was no copyright law in vaudeville, either, but a vaudevillian would starve before he would steal another actor's stuff."[14] Isn't it still true that imitation is the sincerest form of flattery?

Truth or Consequences, which was launched on behalf of Procter and Gamble's flagship product, Ivory soap, soon turned its focus to that firm's major washday brand. Within five months of its premiere the show was plugging Duz detergent "in the big red box." The product became synonymous with the series, linked to it for a decade during its heyday and easily its best-remembered sponsor. Commercials often featured the sound of a washing machine working overtime while some vocalists plugged the sponsor's suds.

> SFX: Water sloshing to agitator action for several beats
> MALE CHORUS: D-U-Z, D-U-Z …
> FEMININE SOLOIST (*over chorus, which continues to repeat D-U-Z, D-U-Z*): Put Duz in your washing machine
> Take your clothes out bright and clean
> When you Duz your wash you'll sing
> ALL: "D-U-Z does everything!"

Edwards often sang along and contributed to the commercials in cheery exchanges with the announcer. Sometimes he would refer to the ditty, whose words were frequently altered, as "the washday song." That seemed peculiar, since competitor Lever Brothers pushed its Rinso brand detergent at that time on radio commercials that included a bouncy jingle with the lyrics "Rinso white! Rinso bright! Happy little washday song!"

At least nine announcers, all well established to radio listeners for other programs on which they already appeared, assisted Edwards over the long run of *Truth or Consequences*.

The first, Clayton (Bud) Collyer, became a Duz pitchman on several other Procter and Gamble series, including *The Goldbergs*, *The Guiding Light* and *Road of Life*. He is profiled in the chapter on *Break the Bank*.

Well known sportscaster Mel Allen took a turn announcing before the *Truth or*

Consequences microphone, too. A native of Birmingham, Alabama, he was born February 14, 1913. When CBS officials heard him give the play-by-play account of a baseball game between his alma mater, the University of Alabama, and Tulane University, they signed him as a New York disk jockey and newscaster. Allen was soon introducing *The Army Hour, Command Performance, Duffy's Tavern, Kitty Foyle, The Saturday Night Swing Club* and *This Day Is Ours*.

By 1939 Allen had returned to his first love, that of covering major league baseball. For two decades he was designated "the voice of the Yankees." He tackled kickoff events, sports roundups, All-American awards banquets and games of the week. For his broadcasting expertise he received the initial Ford C. Frick Award, named in honor of a late baseball commissioner. Allen died June 16, 1996, at Greenwich, Connecticut.

Ed Herlihy, another *Truth or Consequences* announcer, was a reliable studio support with the capability to manage a wide range of general utility tasks before the microphone. Born at Dorchester, Massachusetts, on August 14, 1909, he joined NBC in 1935 and is acclaimed for several long runs. For 15 years he oversaw *The Horn and Hardart Children's Hour*, the radio show's audience that Ralph Edwards "borrowed" while recording the *Truth or Consequences* audition disc. (Edwards was the show's host at the time.) Herlihy was commercial spokesman for the Kraft Foods Company for 42 years, one of the longest associations in broadcasting. For 25 years, his was the voice in movie theaters on the Universal-International newsreels.

On radio Herlihy announced *The Adventures of the Thin Man, America's Town Meeting of the Air, The Army Hour, The Big Show, Brave Tomorrow, Coast to Coast on a Bus, Dick Tracy, The Falcon, Hearts in Harmony, The Henry Morgan Show, Honeymoon in New York, Information Please, Inner Sanctum Mysteries, Irene Rich Dramas, Just Plain Bill, The Kraft Music Hall, Life Can Be Beautiful, The Martin and Lewis Show, Melody Puzzles, Mr. District Attorney, The O'Neills, People Are Funny, The Pet Milk Show, Rosemary, Thanks for Tomorrow, That's a Good One, This Small Town, Vacation with Music, Vic and Sade, Weekend,* and *Your Radio Reporter.*

Milton J. Cross, meanwhile, is best recalled as the well recognized voice of the Metropolitan Opera. He introduced and commented on these legendary Saturday matinee broadcasts for 43 years (1931–1975). Born in New York City April 16, 1897, he either announced or hosted these series: *The A & P Gypsies, America's Town Meeting of the Air, Betty and Bob, Bughouse Rhythm, The Chamber Music Society of Lower Basin Street, Coast to Coast on a Bus, Don't Forget, General Motors Concerts, Information Please, The Jeddo Highlanders, The Lucky Strike Music Hall, The Magic Key, Melody Highway, Metropolitan Opera Auditions of the Air, Musical Americana, The Piano Playhouse, Raising Your Parents, The Raymond Paige Orchestra, Roxy and His Gang, The Slumber Hour* and *This Is Your FBI.*

In 1929 the American Academy of Arts and Letters conferred upon Cross its highest honors for a radio announcer. He died January 3, 1975.

Jay Stewart — in addition to announcing several radio series (*Duffy's Tavern, The Great Gildersleeve, The Open House, Take It or Leave It, That's a Good Idea and That's Life*) — invested much of his career as a host of radio audience participation shows, including: *The Carnation Family Party; Jay Stewart's Fun Fair; Meet the Missus; Surprise Package; What's Doin', Ladies?,* and *The Wizard of Odds.* On TV he hosted *Fun Fair* and announced the durable game series *Let's Make a Deal.* Stewart died September 17, 1989, at age 71.

Another of *Truth or Consequences'* popular announcers, Harlow Wilcox, was born at Omaha, Nebraska, March 12, 1900. His most enduring assignment from 1937 to 1953 was to introduce and play foil to *Fibber McGee and Molly.* Wilcox was also interlocutor for *The Adventures of Frank Merriwell, Amos 'n' Andy, Arnold Grimm's Daughter, Attorney at Law, The Baby Snooks Show, The Ben Bernie Show, Betty and Bob, Blondie, Boston Blackie, The Frank Morgan Show, Hap Hazard, Hollywood Premiere, Ice Box Follies, The King's Men, Mayor of the Town, Myrt and Marge, The Passing Parade, Pennzoil Parade, The Phil Baker Show, Suspense, Tony Wons' Scrapbook* and *The Victor Borge Show.* He died in Hollywood September 24, 1960.

Announcer Ken Roberts is profiled in the chapter on *Take It or Leave It.*

Verne Smith, meanwhile, commanded narrational duties on *The Adventures of Ozzie and Harriet, A Day in the Life of Dennis Day, Furlough Fun, Jubilee, The Judy Canova Show, Kay Kyser's Kollege of Musical Knowledge, The Louella Parsons Show, Our Miss Brooks, The Roy Rogers Show, A Tale of Today* and *Your Dream Has Come True.* He also carried a running part on *Arnold Grimm's Daughter.*

Finally, Ken Carpenter, Bing Crosby's longtime sidekick, also introduced *Truth or Consequences.* Born at Avon, Illinois, on August 21, 1900, Carpenter announced *The Al Jolson Show, The Bing Crosby Show, Command Performance, The Edgar Bergen and Charlie McCarthy Show, The General Electric Theater, The Great Gildersleeve, The Halls of Ivy, The Kraft Music Hall, The Life of Riley, Lux Radio Theater, Meet Corliss Archer, One Man's Family, Packard Mardi Gras, The Passing Parade* and *Three Sheets to the Wind.*

He often presided over sporting events, like Rose Bowl football games and Santa Anita handicaps, in addition to prestigious Hollywood celebrations. Carpenter died in Santa Monica, California, on October 19, 1984.

Several others in supporting roles on *Truth or Consequences* maintained duties that were vital to the success of the series.

Keyboard artist Buddy Cole backed up the amusing antics right on cue. His professional career included musical stints (at times as bandleader or with the Buddy Cole Trio) on *Botany Song Shop, The Hoagy Carmichael Show, Hollywood Showcase, The Rosemary Clooney Show* and *Sincerely, Kenny Baker.* In 1941–42, while at the tender age of 25, he hosted and sang for a CBS dramatic series called *Treat Time* that was centered on the lives of eminent composers. Cole died at 48 on November 15, 1964.

Sound effects on *Truth or Consequences* was handled by Lloyd J. Creekmore (of *The Joe Penner Show* and *Reunion of the States*) and Bob Prescott (with credits including *Death Valley Days, Gangbusters, The Goldbergs, Inner Sanctum Mysteries* and *The March of Time*).

Among the show's writers were several adaptable artisans. Plying their literary trade elsewhere were Carl Jampel (who also wrote for *Archie Andrews* and *Glamour Manor*) and Mort Lewis (who did the same for *Behind the Mike, The Gibson Family, Stroke of Fate* and *The Telephone Hour*). Head writer Phil Davis was so versatile that he not only contributed to the writing of *True or False* but also wrote for practically every sit-com in TV's early days, including *The Ann Sothern Show, The Donald O'Connor Show, The Donna Reed Show, Family Affair* and *My Mother, the Car.* Bill Burch, meanwhile, yet another of *Consequences'* scribes, produced Gene Autry's *Melody Ranch* while directing its companion series *The Adventures of Champion.* And Ed Bailey was competent not only as a director (of this show) but as a sound effects technician, too, pursuing that craft on such series as *Bachelor's Children, Back-*

stage Wife, Lights Out, and *Vic and Sade.* Talented virtuosos, these.

In mid–2000 longtime Edwards staffer Sue Chadwick, who was initially employed by the programming innovator in 1947, referred to her boss as a "gentle" man. She noted that, at that juncture, "he still comes into the office (at Ralph Edwards Productions in Hollywood) a couple of days a week to sign letters and do whatever needs to be done." Then, with a smile in her voice, she added, "Ralph never knew how to do anything but work."

Truth or Consequences, the grand-daddy of the stunt shows on radio and television, helped Americans overcome any tendency they might have had to take life seriously. While its early years overlapped one of the most traumatic periods in the nation's history, the series encouraged people to experience the sunny side of life. As it brought listeners to the peak of insanity, this zany, riotous barrel of laughs glued 20 million individuals to their radio sets every Saturday night for 10 years.

Can you think of another entertainment form in the 1940s that might have even come close?

16

Welcome Travelers

Premise: Here you had a program following the assumption that people like to talk about themselves— if they can do it with strangers, not simply the individuals they've known all their lives! *Welcome Travelers'* co-creator and host, Tommy Bartlett, maintained that, given an opportunity, folks would "open up" and candidly share their good fortunes and misfortunes while millions of eavesdroppers tuned in. He was right. He further believed that people on a journey are more likely to spill their guts than those who remain quietly at home. He set out to prove his suppositions on this little imaginative human-interest drama. It was a half-hour of live entertainment that allowed people from all walks of life to share what they would out of their backgrounds, hearts and minds. Voluntary program guests were recruited daily at Chicago airport, bus and train terminals. Some were on their way to the city, some were merely passing through it, while all were on a journey to someplace else. In a genuinely friendly, relaxed environment, Bartlett adopted a laid-back attitude, helping those travelers reveal some of their innermost secrets. It was an intensive study in human nature, prompting the critics to both laud and castigate the show. For seven years it aired on radio. After being on television for a couple of years, the format was drastically altered from the typically genteel stories shared by program guests in the past. In their place were tales of heartwrenching woe. Falling ratings resulted in yet additional tampering with the show, abandoning its original premise, city of origin and host to proceed in totally new directions— with even a name change. As its audience continued to dwindle, the sponsor withdrew and the last vestiges of a once commanding daytime audience participation series vanished. But for those who recall its radio days with fondness, the show was definitely something live and spontaneous, one that few competitive ventures could equal.

Creators: Tommy Bartlett, Les Lear

Director: Bob Cunningham

Master of Ceremonies: Tommy Bartlett

Announcer: Jim Ameche

Sponsor: Household cleaning goods and personal care products manufacturer Procter & Gamble underwrote this series throughout its weekday runs on both radio and television.

Ratings: High: 6.3 (1950–51); Low: 4.0 (1953–54); Median: 5.1 (seven seasons). While the median rating was good enough to keep it on the air, the show would be considered a failure if compared to some of daytime's durable soap operas, several of them boasting double-digit figures. Nevertheless, as with every series, this drew a loyal contingent of fans who remained faithful throughout the run.

On the Air: June 30, 1947–July 8, 1949, ABC, weekdays, 12 Noon ET; July 11, 1949–Sept. 24, 1954, NBC, weekdays, 10 A.M.

*   *   *

Tommy Bartlett was convinced that people on a journey are more likely to let their hair down and chat with strangers than they are to talk with folks in their own hometowns. He told a journalist: "You can really hear them on a train, plane, boat or bus. That's when people throw off their restraints and tell others not only the things they have done, but what they think about it."[1] For seven years on radio, and three-and-a-half years on television, he put his idea to the test before daytime audiences who tuned in to *Welcome Travelers*.

Emanating live five days a week from the College Inn of Chicago's Sherman Hotel, the show dispatched a cadre of scouts to local train and bus depots—and, later, airline terminals—to pluck prospective interviewees who were passing through the city on their way to somewhere else. Those subjects who seemed ripest for the assignment were generally uninhibited, often possessed amiable, extroverted personalities and frequently told something that piqued the curiosity of the *Welcome Travelers* staff—enough to suggest that they might make interesting program guests.

Those appearing on the show were encouraged to relate unusual tales about themselves and possibly the circumstances that had brought them to Chicago. Some-

times they were asked about life in their hometowns and the states they represented. Some shared highly emotional issues, while others told of romantic encounters or even spoke of troubled concerns, situations that had left them destitute or alone. These were first-person, human-interest accounts that drew millions of listeners who were enchanted and inspired by the candor that they heard. It was all highly absorbing, this eavesdropping into someone else's life.

The program's visitors represented a panorama of Americana, coming from all walks of life and every social stratum. A racially mixed contingent, they hailed from widely separated geographic territories. They sustained highly divergent opinions on many topics—some were outspoken—and occasionally they lobbied for great causes in their fleeting moments of fame.

Presented on a show that was daily introduced in a manner comparable to that of a train barker, they told their stories to Tommy Bartlett, the program's co-creator and master of ceremonies. Bartlett, according to a biographer, was considered "among the most able and least offensive emcees in the area of human-interest stories."[2]

For their part, participants were rewarded with gifts of valuable merchandise after their on-air respites. A studio audience typically averaging 1,000 members witnessed all of this. And for the most part they, too, had been recruited at Chicago train, bus and air terminals, where *Welcome Travelers* dispensed tickets every weekday to the show.

Shortly after daybreak each morning a crew of quick-witted, affable, well-groomed young men fanned out to the city's multiple rail, bus and air terminals. Studying the incoming travelers, these staffers—having gained a sixth sense based on multiple previous encounters—quickly spotted worthy guests. Introducing themselves by offering a ticket for the broadcast, the young scouts engaged their quarry in dialogue about their travels while simultaneously sizing up who might become enticing interviewees.

Later, at the Sherman Hotel, prospective program guests completed questionnaires about themselves. (For two years, from June 30, 1947, through July 8, 1949, the half-hour weekday program aired at 12 noon Eastern Time on ABC. When it moved to NBC on July 11, 1949, it was on at 10 A.M.)

While the travelers enjoyed a sumptuous complimentary breakfast, the program's staff— working at top speed —culled from a stack of forms the most interesting questionnaires, concurrently carrying on verbal exchanges with their authors. The assistants next put together vita sheets on each one. These were given to *Welcome Travelers* director Bob Cunningham. From them he selected the actual program guests and presented them to Bartlett. He also suggested the route that a subject's interview might take. At that juncture, Bartlett took over.

In 1948 the show's scouts approached Mr. and Mrs. Russell Thiel of Philadelphia, who were on their way to a blind youth's wedding in Chicago. Pursuing that, they uncovered a fascinatingly heartwarming tale of a self-deprecating couple who for years had opened their home to servicemen who had lost their sight while on active duty. Taking in boys released from the Philadelphia Naval Hospital and the Army's Valley Forge Hospital, the Thiels fed them, entertained them, provided a place for them to sleep for as long as they cared to stay, and carried them to ball games and public events—financing all of it out of their own pockets. On occasion, as many as 20 sight-impaired young men slept at the Thiel home; their hosts and their three children sometimes gave up their own beds to sleep on the floor. It was a touching account of how one family saw an opportunity to tem-

porarily improve the circumstances of some of life's unfortunates.

On another occasion, in 1950, *Welcome Travelers* introduced the John Walsh family of Quincy, Massachusetts, to its radio audience. The Walshes were en route to a new life in Fresno, California. Only a few years earlier the couple had set a record by giving birth to six children (three sets of twins) within 24 months. They had had another child after that. By then, with nine mouths to feed, they were living hand-to-mouth in a rented home, that had just been sold from under them, while on a weekly income of $50 to $65.

A Fresno contractor, meanwhile — also a father of twins whose wife had recently appeared on *Welcome Travelers*— heard them and offered to design and build an affordable home for the Walshes. Fresno locals lined up a better job for John Walsh, neighbors provided furniture and the radio show kicked in a new refrigerator. It was an encouraging portrayal of one family's initial steps toward recovery from financial collapse.

In the course of time, it was probably inevitable that the program would be "taken" by some unscrupulous charlatans who sought personal gain at the expense of integrity. Occasionally, the show was put in the position of separating fact from fiction while dealing with human nature of many stripes. More than once a guest claimed to be down on his luck and stranded. A runaway youth gained a sympathetic following while pretending to be an orphan en route to a relative's home.

Sometimes the staff of *Welcome Travelers* uncovered situations requiring special preparation. The nation rejoiced when a childless couple got their first look at their newly adopted baby while the show was on the air. By contrast, there was heartbreak when two mothers appealed to a kidnapper to return their children unharmed. There was also a sobering moment when a

Is that a look of ecstasy or agony? Tommy Bartlett created and hosted the human-interest *Welcome Travelers* series in which real people on real journeys told their peripatetic tales. Among his guests were a couple of dudes from the Lone Star state who attempted to outfit the genial Bartlett with Western style brogans. Could it have been that the host's feet were simply too big for his boots? (Photofest)

terminal cancer patient candidly told how he intended to use the remaining months of his life. The spontaneity of such human drama invariably touched many in the audience and kept them coming back for more.

Nor was *Welcome Travelers* beyond taking on some extraordinary challenges, either. The U.S. Air Force requested that the program take a journey to Germany in 1949 to entertain fliers following a Berlin airlift. A 29-member entourage made the 10-day trek to Europe, airing 11 broadcasts and performing in several additional shows.

The program bore a trivial likeness to another interview series, *We, the People*— one of a handful of human-interest features proliferating in the 1940s. *People* aired as a separate show between 1937 and 1951, having been introduced in 1936 as a segment of *The Rudy Vallee Hour*. A portion of *People* was scripted, and some of its guests with the better yarns to relate could hardly read their lines with sufficient competence to make them sound believable. *Welcome Travelers* was far more spontaneous.

Sometimes these new human-interest series arrived to critical acclaim, frequently not without repercussions. An illustration should suffice.

In early 1954 the Providence (Rhode Island) *Journal-Bulletin* reported that it would no longer include the popular human-interest series *Strike It Rich* in its published daily radio and television schedules. The daily paper cited specific shows that "deliberately exploit human want and misery for commercial gain."[3] Two other programs, allegedly of similar ilk — the newspaper called them "agony programs" — would also no longer be listed: *Welcome Travelers* and *On Your Account*, the latter an NBC-TV commodity on which contestants told hard-luck tales to a jury who picked those they believed to be most deserving of the group. Could this have been guilt by association, perhaps, or at least so

in the case of *Welcome Travelers*? (Looking at it from this vantage point, it's a wonder that *Queen for a Day* didn't incur the wrath of the Rhode Island rag, too, with its daily tales of feminine anguish, pathos and despair.)

The fact is that by the time it left radio on September 24, 1954, and was airing exclusively on television, *Welcome Travelers'* direction shifted dramatically from its radio days: Previously, for the most part, it highlighted sagas of a more frivolous nature. Yet, "Inspired by the success of *Strike It Rich*, the tales had become litanies of woe," explained TV chronicler Wesley Hyatt.[4] He cited a lady who experienced a nervous breakdown upon hearing of her only daughter's nuptials. Then there was a widow who obviously was ill-prepared to meet her financial obligations when asked to fork over a colossal sum following her late spouse's demise.

Meanwhile, the tube version of the show premiered on NBC-TV September 8, 1952, at 3:30 P.M. Eastern Time. It shifted the following year to 4 o'clock (on August 3, 1953). But not until it left NBC did it become more aggressive in its appeal to audiences. The series debuted on CBS-TV July 5, 1954, at 1:30 P.M. as sponsor Procter & Gamble pulled the plug on the soap opera *The First 100 Years* airing in that time period. That drama, incidentally, survived for only a year-and-a-half.

Tommy Bartlett, the radio host, also presided over the televised series until suddenly, on May 6, 1955, the rug was pulled out from under him. The human-interest program abruptly left Chicago, with its misery yarns behind it. The following week it unceremoniously opened in New York City.

In *Welcome Travelers'* revised format, singer Jack Smith, who had only a short time earlier broadcast weeknights on CBS Radio, jousted with a trio of sightseers who had come to town. Guests estimated where a spinning compass would stop and answered quiz questions posed by the host. Contestants who qualified to enter a Treasure Room by correctly responding to a complex query put to them by Smith went home bearing U.S. defense bonds as payoffs.

Less than six months later, on October 31, 1955, *Welcome Travelers* experienced yet another transformation, this time resulting in both format *and* title changes. Under its new banner, *Love Story*, the program focused on Smith and co-host Pat Meikle interviewing couples who competed for cash and merchandise prizes. It was an ignoble effort.

Tommy Bartlett's original concept had been radically diluted, and TV watchers were less than enthralled. Nearly nine years after *Welcome Travelers* debuted as a popular midday radio feature, it had evolved (digressed?) into unrecognizable clutter. *Love Story*, sounding more like a soap opera than a game show, was canceled on March 30, 1956, five months after its debut. Procter & Gamble replaced it the following week with the premiering *As the World Turns*. Given the history of that daytime drama, somebody obviously made a wise choice there.

Nevertheless, while it operated under the premise that initially inspired Bartlett and his co-creator, Les Lear, *Welcome Travelers* often proved Bartlett's theory daily: "People seem to open up when they're traveling."[5]

Born in Milwaukee on July 11, 1914, Bartlett became a high school dropout. Early in life he was fascinated with hearing people talking over the airwaves without the benefit of wires connecting their voices to his crystal set. At 14 he started announcing for his hometown's WISN. (He claimed his first "role" was that of a barking dog.) Five years hence, he advanced to Chicago's far more powerful WBBM, where he announced for *Meet the Missus* and *The Missus Goes to Market*, both regional series. It would be 13 years before he would preside over his own audience-participation show.

In 1939 he announced a short-lived CBS program titled *News and Rhythm*. He hosted broadcasts of Carl Hohengarten's Orchestra. Yet despite these, his on-air credits were minimal until *Welcome Travelers* was sold to Procter & Gamble.

In 1950 he narrated a radio remote from the Chicago Rail Fair. The broadcast booth on that occasion sat adjacent to a booth for Cypress Gardens, a Florida attraction that boasted daily water-ski shows. The encounter led Bartlett to develop his own Midwestern ski show at nearby Wisconsin Dells. That venture, known as Tommy Bartlett's Ski, Sky and Stage Show, Robot World and Exploratory, eventually lured thousands of summer visitors.

A confirmed bachelor, Bartlett maintained a Chicago apartment near his broadcasting studios. He was an experienced pilot, owned an airplane and spent many weekends journeying — just as his broadcast subjects did — to somewhere else.

Les Lear, his partner in creating and owning *Welcome Travelers*, made no other known contributions to the broadcasting industry.

The program's director, Bob Cunningham, announced for a couple of other series, *The Peabodys* (1946–47) and *The Crime Files of Flamond* (1952–57).

But it was Jim Ameche, *Welcome Travelers'* announcer, who spent nearly his entire career doing other shows in radio. Each day he would introduce this one as "the program that brings you actual stories, amusing, inspiring, unforgettable, of people just like you." Born at Kenosha, Wisconsin, on August 6, 1915, he received a message in 1933 from older sibling Don Ameche — who was already firmly entrenched in network radio — urging him to come to Chicago. An audition was scheduled for the namesake role of *Jack Arm-*

strong, the All-American Boy, a juvenile adventure serial that was soon to premiere.

At 18, the younger Ameche won the part that reportedly paid him $59.50 for five weekly appearances. Yet his identity was kept closely guarded. "Nobody ever knew I was on the show," he attested. "There was an unwritten law against revealing who played Jack."[6]

While Jack Armstrong may have been his best-known character, Jim Ameche worked on many other radio mainstays as host, announcer, cast member or in the lead role: *The Amos 'n' Andy Show; At Home with Faye and Elliott; Attorney at Law* (in which he played the lead, Terry Regan); *Big Sister; Broadway Matinee; Grand Central Station; Grand Hotel* (replacing brother Don Ameche as the lead); *Grand Marquee; Here's to Romance; Hollywood Open House; Love Story Theatre; Lux Radio Theater; Mercury Summer Theater; The Rinso-Spry Vaudeville Theater; Romance, Rhythm and Ripley; Silver Eagle, Mountie* (he played the lead here, too); and *Woodbury Hollywood Playhouse.*

Ameche hosted the NBC-TV *Festival of Stars* in the summer of 1957, a dramatic anthology featuring episodes of *The Loretta Young Show* in which the actress hadn't appeared. In 1975 he became a disc jockey at Tucson, Arizona's KCEE. His death occurred in that city on February 4, 1983.

There were fewer principals on *Welcome Travelers* than on most other daytime series. What the series missed in a reduced staff, however, it more than made up for by drawing listeners to their sets, often mesmerized by the insightful glimpses allowed into the lives of people representing all walks of life. It was reality radio that obviously provided the spontaneity and candor few series could.

Tommy Bartlett offered this philosophy: "If people would take time out to know about other people, to really learn what makes them tick, then all people would be *all* right."[7]

At least while *Welcome Travelers* was a radio series, it worked on that notion every day.

17

You Bet Your Life

Premise: Correctly identified as a "comedy-quiz" by most media observers, this whimsical 30-minute feature was a hybrid relying upon dual genres for sustained popularity. While intentionally a game show drawing upon rudimentary forms that had been successfully applied by several other programs (e.g., risk one's winnings for double or nothing), that was merely a cover, this little jewel was essentially a showcase for the wisecracking jibes of its irascible host, Groucho Marx. Years before, he had enjoyed a screen career, acting alongside his siblings, the notoriously unrestrained Marx Brothers. Now this uncontrollable rowdy was unleashed on another medium. He would have his way with contestants who might be justifiably leery—some of his barbs were definitely more biting than witty. While he didn't display a mean streak, each week he enjoyed titillating his audiences by toying reprehensibly with the couples before him. Those individuals, incidentally, were men and women who had never met before that show, and who possessed discernible characteristics that were totally opposite of one another. A cantankerous Marx coolly and calculatingly met them. Under the guise of

interviewing, he taunted them, zapping them with insults while provoking laughter from the audience. While he did his thing, the show was becoming one of the most innovative on the air. It popularized the use of transcription tape, introduced broadcasting's first rerun as well as its first simulcast, was among series leaders in adding a laugh track, fostered improved understanding between ethnic factions, schemed behind the scenes to place specific individuals on-stage for its host to interview, and prepared in advance nearly everything Marx said. Not every series acquired that many distinctions. No matter, it was fun, and at its peak the program attracted 40 million listeners and viewers every week. To last for 14 years—nine on radio and 11 on TV (with some overlap)—it definitely had to be doing something right.

Creator-Producer: John Guedel
Producer: Harfield Weedin
Directors: Bob Dwan, Bernie Smith
Master of Ceremonies: Groucho Marx
Announcers: Jack Slattery, George Fenneman
Writers: Hy Freedman, Ed Tyler
Bandleaders: Billy May, Jerry Fielding, Jack Meakin

Sponsors: From its inception through Dec. 28, 1949, the show was underwritten by the Elgin-American Compact Co. for that firm's line of compacts, cigarette cases and dresser sets. Effective Jan. 4, 1950, through the final radio broadcast, DeSoto-Plymouth automobile dealers of the Chrysler Corp. subscribed the program.

Ratings: High: 16.9 (1949–50); Low: 3.2 (1955–56); Median: 9.7. During the first five seasons the figures never fell below double digits.

On the Air: Oct. 27, 1947–Dec. 22, 1947, ABC, Monday, 8 P.M. ET; Dec. 31, 1947–April 28, 1948, ABC, Wednesday, 9:30 P.M. ET; Sept. 22, 1948–May 25, 1949, ABC, Wednesday, 9:30 P.M.; Oct. 5, 1949–Dec. 28, 1949, CBS, Wednesday, 9:30 P.M.; Jan. 4, 1950–June 28, 1950, CBS, Wednesday, 9 P.M.; Oct. 4, 1950–June 27, 1951, NBC, Wednesday, 9 P.M.; Oct. 3, 1951–Sept. 19, 1956, NBC, Wednesday, 9 P.M. (Reruns were broadcast during the summers, effectively keeping the show on the air year-round.)

* * *

This was a series that could nearly be run on catchphrases.

When the show came on the air, announcer George Fenneman introduced its star — the irreverent, irascible, invincible comic-quizmaster Groucho Marx — by chanting: "And now … HERE HE IS … the ONE … the ONLY …" before the studio audience in unison completed the exclamation, "GROUCHO!"

During the quiz portion of the program, when a couple appearing before the host was fielded a question, Marx repeatedly cautioned: "Only one answer between you. Think carefully, and no help from the audience."

When a pair risked and lost all their money, Marx allowed: "Nobody goes home broke." Then he asked them a question for a small consolation prize, most frequently: "Who was buried in Grant's tomb?"

Presenting the concept of the "secret word" to each twosome, Marx employed dual catchphrases that joined the national lexicon: "Say the secret word and divide a hundred dollars" he'd advise, then remind the contestants: "It's a common word, something you see around the house every day."

At the conclusion of each show for DeSoto and Plymouth automobile dealers, Marx wiggled his furry eyebrows and signed off: "And tell 'em Groucho sent you!"

After some 400-plus original radio performances and nearly 200 more on TV, *You Bet Your Life* was known by audiences so well that they could say those familiar words right along with its star. Millions of applications of those terms must have been widely exercised on a daily basis.

An early paradigm of today's TV talk show, *You Bet Your Life* exemplified the most rudimentary elements of encounter and repartee on radio. Uniquely combining human interest and razor-sharp wit, it engaged "the best use of contestants of any quiz show."[1] It was also portrayed as "one of the most successful game shows ever"[2] while it "cast aside more industry barriers and social taboos than possibly any other program."[3] A revered analyst claimed "this is probably the first radio show that without material change holds interest on television."[4] The series had other distinguishing features, to be explored presently, but none so inimitable as those of the host himself.

While other subsequent programs attempted to duplicate the irrepressible antics of Groucho Marx, none did so with comparable flourish. Perceptive observer Gerald Nachman painted a text portrait that succinctly, yet indelibly, recalls Marx to any who ever heard or saw the program: "Perched on a stool, benignly puffing his cigar, he was the very picture of

In the end, whether it was in the movies or as quizmaster of *You Bet Your Life*, you could almost bet the rent that Groucho Marx would gain a kiss from a pretty girl. That may have been his characteristic piece de resistance, no matter what the occasion. The irascible Marx was also known for a sarcastic wit that often provoked gales of laughter among audiences as he probed defenseless guests. (Photofest)

quizmasterly decorum, a decoy for the viper lurking beneath."[5] Behind that bespectacled, mustachioed countenance beat the heart of a cunning, impish rogue who was simply waiting to have a crack at an unsuspecting guest. Critics tended to agree; Marx possessed a "rapierlike wit and sarcastic asides."[6]

Succinctly, in a few terse words, Bernie Smith — a *You Bet Your Life* director — explained the show's hypothesis: "The idea is to find a remarkable personality and let Groucho throw rocks at him."[7]

Once, when a contestant became tongue-tied, unable to respond to Marx's questions, the quick-witted emcee offered this rejoinder: "Either he's dead or my watch has stopped!"

Another time a lady answered his inquiry about her age by telling him she was "approaching forty." That merely opened the door for him to ask: "From which direction?"

When a tree surgeon appeared, the gleeful host wanted to know: "Have you ever fallen out of any of your patients?"

The often-lecherous Marx, told by an attractive young coed that she went to "a college for girls," exclaimed, "That's the reason I'd want to go, too!"

When a gentleman announced that he had gone to San Francisco State, Marx immediately quipped: "College or reformatory?"

Taking on everyone from small-town mayors to beauty queens, and even the idyllic classical baritone John Charles Thomas and the prodigious General Omar N. Bradley, Marx deflated them all. No one was immune to his frequent and often caustic barbs.

Notwithstanding the depiction of an overbearing quizmaster with disdain for every game-player, some observers still viewed him differently. "He has the happy faculty to extract laughter, not at the expense of the contestants, but from an off-guard zanyism that has a quality of freshness about it," *Variety* noted.[8] Referring to Marx as "radio's first *uncongenial* quizmaster," another claimed he was "an antidote to every vapid, sugary quiz-show MC on the air."[9]

He also maintained a warmth that his producers insisted was genuine. Possessing a keen sense of social responsibility, Marx infrequently expressed positions on the air favoring racial forbearance and global harmony. His show helped dissolve long-standing tensions between Caucasian and Negro musicians, for instance. Under the leadership of Jerry Fielding, the show's orchestra leader from 1948 to 1954, qualified black musicians were hired in spite of network protests. Members of other sects also gained ground because of *You Bet Your Life*'s efforts. Director Bernie Smith recalled: "I realized the audience was made up of a whole lot of minorities. We're all minority groups."[10] On nearly every broadcast an ethnic faction was represented. A serious attempt was made to place them in sympathetic situations.

Julius Henry (Groucho) Marx emanated from a family of Jewish immigrants where matriarchal influence claimed the upper hand. Sam, the patriarch, was a tailor by trade but never too successful. Minnie Marx, Sam's wife and a stage-struck mom — with the encouragement of Al Shean, her uncle (whose claim to fame was the vaudeville act of Gallagher and Shean) — guided four of their five sons into show business. Groucho, born October 2, 1890, while the family lived in tenement housing on Manhattan's upper east side, was the third sibling in birth order: Chico, Harpo, Groucho, Gummo and Zeppo. All but Gummo spent their lives as professional entertainers.

Following in their kin's footsteps, while still young, the other brothers joined their mother and an aunt on the vaudeville circuit. Initially they appeared as "Six Musical Mascots" and later as "The Four Nightingales" and still later as "The Four Marx Brothers." Each lad was multitalented, gaining proficiency with a variety of musical instruments. Groucho, for example, adroitly played the guitar, piano, mandolin and harp. Others were accomplished on some of those same instruments, plus flute, trombone, cornet, zither, violin, saxophone and cello.

In time the Marx Brothers became the foremost madcap comic act on the Broadway stage. Their success led them into motion pictures for Paramount, Metro-Goldwyn-Mayer and RKO, with their best known films being *The Cocoanuts, Animal Crackers* and *Monkey Business* (released in 1932), *Horsefeathers* and *Duck Soup* (both 1933), *A Night at the Opera* (1935), *A Day at the Races* (1936), *Room Service* and *At the Circus* (1938), *Go West* (1940) and *The Big Store* (1941, which laid an egg compared to their earlier attempts, effectively ending their celluloid pursuits). While Gummo never appeared in films, Zeppo also grew tired of them after awhile, quitting to open the Zeppo Marx talent agency in Hollywood.

A couple of the four performing Marxes found their way into radio for 26 weeks during the 1932–33 season. On Monday evenings, Chico and Groucho split a $6,500 weekly income while appearing on the Blue network's *Five Star Theatre* in a zany series about a malpractice lawyer and his bungling assistant: *Flywheel, Shyster and Flywheel, Attorneys at Law.* (Harpo, the family's silent character, would have been absolutely out of place in an audio medium; his forte was in honking a horn, chasing blondes and playing the harp, which steered him toward visual forms.)

A critic made light of the demands of the Marxes' initial radio showcase:

> A few years earlier they had been presenting four shows daily in vaudeville; more recently, it had been seven performances a week on Broadway. They were now being paid a princely sum to stand before a microphone each week for half an hour ... to read from a script that they had barely bothered rehearsing. True, the brothers did have to cap each skit with a brief paean to the wonders of Essolube [motor oil] — but if Walter Winchell could sell Jergens lotion and Rudy Vallee could warble for Fleischmanns yeast, then the Marx Brothers could spend sixty seconds hawking gasoline for Standard Oil.[11]

Those 26 weeks ended, the boys returned to Hollywood in spring 1933 and made more films. (Standard Oil failed to renew.) A subsequent attempt in radio, in fact, was less successful than the first. A year later Groucho and Chico signed with the American Oil Company for a series that would lampoon the news of the world. *The Marx of Time* was pulled from CBS's Sunday-night-at-seven schedule after just eight weeks. (It was the last broadcast series in which Groucho was to routinely appear with another member of his family. A biographer summarized: "Chico sounded stiff and studied over a microphone. He appeared irregularly on musical programs, usually as a pianist or guest bandleader, rather than the Italian caricature he perfected in films. As late as 1952, he produced an unsuccessful pilot program, *The Little Matchmaker*, in which he played Chico Revelli, a marriage broker. By this time, however, his ethnic characterization was at best stale, and the show never became a series."[12])

Nor did Groucho fare much better without his family in a third radio attempt, an omnibus Hollywood talk and variety affair called *The Circle*. (Like so many of its contemporaries — including Bing Crosby's *Kraft Music Hall* and Frank Sinatra's *Songs by Sinatra* — *The Circle* sought to stifle studio audience reactions, allowing laughter but not applause. That oversight would be corrected within a brief span by none other than Crosby and Sinatra.) *The Circle* debuted on January 15, 1939, on NBC Red and featured stunning celebrities like Ronald Colman and Carol Lombard, in addition to Groucho. Even with such prominent figures, the show's Crossleys lingered in the ratings basement and the program left the air on July 9, 1939, never to return. (Marx enjoyed a couple of minimal successes in radio in the mid–1940s; he was a semi-regular in the casts of *Orson Welles' Almanac* and *The Radio Hall of Fame*. From 1950 to 1952 he appeared intermittently on NBC's *The Big Show*.)

Despite numerous guest shots on others' shows (*Rudy Vallee, Ed Sullivan, Burns and Allen*, and many more), Marx was skittish by then about permanent employment opportunities offered him in radio. In 1941 he turned down the starring role in the future hit *The Life of Riley*. The part would eventually go to William Bendix, who would help make it one of radio's most memorable comedy series. When he later tried out as quizmaster for *Take It or Leave It*, Marx was passed over for another candidate. No wonder he was skeptical of radio, having experienced multiple difficulties in finding his métier there. A temporary confirmation arrived in the 15 months he hosted the musical variety series *Blue Ribbon Town* for CBS in 1943–44. Yet some reviewers tagged Marx's wisecracking as acerbic instead of amusing. Kenny Baker relieved him of duty, and a few weeks later, adding insult to injury, the series was renamed *The Kenny Baker Program.*

Imagine Marx's reaction, then, when young up-and-coming producer John Guedel approached him with a premise for yet another quiz program, to potentially be headlined by Marx. This was the same Guedel who was responsible for putting *Art Linkletter's House Party* and *People Are Funny* on the air while encouraging Ozzie Nelson to launch *The Adventures of Ozzie and Harriet*, all three of those considered huge broadcasting successes. (Early on, Guedel had envisioned *You Bet Your Life* as a five-night-a-week quarter-hour quiz with a conventional host, his preference being Garry Moore. He hadn't been able to sell his concept, however, and was still looking over his options when a chance encounter with Marx changed his direction completely.)

Guedel was reportedly in the backstage wings during a Walgreen Drugs radio special that featured Bob Hope and Groucho Marx. When Hope tossed his prepared script aside and began ad-libbing his lines, Marx did the same, creating some of the most amusing banter a studio audience had ever witnessed. Following the show, Guedel informed Marx: "Hiring you to read a script is like using a Cadillac to deliver coal."[13] The producer inquired if Marx could dialogue spontaneously for infinite periods. "I've ad-libbed a whole Broadway show many a time," Marx countered.[14] In fact, it was virtually impossible for him *not* to do it, he assured him, conceding that he detested scripted material.

Guedel told *Radio Life*: "I figured he'd be great working with people out of an audience. When the people were being funny, Groucho could be the perfect straight man;

when the people played it straight, Groucho couldn't miss with his own comedy. With Groucho, I figured we'd be protected from both sides."[15]

Even though Guedel was throwing Marx a life preserver to save his sinking career, the latter could hardly have embraced it, given his faltering previous encounters in radio. It would also be a dramatic plummet from his Marx Brothers days, the comedian theorized. But Guedel was persistent. Still unconvinced, Marx was persuaded at last to fork over $125 out of his own pocket, matched by a similar sum from Guedel, to make an audition tape before a *House Party* audience one day following that show's airing.

Guedel peddled the recording to the national radio networks, and all four quickly turned it down, viewing Marx in a spiraling state of decline. One observer compared Marx's sagging career with that of Milton Berle, "radio's most notable failure."[16]

Fortunately, the rejection didn't end in dejection, for Guedel tried another approach. Reading in *Variety* that the Elgin-American Compact Company (which also made cigarette cases and dresser sets) expected to sign Phil Baker as host of a new quiz called *Everybody Wins*, Guedel offered Elgin-American Groucho instead. (Phil Baker had, incidentally, become the *Take It or Leave It* quizmaster when Marx failed in his own quest there.) Elgin-American's president bought the show at once, unaware that most industry observers by then viewed Marx as a "has-been," with some producers even reluctant to book him for guest appearances.

Two weeks later, on October 27, 1947, Groucho debuted on ABC in *You Bet Your Life*. Only five weeks had elapsed since the demonstration disc was cut! Baker, on the other hand, subsequently fired his press agent for leaking the intended pact to the trade papers before Elgin-American could ink it.

At that time some stalwarts in show-biz viewed a quizmaster as the lowest performer on the totem pole. As could be expected, media analysts were quick to respond to what might be perceived as a plunge by the aging Marx; he hadn't succeeded in radio previously, and he hadn't appeared on the screen since the Marx Brothers' colossal flop a half-dozen years earlier. His relegation to a quiz show master of ceremonies was, in the opinion of *Newsweek*, "like selling Citation to a glue factory."[17]

The show's initial outing could hardly have been termed an overnight success. Even though Marx had mingled with the guests beforehand, and nothing had been left to chance by his lines being wholly scripted, difficult moments still occurred when the players and the host seemed doubtful. The folks at home caught that, too. "Most listeners felt his [Marx's] genuine comic talent was underused," fathomed one authority. "Only occasionally did his explosive banter register several notches above the level of the average quizmaster and carry a quality of freshness.... It remained a rather unoriginal quiz with a run of uninspired participants."[18]

The formerly chaotic comic's penchant for breaking up audiences with contemptuous gibes in theaters and movies simply wasn't happening in radio. Newsmen assigned to cover the electronic media weren't amused. Wrote one: "Trouper that he is, Mr. Marx works hard and does his best, but the show never really comes off. Somewhere along the line the delightful silliness of Mr. Marx's act has been confused with the exhibitionistic absurdity of the average radio quiz. One happy day Mr. Marx will break into radio; he will be assigned a program without a stylized format."[19]

John Guedel realized that he must take drastic steps to improve the situation at once or see his fledgling (and floundering)

quiz show go down the drain. To fix it he determined that the quiz segments would be performed in an essentially no-nonsense manner. The host would never meet his guests in advance and would be given only minimal data about each one (perhaps an occupation, hometown, a unique hobby or interest, or possibly an unusual name, and little more). Finally, gagwriters would be hired to augment the host's repertoire of seemingly endless jokes.

"Groucho was fast and funny ... but hardly fail-safe," a radio historiographer explained, "and he felt better going into battle with a few ripostes up his sleeve."[20] To implement that feat without giving it away, Guedel had cue cards printed and projected onto a screen situated above Marx. While it appeared to studio (and later, television) audiences during a big laugh on-stage that the emcee was demurely gawking into space, his head tilted slightly heavenward, he was really receiving more from upstairs than the uninitiated knew: Marx was getting his next ad lib from on high, thus being guided — joke by joke — through the entire show!

But Guedel wasn't nearly done yet. He took several other substantive measures to insure the longevity of his latest attraction.

The networks had individually and collectively maintained a longstanding policy against taping programs in advance for broadcast at a later time. The principal argument for this tactic was to insure that performers couldn't sell their material that was intended for the network to various outlets that might include local affiliates and perhaps even competing webs.

Rules are sometimes made to be broken, however, and one of radio's biggest stars finally did just that. Crooner Bing Crosby, who was something of an industry maverick, didn't like being tied to a certain studio and schedule for broadcasting — he wanted to be free to roam the globe whenever he took a notion. To keep him satisfied and under contract, the chain permitted him to begin using the magic of tape to record his shows in advance. As anyone could anticipate, with the camel's nose already under the tent it would be only a matter of time before the animal's whole body was inside!

Guedel seized upon that revolution to shore up his faltering series. By taping *You Bet Your Life* for an hour, then creatively plucking out the choicest morsels for a half-hour radio program, he could give listeners "concentrated Marxiana."[21] (The show was initially recorded on 33-1/3 rpm discs played on turntables. Before the first season ended, however, reel-to-reel audiotape was introduced. ABC's Bing Crosby became the first to try·it on the air. Marx's show quickly followed suit, and before long, almost all ABC primetime series adopted audiotape.)

Transcription turned out to be *You Bet Your Life*'s saving grace. Marx was placed at ease, knowing any fluffs and flat spots would never be heard outside the studio. Now he jabbed and jabbered at contestants for as long as he liked, until enough zingers for a weekly broadcast were amassed. A 16-minute rough-and-tumble exchange, for instance, might be pared down to a lively on-air interview requiring but a fourth of its original time. "Not even Groucho was as funny as he seemed," Guedel admitted. "He would press at first. He'd keep going-going-going until he got what he was after. Hell, we wouldn't ever have finished a show [without tape]. It would have been a thirteen-week show. Instead it was a fourteen-year show."[22]

Taping the shows soothed a sponsor's ambivalence about Marx's proclivity for telling ribald tales, too. Passing tapes in front of network censors before airing them eliminated that deep-seated concern.

Not only did transcription give a boost to Groucho's show, it also had the net effect of popularizing the use of recording tape in general, leading many other shows to adopt it.

After a year, *You Bet Your Life* escalated from a pathetic ninety-second in the ratings to the top 10. Marx's confidence as a humorist was reaffirmed and his lifeless career rejuvenated. In 1948 the show won a prestigious Peabody Award from the School of Journalism at the University of Georgia. It was the first time a quiz program had ever won *anything*. In 1950 Marx was presented an Emmy as television's "Most Outstanding Personality," an acknowledgment by the industry that it had been premature in writing off his career only a few years before.

The show continued to enjoy ratings success, landing fifth among all radio programs by April 1953. The top five, in order, were: *Amos 'n' Andy, The Jack Benny Program, Lux Radio Theater, The Edgar Bergen and Charlie McCarthy Show, You Bet Your Life*. (Despite this, Marx continued to remain ambivalent: "I am now fifth in the national ratings, but I can't find anyone who admits they still have a radio, much less listens to one. The rich people are the ones who have the TV sets. The paupers, or schlepper crowd, still hang on to their portable radios, but unfortunately they're not the ones who buy Chryslers and DeSoto station wagons."[23] His sponsor at the time was the DeSoto-Plymouth Division of the Chrysler Corporation, which was reportedly earmarking $27 of every new automobile sale to the Marx show, then aired on both radio *and* television. By the mid–1950s, the program had a combined weekly broadcast audience of 40 million, a figure very few other shows could ever boast in that epoch.)

Guedel took still further steps to insure his program's continued success. One was the creation of a laugh track, one of the first shows to add one. One player's spontaneity sparked such a generous outburst of hilarity that the audience's response was preserved for still further use and incorporated into several other NBC programs. Said the man: "I was living with a 300-pound gent when the bedroom caught on fire. In my haste I mistakenly seized *his* slacks and shoes and put 'em on. I was descending the ladder when a shoe came off. As I tried to grab it I let go of the slacks I had been clutching tightly. A horde of 500 people below me looked up and they saw my dilemma."

Yet another tack the show would pursue — which may have been its most defining scheme yet — was its method of selecting contestants. Very few guests were yanked from the studio audience. On the contrary, carefully orchestrated machinery operating in the background allowed the show to pair precise individuals who would, often without trying, generate rib-tickling repartee with Marx. So well oiled was the mechanism of securing guests that it included a full-time staff of 12 people whose jobs were to scour the nation, turning up folks with whom Marx could have fun. The objective was to find potential contestants who were fascinating, fluent and candid. "What finally saved the show," claimed an author, "were guests with a high ribbing potential — contestants with, say, twelve children, a silly job, a bizarre hobby, a deadly personality, or a 46-inch bustline."[24]

Around 200 potential game-players were recruited weekly. The *You Bet Your Life* staff interviewed about 10 percent of them, from whom either four or six were selected. (At varying times the show featured two and three couples.) In talking with the candidates, the gagwriters exploited every response for funny yarns, preparatory to providing cue cards for Marx.

A key factor in the selection process was to link duos consisting of individuals who were decidedly opposite one another. Director Bernie Smith explained that if both were alike, "one of them gets lost."[25] Thus, a prince and a pauper, an intellect and a school dropout, a confirmed bachelor and an old maid, an opera concert-goer and a rock 'n' roller, and a cotton picker and a CEO would provide sure grist for the Marx mill. One could anticipate finding the rube and urbane, and the obscure and legendary, side-by-side on broadcasts. During a taping session, these "couples" — who had never previously met — were cordoned off in soundproof rooms. This prevented them from learning how much money the other players had won, which could tell them how much they must win to qualify for a bonus round.

Marx, meanwhile, discerned the assets and liabilities of the characters before him. Seeking anything that could be turned into laughter, he allowed contestants to sing if they wanted to (and he joined in with them in their often tacky attempts); he encouraged them to read their own poetry aloud; and he pushed them to recite funny tales. These sitting ducks became willing stooges for the master of insult (a forerunner to Don Rickles and many other successors).

Most guests were incredibly witty, whether they intended to be or not. Bernie Smith declared that none were coached and they were told only to be themselves, to speak up and not be afraid to talk back. Marx liked players who would spar with him, making their segments far more interesting to the typical listener than otherwise. What he didn't care for, and freely admitted, was a presumptuous smart aleck who believed he could set in motion the direction of their dialoguing. "Oh, a wiseguy, eh?" Marx would allow upon discerning such a customer, who would then be in for a rough go of it during the balance of his time on-stage. It was reminiscent of The Three Stooges, one of whom was constantly turning up a "wiseguy" — and whose careers coincidentally paralleled the Marx Brothers' in celluloid.

As for the guests, some real dillies

turned up, including a young Cleveland housewife whose name would be a household word in entertainment circles within a decade — Phyllis Diller! There was William Blatty, then writing a book called *The Exorcist*. And there were lots of common names, like Anna Badnovic, who came from a Yugoslavian hamlet where *everybody* boasted the surname Badnovic! But without doubt, the best of them all — even Groucho would later say so himself, confirming the guest as "the most naturally funny person who ever appeared" on the show — was a low wage–earner in San Antonio, Texas, with the name Ramiro Gonzalez Gonzalez.

It so happened that popular radio quizmaster Walter O'Keefe was in San Antonio presiding over a local telethon. During that benefit, Gonzalez — of the WOAI-TV crew — performed a comedy routine and danced with Dagmar, a stunningly beautiful national TV celebrity who could boast of sexy, statuesque features. The bit was so comical that, on his return to the West Coast, O'Keefe reported his observations to Marx, and encouraged him to get the amusing Mexican for his show. In his autobiography, *The Secret Word Is Groucho*, Marx noted that arrangements were soon made to transport Gonzalez to Hollywood.

As could be expected, the host had great fun with his guest's double name:

"What does your wife call you — Ramiro or Gonzalez?" inquired the quizmaster.

"She call me Pedro," came the reply.

"And where are you from, Mr. Gonzalez Gonzalez ... Walla Walla?" Marx asked.

"I from San Antonio, Te-has," said Gonzalez.

Following this tête-à-tête, Gonzalez demonstrated his dancing prowess by shuffling across the stage with a striking young lady who had been selected as his quiz partner. Then he spent the game eyeballing the ceiling, hoping that the duck bearing the "secret word" would descend on him. After three questions, Gonzalez begged to quit, saying that what he had already won would buy plenty of beans and tortillas for his wife and kids. The audience dissolved into convulsive, uncontrollable laughter.

The public was so taken by this man that many people later referred to him as "the Mexican Jerry Lewis." (Lewis was a popular comedian of the day, the same individual who would devote much of his later life to a crusade against Muscular Dystrophy.) Movie actor John Wayne included Gonzalez in several western films. Gonzalez gained further notoriety by appearing at county fairs and rodeos. In his honor, the city of San Antonio named a municipal park for him, recognizing his role in fostering improved Mexican-American affairs.

While the *You Bet Your Life* game itself was truly secondary to those side-splitting exchanges between Marx and his guests — John Dunning called it "mere window dressing for the antics of the quizmaster"[26] — the quiz was played for real. Although in the beginning the top prize winners didn't go home with a lot of loot measured by today's expected levels, the monetary rewards continued to improve over the years — especially with the advent of the televised era — and saw some contestants divide cash prizes bearing five figures.

Like *Truth or Consequences* before it, *You Bet Your Life*'s origins sprang from an old parlor game. In the earliest days, three couples were each given $20 and instructed to bet as much of it as they were willing to risk on four questions from a category of their own choosing. Following the double or nothing pattern of several other series (including *Double or Nothing* and *Take It or Leave It*), the game escalated with a win-

or-lose concept. Teams could go broke or ultimately win as much as $320 in the qualifying round by doubling the full value of their original $20 with each successive question. The starting amount was later raised to $100, giving players an opportunity to divide as much as $1,600 in the initial round. Eventually the game was changed to allow couples to miss one question, reducing their earnings while remaining in the game. Missing two questions in succession disqualified them from further play.

(Typical questions asked on the program: What were the first words sent over the telegraph by its inventor, Samuel Morse? Answer: *What hath God wrought?* What river separates Manchuria from Korea? Answer: Yalu. Who was our only bachelor president? Answer: *James Buchanan.* What plants do silkworms feed on? Answer: *Mulberry.*)

Near the end of the show the couple earning the highest cash amount returned to play a bonus round. This included a single general knowledge question valued at $500 (later $1,000). That figure increased weekly by the same amount when couples were unable to answer a question correctly. The bonus prize, too, was again inflated during the television era as a wheel of fortune was added to the show's visual properties. Teams chose two numbers between one and 10, one for $5,000, the other for $10,000. The bonus round question's value was determined by where the spinning wheel stopped. If neither of a couple's chosen numbers came up, they played for $2,000.

And for those couples who risked and lost everything in the qualifying round there was the *It Pays to Be Ignorant* consolation prize. Twenty-five dollars (later $100) was awarded for answering "Who was buried in Grant's tomb?" or a similar easy query. At least once, nevertheless, a couple even missed *that* one!

There was also the "secret word," which was normally explained as "a common word, something you see around the house every day." Announcer George Fenneman, out of earshot of the contestants, launched each broadcast with a statement similar to this one: "Ladies and gentlemen, the secret word tonight is chair, C-H-A-I-R." Marx inquired: "Really?" Fenneman retorted: "You bet your life!" The band burst into a rousing rendition of Marx's trademark theme, "Hooray for Captain Spaulding," devised by screenwriters Bert Kalmar and Harry Ruby for the Marx Brothers' *Duck Soup* movie.

The "secret word" concept had its origins in Guedel's *People Are Funny* show. There, host Art Linkletter gave contestants $100 when an alarm clock rang while he interviewed them. *You Bet Your Life* director Bernie Smith borrowed the idea and replaced the alarm clock with a toy duck bearing Marx's characteristic features. The secret word itself could just as easily have been *wall, telephone, hand, water, table, floor, radio* or hundreds of other items one usually encounters in a day.

If either member of a couple playing the game or being interviewed said the chosen word, pandemonium broke loose. The band's trumpeter blasted a few bars of "Reveille" on his horn, while the duck — wearing horn-rimmed glasses and mustache, complete with bushy eyebrows and holding a cigar — dropped from the ceiling with a card on which the "secret word" was printed. Near the end of the TV era, model Marilyn Burtis was substituted for the duck; she would descend on a trapeze, holding a placard with the word on it, to Marx's delight. By saying the "secret word" a couple divided $100. Marx and Guedel, who jointly owned the show, paid the $100 out-of-pocket in cash and on the spot. The sponsor picked up the tab for all the other prize money.

Returning briefly to Marx's strongly avowed preference for ad-libbing, Leonard

Maltin tells a perceptive story in which Marx's predilection appears compromised on at least one occasion. It concerns an encounter Marx had with Jack Benny's gagwriters when Marx was about to make a guest appearance on Benny's show. Sent in advance by Benny to Marx's home to let him see the script, the scribes returned to report that Marx was characteristically caustic and unreceptive to their overtures. "Well, we won't use him, then," was Benny's response, defending his staff's work. Some years later the two great comedians met at a local country club. Marx asked Benny why he never had him on his show. Benny replied: "I'd be happy to have you on my show, but only if you use the script my writers write for you."[27] Marx agreed and appeared the following week, presumably reading his lines exactly as written, in obvious contrast to his passionate fondness for ad libs.

John Guedel, ever the entrepreneur, realized an opportunity to exploit his new quiz show even further as the end of the 1947–48 radio season approached. Most programs traditionally took a summer hiatus after 39 weeks of broadcasting, replaced by a fill-in series that held the time slot open for the regular show returning in the fall. Knowing there could be a need to jump-start the quiz show again in the fall, and fully aware of the existence of the show on tape, Guedel concocted a story for ABC Radio officials. He told them that, since the average listener heard only 3.4 shows per season (a fictitious number he had dreamed up), the network could profit by replaying the 13 better You Bet Your Life programs during Marx's absence. The network bought it and the rerun was born, the first time ever for it to be successfully employed. More than five decades later it is still with us, showing no sign of abatement any time soon!

A year later, as the second season ended, it occurred to Guedel that the prop-erty had the potential to be quite durable as well as lucrative. He informed Marx: "It's never going to be a total smash unless we move it from ABC to one of the two other major networks. We're going to want to sell the show to TV, but it's not moving there unless the ratings are even higher."[28] It was just the kind of music that would play on the heartstrings of CBS chairman William Paley, for he was at that moment conducting talent raids on the other networks to amass a considerable fortune for his web. Having already acquired Amos 'n' Andy, he would ultimately obtain most of NBC's Sunday night properties, including Jack Benny, Edgar Bergen and Charlie McCarthy, Red Skelton, and more; and he would welcome the likes of ABC's Bing Crosby and Marx's You Bet Your Life.

The comedy-quiz thus shifted to CBS at the start of the 1949–50 season. By December 1949, CBS could boast of being home to 16 of radio's top 20 Nielsen-rated shows. Life's stay at CBS was short-lived, however. Elgin-American, which had sponsored the program since its inception, pulled out after 13 weeks at CBS. But waiting to sign for the series was the DeSoto-Plymouth Division of the Chrysler Corporation, which took it over without missing a week, on January 4, 1950.

Even though You Bet Your Life would be a resident at CBS for only another 26 weeks, its acquisition by DeSoto-Plymouth and a move to NBC in the autumn of 1950 was a stroke of good luck. The two—sponsor and network—collaborated to launch the TV series at that time, significantly expanding the program's stature and image. The year at CBS helped prepare the way; Guedel correctly understood that to become a smash hit and make it to TV at last, the series required exposure that one of the two major networks could provide. During the CBS year the show scored its highest radio ratings in history, never to be equaled across its nine-year run in that medium. *You Bet Your Life* remained on radio from October 27, 1947, through September 19, 1956.

The video version, with the same host, announcer and orchestra, debuted on NBC-TV at 8 P.M. Eastern Time, Thursday, October 5, 1950. An analyst noted that it was "TV's cheapest major show, requiring only a curtain, a stool, and a duck on a wire."[29] Director Bernie Smith called it the "staidest TV show ever devised,"[30] and in truth, the most animated thing about the tele-version was Marx's eyebrows. To be sure, it was a brusque disparity to his ongoing movement in films. No matter. The series on the tube grew steadily in popularity, eventually landing in video's top 10, precisely as it had done earlier in radio.

It was also continuing to make its owners wealthier men than they already were. By the mid–1950s, with the show playing on two mediums, Marx revealed in an autobiography that he had an NBC contract providing him with $4,800 per week for 39 weeks, plus $760,000 annually for 10 years—not bad for a kid who began life on New York's upper east side with few of the essentials, let alone any amenities! His contemporary—Guedel—wasn't going to the poor house either. From that one show (remember, he co-owned *House Party* and *People Are Funny*) he was carrying home $300,000 a year plus 13 percent of the net profits. If ever two fellows had the magic touch, they were Guedel and Marx!

Guedel wasn't done with being innovative yet, however. When the show went to television, he came up with the idea for broadcasting's first permanent simulcast. Using a *single* soundtrack, he would squeeze out adaptations for both radio and television. He employed eight 35mm cameras for the TV series, collecting up to 90 minutes' worth of film for each half-hour show. Guedel was successful in transferring it to radio by editing out sight gags for the audio

transcription that a hearing-only audience wouldn't comprehend.

You Bet Your Life emanated from the old NBC studios at Sunset and Vine in Hollywood, later to become the site of a bank. (It was the same address used by Ralph Edwards for many years on *Truth or Consequences*, which was among the network's stable of West Coast–originated shows.)

Airing on NBC Radio at 9 o'clock Wednesday nights, *Life* was replayed 23 hours later on NBC-TV Thursday nights at 8 o'clock. One scribe perceived: "The duplication indicated that NBC had conceded publicly that a prime-time televiewer by 1950 was not apt to turn on his radio."[31] It suggested that the network gave no pause when considering that gags witnessed on Thursdays might have already been heard by substantial numbers the day before. It was a vivid indication of the direction both NBC and DeSoto-Plymouth saw broadcasting's fortunes heading. The automobile dealers continued to carry the radio version of the comedy-quiz program for the next six seasons alongside those telecasts, nonetheless. (The show remained under DeSoto-Plymouth sponsorship on television, too, until its parent corporation decided to cease production of the DeSoto line in December 1960. For the remainder of that season, its last on the air, the series was underwritten by P. Lorillard, Incorporated for Old Gold cigarettes, and by the Toni Division of the Gillette Corporation for Toni and Prom home permanents, Tame creme rinse and White Rain shampoo.)

Diminishing audio ratings continued to point to a day when the plug would ultimately be pulled on radio. In the 1950–51 season the program's Neilsens were a respectable 13.7; six years later they had fallen more than 10 points to a dismal 3.2. Even most daytime series maintained higher figures than that! Conversely, the TV numbers were escalating; that version—like its radio counterpart years before it — was consistently placing among video's top 10.

Like the radio show, the TV venture aired repeats of the better programs from the previous season as a summer replacement, calling them *The Best of Groucho*. (The first summer, however — 1951 — *It Pays to Be Ignorant* occupied that slot.) It was another financial windfall for intrepid owners Guedel and Marx. In its final broadcast season the fall-winter-spring series was retitled simply *The Groucho Show*. It departed the airwaves for the final time on September 21, 1961, 11 years after its TV debut and nearly 14 years after its radio premiere. Its home audience was still comprised of millions of faithful viewers to the very end.

The series had enough life in it — and, more importantly, believers within the industry — to try for several comebacks, nonetheless, including a couple of reincarnations.

The first variation was an attempt by Marx himself to perpetuate what he had started years before with a CBS-TV entry titled *Tell It to Groucho*. The show's premise had the former quizmaster chastising his guests as they arrived to talk about their jobs, spouses, hobbies, personal concerns or whatever. Sound familiar? The program debuted on January 11, 1962, less than four months after Marx's highly successful comedy-quiz had departed. But audiences are sometimes fickle (out of sight, out of mind?). The series didn't last long enough to even be rated; it was dropped May 31, 1962, effectively bringing to a close Marx's career in headlining his own show.

A few years before his death in the late 1970s, Marx unsuccessfully attempted to persuade NBC to syndicate *You Bet Your Life*, using the original black-and-white videotapes. NBC, the first network to convert all of its programming to color, wasn't interested, however. It was convinced that the show's momentum had long passed.

Months later Guedel was called by NBC, informing him that a need for storage space required the web to dump all 11 years' worth of the show's videotapes, though he could have a copy. Ever the opportunist, Guedel implored the network that he wanted *every* print! Sixteen hundred copies soon arrived. Beginning with KTLA in Los Angeles, he and Marx signed the station to show the reruns late at night for just $54.88 a pop. The pair soon leased the rights from NBC and placed the show into national syndication. Before long they were splitting in excess of $50,000 annually for reruns while discovering that a whole new Groucho cult had emerged.

Also in the 1970s, long after he had written his last autobiography and virtually stopped making guest appearances, Marx performed a comedy concert at Carnegie Hall. Like most everything he did in life, it was recorded on videotape for posterity. Marx died August 19, 1977, at Los Angeles.

A recently issued biography of Marx's life portrays an individual who, out of the public limelight, lived a rather shallow, sad existence in private. He was married and divorced three times; and his first two wives and one of his daughters suffered the scourge of alcoholism. In his latter days Marx fell prey to a feminine conniver who, as his companion, soon managed his assets. She allegedly diverted much of his resources for personal gain. This resulted in tumultuous legal strife between his survivors and her after his death.

Author Stefan Kanfer (*Groucho: The Life and Times of Julius Henry Marx*) places most of the fault for Groucho's poignant life on his mother, claiming she kept him at a distance while doting on Chico and Harpo. Groucho aspired to a medical career, and desperately desired the formal education he was denied. He blamed his mother and bitterly resented the fact that she "forced" him into show business. He "never did have much of a childhood," Kanfer states, "and as a consequence his adult life was marked with immaturity and contradiction. He was a socially ambitious scamp, a loving and insensitive father, a faithful and contemptuous husband, a scripted ad-libber, an infantile grownup, a fearful iconoclast, and, above and below all, a depressive clown."[32] It's a fairly bleak testimonial to one who outwardly brought laughter and joy to millions for so many years.

On September 8, 1980, a newly syndicated version of *You Bet Your Life*, starring comedian Buddy Hackett, was placed in circulation by Hill-Eubanks Productions and MCA Television. Bob Eubanks, who was to become a venerable TV game show host himself in later years, was among the backers. The show displayed a number of the characteristics of its former self.

Contestants were interviewed by Hackett, then competed in a general knowledge quiz. The first question had a $25 value, and each successive question was worth double the previous one's sum, to a maximum of $400. At that point couples could triple their winnings on an additional question or lose half of their cash if they missed. The pair earning the most money was given a shot at picking an egg from "Leonard the Duck" as a bonus prize. The series lasted for one year.

A second reincarnation, taped in Philadelphia for Carsey-Werner Productions, was also syndicated. Premiering August 31, 1992, it featured comedian Bill Cosby as host. (Marcy Carsey and Tom Werner produced Cosby's highly rated 1980s comedy series *The Cosby Show*.) Each show began with a black goose attired in a Temple University sweatshirt (Cosby's alma mater) dropping down to reveal the "secret word." Saying the word would net a player $500. A team was given $750 to risk on three questions from a pre-selected category. At the show's end, the team with the largest earnings returned for a bonus question. A trio of cards, two bearing pictures of the black goose, were placed face down on a table. If a team chose one of those, they played for double their previous earnings. For a correct answer, the remaining card netted the team $10,000. This series lasted a year, ending September 3, 1993.

Black goose? One could almost hear John Guedel asking, as Joe Penner did before him, "Wanna buy a duck?"

Marx made what he did on *You Bet Your Life* appear so easy that — with his exposure on TV — several comedians attempted to copy his phenomenal success. Other broadcast games with strong infusions of comedy included: *Can You Top This?*, *Laughs for Sale*, *Stop Me If You've Heard This One*, *Tag the Gag* and *What's the Joke?* Television offered its viewers several cartoon games, meanwhile: *Draw Me a Laugh*, *Draw to Win*, *Droodles* and *Laugh Line*.

A number of comedians also tried to equal Marx as a game show host on the tube, but none ever fared as well. Among them: *Judge for Yourself* with Fred Allen, *Do You Trust Your Wife?* with Edgar Bergen and Charlie McCarthy, and *You're in the Picture* with Jackie Gleason. In fact, the only TV comedy-quiz to approach decent ratings was *Two for the Money* with Herb Shriner. After four years, Shriner tired of it and was replaced by Sam Levenson and Mason Gross, neither of whom could keep the Shriner momentum going.

When the original *You Bet Your Life* began on radio — having made an audition tape with *House Party*'s audience — it "borrowed" the services of Jack Slattery, *House Party* announcer. (Both Slattery and Guedel are profiled in that program's chapter.) Guedel soon conducted an audition for a permanent announcer for *You Bet Your Life*. Forty-two men appeared in quest of the role, but George Fenneman was the instant winner. Cited by a radio historiographer as the "eternal straight man," Fenneman was to become the "ideal foil" for Marx.[33] Another radio historian referred to Fenneman as "Groucho's good-natured whipping boy," certifying him as being "as mild-mannered as Groucho was ill-mannered."[34] In choosing Fenneman, Guedel allowed: "Right away, I felt the contrast. George was the guy on the top of the wedding cake. They were the odd couple."[35] Marx bullied the announcer relentlessly, though Fenneman failed to take it personally.

"At the beginning I was young and resilient, and I didn't have the good sense to know I was being insulted," the suave, devilishly handsome Fenneman conceded. "It was part of the character he was building for me that became wonderfully salable in years to come. I'd have to be a clod to badmouth the man who made it possible."[36] In a 1987 interview with author Tom DeLong he also claimed: "I pinched myself regularly to make sure that a kid who planned to be a schoolteacher could find himself on the same stage with one of the master wits of all time."[37] (Fenneman was obviously overcome by his good fortune, and one of the reasons for it had purse strings attached. The reruns Marx and Guedel peddled to late-night TV, for instance, brought Fenneman a tidy $100,000 in residuals for doing absolutely *nothing*, seven times what he earned when he *was* working!)

It was Fenneman's voice that radio and TV audiences heard from a backstage soundproof booth reminding them how much money the couples who appeared earlier had won, as well as what the "secret word" was. Fenneman also kept on top of how much the couples were winning with each question asked. Sometimes he would caution: "You have one wrong now; don't get the next one wrong or you're out of the game."

The popular announcer was born in Peking, China, on November 19, 1919. While he is remembered for his association with Marx over 14 years, had *You Bet Your Life* not intervened, Fenneman likely would have been better recalled for his ties to yet another major media figure, Jack Webb. Fenneman was the announcer on three radio series in which the actor starred: *Pat Novak for Hire, Pete Kelly's Blues* and — most prominently — *Dragnet*, the latter series on radio *and* television. In addition, Fenneman announced for radio's *Gunsmoke* and *On Stage America* while appearing in supporting roles on *I Fly Anything* and *Too Many Cooks*. He also hosted three other TV series with brief runs, including a couple of game shows: *Anybody Can Play* (ABC-TV, 1958), *Your Surprise Package* (CBS-TV, 1961–62) and *Your Funny, Funny Films* (ABC-TV, 1963). He died on May 29, 1997.

Two men prominently connected with *You Bet Your Life* left no other recorded legacies: gagwriters Hy Freedman and Ed Tyler. There were three musical directors, however, whose contributions were well certified in the industry: Billy May, Jerry Fielding and Jack Meakin.

May conducted orchestras for *The Adventures of Ozzie and Harriet, Forever Ernest* and *The Stan Freberg Show* on radio, plus *The Milton Berle Show* (NBC-TV) and *Naked City* (ABC-TV).

Fielding held the baton for *The Hardy Family* and *The Jack Paar Show* on radio, and *The Lively Ones* on NBC-TV. He was 57 when he died on February 17, 1980.

Meakin, born September 28, 1906, at Salt Lake City, died December 30, 1982, at Rancho Mirage, California. In between, the Stanford alumnus, who launched his professional career as a pianist at NBC in San Francisco in 1929, directed music for numerous radio features: *The Abbott and Costello Show, Arch Oboler Plays, Bughouse Rhythm, The Chamber Music Society of Lower Basin Street, The Great Gildersleeve, Hedda Hopper's Hollywood, Honest Harold,*

The Hour of Charm, The Jack Meakin Orchestra, Jonathan Trimble Esquire, Kay Kyser's Kollege of Musical Knowledge, Silver Theater, Summerfield Bandstand, This is Hollywood, Tonight at Hoagy's and *Your Hit Parade.* He directed the melody for Marx's brief stint on CBS-TV in 1962, *Tell It to Groucho.*

Directors Bob Dwan and Bernie Smith earned minimal credits beyond *You Bet Your Life.* Dwan directed *Today's Children* on radio and, together with Smith, *Tell It to Groucho* on TV. Smith was also West Coast producer for radio's *We, the People.* He died at 75 on January 9, 1990.

Producer Harfield Weedin directed radio's *Marvin Miller, Storyteller* series and produced ABC-TV's *Dr. I.Q.* quiz. He died June 8, 1993, at age 77.

Despite all of its pre-show manipulations, *You Bet Your Life* was enormously popular and successful where Groucho Marx's several imitators failed. He was, after all, the ONE ... the ONLY. While his zingers were prepared in advance by some of the airwaves' most resourceful gagwriters, perhaps no one on the horizon who gazed at those cue cards overhead could have made the deliveries seem as satisfying.

Appendix: An Annotated Guide to Network Radio Audience Participation Shows

This guide does not purport to be an exhaustive list of all the programs of the genre, although it is believed to be the most comprehensive published to date. While sources tapped for the compilation were not limited to the following, these were most frequently consulted and are listed alphabetically by authors (with titles appearing in the Bibliography section): Buxton and Owen (1997), DeLong (1991), Dunning (1998), Fabe, Hickerson (1996), Summers, Swartz and Reinehr, Terrace.

The Abbott and Costello Children's Show. A spin-off from the original targeting the younger set with comedy, music, awards, games, guests and juvenile talent. Boys and girls competed in a "Bubble or Nothing" silly quiz (which involved chewing gum). *ABC, 1947–49*

Add a Line. Master of ceremonies John Nelson read a rhyme, and contestants recalled the final line. *ABC, 1949*

Adventures in Photography. A news and quiz combination. *NBC Blue, 1939–40*

Albert L. Alexander's Mediation Board. A team of teachers and sociologists counseled the hapless on personal problems, including infidelity and marital discord. *MBS, 1943–52*

The Alibi Club. Audience participation series. *CBS, 1939*

Allie Lowe Miles. Offered advice to inquirers about matters of the heart. (She appeared with Sedley Brown on a similar series during this era, *Husbands and Wives*.) *MBS, 1935–38*

Amazing America. Bob Brown hosted a factual knowledge game tied to locales and awards by Greyhoud Bus Lines. *NBC, 1940*

America Calling. Dialogue by telephone between overseas GIs and their loved ones. Similar to *Transatlantic Call* several years earlier. *CBS, 1952–53*

American Forum of the Air (a.k.a. **Mutual Forum Hour**). Moderator Theodore Granik took questions from the audience for guests to consider following sometimes heated debates on the hot topics of the day. *MBS, 1937–49; NBC, 1949–56*

American School of the Air. Considered "the most outstanding show in educational radio," it was offered as a teaching supplement, integrated into the curriculums of thousands of the nation's schools. *CBS, 1930–48*

The American Women's Jury. A dozen housewives rendered a daily verdict in cases of listener concerns over in-laws, infidelity and more home life issues. Deborah Springer was Judge Emily Williams; Bill Syran, prosecutor Robert Coulter; Evelyn Hackett, defense attorney Jane Allen. *MBS, 1944–45*

Americans at Work. Vocational guidance, a typical day for an employee, and interviews with industry officials and staff were featured. *CBS, 1938–40*

America's Town Meeting of the Air. Public affairs discussion, moderated by George V. Denny Jr., and interaction with the studio audience. *NBC Blue, then ABC, 1935–56*

The Anniversary Club. Actor Ben Alexander was master of ceremonies for an audience participation show. *1940s*

Answer Auction. Details unavailable. *CBS, 1940*

The Answer Man. Facts supplied by Albert Mitchell, "The Answer Man." *MBS, 1937–52*

Answer Me This. Inquiries and replies on geography, science and educational topics formed a basis for dramas. *NBC, 1936*

Answers by the Dancers. An early dance-interview show conducted by musical maestro Horace Heidt. *NBC Blue, 1932*

Archie Andrews. A teen sit-com about a family, starring Bob Hastings most of the run. The studio audience played a role in commercials, singing rowdily: "Tender beef, juicy pork, known from the West Coast to New York ... Swift's premium franks!" *NBC Blue, 1943–44; MBS, 1944; NBC, 1945–53*

Are You a Genius? A child competing in this knowledge match was declared "genius of the day" for earning the most points. One feature was a "worst joke" contest. Ernest Chappell hosted. *CBS, 1942–43*

The Army-Navy Game (a.k.a. **Army-Navy House Party**). Fred Uttal was master of ceremonies for a quiz featuring soldiers vs. sailors. *NBC Blue, 1942–43; MBS, 1943, 1944*

Art Linkletter's House Party. Gimmicks, games, guests, kids, advice and variety characterized Linkletter's daily exchanges. [see Chapter 1] *CBS, 1945–48, 1950–67; ABC, 1949*

Arthur Godfrey's Talent Scouts. Presented semi-professional talent, as opposed to rank amateurs on similar series. Winning first place netted a spot on Godfrey's daily morning show on CBS for several days. [see Chapter 2] *CBS, 1946–56*

The Ask-It-Basket. Jim McWilliams ("radio's original question-and-answer man") was emcee to late 1940, followed by Ed East. Listeners provided questions. *CBS, 1938–41*

Ask Me Another. A player continued for as long as he could answer Happy Felton's questions (at $10 each). *NBC, 1946*

The Atwater Kent Auditions (a.k.a. **National Radio Auditions**). Amateur talent contended, beginning in local contests; annually, 10 national finalists were selected and competed for a top prize of $5,000 plus study at an established music institution. Graham McNamee presided. *NBC, 1927–32*

Auction Gallery (a.k.a. **Victory Auction** and **Radio Auction**). Studio guests and listeners bid on objects presented by auctioneer Dave Elman. Only recognized collectors and antique dealers were admitted to the studio. Items were described and integrated into brief dramas. Listeners could wire or mail in their bids within one week. *MBS, 1945–46*

Auction Quiz. Questions provided by listeners as studio guests bid for chances to answer in an auction motif. Chuck Acree was quizmaster. *NBC Blue Midwest, 1941–42*

Author, Author. Listener-submitted plots were turned into plausible situations by a brainy panel moderated by Sidney J. Perelman. *Ellery Queen* was featured. *MBS, 1939–40*

Band remotes. Live popular music shows from hotels, restaurants, ballrooms, dance halls and military camps, on all networks, normally starting at 11 P.M. ET in 30-minute timeslots, and aired primarily between 1935 and 1950. Audience members frequently danced to the music. For a comprehensive list, see John Dunning's *On the Air*, pp. 65–74.

The Baron and the Bee. Jack Pearl, "teller of tall tales," as Baron Munchhausen, and straight man Cliff Hall as Sharlie, were featured in a comedy quiz spelling bee in which dual-member teams vied for cash prizes. *NBC, 1953–54*

The Battle of the Sexes. Purporting to determine "once and for all" the brighter gender, dual four-member teams (male, led by Frank Crumit; female, led by Julia Sanderson, his wife) competed in a general fact quiz. They left in July 1942 when the format changed to a spelling bee with soldiers vs. feminine canteen staff. Jay C. Flippen and Walter O'Keefe hosted then. *NBC, 1938–43; NBC Blue, 1943–44*

Beat the Band. Garry Moore, followed by Loretta Sell ("the incomparable Hildegarde"), emceed a game soliciting wacky music riddles from listeners. *NBC, 1940–41, 1943–44*

Beat the Clock. Bud Collyer presided as players performed stunts before the time ran out. An eminently more popular TV run (1950–61) followed the radio stint. *CBS, 1949*

Ben Bernie's Musical Quiz (a.k.a. **Musical Mock Trial**). Bernie, "the old maestro," presided as masculine vs. feminine teams fought for merchandise in a music-oriented question-and-answer face-off. *CBS, 1938–40*

The Better Half (a.k.a. **Raising a Husband**). Tom Slater (to 1944), then Tiny Ruffner

hosted this often hilarious stunt game with husbands and wives competing against each other to determine ultimate prowess. *MBS, 1942–50*

The Big Break. Performances by undiscovered talent, with Eddie Dowling as master of ceremonies. *NBC, 1947*

The Big Talent Hunt. Presenting people with atypical skills (e.g., one-man bands, yodelers, jugglers), hosted by Jim Backus. *MBS, 1948*

Blind Date. Frances Scully (to 1943) and Arlene Francis were hostesses as GIs from the studio audience vied for dates with glamorous women. *NBC, 1942–43; ABC, 1943–46*

Bob Elson Aboard the Century. Sportscaster Bob Elson set up a microphone weeknights at Chicago's LaSalle Street station to interview the rich and famous traveling to and from New York via a prestigious train, The Century. *MBS, 1946–51*

The Bob Hawk Show (a.k.a. **Thanks to the Yanks**). Comedy by the host was interspersed in a quiz. Winners were designated as a "lemac" (sponsor "Camel" spelled in reverse) and sung to by the audience. *CBS, 1942–47, 1948–53; NBC, 1947–48*

The Bob Smith Show. Determining a "mystery year" was the object of a quiz sandwiched between the music. *NBC, 1954*

Break the Bank. Bert Parks became the first full-time host of this high-paying quiz as teams tested their knowledge skills. Clayton "Bud" Collyer later presided over a daytime version. [see Chapter 3] *MBS, 1945–46; ABC, 1946–49, 1951–53; NBC, 1949–51, 1953–55; MBS (concurrently), 1954–55*

Breakfast at Sardi's (a.k.a. **Breakfast with Breneman, Breakfast in Hollywood, Welcome to Hollywood**). Lively, often corny human-interest series hosted by Tom Breneman to April 1948, then Garry Moore, Cliff Arquette, John Nelson and Jack McElroy. *NBC Blue, then ABC, 1942–51; NBC, 1952–54*

The Breakfast Club. A riotous homespun potpourri of comedy, music, sketches, guests, recognitions and tributes featuring Don McNeill as master of ceremonies and a collage of "regulars." [see Chapter 4] *NBC Blue, then ABC, 1933–68*

Breezing Along (a.k.a. **Singo, Rhymo**). In "Swing-Go," set in a musical-variety motif, players tried to finish a rhyme with a song title. David Ross was emcee. *NBC Blue, 1939–40*

Bride and Groom. Betrothed couples were interviewed, wedded in an offstage chapel during the show and returned to the platform to receive gifts galore. John Nelson presided. [see Chapter 5] *ABC, 1945–50*

Budding Talent (a.k.a. **Budd Hulick**). Hulick ("Budd" of *Stoopnagle and Budd*) hosted the talent. *NBC Blue, 1938–39*

Bull Session. Featuring collegians in extemporaneous discussions on a wide variety of topics. *CBS, 1939–40*

By Popular Demand. Listener-requested songs, hosted by "Bud" Collyer, sung by Harry Babbitt and Mary Small. *MBS, 1946*

Calling All Detectives. Vincent Pelletier offered clues to culprits in crime dramas. Surrendering five minutes for local announcers to make phone calls, listeners guessed whodunit. Then the show resumed with the answer. *MBS, 1950*

Can You Top This? A joke-swapping panel with Ward Wilson as host, Peter Donald as audience quipmeister and panelists "Senator" Ed Ford, Harry Hershfield and Joe Laurie Jr. If listener submissions topped panel members' gags on a studio applause meter, cash prizes were awarded. [see Chapter 6] *MBS, 1940–45, 1948–50; NBC, 1942–48, 1953–54; ABC, 1950–51*

Candid Microphone. A forerunner of TV's *Candid Camera*, this Allen Funt outing duped unsuspecting targets into believing zany situations were on the level. Their reactions were transcribed, with the "victims" later branded as "good sports." *ABC, 1947–48; CBS, 1950*

Caravan. A quiz with John Reed King as emcee. *ABC, 1952*

The Carnation Family Party. Jay Stewart hosted a game in which contestants were required to confirm or deny specific information about themselves. *CBS, 1950–51* (Appeared with a different format on *NBC Blue, 1938* and *NBC, 1942*)

Cash on Delivery. *MBS, 1940*

Catch Me if You Can. Bill Cullen emceed this quiz in which two players climbed a mythical ladder to a "golden door," the first there trying to untangle clues for prizes. *CBS, 1948*

Chance of a Lifetime. John Reed King ran a game of chance pitting four players in a race against time. *ABC, 1949–52*

Choose Up Sides. Henry McLemore oversaw two teams trying to answer listener-submitted sports questions. *CBS, 1940–41, and partial summer replacement for Kate Smith, 1940–49*

Cinderella, Inc. A quartet of American housewives was brought to New York, lodged in luxurious digs, outfitted in pricey garments, escorted to entertainment venues and indulged throughout their stay. Before going home, they shared reactions with host Bob Dixon. *CBS, 1940, 1946–47*

The Cliché Club. Walter Kiernan moderated a panel trying to unravel a listener-submitted phrase. *ABC, 1950*

Club Matinee. A showcase for new talent, it was T. Garrison Morfit's network debut. In a "Rename the Morfit" contest, a listener gave him a new moniker: Garry Moore. Ransom Sherman also presided. *NBC Blue, 1937–42; ABC, 1945–46*

College Quiz Bowl. Allen Ludden oversaw two collegiate teams answering questions for $500 grants. *NBC, 1954–55*

Comedy of Errors. Jack Bailey emceed as studio guests attempted to spot mistakes in short skits. *MBS, 1949–52*

Community Sing (a.k.a. **Summer Hotel**). Studio audience singing, plus musical acts and comedy by Milton Berle, one of his earliest radio stints. Berle and Wendell Hall hosted in New York, and Billy Jones and Ernie Hare ("The Happiness Boys") hosted in Philadelphia. *CBS, 1936–37*

Consumer Quiz. Fred Uttal presided as a quintet of feminine contestants answered shopping-related questions. (An unrelated, similar-titled series, *Consumer's Quiz*, aired on MBS, 1940–42.) *CBS, 1946*

Contact Dave Elman. Listeners were invited to exploit radio to get in contact with other individuals. *MBS, 1940–41*

Coronet Quick Quiz. Charles Irving asked eight rapid-fire questions and gave answers as listeners tested aptitudes to quickly respond in a five-minute quiz. *NBC Blue, 1944–45*

Correction Please. Studio contestants amended errors in multiple-choice answers to questions by bidding up to the $10 they had been given to play the game. Jim McWilliams, then Jay C. Flippen, hosted. *CBS, 1943–44; NBC, 1945*

County Fair. Jack Bailey, Peter Donald and Win Elliot hosted a game from a pretend midway, with contests between audiences and celebrities. *NBC Blue, 1945; CBS, 1945–50*

The Court of Human Relations. Audiences rendered verdicts for dramas concerning actual legal cases. Tales came from stories in sponsor *True Story* magazine. *NBC, 1934, 1935–38; CBS, 1934–35; MBS, 1938–39*

The Court of Missing Heirs (a.k.a. **Are You a Missing Heir?**, **The Board of Missing Heirs**). Files of people with unclaimed inheritances were enacted; 150 real heirs were located via county probate records. Creator James Waters hosted. *CBS, 1937–38; Midwest, 1939–42; ABC, 1946, 1947*

Crackpot College. *CBS, 1940*

Crossword Quiz. Allen Prescott, then David Gilmore were masters of ceremonies. *ABC, 1948*

Daily Dilemmas. A game, hosted by Jack Barry, featured skits depicting real-life crises. Studio audience members tried to determine those dramas' aims. Audience panels evaluated the quality of the responses. *MBS, 1946–48*

Darts for Dough. A game combining physical skill and mental dexterity. Players threw darts at a board for cash prizes based on ability to answer queries. Doing a stunt let any continue who missed a question. *NBC Blue, then ABC, 1944–47*

Dave Elman's Auction Gallery. Auctioneer Elman took bids from studio guests and listeners by telephone. *MBS, 1945*

Deadline Dramas. Listeners submitted plots of up to 20 words; a cast of three had two minutes to plan a seven-minute playlet, performed to the incredulity of radio and studio audiences. Cast: (variously) Joan Banks, William Fadiman, Elsie Gordon, Bob White, Ireene (sic) Wicker. *NBC, 1940–41; NBC Blue, 1943–44*

Dealer in Dreams. Quiz series. *CBS, 1940*

Dear Columbia. Fan mail dramatizations. *CBS, 1935–38*

Detect and Collect. Rivals began with $25 and five chances to name an object behind a curtain. For wrong guesses, they forfeited $5. Wendy Barrie emceed. In a revised version, Vincent Lopez hosted a musical game whereby listeners at home tried to figure out how often a certain tune was scattered among other songs. *CBS, 1945–46*

Dr. Christian. A rural physician contemplated the physical maladies and emotional anxieties in the lives of residents. "The only show in radio where the audience writes the script," the drama typically received 10,000 manuscripts annually and aired 52. Jean Hersholt starred. [see Chapter 7] *CBS, 1937–54*

Doctor Dollar. An early, simplified quiz awarding dollars as cash prizes for questions answered. *NBC, 1937*

Dr. I.Q., the Mental Banker. A demonstration of quick wits as Dr. I.Q. (Lew Valentine, Jimmy McClain) asked rapid-fire questions and paid silver dollars for right answers. [see Chapter 8] *NBC Blue, 1939; NBC, 1939–49; ABC, 1950*

Dr. I.Q. Jr. A juvenile spin-off, with Dr. I.Q. (Jimmy McClain, Lew Valentine) from the adult version, and silver dimes replacing silver dollars. Quick-paced, like the original, but with easier questions. *NBC, 1941, 1948–49*

Dr. Peter Puzzlewit. *NBC, 1937*

Dollar a Minute. Bill Goodwin refereed as those with talent or gripes paid a buck a minute to air them. *CBS, 1950–51*

Don't Forget. Players began with $5 and accrued 68 cents for correct answers in a quiz emceed by Allen Prescott. The 68-cent formula resulted via the show being broadcast on the sixth day of the week at eight o'clock. *NBC Blue, 1939–40*

Don't You Believe It. Alan Kent and Tom Slater originally co-hosted the series, followed by Toby Reid in 1946. *MBS, 1938–39; NBC Blue, 1944; CBS, 1946–47*

Double or Nothing. Masters of ceremonies for a risk-all quiz to duplicate earnings were Walter Compton, John Reed King, Todd Russell and Walter O'Keefe. [see Chapter 9] *MBS, 1940–47; CBS, 1947–48; NBC, 1948–53; ABC, 1954–54*

Doubleday Quiz Show. *MBS, 1949, 1950*

Dough Re Mi. Hope Emerson guided players in a test of their musical knowledge. *NBC, 1942–43*

Down You Go. Bergen Evans offered a cryptic clue to a well-known listener-submitted phrase, quotation or slogan. Four permanent panelists played the game; for each missed guess, $5 was sent to the home contributor. *MBS, 1952–53*

Dunninger, the Mentalist (aka **The Dunninger Show**). Mind-reading demonstrations featuring Joseph Dunninger, and musical variety. *NBC Blue, 1943–44; NBC, 1945, 1946*

Earn Your Vacation. Jay C. Flippen, then Steve Allen, hosted a contest where players met harder and harder questions to win trips. *CBS, 1949–50*

Ed East and Polly. The Easts hosted a collection of gags, contests and interviews, similar to *Art Linkletter's House Party*. Its original

format segued into *Ladies Be Seated* in 1944. *NBC Blue, 1943–44; NBC, 1945*

Elmo Roper. The survey-taker solicited and reported public opinion on a myriad of topics. *CBS, 1948–50*

Emily Post (aka **How to Get the Most Out of Life**). The manners expert and celebrated newspaper columnist responded to listeners' queries. *CBS, 1930–31, 1937–38; NBC Blue, 1931–33, 1934; NBC, 1938–39*

Enough and on Time. Quiz series. *NBC Blue, 1943*

Especially for You. Game show. *1940*

Everybody Wins. Phil Baker ran a quiz where the winners won and losers did, too, gaining consolation prizes. *CBS, 1948*

Everything for the Boys. A dual concept: 20-minute dramas with actor Ronald Colman, supervised by writer-director Arch Oboler; and shortwave exchanges between GIs in combat zones and family members at home. *NBC, 1944*

Facts Unlimited (aka **Ideas Unlimited**). Quiz. *NBC, 1950*

Fame and Fortune. The Tommy Dorsey Orchestra, and vocalists Connie Haines and Frank Sinatra, performed compositions by rank amateurs. The best song was picked by studio audience applause, its writer receiving $100. *NBC Blue, 1940–41*

Finders Keepers. For a cash prize, studio contestants vied to identify a mistake in dramatic scenes. Hosts: Bob Sherry, Happy Felton. *NBC, 1944–45*

Fish Pond. Win Elliot hosted; players were equated with fish. Fishes performed a song, comedy routine or other act. The fish pond (studio audience) decided if they were keepers (and prize-winners) or to be thrown back. *ABC, 1944*

Five-Minute Mysteries. Following five-minute dramas, listeners supplied clues leading to plot solutions. *NBC, 1940, 1945–48*

The Five Mysteries Program. A panel of listeners and studio guests suggested solutions to five mini-mysteries just heard. Cash prizes were awarded. *MBS, 1947–48, 1949–50*

For Your Approval. Series auditions, retrieving the earlier *Forecast* concept on CBS, with Jock MacGregor. *MBS, 1946–47*

Forecast. Series auditions for potential CBS radio shows. *CBS, 1940, 1941*

Free for All. *CBS, 1947*

Fun Fair. Based on people and their pets, with Jay Stewart hosting. *1940s*

Fun for All. Bill Cullen and Arlene Francis cohosted music, contests and comedy sketches. *CBS, 1952–53; ABC, 1953*

Fun in Print. Studio guests vs. famous authors in question-and-answer rounds. Sigmund Spaeth presided. *CBS, 1940*

Funny Side Up. One of Bert Parks' last assignments as a radio quizmaster. *CBS, 1959*

Gag Busters. A comedy quiz with master of ceremonies Milton Berle. *1939*

Game Parade. Small cash prizes were awarded to winners of the question-and-answer rounds in a quiz involving five youngsters. Arthur Elmer presided. *NBC Blue, 1942–43*

Gateway to Hollywood. Thirteen couples, novice actors all, performed in simple dramas—one pair weekly—over a 13-week span. One couple was awarded a contract with RKO Pictures. John Archer and Gale Storm were "discovered" on the show. Film producer Jesse L. Lasky hosted. *CBS, 1939*

G.E. College Bowl. Allen Ludden, later Robert Earle, emceed a collegian question-and-answer marathon. *NBC, 1953*

Get Rich Quick. Shades of *Stop the Music!* To win, you had to be listening when Johnny Olsen called, asking for the name of a figure or article in a skit just presented. *ABC, 1948*

G.I. Laffs. A gagfest with songs by Martha Mears and jokes supplied by servicemen. William Gargan hosted. *CBS, 1945*

Give and Take. Players chose gifts, then tried to win them in question rounds as John Reed King emceed. *CBS, 1945–53*

Go for the House. John Reed King hosted seven married couples who vied in quiz rounds for household furnishings and, ultimately, a six-room house and lot. *ABC, 1948–49*

Go Get It (aka **Melody Treasure Hunt**). Joe Bolton and Tom Slater were at the helm for this contest. *MBS, 1941–43*

Gold Is Where You Find It. James Fleming was master of ceremonies for a game series. *CBS, 1941*

Good Listening. Songs broken up by audience "plants" put some contestants off from answering the questions about those tunes. Lionel Kaye was emcee. *CBS, 1943*

Goodwill Court. Offered free legal advice to unidentified subjects willing to share their woes before a microphone. After two months, the N.Y. Supreme Court banned adjudicators and attorneys from appearing. A.L. Alexander was mediator. *NBC, 1936–37*

The Goodwill Hour (aka **The John J. Anthony Program**). High-school dropout Lester Kroll, claiming to hold three degrees, gave advice on human relationships and focused on marital and financial discord under the moniker John J. Anthony. Catchphrase: "Ask Mr. Anthony." *MBS, 1936, 1937–40; Blue, 1940–43; MBS, 1943–44, 1945–46, 1947, 1949, 1951–53, 1957*

Grand Slam. Irene Beasley was the singing hostess in a lively quest for a $100 bond prize between contestants and listeners submitting five-part questions. *CBS, 1946–53*

The Great Day. John Reed King emceed as GIs told why they should receive $100. Winners were picked by audience applause. *MBS, 1952–53*

The Grouch Club. A forum for listener complaints, hosted by Jack Lescoulie. *CBS West Coast only, 1938–39; NBC, 1939–40*

Guess Where. With June Walker hosting, players tried to identify locales portrayed in brief skits. *MBS, 1939, 1943*

Guess Who? Peter Donald, then Happy Felton, presided over a guessing game involving hidden identities. *MBS, 1944–49*

Hagen's Spelling Bee. A word bee competition for children, launched by physician Dr. Harry Hagen. *CBS, 1936–37*

Happy Landing. Quiz with Clayton "Bud" Collyer. *ABC, 1950*

Health Quiz. *MBS, 1951; CBS, 1951*

Heart's Desire. Human-interest giveaway with strong ties to *Strike It Rich* premise, and Ben Alexander as MC. *MBS, 1946–48*

Here's the Clue. Tips offered to solve a puzzle. *CBS, 1941*

Hint Hunt. *CBS, 1947–49*

History Is Fun. Quiz with MC Ted Malone. *NBC Blue, 1943*

Hit the Jackpot. Bill Cullen bestowed extravagant gifts on listeners who solved mysteries from the clues that were hidden in songs and narratives. *CBS, 1948–49, 1950*

Hits and Misses. Quiz series. *CBS, 1946–51*

Hobby Lobby. Human-interest platform for people with unusual pastimes. Dave Elman, then Bob Dixon presided. *CBS, 1937–38, 1939–40, 1941–43, 1945–46; NBC, 1938, 1950; NBC Blue, 1938–39; MBS, 1949*

Holland Housewarming (aka **The Housewarming**). A guest of honor was benefited weekly at a housewarming party hosted by Don McNeill, with the Benny Goodman Orchestra. *NBC, 1941*

Hollywood and Vine. Interviews with passersby. *ABC, 1946*

Hollywood Calling. George Murphy presided as celebrated film figures telephoned listeners to test their movie familiarity. A grand prize exceeded $30,000. *NBC, 1949–50*

Hollywood Grabbag. Game show. *MBS, 1940*

Hollywood Jackpot. For commodity bonanzas, players recalled memorable film dialogue. Kenny Delmar hosted. *CBS, 1946–47*

Hollywood Premiere. Audiences submitted queries to hostess Louella Parsons, who asked them of guest stars performing in 20-minute film adaptations. *CBS, 1941*

Hollywood Quiz. *MBS, 1949–50*

The Home Symphony Orchestra. Ernest LaPrade conducted as listeners played instruments while orchestral works aired. Music could be purchased from the network or local dealers. Brief guidelines preceded selections. *NBC Blue, 1937–38*

Honeymoon in New York. Interviews with betrothed couples conducted by Durward Kirby, who presented merchandise prizes, á la *Bride and Groom*, running simultaneously on ABC. *NBC, 1945–47*

Hope Chest. Giveaway series. *CBS, 1946*

How Did You Meet? Human-interest interviews. *NBC, 1941*

How To. Human-interest discussions, with Roger Price moderating a problem-solving panel. *CBS, 1955*

How'm I Doin'? Two players given $30 each faced a trio of questions that added to or depleted their stashes by $10 a pop. The game ended if one ran out of money. Bob Hawk emceed. *CBS, 1942; NBC, 1942*

How's the Family? Marshall Kent presided as married couples answered questions for merchandise gifts. *MBS, 1953*

Husbands and Wives. Domestic squabbles were aired to host Sedley Brown and hostess Allie Lowe Miles, as well as to the rest of the country. *MBS, 1936; NBC Blue, 1936–37*

If I Had the Chance. Host Cal Tinney spotlighted people's suppressed desires. *NBC Blue, 1938–39*

I'll Buy That. *CBS, 1953*

I'm an American. Interviews with naturalized citizens. *NBC, 1940–42*

Information Please. An award-winning panel of intellects, moderated by Clifton Fadiman, tested their powers in response to listener-submitted queries. [see Chapter 10] *NBC Blue, 1938–40; NBC, 1940–46; CBS, 1946–47; MBS, 1947–48, 1950–51*

It Happens Every Day. Arlene Francis and Bill Cullen interviewed characters and told curious yarns. *CBS, 1951–53*

It Pays to Be Ignorant. A quiz show spoof with quizmaster Tom Howard and contestants facing dumbbell panelists Lulu McConnell, Harry McNaughton and George Shelton. *MBS, 1942–44; CBS, 1944–49, 1950; NBC, 1951*

It Pays to Be Married. Quiz series. *NBC, 1953–55*

It's a Living. Human-interest interviews with individuals in bizarre or extraordinary occupations, hosted by Ben Alexander. *MBS, 1948*

It's Our Turn. Teen comments on current events, hosted by Hugh Downs. *NBC, 1948*

It's Up to You. Dale Baxter hosted as competitors performed stunts; audience applause picked winners. *NBC Blue, 1939*

Jack Dempsey's Sports Quiz. Mark Goodson's first turn as a network master of ceremonies. *MBS, 1942*

Jay Stewart's Fun Fair. A show of pets, with owners showing them, responding to questions about them and competing in a game for prizes. *ABC, 1949, 1950–51*

The Joe DiMaggio Show. Sports figures were introduced and true stories dramatized in the lives of well-known athletes. Children earned prizes for answering questions in a sports quiz in which DiMaggio was "umpire" and Jack Barry was "pitcher." *CBS, 1949–50*

John Barclay's Community Sing. A sing-along. *CBS, 1936*

The Johnny Olsen Show (aka **Johnny Olsen's Rumpus Room, Johnny Olsen's Get-Together, Johnny Olsen's Luncheon Club**). Music and variety with Johnny and Penny (Mrs.) Olsen featured in exchanges with audiences and special guests. *ABC, 1946, 1949, 1950–51; MBS, 1949, 1954–57*

Juvenile Jury. Unrehearsed and unscripted, a kids' panel, presided over by Jack Barry, attempting to answer listeners' queries on topics like makeup, allowances, morality and discipline. *MBS, 1946–51; NBC, 1952–53*

Kay Kyser's Kollege of Musical Knowledge. A music quiz with quizmaster Kyser, "the old professor." A blend of corn, contests and melody. *MBS, 1938, 1939–40; NBC, 1938–48*

(partially concurrent with MBS); ABC, 1948–49

Kelly's Courthouse: Following a six-minute mystery that stopped short of divulging the culprit, studio contestants tried to identify the guilty party with the aid of three musical clues. Fred Uttal hosted. *NBC Blue, 1944*

Kiss and Make Up. Milton Berle was the judge in a contrived courtroom where married couples aired complaints about their mates. A studio panel determined the partner "at fault." The show's title was applied as a penalty. *CBS, 1946*

Ladies Be Seated. A continuation of *Ed East and Polly* (an earlier show); when the Easts departed in 1946 it was taken over by Johnny and Penny Olsen, and later by Tom Moore, who conducted games, sing-alongs and interviews. *ABC, 1944–50*

Ladies Fair. Tom Moore presided over a women's gabfest with games, music and interviews. *MBS, 1950, 1951–54*

Lady Be Beautiful. One of the airwaves' first makeover shows, in which Ben Alexander brought a woman to the stage for critical appraisal by beauty specialists before a conversion from head to toe. *MBS, 1946*

Lawyer Q. Radio actor Karl Swenson, later Dennis James, conducted this quiz. After dramatic reenactments, twelve jurors from an audience tried to match guilty and not guilty verdicts with real ones for cash. *NBC Blue, 1941; MBS, 1947*

Leave It to the Girls. Originally a discussion of listener-submitted concerns by a feminine panel quartet, it dissolved into comical issues relating to male-female relationships. A prominent gentleman (e.g., Henry Morgan, Georgie Jessel) countered the male bashing. Hosted by Ted Malone, with Paula Stone as moderator. *MBS, 1945–49*

Let's Laugh and Get Acquainted. Jack Gregson interviewed couples from the audience, reviewed topics of interest, then awarded merchandise prizes. *NBC, 1946*

Let's Play Games. *MBS, 1937–38, 1949*

Let's Play Reporter. Contestants tried to recall facts from stories submitted by listeners and told by host Frances Scott. Prizes were $1 per correct response. *NBC, 1943*

Let's Pretend. Fairy-tale reenactments. The audience, primarily kids, provided well-rehearsed sounds for traveling to Let's Pretend land while delivering appropriate responses called for during narrator Uncle Bill's commercials for Cream of Wheat. *CBS, 1934–54*

Let's Talk Hollywood. George Murphy moderated a panel of West Coast celebrities trying to answer listener-submitted questions on films and stars. Stumping the panel netted the contributor a free pass to a theater for a year. *NBC, 1948*

Life Begins at 80. Jack Barry moderated as octogenarians discussed issues suggested by listeners and guests. So candid was the panel that the program was taped to delete indelicate slips of the tongue. *MBS, 1948–49; ABC, 1952–53*

Listen Carefully. Quiz with Jay Jostyn as emcee. *MBS, 1947*

Live Like a Millionaire. Jack McCoy welcomed the children who introduced their parents offering amateur talent. Winners, determined by audience applause, earned a week's tax on a million dollars. *NBC, 1950–52; ABC, 1952–53*

Lucky Partners. In the early version, Paul Brenner was quizmaster; Carl Cordell followed. *MBS, 1948, 1957–58*

Lucky Stars. More undiscovered talent competed as Jack Kiltie served as master of ceremonies. *NBC, 1946*

Major Bowes' Original Amateur Hour. Those with "busfare and a harmonica" made a grab for the brass ring as large numbers attempted to have their talent discovered at this established venue. *NBC, 1935–36; CBS, 1936–45;* Reprised as *Ted Mack's Original Amateur Hour: ABC, 1948–52*

Major Bowes' Shower of Stars. A continuation of Bowes' earlier show, it returned *Original Amateur Hour* winners to the microphone and introduced more novices. *CBS, 1945–46*

The Man of Magic. Mentalist Felix Greenfield offered mind-reading exhibitions using subjects at home and in the studio. *MBS, 1944*

The March of Games. Listeners acquired *Junior Encyclopedia* sets by submitting best questions on this test of knowledge featuring five children. The high scorer won $5, and runner-up $3. The "youngest emcee in radio," Arthur Ross, 14 at the start, presided. Nila Mack produced-directed, often presenting kids from the *Let's Pretend* cast. *CBS, 1938–41*

Marriage Club (aka **Marriage Club, Inc.** and **Your Marriage Club**). Haven MacQuarrie presided as wedded pairs shared their domestic struggles before contending in a quiz for merchandise awards. *NBC Blue, 1940; CBS, 1940–41*

Married for Life. Bill Slater interviewed betrothed couples, and a narrative of their love story was presented. Gifts were awarded. Mutual's response to NBC's *Honeymoon in New York* and ABC's *Bride and Groom. MBS, 1946, 1947*

Meet Me in Manhattan. Walter Kiernan guided a fleeting audience participation series. *ABC, 1946*

Meet the Missus. In the tradition of *Art Linkletter's House Party*, this interview/caper/gift-giving show plucked women from the audience at Earl Carroll's Hollywood restaurant. Emcees: Jack Bailey, Ed East, Harry Koplan, Harry Mitchell and Jay Stewart. *CBS (predominantly West Coast), 1944–50*

Meet Your Lucky Partners. Paul Brenner conducted a match involving a listener by telephone and a studio audience member paired to answer questions for prizes. *MBS, 1948*

Meet Your Match. Tom Moore and Jan Murray separately emceed as a player selected an opponent from the studio audience. Question rounds followed. *MBS, 1949; NBC, 1949–50, 1952–53*

Melody Puzzles. Fred Uttal supervised skits that included clues to song titles, which contestants tried to guess. *MBS, 1937–38; NBC Blue, 1938 (partial overlap with MBS run)*

MGM Screen Test. Talent show with Dean Murphy. *1940s*

Midweek Hymn Sing. Over 100,000 requests were received from listeners for favorite sacred music selections to be performed by baritone Arthur Billings Hunt. *NBC, 1926–36*

The Missus Goes A-Shopping. John Reed King oversaw stunts and gimmicks on missions linked with shopping. *CBS, 1941–51*

Mr. Adam and Mrs. Eve. Frank Crumit and Julia Sanderson ran a highly partisan question marathon involving four men in spirited competition with four women. It abruptly ended with Crummit's demise, September 7, 1943. *CBS, 1942–43*

Money-Go-Round. Players answered questions for cash about vocals sung by the Larry and Ginger Duo. Benay Ventua hosted. The series lasted three weeks. *NBC Blue, 1944*

Money on the Line. A telephone game show. *CBS, 1944*

Mother Knows Best. Warren Hull was MC for a potpourri of games and tunes especially for women. *CBS West Coast and WCBS (New York), 1947–48; CBS, 1949–50*

Movie Quiz. Jack Bailey tested contestants' capacities for identifying scenes and stars in current attractions by hearing extracts from film sound tracks. *ABC, 1945*

Murder Will Out. Following a dramatized real-life mystery, four studio contestants competed to name the killer and tell the clue that led them there. *NBC Blue, 1945–46*

Musical Mock Trial. "Judge" Ben Bernie officiated as six studio contestant "jurors" decided if tuneful selections were related to narratives that the judge read. *CBS, 1940*

Musical Treasure Chest (aka **Tums Treasure Chest, Dixie Treasure Chest**). Horace Heidt conducted a jackpot quiz of melodious inquiries. *NBC, 1940–44*

Musico. A short-lived quiz produced by Louis Cowan with a musical question theme. *CBS, 1940*

Mystery File. Criminal cases were reenacted, after which contestants tried to solve the crimes based on clues in the dramatizations. Walter Kiernan hosted. *ABC, 1950–51*

Mystery History Quiz. *MBS, 1939–40*

Name It and It's Yours. Children's quiz. *NBC Blue, 1939*

Name It and Take It. Ed East was the quizmaster of this Milton Biow property. *NBC Blue, 1939–40*

Name That Tune. With a $500 jackpot for recognizing a trio of mystery songs, this was NBC's response to a music-quiz craze. Two players met for five rounds. Red Benson hosted, while the winner pursued the jackpot. *NBC, 1952–53*

Name the Movie. A celebrated icon read lines from films as players vied for gifts. Marvin Miller emceed. *ABC, 1949*

Name the Place. Ben Grauer read descriptions of cities, states and nations as players guessed locales. *NBC Blue, 1939; NBC, 1939 (concurrent with NBC Blue)*

Name Three. Bob Hawk was master of ceremonies on a quiz requiring a trio of answers to his questions. *MBS, 1939–40*

Name Your Music. Tommy Cauthers and Margaret Carroll officiated on this melodious quiz. *NBC, 1946*

National Amateur Night. Ray Perkins hosted as five judges voted on novice talent acts. Poor performers were booted; winners earned minor radio deals. *CBS, 1934–36; MBS, 1936*

Never Too Old. Art Baker interviewed the elderly (minimum age of 70) in this human-interest fare. *MBS, 1945*

News Game. Hospitalized GIs gained cash prizes as news authorities gave answers over a ticking clock to current events queries from NBC newsman Kenneth Banghart. *NBC, 1954*

A Night with Horace Heidt. Another amateur talent showcase with the same famous leader. *NBC Blue, CBS, NBC (variously under this title and several others), 1932–53*

Noah Webster Says. Players tried to define five listener-submitted terms. The first word was worth $1; successors doubled in value to the fifth, worth $50. Haven MacQuarrie hosted. *NBC West Coast, 1942, 1945–51 (continuity undocumented); NBC, 1942–43, 1945; NBC Blue, 1943*

Nobody's Children. Walter White Jr. introduced orphaned and sometimes homeless juveniles who were interviewed by Hollywood stars. A discussion of each child's case ensued. *MBS, 1939–41, and West Coast only in 1941, 1942*

Old-Time Spelling Bee. Word competition. *MBS, 1936–37*

Old Town Auction Block. "Colonel" Robert Brown conducted this bidding game that aired only twice. *NBC Blue, 1941*

On Your Mark. "Bud" Collyer quizzed players. *MBS, 1948–49*

One Thousand Dollar Reward. Following a 25-minute felony drama — minus the solution — host John Sylvester called a listener chosen from a postcard drawing. The fan earned $1,000 for cracking the crime. *NBC, 1950*

The Original Amateur Hour. Major Bowes' program was amended and Ted Mack spotlighted the talent this time. *ABC, 1948–52*

Paging the Judge. Guest judges picked winners as audience participants tested their aptitude for solving troubles in prearranged situations. Robert Paige hosted. *ABC, 1953–54*

Palmolive Community Sing. Tinhorns, unschooled and off-the-street voices dominated as evangelistic vocalist Homer Rodeheaver hosted a join-in musical outing. *CBS, 1936*

Pass the Buck. *CBS, 1949*

Payroll Party. Nicholas Girrard emceed as housewives attempted some bizarre stunts for cash awards. *ABC, 1952*

People Are Funny. In many aspects, a replay of *Truth or Consequences*, with outlandish stunts the motif for an Art Linkletter–hosted

mirthful melee. *NBC West Coast, 1939–42 (other titles); NBC, 1942–51, 1954–60; CBS, 1951–54*

People's Platform. Current events panel, moderated by Lyman Bryson to 1946, then Dwight Cooke. Panel guests included Tallulah Bankhead, Irving Berlin, Samuel Goldwyn, Herbert Hoover, Groucho Marx, Harold Stassen and others of their caliber. Common citizens gave opposing views. *CBS, 1938–52*

The People's Rally. Combination quiz, issue-oriented debate and public affairs poll, this potpourri featured quizmaster Bob Hawk and discussion leader John B. Kennedy. Silly questions comprised the quiz; debates presented two sides to issues, the audience then voted for an opinion. *MBS, 1938–39*

The Personal Column of the Air. Reader letters were dramatized as authors sought to reconnect with lost friends and relatives via a broadcast. *NBC Blue, 1936; NBC, 1936–37*

The Philip Morris Musical Game. A Milton Biow–owned entry among melody contests. *CBS, 1940*

The Phrase That Pays. Red Benson, then Ted Brown emceed as a contestant tried to identify a listener-submitted phrase, with three clues given. Prizes were based on the clues; if a player failed entirely, the contributor won. *NBC, 1953–55*

Pick a Date. Picking a memorable year in her life, a lady faced queries about some prominent actions transpiring that year. Buddy Rogers was master of ceremonies. *ABC, 1949–50*

Pick and Play with Bob and Ray. Comedians Bob Elliott and Ray Goulding led studio players to choose a number and reply to questions linked to it. A merchandise jackpot awaited those who could respond correctly to every query. *NBC, 1953*

Pin Money Party. Game show. *NBC, 1940–41*

Play Broadcast. Contenders from a studio audience listened for winning clues in comedy sketches by Marvin Miller, who acted in diverse roles. *MBS, 1940–41*

Pop the Question. When a contestant popped a balloon of a specific color on a dart board, a question of predetermined complexity and prize value was asked. *MBS, 1954–56*

Pot o' Gold. The first big money giveaway; Ben Grauer, Rush Hughes and Happy Felton hosted. All one had to do to win $1,000 was be at home and answer the phone. Copycat series followed. *NBC, 1939–40; NBC Blue, 1940–41; ABC, 1946–47*

Professor Puzzlewit. Larry Keating filled the title role. *NBC West Coast, 1937–39*

Professor Quiz (aka **Professor Quiz and His Brainbusters**). Psychiatrist Craig Earl guided five contenders for silver dollar prizes, wading through listener-submitted queries on "the first true radio quiz." *CBS, 1936–41; ABC, 1946–48*

Queen for a Day. Dud Williamson initially presided over a woe-filled melee of perceived needs by women competing for notoriety and gain. Jack Bailey is best identified as the longtime emcee, however. [see Chapter 11] *MBS, 1945–57*

Quick as a Flash. Ken Roberts, Win Elliot and Bill Cullen, in order, presided as six players tried to solve questions with clues. Pressing a key caused a flash of one's assigned light color, indicating readiness to guess. Any who miscued here were out of the game. *MBS, 1944–49; ABC, 1949–51*

Quicksilver. With a disguised microphone, Ransom Sherman approached passersby on streets asking for help in solving listener-submitted riddles. Right replies netted five silver dollars; wrong replies, one. *NBC, 1939; NBC Blue, 1939–40*

Quixie Doodles (aka **Bob Hawk's Quixie Doodle Quiz, Colonel Stoopnagle's Quixie Doodle Quiz**). Hawk and F. Chase Taylor (Stoopnagle) hosted as teams contended, answering satirical, nonsensical questions. *MBS, 1939–40; CBS, 1940–41*

The Quiz Kids. Five precocious juveniles (three "regulars" and two guests), intellects all, faced stumpers submitted by listeners.

Joe Kelly moderated. *NBC, 1940, 1946–51; NBC Blue and ABC, 1940–46; CBS, 1952–53*

Quiz of Two Cities. Rival audiences (in theory, at least) competed as Michael Fitzmaurice hosted, playing to a list of municipalities — e.g., Minneapolis vs. St. Paul, New York vs. Chicago, Los Angeles vs. San Francisco. *MBS, 1944–47*

The Quiz Quotient. *CBS, 1943*

Quizathon. *MBS, 1949*

Quizdom Class. *ABC, 1946–49*

Quizzer's Baseball. Dual three-member teams gained basehits, doubles or homeruns by the response time of their answers to questions fired by opposing pitchers Glenda Farrell and Budd Hulick. Harry Von Zell umpired. *NBC, 1941*

Quizzical. An ethnic version of *Kay Kyser's College of Musical Knowledge* and a road show for Cab Calloway's band. Contestants rolled dice, the numbers representing questions about music that they were to answer. *NBC Blue, 1941–42*

Raising Your Parents. A forum of letters from troubled youth on issues like discipline and neglect, submitted for support and advice to a juvenile panel. Opera lover Milton Cross hosted; Dan Golenpaul (soon to create *Information Please*) produced. *NBC Blue, 1936–37*

Rate Your Mate. Spouses predicted how their partners would answer questions, earning up to $100 for accuracy. Joey Adams was master of ceremonies. *CBS, 1950–51*

Rebuttal. Folks who felt they had been exploited in the media offered "their side" of a dispute. John W. Vandercook introduced them with a brief review. *MBS, 1950*

Request Performance. Listener letters called for favorite artists and dramatic sketches. *CBS, 1945–46; MBS, 1947*

Reunion USA. Returning GIs in rehabilitation. *ABC, 1945*

RFD America. Joe Kelly, then Ed Bottcher emceed as a quartet of farmers contended to be "Master Farmer of the Week" by pursuing rural quiz questions. The titlist returned weekly to face new challengers until replaced by another winner. *MBS, 1947–48; NBC, 1948, 1949*

Rhymo. Players gave the last line or final few words of a four-line jingle, relying on a song host-conductor Johnny Green's orchestra played as a clue. *CBS, 1940*

Richard Maxwell (aka **A Friend in Deed, Hymns You Love**). Hymn-singing tenor Maxwell, the "good Samaritan of the air," organized Good Neighbor clubs to aid listeners down on their luck, people sending in details of sad plights. *NBC Blue, 1934–35; CBS, 1936–40, 1941; MBS, 1945–46*

Right Down Your Alley. Aired from New York City bowling lanes, Bill Slater and Don Gardner quizzed competitors who then rolled to match predeliberate scores. *ABC, 1946*

Rock 'n' Roll Dance Party. Count Basie's orchestra supplied the bop-hop tunes as Joe Williams hosted. *CBS, 1955, 1956*

Santa Cataline Fun Quiz. *CBS, 1940*

Say It with Music. Art Linkletter, host. *MBS, 1940, 1950*

Scout About Town. Anna May Dickey and Hunt Stromberg Jr. welcomed undiscovered talent. *MBS, 1946*

Scramby Amby. Scrambled words submitted by listeners figured in a quiz hosted by Perry Ward. Music and verbal clues helped players find answers. *NBC West Coast, 1943; NBC Blue West Coast, 1944; NBC Blue, 1944–45; MBS, 1946–47*

Screen Test. Aspiring actors appeared with established ones in brief skits as John Conte presided. *MBS, 1944*

Scripteasers. Buddy Rogers, then Benny Rubin emceed a quiz in which a skit hinted at a specific song title. *NBC, 1937*

The Sears Grabbag. A jackpot quiz. *1940*

Second Chance. Quiz. *NBC, 1954–55*

Second Honeymoon. Judges selected a housewife who "told the best story" to emcee Bert Parks about why she wanted a follow-up wedding trip. The winner got the trip and a new wardrobe. *ABC, 1948–49, 1949; MBS, 1949–50*

Service with a Smile (aka **The Army Show, Army Camp Program**). Garry Moore emceed as GIs performed talent acts from military facilities. *NBC, 1941–42*

Sez Who? Panelists guessed celebrities' voices as Henry Morgan, later John Cameron Swayze, moderated. *CBS, 1957–58*

Shoot the Moon. A jackpot quiz with Clayton "Bud" Collyer as master of ceremonies. *ABC, 1950–51*

Sigmund Spaeth's Music Quiz. The "tune detective," who earlier proved composition copyright infringements, was master of ceremonies for a melody-minded contest. *MBS, 1947*

Sing Along (aka **Sing Along with the Landt Trio**). Featuring self-taught harmonizers Daniel, Jack and Karl Landt; musical arrangements were purposely selected so home audiences could vocalize with the performing brothers. *CBS, 1942–43, 1948*

Sing for Your Dough. Lew Valentine led a community sing. On signal, all but a few (who were before mikes) quit; those at mikes earned two dollars for continuing. *NBC Blue, 1942*

Sing for Your Money. Musical game show. *MBS, 1940*

Sing for Your Supper. Tommy Tucker hosted, and Tucker's band played, as a quartet of contestants vied for prizes, singing a song while performing a prearranged stunt. *MBS, 1949*

Sing It Again. Dan Seymour conducted this dual mix: In one half, novice composers performed new arrangements of popular songs; in the other, rhymed clues were offered to help quiz players properly guess a recorded voice. *CBS, 1948–51*

The Singing Bee. Host Welcome Lewis and vocalist Art Gentry teamed on a musical quiz. *CBS, 1940–41; NBC Blue, 1942–43*

Singo. On this Welcome Lewis-Art Gentry outing, listeners submitted three song titles that told a story or asked a question. A GI was picked by a studio player, with whom he would divide a four-dollar prize. *NBC Blue, 1944*

The $64,000 Question. Emcee Hal March carried the big money giveaway to new heights, with a glass isolation booth, a strongbox holding questions and, finally, a scandal forcing the genre off the air. A simulcast of the TV show seen by 55 million added another million via radio. *CBS, 1955–58*

Skyrider Quiz. *MBS, 1944–45*

Slanguage Quiz. A colloquial speech game. *NBC Blue, 1944*

Smilin' Ed's Buster Brown Gang. A fictional adventure story, letters from young listeners, chats with an imaginary cast (e.g., Midnight the Cat, Squeaky the Mouse, Froggy the Gremlin), songs, guests and studio audience assistance with commercials for Buster Brown shoes embraced a boisterous half-hour headed by jolly Ed McConnell. *NBC, 1944–53*

So This Is Love. Eddie Dunn was emcee of a romantic-themed quiz that aired daily for four weeks. *MBS, 1947*

So You Think You Know Music. Ted Cott presided as players tried to answer queries about many phases of melody. *CBS, 1939–40; NBC, 1940–41; MBS, 1945–46*

So You Want to Lead a Band. Conductor Sammy Kaye picked audience guests harboring a wish to conduct an orchestra and allowed them to lead his. A $1,000 prize went to the best instant maestro in a later conducting contest. *ABC, 1946–48*

Somebody Knows. $5,000 was offered any listener who could help the police solve an actual murder case based on the premise "somebody knows who did it." Jack Johnstone narrated the playlets. *CBS, 1950*

A Song Is Born. Four composers— three novices and a professional — performed their compositions. Stories about the songs were read or dramatized. Each received $25, with the best song (as voted by a panel) published. *NBC, 1944*

Songo. A jackpot quiz. *1940*

Songs for Sale. Jan Murray and Richard Hayes hosted as the works of novice composers were performed, appraised by a panel of pros and put up for sale. Simulcast. *CBS, 1950–51*

Spelling Bee (aka **The National Spelling Bee**). Paul Wing, then Joe Gannon, emceed as teams (often collegiate) vied in spelling galas. *NBC Blue, 1937, 1938; NBC, 1938–40*

Spelling Beeliner. A spelling marathon. *CBS, 1940*

Spend a Million. Contestants received $1,000, bought gifts after answering questions correctly and kept those gifts by being the first out of money. Joey Adams, MC. *NBC, 1954–55*

Spin to Win. Warren Hull presided as calls were made to ask listeners to name the record just played; qualifiers could try for a $15,000 jackpot by naming a song played in reverse. (In 1940–41 Hull conducted a game with a similar title, *Spin and Win*, on NBC Blue.) *CBS, 1949*

Sports Pop-offs. A sports motif game show. *CBS, 1940*

S.R.O. A permanent panel, moderated by Betty Furness, tried to answer listener-submitted questions. If the panel was stumped, a contributor selected a savings bond or theater tickets as a prize. The show lasted four weeks. *ABC, 1953*

Star for a Night. Novice or aspiring actors won merchandise prizes for their capacities to perform in brief sketches. Paul Douglas was host. *NBC Blue, 1943–44*

Stars and Starters. A recognized performer and a novice joined in a drama or song as Jack Barry emceed. *NBC, 1950*

Stars in Khaki 'n' Blue. Amateur acts from the armed services, with Arlene Francis as hostess. *NBC, 1952*

Stillicious Kids Quizeroo. A juvenile game show. *CBS, 1940*

Stooperoos. A man and woman responded to weird situations. The zaniness of replies helped audiences decide on winners. F. Chase

Taylor (Colonel Stoopnagle) emceed. *CBS, 1943*

Stop and Go. Ken Murray, then Joe E. Brown hosted as GIs traveled on a pretend trip with quiz answers worth $2 a pop; winners were the first to win $8. *CBS, 1943–44; NBC Blue, 1944–45*

Stop Me if You've Heard This One. With strong *Can You Top This?* ties, jokes were solicited from listeners for a panel of quipsters (variously Morey Amsterdam, Jay C. Flippen, "Senator" Ed Ford, Harry Hershfield, others). Panelists yelled "Stop!" if they could finish a gag read by Milton Berle, later Roger Bower. *NBC, 1939–40; MBS, 1947–48*

Stop That Villain. "Rogue" Jack Bailey confused players with misleading clues, while "hero" Marvin Miller gave helpful hints toward correct quiz answers. *MBS, 1944*

Stop the Music! "The show that ended Fred Allen's radio career" saw emcee Bert Parks (later, Bill Cullen) calling homes for valuable prizes, inquiring what tune had just been presented. [see Chapter 12] *ABC, 1948–52; CBS, 1954–55*

Story to Order. Lydia Perera was storyteller for a juvenile series of tales developed from listener ideas. *NBC, 1945*

Strike It Rich. People down on their luck found friends in quizmasters Todd Russell (initially) and Warren Hull (thereafter) and "the show with the heart," with multiple means to help the hapless, even if they failed in the quiz. [see Chapter 13] *CBS, 1947–50; NBC, 1950–57*

Stump the Authors. Editor Sidney Mason moderated a panel of a trio of scribes who were given a half-minute to design an original story from audience proposals. *ABC, 1946*

Suit Yourself. Quiz game. *ABC, 1945*

Surprise Package. Jay Stewart reigned over a prize-winning stunt marathon with audience members competing. *ABC, 1950*

Surprise Party. Stu Wilson was master of ceremonies on this audience participation outing. *CBS, 1946–47*

Swap Night. An early call-in series on which listeners traded items they no longer needed. *NBC Blue, 1942*

Take a Card. A quartet of players drew four cards each from a deck of 52 before Wally Butterworth asked a question about one card. That player earned cash that was tied to the card's face value, if he replied correctly. *MBS, 1943*

Take a Number. Al "Red" Benson, Happy Felton and Bob Shepherd steered this game involving listener-submitted queries. Players responding correctly most often qualified for a jackpot round with much larger prizes. *MBS, 1948–55*

Take It or Leave It (aka **The $64 Question**). Interviews were as important as the quiz in which the contestants could take their money and quit or risk it all for higher figures. Emcees: Bob Hawk, Phil Baker, Garry Moore, Eddie Cantor, Jack Paar. [see Chapter 14] *CBS, 1940–47; NBC, 1947–52*

Talent Search, Country Style (aka **Saturday Night, Country Style**). Amateur country music acts performed after emcee Tom George introduced the newcomers. *CBS, 1951–56*

Talk Back. Happy Felton presided. *ABC, 1950–51*

Talk Your Way Out of This One (aka **Talk Your Way Out of It**). A situational game where players improvised. Peter Donald hosted in 1949 when the title changed. *CBS, 1941; ABC, 1949*

Teen Town. Spotlighting gifted teenagers, Dick York presented talented youths. *ABC, 1946*

Tello-Test. A daily quiz series. *MBS, 1945–51*

Texaco Opera Quiz. Milton Cross fielded listener-submitted questions to a panel of operatic experts during regular intermissions of Metropolitan Opera broadcasts. *NBC, 1940– (final date undocumented)*

That's a Good Idea. Dramatic vignettes of workable ideas submitted by listeners "for the betterment of mankind," for which their originators were paid five dollars. David Vaille narrated. *CBS, 1945*

That's Life. "Anything that encouraged laughter at another's weaknesses" describes a breathless rapid-fire question show emceed by Jay C. Flippen. Those wishing to perform, share a tale or gripe were welcome. *CBS, 1946–47*

There's Money in Your Name. Frank Small, quizmaster. *1948*

Think Fast. Mason Gross moderated a permanent panel facing listener-submitted questions. *ABC, 1949–50*

The Thirteenth Juror. The listener played a 13th juror, deciding what actually transpired in a mystery drama anthology. Vincent Price was featured. *NBC, 1949*

This Amazing America. Bob Brown inquired of players little-known facts about the national landscape. *NBC Blue, 1940*

This Is Fort Dix. A human-interest feature wherein GIs reported to the folks back home on what they had been doing while in the service. Tom Slater hosted. *MBS, 1940–44*

This Is Life. Vincent Pelletier read listeners' messages about missing relatives, friends or property in an effort to restore them. Charities were helped, too. *MBS, 1941–43*

This Is My Story. Listeners submitted 500-word narratives that were enacted as plays. Every 12 weeks the writer of the best tale — judged by Hedda Hopper, Leo McCarey and Barbara Stanwyck — gained a $1,000 war bond. Runner-ups got $250 and $100. *CBS Pacific Coast Network, 1944–45*

This Is Your Life. Ralph Edwards surprised unexpecting subjects, recounting major events in their lives while presenting those who impacted them. They were showered with gifts and cash. The show grew from *Truth or Consequences*, another Edwards radio success. *NBC, 1948–50; CBS, 1950*

Three for the Money. Predicting audience reaction to songs (based on applause) was a feature of a process involving a trio of players. Clayton "Bud" Collyer presided in rounds that offered top prizes of $300, $500 and $5,000. *MBS, 1948*

Three's a Crowd. John Reed King was emcee. *MBS, 1948*

Time's a-Wastin'. Clayton "Bud" Collyer emceed as players tried to answer queries in 10 seconds, the value of prizes decreasing at $100 per second of hesitancy. *CBS, 1948*

Title Tales. Five listener-submitted song titles formed the basis for a story told by a permanent cast. Their failure netted the listener $50. Sylvia Rhodes hosted. *MBS, 1940*

Transatlantic Call (aka **People to People**). Phonograph records requested by GIs overseas were played, and families were connected with their servicemen via on-air phone calls. *CBS, 1943–46*

Transatlantic Quiz. Listeners supplied questions for a four-member panel, half in London, half in New York. Hosts: Lionel Hale, Ronny Waldman (U.K.); Alistair Cooke (U.S.). Similar to a global *Information Please*. *NBC Blue, 1944–45*

True Adventures (aka **Your True Adventures**). Real-life tales from listeners dramatized. Narrator Floyd Gibbons doled out $25 weekly and $250 monthly for the best ones. *CBS, 1937*

True or False. Players met seven increasingly tough true-false queries before a 1948 format change. Then they faced questions on people in the news, answering four out of five for $2,500. Henry Hagen, later Eddie Dunn, emceed. *MBS, 1938, 1948–49, 1950–51, 1953, 1954–56; NBC Blue, 1938–43*

Truth or Consequences. Emcee Ralph Edwards turned a quiet parlor game into a rollicking mania of zany stunts that captured national attention for a full decade. [see Chapter 15] *CBS, 1940, 1950–51; NBC, 1940–50, 1952–54, 1955–56*

Try and Find Me. A Walt Framer game show based on clues referring to locales. *CBS, 1945–46; ABC, 1946*

Twenty Questions. A permanent panel, moderated by Bill Slater or Jay Jackson, attempted to identify a person, place or object within 20 questions. If they failed, the listener submitting the stumper won a gift. *MBS, 1946–54*

Two for the Money. After comedian Herb Shriner's monologue, three pairs of game players competed, with the winners going for a bonanza prize round. *NBC, 1952–53; CBS, 1953–56*

Uncle Jim's Question Bee. Jim McWilliams (later, Bill Slater) asked queries of three men and three women for a $25 top prize. Considered the airwaves' second game show, after *Professor Quiz. NBC Blue, 1936–39, 1940–41; CBS, 1940*

Victory Tunes (aka **Chesterfield Time, Pleasure Time**). Fred Waring and his orchestra honored the musical requests of World War II GIs. *NBC, 1939–44*

Visiting Hour. Ted Husing conducted interviews of wounded GIs at military base medical facilities. *CBS, 1944*

Vox Pop (aka **Sidewalk Interviews**). Spontaneous chats with passersby at street corners and hotel lobbies. Variously featuring Parks Johnson, Jerry Belcher, Wally Butterworth, Neil O'Malley, Warren Hull. *NBC Blue, 1935, 1941 (concurrent with CBS); NBC, 1935–39; CBS, 1939–47; ABC, 1947–48*

Walk a Mile. Win Elliot, then John Henry Falk asked queries for cigarette carton gifts. "I'd walk a mile for a Camel" said the sponsor's slogan, hence the title. *NBC, 1952–54*

Watch and Win. Ben Alexander was emcee of the game. *1940s*

We Americans. Interviews conducted by Walter Pitkin of fellow countrymen from all walks of life. *CBS, 1935*

We Deliver the Goods. Maritime heroes shared personal tales, and host Howard Culver read true adventure stories of the Merchant Marines that were broadcast from a Santa Catalina Island training station. *CBS, 1944*

We, the People. Human interest. Hosts: Phillips H. Lord, Gabriel Heatter, Milo Boulton, Dwight Weist, Dan Seymour, Burgess Meredith, Eddie Dowling. *NBC Blue, 1936–37; CBS, 1937–49; NBC, 1949–51*

We, the Wives. Quizmaster Chuck Acree presided over this competition among housewives. *MBS, 1939; NBC, 1939–40*

We Want a Touchdown. Red Barber played quizmaster for a football series. *MBS, 1938, 1939*

Welcome Neighbor. Interviews by Dave Driscoll and Tom Wolf of visitors from everywhere to the World's Fair. *MBS, 1939*

Welcome Travelers. Human-interest interviews conducted by Tommy Bartlett involving people on journeys to, from and through Chicago. [see Chapter 16] *ABC, 1947–49; NBC, 1949–54*

We've Got Your Number. *MBS, 1945–46*

What Am I Offered? Bob Dixon was emcee. *MBS, 1947–49*

What Makes You Tick? John McCaffery, later Gypsy Rose Lee, presided as subjects rated themselves in 10 psychosomatic areas. Guest psychologists then evaluated their responses. *MBS, 1948; ABC, 1948, 1950–51; CBS, 1948–49*

What Would You Have Done? Ben Grauer presented a crisis to guests who told how they would have resolved the situation. Audience applause determined the winners. *NBC Blue, 1940*

What's Doin' Ladies? Audience participation series conducted by Jay Stewart, emcee. *ABC, 1943–48*

What's My Line? Hosted by John Daly, this successful TV panel show, in which occupations were guessed, came to radio, a reversal of an established trend. *NBC, 1952; CBS, 1952–53*

What's My Name? A giveaway paying $10 for naming mystery subjects on a first clue, thinning by $1 per added clue. A first clue in 1948 was worth $100, followed by $50 and $25. Until someone won, $500 weekly went into a jackpot. Arlene Francis was hostess, paired with many males: Budd Hulick, Fred Uttal, John Reed King, Ward Wilson, Carl Frank. *MBS, 1938–39, 1942; NBC, 1939–40, 1941, 1943; ABC, 1948, 1949*

What's the Name of That Song? Dud Williamson, Bob Bence and Bill Gwinn, in order, paid $30 to contestants guessing three tune titles, $15 for two, $5 for one. *MBS, 1944–47, 1948*

What's Your Idea? Listeners submitted thoughts about radio to host Don McNeill, then to Nelson Olmsted. *NBC, 1941*

Where and When? A quiz surrounding a contestant's knowledge of impacting events that had already occurred. *NBC, 1940*

Where Are We? Budd Hulick presided. *MBS, 1939, 1940*

Where Are You From? Henry Lee Smith emceed. *MBS, 1940–41*

Where Have You Been? Horace Sutton moderated a permanent panel trying to guess guests' travel history. *NBC, 1954–55*

Which is Which? Players guessed if voices they heard were celebrities or impostors. Ken Murray paid $50 to winners; $5 to losers, and $45 to a national war fund. *CBS, 1944–45*

Whiz Quiz. General knowledge questions, fielded by Johnny Olsen, were answered for merchandise prizes. *ABC, 1948*

Who Are You? Clues led players to identities. *MBS, 1940*

Who-Dun-It? From the files of mythical Inspector Slade (Santos Ortega), brief mysteries were aired. For $100, host Bob Dixon directed players to identify the guilty party. A musical clue assisted in solving a jackpot case. *CBS, 1948*

Who Knows? A quiz based on the case records of psychic phenomena book author Dr. Hereward Carrington. *MBS, 1940–41*

Who, What, When, Where? A game based on recalling details, with Francis Scott as quizmaster. *NBC, 1943*

Winchell Column Quiz. Announcer Ben Grauer conducted an audience participation contest revolving around a popular broadcast colleague, Walter Winchell. *NBC Blue, 1938*

Winner Take All. One player with a buzzer, one with a bell sought chances to answer queries asked by Bill Cullen, Ward Wilson and Clayton "Bud" Collyer. *CBS, 1946–49, 1951–52*

The Wizard of Odds. Jay Stewart, then Walter O'Keefe emceed, as players—with $5 each—bid to answer queries; replies increased or decreased stashes. *NBC, 1949–53; CBS, 1953–54*

Wonderful City. Human-interest (for worthy causes). Harry Wismer presided. *MBS, 1953, 1954–55*

The Word Game. Franklin P. Adams was quizmaster for a spelling bee and word-usage competition. *CBS, 1938*

Yankee Doodle Quiz. Ted and Verlia Malone conducted a competition based on American history. *NBC Blue, 1943, 1944*

You Bet Your Life. Jester Groucho Marx, late of cinema fame, sparred with odd couples, making light of them before conducting the quiz. Primarily a forum for Marx's antics, the game was purely secondary. [see Chapter 17] *ABC, 1947–49; CBS, 1949–50; NBC, 1950–56*

You Decide. Quiz series. *CBS, 1941*

Your Dream Has Come True. Game of chance. Ian Keith was master of ceremonies. *NBC, 1940–41*

Your Happy Birthday. Quiz with Edmund "Tiny" Ruffner (height: 6' 7") as "The Birthday Man." *NBC Blue, 1941*

Your Lucky Strike (aka **The Don Ameche Show**). A twist on amateur showcases as host Ameche presented unknown talent performing and telling human-interest tales. Three women at home were chosen to pick the winners by phone. *CBS, 1948–49*

Your Sports Question Box. Sports inquiry game. *ABC, 1947*

Your Unseen Friend. Dramatic sketches rooted in troubles sent in by listeners. Narrator Maurice Joachim, the "unseen friend," clarified the skits and offered advice to unravel some related concerns. *CBS, 1936–38*

You're in the Act. Nils T. Granlund conducted an audience participation series. *CBS, 1946*

You're the Expert. Fred Uttal hosted, and a guest judge chose winners, as players solved actual problems. "Best" answers netted $25, followed by $10 and $5. *CBS, 1941*

Yours for a Song (aka **Conti Castille Show**). Bert Parks hosted a musical game and conducted audience sing-alongs. *MBS, 1948–49*

The Youth Opportunity Program. Amateur talent-thons in many locales hosted by bandleader Horace Heidt. *NBC, 1947–51*

Youth vs. Age. Cal Tinney, then Paul Wing presided as listener-submitted questions were asked of adult and teen teams. The high-scoring group won a dollar per correct answer. *NBC, 1939, 1940; NBC Blue, 1939–40*

Youth Wants to Know. A teen panel questioned a guest in that individual's area of expertise. *NBC, 1952–53*

Chapter Notes

Preface

1. Hawk, Bob. "This Quiz Business." *Radio and Television Mirror*, March 1949, p. 30.

2. DeLong, Thomas A. *Quiz Craze: America's Infatuation with Game Shows*. New York: Praeger Publishers, 1991, p. x.

3. Wolfe, Charles Hull. *Modern Radio Advertising*. New York: Funk & Wagnalls Co., in association with Printers' Ink Publishing Co., Inc., 1949, pp. 193–194.

4. Ansbro, George. *I Have a Lady in the Balcony: Memoirs of a Broadcaster*. Jefferson, N.C.: McFarland and Co., Inc., 2000, p. 44.

5. Cox, Jim. *The Great Radio Soap Operas*. Jefferson, N.C.: McFarland & Co., Inc., 1999, p. 4.

6. Nachman, Gerald. *Raised on Radio*. New York: Pantheon Books, 1998, p. 9.

Chapter 1

1. Fabe, Maxene. *TV Game Shows: A Behind-the-Screen Look at the Stars, the Prizes, the Hosts and the Scandals!* Garden City, N.Y.: Doubleday & Company, Inc., 1979, p. 168.

2. DeLong, Thomas A. *Quiz Craze: America's Infatuation with Game Shows*. New York: Praeger Publishers, 1991, p. 56.

3. Maltin, Leonard. *The Great American Broadcast: A Celebration of Radio's Golden Age*. New York: Penguin Putnam Inc., 1997, p. 297.

4. Dunning, John. *On the Air: The Encyclopedia of Old-Time Radio*. New York: Oxford University Press, 1998, p. 333.

5. Nachman, Gerald. *Raised on Radio*. New York: Pantheon Books, 1998, p. 338.

6. Ibid., p. 340.

7. DeLong, Thomas A. *Radio Stars: An Illustrated Biographical Dictionary of 953 Performers, 1920 through 1960*. Jefferson, N.C.: McFarland & Company, Inc., 1996, p. 19.

8. Nachman, p. 340.

9. Nachman, p. 339.

10. "Houseparty." *Radio Album Magazine*, Winter 1949, p. 72.

11. Dunning, 1998, p. 334.

12. Nachman, p. 341.

13. Nachman, p. 338.

14. Ibid., p. 339.

Chapter 2

1. Slide, Anthony. *Great Radio Personalities in Historic Photographs*. Vestal, N.Y.: The Vestal Press, Ltd., 1982, p. 52.

2. Singer, Arthur J. *Arthur Godfrey: The Adventures of an American Broadcaster*. Jefferson, N.C.: McFarland & Company, Inc., 2000, p. 1.

3. DeLong, Thomas A. *Radio Stars: An Illustrated Biographical Dictionary of 953 Performers, 1920 through 1960.* Jefferson, N.C.: McFarland & Company, Inc., 1996, p. 107.

4. Jack Perkins, hosting a video biography, *Arthur Godfrey: Broadcasting's Forgotten Giant,* originally shown in 1996 on the Arts & Entertainment cable network.

5. Singer, Ibid.

6. Dunning, John. *On the Air: The Encyclopedia of Old-Time Radio.* New York: Oxford University Press, 1998, p. 43.

7. Lackmann, Ron. *Remember Radio.* New York: G.P. Putnam's Sons, 1970, p. 94.

8. Nachman, Gerald. *Raised on Radio.* New York: Pantheon Books, 1998, p. 355.

9. Dunning, 1998, p. 47.

10. *Time,* quoted without specific reference in DeLong, 1996, p. 108.

11. Nachman, p. 354.

12. Singer, p. 3.

13. Ibid., p. 2.

14. Ibid.

15. Smith, Sally Bedell. *In All His Glory: The Life of William S. Paley, The Legendary Tycoon and His Brilliant Circle.* New York: Simon and Schuster, 1990, pp. 260, 270.

16. Singer, p. 76.

17. Buxton, Frank and Bill Owen. *The Big Broadcast, 1920–1950,* Second Edition. Lanham, MD: The Scarecrow Press, Inc., 1997, p. 15.

18. Nachman, p. 260.

19. Nachman, p. 354.

20. *Arthur Godfrey's Talent Scouts* broadcast, September 26, 1949.

21. Ibid., November 12, 1950.

22. Nachman, p. 354.

23. Dunning, 1998, p. 46.

24. Singer, p. 160.

25. Arts & Entertainment cable network biography, 1996.

26. Dunning, 1998, p. 47.

Chapter 3

1. Dunning, John. *On the Air: The Encyclopedia of Old-Time Radio.* New York: Oxford University Press, 1998, p. 112.

2. Ibid.

3. "Radio Reviews." *Variety,* October 24, 1945, p. 38.

4. Dunning, 1998, p. 112.

5. Nachman, Gerald, *Raised on Radio.* New York: Pantheon Books, 1998, p. 324.

6. DeLong, Thomas A. *Radio Stars: An Illustrated Biographical Dictionary of 953 Performers, 1920 through 1960.* Jefferson, N.C.: McFarland & Co., Inc., 1996, p. 210.

7. DeLong, Thomas A. *Quiz Craze: America's Infatuation with Game Shows.* New York: Praeger Publishers, 1991, p. 115.

8. Nachman, Gerald, p. 325.

9. DeLong, 1996, p. 210.

10. Fabe, Maxene. *TV Game Shows.* Garden City, N.Y.: Doubleday & Company, Inc., 1979, p. 117.

11. DeLong, 1991, p. 108.

12. DeLong, 1996, p. 151.

13. DeLong, 1991, pp. 100–101.

14. Fabe, Maxene, *TV Game Shows.* Garden City, N.Y.: Doubleday & Company, Inc., 1979, p. 127.

Chapter 4

1. Dunning, John. *On the Air: The Encyclopedia of Old-Time Radio.* New York: Oxford University Press, 1998, p. 115.

2. Reported in *Don McNeill and the Breakfast Club Celebrate 20 Years of Corn,* a premium booklet released by the show in 1953, p. 23.

3. Kirby, Durward. *My Life ... Those Wonderful Years!* Charlotte Harbor, Fla.: Tabby House Books, 1992, p. 96.

4. Dunning, 1998, p. 115.

5. Ibid.

6. Ibid., p. 116.

7. Nachman, Gerald. *Raised on Radio.* New York: Pantheon Books, 1998, p. 359.

8. Ibid., p. 359.

9. Ibid., p. 358.

10. Appearing in *The 1954 Breakfast Club Yearbook: A Collection of Favorite Poems, Photographs and Stories.* Chicago: Don McNeill Enterprises, Inc., 1954, p. 16.

11. Ibid.

12. Ibid., pp. 358, 359.

13. *Don McNeill and the Breakfast Club Celebrate 20 Years of Corn*, p. 6.

14. Dunning, 1998, p. 113.

15. Ibid., p. 356.

16. Singer, Arthur J. *Arthur Godfrey: The Adventures of an American Broadcaster.* Jefferson, N.C.: McFarland & Company, Inc., Publishers, 2000, p. 152.

17. Dunning, p. 117.

18. Brooks, Tim and Earle Marsh. *The Complete Directory to Prime Time Network TV Shows, 1946-Present.* Fourth Edition. New York: Ballantine Books, 1988, p. 212.

19. Hyatt, Wesley. *The Encyclopedia of Daytime Television.* New York: Billboard Books, 1997, p. 69.

Chapter 6

1. Landry, Robert. "Radio Reviews," *Variety*, December 11, 1940, p. 39.

2. Dunning, John. *On the Air: The Encyclopedia of Old-Time Radio.* New York: Oxford University Press, 1998, p. 135.

3. Dunning, John. *Tune in Yesterday: The Ultimate Encyclopedia of Old-Time Radio, 1925–1976.* Englewood Cliffs, N.J.: Prentice-Hall, Inc., 1976, p. 110.

4. Dunning, 1998, p. 349.

5. Ibid.

6. Ibid., p. 350.

Chapter 7

1. Dunning, John. *On the Air: The Encyclopedia of Old-Time Radio.* New York: Oxford University Press, 1998, p. 202.

2. Nachman, Gerald. *Raised on Radio.* New York: Pantheon Books, 1998, p. 379.

3. Ibid.

4. Dunning, p. 202.

5. Grams, Martin Jr. *Radio Drama: American Programs, 1932–1962.* Jefferson, N.C.: McFarland & Company, Inc., Publishers, 2000, p. 139.

6. Maltin, Leonard. *The Great American Broadcast: A Celebration of Radio's Golden Age.* New York: Penguin Putnam Inc., 1997, p. 56.

7. Dunning, p. 203.

8. Grams, pp. 140–148.

9. DeLong, Thomas A. *Radio Stars: An Illustrated Biographical Dictionary of 953 Performers, 1920 through 1960.* Jefferson, N.C.: McFarland & Company, Inc., Publishers, 1996, p. 269.

10. Slide, Anthony. *Great Radio Personalities in Historic Photographs.* Vestal, N.Y.: The Vestal Press, Ltd., 1982, p. 107.

11. Nachman, p. 268.

12. Ibid.

13. Maltin, p. 145.

14. Ibid., pp. 144–145.

Chapter 8

1. Nachman, Gerald. *Raised on Radio.* New York: Pantheon Books, 1998, p. 322.

2. Ibid., p. 325.

3. Dunning, John. *On the Air: The Encyclopedia of Old-Time Radio.* New York: Oxford University Press, 1998, p. 204.

4. Ibid., pp. 204–205.

5. DeLong, Thomas A. *Quiz Craze: America's Infatuation with Game Shows.* New York: Praeger Publishers, 1991, p. 22.

6. Dunning, 1998, p. 205.

7. Ansbro, George. *I Have a Lady in the Balcony: Memoirs of a Broadcaster in Radio and Television.* Jefferson, N.C.: McFarland & Company, Inc., 2000, p. 187.

8. Nachman, p. 324.

9. Dunning, John. *Tune in Yesterday: The Ultimate Encyclopedia of Old-Time Radio, 1925–1976.* Englewood Cliffs, N.J.: Prentice-Hall, Inc., 1976, p. 163.

Chapter 9

1. Dunning, John. *Tune in Yesterday: The Ultimate Encyclopedia of Old-Time Radio, 1925–1976.* Englewood Cliffs, N.J.: Prentice-Hall, Inc., 1976, p. 167.

2. DeLong, Thomas A. *Quiz Craze: America's Infatuation with Game Shows.* New York: Praeger Publishers, 1991, p. 105.

3. *Radio and Television Mirror*, September 1950, pp. 46–47.

Chapter 10

1. Maltin, Leonard. *The Great American Broadcast: A Celebration of Radio's Golden Age*. New York: Penguin Putnam Inc., 1997, p. 25.

2. DeLong, Tom. *Radio Stars: An Illustrated Biographical Dictionary of 953 Performers, 1920 through 1960*. Jefferson, N.C.: McFarland & Co., Inc., 1996, p. 92.

3. Dunning, John. *Tune in Yesterday: The Ultimate Encyclopedia of Old-Time Radio, 1925–1976*. Englewood Cliffs, N.J.: Prentice-Hall, Inc., 1976, p. 304.

4. Nachman, Gerald. *Raised on Radio*. New York: Pantheon Books, 1998, p. 332.

5. John Kieran quoted in Dunning, John. *On the Air: The Encyclopedia of Old-Time Radio*. New York: Oxford University Press, 1998, p. 341.

6. DeLong, Tom. *Quiz Craze: America's Infatuation with Game Shows*. New York: Praeger Publishers, 1991, p. 31.

7. Clifton Fadiman, quoted in Ibid., p. 32.

8. Dunning, 1998, p. 341.

9. DeLong, 1991, pp. 26–27.

10. Ibid.

11. Dunning, 1998, p. 341.

12. Dunning, 1998, p. 342.

13. Nachman, p. 333.

14. Dunning, 1998, p. 346.

15. DeLong, 1991, p. 28.

16. "Clifton Fadiman," *Current Biography, 1941*. New York: Wilson Co., 1942, p. 190.

17. Lamparski, Richard. *Whatever Became Of…? Third Series*. New York: Crown Publishers, Inc., 1970, p. 43.

18. *Current Biography, 1941*.

19. Dunning, 1976, p. 304.

20. DeLong, 1996, p. 5.

21. Sally Ashley. *F.P.A.: The Life and Times of Franklin Pearce Adams*. New York: Beaufort Books, 1986, p. 78.

22. DeLong, 1996, p. 150.

23. Lamparski, p. 87.

24. DeLong, 1991, p. 28.

25. Dunning, 1976, p. 303.

26. Quoted from *Not Under Oath* in Nachman, p. 334.

27. Lamparski, p. 87.

28. Kashner, Sam and Nancy Schoenberger. *A Talent for Genius: The Life and Times of Oscar Levant*. New York: Random House, Inc., 1994, p. 210.

29. Nachman, p. 333.

30. Kieran, John. *Not Under Oath*. Boston: Houghton Mifflin, 1964, pp. 60–61.

31. DeLong, 1996, p. 164.

32. Nachman, p. 252.

33. DeLong, 1996, p. 114.

34. Ashley, p. 217.

35. Kashner, Sam and Nancy Schoenberger, pp. 263–264.

36. Dunning, 1998, p. 346.

37. Nachman, p. 335.

38. Dunning, 1998, p. 560.

39. Ibid.

40. Dunning, 1998, p. 349.

41. Gould, Jack. "A TV Hit for $250." *The New York Times*, February 14, 1954, p. II-11.

42. Nachman, p. 333.

43. Nachman, p. 334.

44. DeLong, 1991, p. 32.

Chapter 11

1. Fabe, Maxene. *TV Game Shows*. Garden City, N.Y.: Doubleday & Company, Inc., 1979, p. 174.

2. DeLong, Thomas A. *Radio Stars: An Illustrated Dictionary of 853 Performers, 1920 through 1960*. Jefferson, N.C.: McFarland & Company, Inc., Publishers, 1996, p. 18.

3. "Reigns of Queens for a Day Span 15 Years with 3,921 Rulers, Mostly Crowned by Bailey." *The Los Angeles Times*, May 1, 1960, p. 3.

4. Tape recording of the performance on May 23, 1952.

5. Andrews, Bart and Brad Dunning. *The Worst TV Shows Ever*. New York: Dutton, 1980, pp. 142–145.

6. Hyatt, Wesley. *The Encyclopedia of Daytime Television*. New York: Billboard Books, 1997, p. 352.

7. Nachman, Gerald. *Raised on Radio*. New York: Pantheon Books, 1998, pp. 350–351.

8. Ibid., p. 351.

Chapter 12

1. DeLong, Thomas A. *Quiz Craze: America's Infatuation with Game Shows.* New York: Praeger, 1991, p. 118; also, *Radio Stars: An Illustrated Biographical Dictionary of 953 Performers, 1920 through 1960.* Jefferson, N.C.: McFarland & Co., Inc., 1996, p. 235.

2. Dunning, John. *On the Air: The Encyclopedia of Old-Time Radio.* New York: Oxford University Press, 1998, p. 639; also, *Tune in Yesterday: The Ultimate Encyclopedia of Old-Time Radio, 1925–1976.* Englewood Cliffs, N.J.: Prentice-Hall, Inc., 1976, p. 573.

3. Nachman, Gerald. *Raised on Radio.* New York: Pantheon Books, 1998, p. 348.

4. *Variety*, June 30, 1948, p. 29.

5. DeLong, 1991, p. 115.

6. "Radio Reviews," *Variety*, March 24, 1948, p. 34.

7. DeLong, 1996, p. 235.

8. Goodson, Mark, "Giveaway Defense," *The New York Times*, July 11, 1948, p. II-7.

9. Fabe, Maxine. *TV Game Shows: A Behind-the-Screen Look at the Stars, the Prizes, the Hosts & the Scandals!* Garden City, N.Y.: Doubleday & Company, Inc., 1979, p. 118.

10. Buxton, Frank and Bill Owen. *The Big Broadcast, 1920–1950.* New York: Viking Press, 1972, p. ix.

11. Nachman, p. 347.

12. Havig, Alan. *Fred Allen's Radio Comedy.* Philadelphia: Temple University Press, 1990, p. 93.

13. Allen, Fred. *Treadmill to Oblivion.* Boston: Little Brown-Atlantic Monthly Press, 1954, pp. 217–218.

14. Ibid., p. 106.

15. Allen, Fred. "In Defense of Radio?" *The New York Herald Tribune*, August 25, 1948, p. 7.

16. Nachman, p. 115.

17. Ibid.

18. Allen, *Treadmill to Oblivion*, pp. 218–219.

19. Fabe, p. 117.

20. Nachman, p. 115.

21. Nachman, p. 114.

22. Block, Hal. "You Can't Top a Refrigerator," *Variety*, July 28, 1948, p. 1.

23. DeLong, 1991, p. 118.

24. Fates, Gil. *What's My Line? The Inside History of TV's Most Famous Panel Show.* Englewood Cliffs, N.J.: Prentice-Hall, Inc., 1998, p. 21.

25. Havig, p. 94.

26. Gould, Jack. "Give Away Curse," *The New York Times*, May 16, 1948, p. II-9.

27. Gould, Jack. "Programs in Review," *The New York Times*, April 4, 1948, p. II-9.

28. Gross, Ben. *I Looked and I Listened.* New York: Random House, 1954, p. 153.

29. Nachman, p. 348.

30. Ibid.

31. Ibid., p. 115.

32. MacDonald, J. Fred. *Don't Touch That Dial!: Radio Programming in American Life, 1920–1960.* Chicago: Nelson-Hall Inc., Publishers, 1979, p. 84.

33. DeLong, 1996, p. 68; also, Cox, Jim. *The Great Radio Soap Operas.* Jefferson, N.C.: McFarland & Co., Publishers, 1999, p. 249.

Chapter 13

1. Fates, Gil. *What's My Line? The Inside History of TV's Most Famous Panel Show.* Englewood Cliffs, N.J.: Prentice-Hall, Inc., 1978, p. 133.

2. Fabe, Maxene. *TV Game Shows.* Garden City, N.Y.: Doubleday & Co., Inc., 1979, p. 158.

3. Gould, Jack. "Radio and Television." *The New York Times*, November 9, 1951, p. 34.

4. Hyatt, Wesley. *The Encyclopedia of Daytime Television.* New York: Billboard Books, 1997, p. 412.

5. DeLong, Thomas A. *Quiz Craze: America's Infatuation with Game Shows.* New York: Praeger, 1991, p. 149.

6. Hyatt, p. 412.

7. Brooks, Tim and Earle Marsh. *The Complete Directory to Prime Time Network TV Shows, 1946–Present.* 4th ed. New York: Ballantine Books, 1988, pp. 752–753.

8. Ibid., p. 753.

9. "Rep. St. George Enters 'Strike It Rich' Fray," *Broadcasting Telecasting.* February 22, 1954, p. 54.

10. "'Strike It Rich' Stricken." *Broadcasting Telecasting.* February 22, 1954, p. 54.

11. Adapted from DeLong, 1991, p. 152.

12. Cohen, Martin. "Strike It Rich, Please Do!" *Radio-TV Mirror*, January 1954, p. 22.

13. Ibid., p. 25.

14. Ibid., p. 80.

15. DeLong, 1991, p. 152.

16. Brooks and Marsh, p. 753.

17. Ibid., p. 752.

Chapter 14

1. Dunning, John. *On the Air: The Encyclopedia of Old-Time Radio*. New York: Oxford University Press, 1998, p. 652.

2. Nachman, Gerald. *Raised on Radio*. New York: Pantheon Books, 1998, p. 322.

3. Ibid., p. 326.

4. Ibid.

5. DeLong, Thomas A. *Radio Stars: An Illustrated Biographical Dictionary of 953 Performers*, 1920 through 1960. Jefferson, N.C.: McFarland & Company, Inc., Publishers, 1996, p. 20.

6. DeLong, Thomas A. *Quiz Craze: America's Infatuation with Game Shows*. New York: Praeger Publishers, 1991, p. 74.

7. Ibid., pp. 74–75.

8. "Radio Follow-up," *Variety*, August 28, 1940, p. 31.

9. "Of the Melancholy Phil," *The New York Times*, March 3, 1946, p. II-7.

10. "Phil Baker," *Current Biography, 1946*. New York: Wilson Company, 1947, p. 25.

11. DeLong, 1996, p. 195.

12. Biow, Milton H. *Butting In ... An Adman Speaks Out*. Garden City, N.Y.: Doubleday, 1964, p. 112.

13. Fabe, Maxene. *TV Game Shows: A Behind-the-Screen Look at the Stars, the Prizes, the Hosts & the Scandals!* Garden City, N.Y.: Doubleday, 1979, p. 191.

Chapter 15

1. Maltin, Leonard. *The Great American Broadcast: A Celebration of Radio's Golden Age*. New York: Penguin Putnam Inc., 1997, p. 203.

2. Nachman, Gerald. *Raised on Radio*. New York: Pantheon Books, 1998, p. 336.

3. "Ralph L. Edwards," *Current Biography, 1943*. New York: Wilson Co., 1944, p. 193; also, Ralph Edwards, "To the Defense of 'Truth or Consequences,'" *The New York Times*, November 8, 1942, p. VIII-12.

4. "Radio Insanity," *Life*, April 2, 1945, pp. 118–120.

5. Ralph Edwards. "The Truth about Truth or Consequences," *Radio and Television Mirror*, January 1949, p. 24.

6. Maltin, p. 137.

7. Nachman, p. 337.

8. "Cause of It All Turns Up." *The New York Times*, January 31, 1943, p. 26.

9. Thomas A. DeLong. *Quiz Craze: America's Infatuation with Game Shows*. New York: Praeger Publishers, 1991, p. 60.

10. *Radio and Television Mirror*, January 1949, p. 87.

11. Ibid., pp. 87–88.

12. Ibid., p. 88.

13. Ibid.

14. Ibid., p. 88.

Chapter 16

1. Bolstad, Helen, "Tommy, the Welcome Traveler." *Radio-TV Mirror*, April 1954, p. 80.

2. DeLong, Thomas A. *Radio Stars: An Illustrated Biographical Dictionary of 953 Performers, 1920 through 1960*. Jefferson, N.C.: McFarland & Company, Inc., Publishers, 1996, p. 25.

3. "'Strike It Rich' Stricken." *Broadcasting Telecasting*, February 22, 1954, p. 54.

4. Hyatt, Wesley. *The Encyclopedia of Daytime Television*. New York: Billboard Productions, Inc., 1997, p. 458.

5. *Radio-TV Mirror*, p. 80.

6. DeLong, 1996, p. 11.

7. Ibid., p. 81.

Chapter 17

1. Nachman, Gerald. *Raised on Radio*. New York: Pantheon Books, 1998, p. 346.

2. Fabe, Maxene. *TV Game Shows: A Behind-the-Screen Look at the Stars, the Prizes, the Hosts and the Scandals!* Garden City, N.Y.: Doubleday & Company, Inc., 1979, p. 141.

3. DeLong, Thomas A. *Quiz Craze: America's Infatuation with Game Shows.* New York: Praeger Publishers, 1991, p. 156.

4. Gould, Jack. "TV Debut Is Made by Groucho Marx." *The New York Times*, October 6, 1950, p. 50.

5. Nachman, p. 343.

6. Brooks, Tim and Earle Marsh. *The Complete Directory to Prime Time Network TV Shows, 1946–Present.* 4th edition. New York: Ballantine Books, 1988, p. 876.

7. Dunning, John. *On the Air: The Encyclopedia of Old-Time Radio.* New York: Oxford University Press, 1998, p. 733.

8. DeLong, Thomas A. *Radio Stars: An Illustrated Biographical Dictionary of 953 Performers, 1920 through 1960.* Jefferson, N.C.: McFarland & Company, Inc., 1996, p. 185.

9. Nachman, p. 342.

10. DeLong, 1991, p. 161.

11. Barson, Michael. "Hello, We Must Be Going: The Short, Happy Life of the Marx Brothers on Radio." *Flywheel, Shyster, and Flywheel: The Marx Brothers' Lost Radio Show*, edited by Michael Barson. New York: Panetheon Books, 1988, p. viii.

12. MacDonald, J. Fred. *Don't Touch That Dial!: Radio Programming in American Life from 1920 to 1960.* Chicago: Nelson-Hall Inc., 1982, pp. 103–104.

13. Fabe, p. 142.

14. Nachman, p. 342.

15. Dunning, John. *Tune in Yesterday: The Ultimate Encyclopedia of Old-Time Radio, 1925–1976.* Englewood Cliffs, N. J.: Prentice-Hall, Inc., 1976, pp. 656–657.

16. Ibid., p. 656.

17. Dunning, 1998, p. 733.

18. DeLong, 1991, p. 158.

19. Gould, Jack. "G. Marx." *The New York Times*, December 7, 1947, p. II-13.

20. Nachman, p. 344.

21. Dunning, 1998, p. 733.

22. Nachman, pp. 344–345.

23. Ibid., p. 345.

24. Ibid., p. 344.

25. Dunning, 1998, p. 734.

26. Dunning, 1976, p. 657.

27. Maltin, Leonard. *The Great American Broadcast: A Celebration of Radio's Golden Age.* New York: Penguin Putnam Inc., 1997, p. 191.

28. Marx, Groucho. *The Secret Word Is Groucho.* New York: G.P. Putnam's Sons, 1976, p. 47.

29. Nachman, p. 346.

30. Ibid., p. 345.

31. DeLong, 1991, p. 160.

32. Runyon, Keith L. "Groucho: the troubled clown." *The Courier-Journal*, June 4, 2000, p. I-15.

33. Dunning, 1976, p. 657.

34. Nachman, p. 343.

35. Ibid.

36. Ibid., p. 346.

37. DeLong, 1991, p. 162.

Bibliography

Audiovisuals

Chadwick, Robert W., producer-director-writer, and Sue Clark Chadwick, writer. *Aren't We Devils?* A videotape featuring the programs of Ralph Edwards. Hollywood: Ralph Edwards Productions, 1992.

Perkins, Jack, Host. *Arthur Godfrey: Broadcasting's Forgotten Giant.* A video biography originally shown on the Arts & Entertainment cable network, 1996.

Scores of broadcast recordings of all the shows for which chapters are included, plus many others referred to in the text.

Books

Aaronson, Charles S., Editor. *1958 International Television Almanac: Who, What, Where in Television and Radio.* New York: Quigley Publications, 1957.

Allen, Fred. *Treadmill to Oblivion.* Boston: Little Brown-Atlantic Monthly Press, 1954.

Andrews, Bart and Brad Dunning. *The Worst TV Shows Ever.* New York: Dutton, 1980.

Ansbro, George. *I Have a Lady in the Balcony: Memoirs of a Broadcaster in Radio and Television.* Jefferson, N.C.: McFarland, 2000.

Ashley, Sally. *F.P.A.: The Life and Times of Franklin Pearce Adams.* New York: Beaufort Books, 1986.

Barson, Michael, Editor. *Flywheel, Shyster, and Flywheel: The Marx Brothers' Lost Radio Show.* New York: Pantheon Books, 1988.

Biow, Milton H. *Butting In ... An Adman Speaks Out.* Garden City, N.Y.: Doubleday, 1964.

Brooks, Tim and Earle Marsh. *The Complete Directory to Prime Time Network TV Shows, 1946–Present. Fourth Edition.* New York, Ballantine Books, 1988.

Buxton, Frank and Bill Owen. *The Big Broadcast, 1920–1950: A New, Revised, and Greatly Expanded Edition of Radio's Golden Age.* New York: Viking, 1972.

____. *The Big Broadcast, 1920–1950.* Second Edition. Lanham, Md.: Scarecrow, 1997.

____. *Radio's Golden Age: The Programs and the Personalities.* Ansonia Station, N.Y.: Easton Valley Press, 1967.

Castleman, Harry and Walter J. Podrazik. *505 Radio Questions Your Friends Can't Answer.* New York: Walker, 1983.

"Clifton Fadiman." *Current Biography, 1941.* New York: Wilson, 1942.

Cox, Jim. *The Great Radio Soap Operas.* Jefferson, N.C.: McFarland, 1999.

DeLong, Thomas A. *The Mighty Music Box: The Golden Age of Musical Radio.* Los Angeles: Amber Crest Books, 1980.

____. *Quiz Craze: America's Infatuation with Game Shows.* New York: Praeger, 1991.

____. *Radio Stars: An Illustrated Biographical Dictionary of 953 Performers, 1920 through 1960.* Jefferson, N.C.: McFarland, 1996.

Don McNeill and the Breakfast Club Celebrate 20 Years of Corn, a premium published by that show in 1953.

Dunning, John. *On the Air: The Encyclopedia of Old-Time Radio.* New York: Oxford University Press, 1998.

____. *Tune in Yesterday: The Ultimate Encyclopedia of Old-Time Radio, 1925–1976.* Englewood Cliffs, N.J.: Prentice-Hall, 1976.

Fabe, Maxene. *TV Game Shows: A Behind-the-Screen Look at the Stars, the Prizes, the Hosts & the Scandals!* Garden City, N.Y.: Doubleday, 1979.

Fates, Gil. *What's My Line? The Inside History of TV's Most Famous Panel Show.* Englewood Cliffs, N.J.: Prentice-Hall, 1978.

Grams, Martin Jr. *Radio Drama: American Programs, 1932–1962.* Jefferson, N.C.: McFarland, 2000.

Gross, Ben. *I Looked and I Listened.* New York: Random House, 1954.

Harmon, Jim. *The Great Radio Comedians.* Garden City, N.Y.: Doubleday, 1970.

Harvey, Rita Morley. *Those Wonderful, Terrible Years: George Heller and the American Federation of Television and Radio Artists.* Carbondale: Southern Illinois University Press, 1996.

Havig, Alan. *Fred Allen's Radio Comedy.* Philadelphia: Temple University Press, 1990.

Hickerson, Jay. *Necrology of Radio Personalities.* Original document and three supplements. Hamden, Conn.: Jay Hickerson, 1996, 1997, 1998, 1999.

____. *The New, Revised Ultimate History of Network Radio Programming and Guide to ALL Circulating Shows.* Third Edition. Plus three supplements. Hamden, Conn.: Jay Hickerson, 1996, 1997, 1998, 1999.

Hyatt, Wesley. *The Encyclopedia of Daytime Television: Everything You Ever Wanted to Know About Daytime TV But Didn't Know Where to Look!* New York: Billboard Books, 1997.

Kashner, Sam and Nancy Schoenberger. *A Talent for Genius: The Life and Times of Oscar Levant.* New York: Random House, 1994.

Kieran, John. *Not Under Oath.* Boston: Houghton Mifflin, 1964.

Kirby, Durward. *My Life ... Those Wonderful Years!* Charlotte Harbor, Fla.: Tabby House Books, 1992.

Lackmann, Ron. *Remember Radio.* New York: G.P. Putnam's Sons, 1970.

____. *Same Time ... Same Station. An A–Z Guide to Radio from Jack Benny to Howard Stern.* New York: Facts On File, 1996.

Lamparski, Richard. *Whatever Became Of ...?* Third Series. New York: Crown, 1970.

MacDonald, J. Fred. *Don't Touch That Dial!: Radio Programming in American Life from 1920 to 1960.* Chicago: Nelson-Hall, 1991.

Maltin, Leonard. *The Great American Broadcast: A Celebration of Radio's Golden Age.* New York: Penguin Putnam, 1997.

Marx, Groucho. *The Secret Word Is Groucho.* New York: G.P. Putnam's Sons, 1976.

McNeill, Don. *The 1954 Breakfast Club Yearbook: A Collection of Favorite Poems, Photographs and Stories.* Chicago: Don McNeill, 1954.

McNeill, Kay. *Don's Other Life ...* Chicago: Mrs. Kay McNeill, 1944.

Mott, Robert L. *Radio Sound Effects: Who Did It, and How, in the Era of Live Broadcasting.* Jefferson, N.C.: McFarland, 1993.

Nachman, Gerald. *Raised on Radio: In Quest of The Lone Ranger, Jack Benny, Amos 'n' Andy, The Shadow, Mary Noble, The Great Gildersleeve, Fibber McGee and Molly, Bill Stern, Our Miss Brooks, Henry Aldrich, The Quiz Kids, Mr. First Nighter, Fred Allen, Vic and Sade, The Cisco Kid, Jack Armstrong, Arthur Godfrey, Bob and Ray, The Barbour Family, Henry Morgan, Joe Friday and Other Lost Heroes from Radio's Heyday.* New York: Pantheon Books, 1998.

Perry, Dick. *Not Just a Sound: The Story of WLW.* Englewood Cliffs, N.J.: Prentice-Hall, 1971.

"Phil Baker." *Current Biography, 1946.* New York: Wilson, 1947.

"Ralph L. Edwards." *Current Biography, 1943.* New York: Wilson, 1944.

Ramsaye, Terry, Editor. *1947–48 International Motion Picture Almanac.* New York: Quigley, 1947.

Schwartz, David, Steve Ryan and Fred Wostbrock. *The Encyclopedia of TV Game Shows.* Second Edition. New York: Facts On File, 1995.

Settel, Irving. *A Pictorial History of Radio.* New York: Grosset & Dunlap, 1967.

Shapiro, Mitchell E. *Television Network Daytime and Late-Night Programming, 1959–1989.* Jefferson, N.C.: McFarland, 1990.

Sies, Luther F. *Encyclopedia of American Radio, 1920–1960.* Jefferson, N.C.: McFarland, 2000.

Singer, Arthur J. *Arthur Godfrey: The Adventures of an American Broadcaster.* Jefferson, N.C.: McFarland, 2000.

Slide, Anthony. *Great Radio Personalities in Historic Photographs.* Vestal, N.Y.: The Vestal Press, Ltd., 1982.

Smith, Sally Bedell. *In All His Glory: The Life of William S. Paley, the Legendary Tycoon and His Brilliant Circle.* New York: Simon and Schuster, 1990.

Summers, Harrison B., Editor. *A Thirty-Year History of Programs Carried on National Radio Networks in the United States, 1926–1956.* New York: Arno Press and *The New York Times,* 1971.

Swartz, Jon D. and Robert C. Reinehr. *Handbook of Old-Time Radio: A Comprehensive Guide to Golden Age Radio Listening and Collecting.* Metuchen, N.J.: Scarecrow, 1993.

Terrace, Vincent. *Radio Programs, 1924–1984: A Catalog of Over 1800 Shows.* Jefferson, N.C.: McFarland, 1999.

Wolfe, Charles Hull. *Modern Radio Advertising.* New York: Printers' Ink, 1949.

Electronic Media

Internet sites specifically devoted to old time radio:

Oldradio.net e-mail discussion forums (two daily)

Periodicals

Broadcasting Telecasting, February 22, 1954.

The Courier-Journal, Louisville, Ky., June 4, 2000.

Life, April 2, 1945.

The Los Angeles Times, May 1, 1960.

The New York Herald Tribune, August 25, 1948.

The New York Times, numerous issues in the 1940s and 1950s.

Radio Album, Winter 1949.

Radio Mirror, Radio and Television Mirror, Radio-TV Mirror, TV Radio Mirror, numerous issues in the 1940s and 1950s.

Time, numerous issues in the 1940s and 1950s.

Variety, numerous issues in the 1930s, 1940s and 1950s.

Index